Fruits Basket

Volume 14

By
Natsuki Takaya

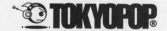

HAMBURG // LONDON // LOS ANGELES // TOKYO

Fruits Basket™

Table of Contents

STORY SO FAR...

Hello, I'm Tohru Honda and I have come to know a terrible secret. After the death of my mother, I was living by myself in a tent, when the Sohma family took me in. I soon learned that the Sohma family lives with a curse! Each family member is possessed by the vengeful spirit of an animal from the Chinese Zodiac. Whenever one of them becomes weak or is hugged by a member of the opposite sex, they change into their Zodiac animal!

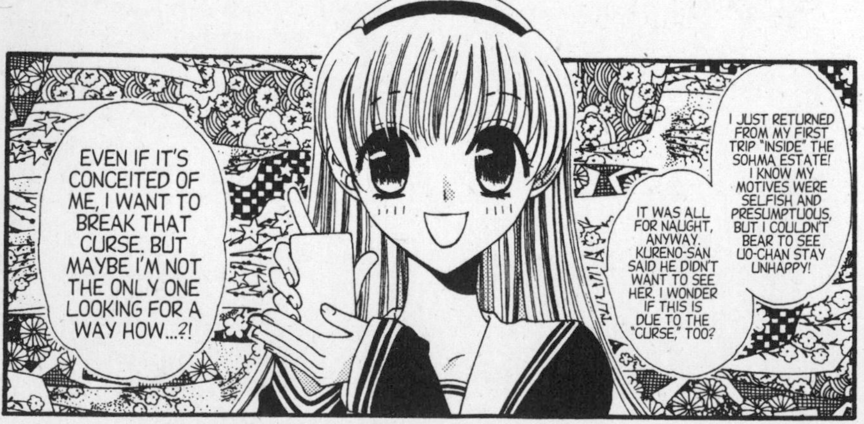
I JUST RETURNED FROM MY FIRST TRIP "INSIDE" THE SOHMA ESTATE! I KNOW MY MOTIVES WERE SELFISH AND PRESUMPTUOUS, BUT I COULDN'T BEAR TO SEE UO-CHAN STAY UNHAPPY!
IT WAS ALL FOR NAUGHT, ANYWAY. KURENO-SAN SAID HE DIDN'T WANT TO SEE HER. I WONDER IF THIS IS DUE TO THE "CURSE," TOO?
EVEN IF IT'S CONCEITED OF ME, I WANT TO BREAK THAT CURSE. BUT MAYBE I'M NOT THE ONLY ONE LOOKING FOR A WAY HOW...?!

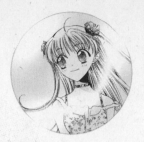

Tohru Honda

The ever-optimistic hero of our story. An orphan, she now lives in Shigure's house, along with Yuki and Kyo, and is the only person outside of the family who knows the Sohma family's curse.

Yuki Sohma, the Rat

Soft-spoken. Self-esteem issues. At school he's called "Prince Yuki."

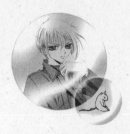

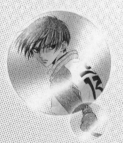

Kyo Sohma, the Cat

The Cat who was left out of the Zodiac. Hates Yuki, leeks and miso. But mostly Yuki.

Kagura Sohma, the Boar

Bashful, yet headstrong. Determined to marry Kyo, even if it kills him.

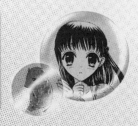

Fruits Basket Characters

Mabudachi Trio

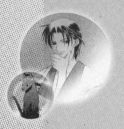

Shigure Sohma, the Dog

Enigmatic, mischievous and a little perverted. A popular novelist.

Hatori Sohma, the Dragon

Family doctor to the Sohmas. Only thing he can't cure is his broken heart.

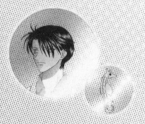

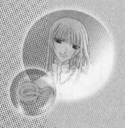

Ayame Sohma, the Snake

Yuki's older brother. A proud and playful drama queen…er, king. Runs a costume shop.

Saki Hanajima

"Hana-chan." Can sense people's "waves." Goth demeanor scares her classmates.

Arisa Uotani

"Uo-chan." A tough-talking "Yankee" who looks out for her friends.

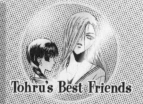

Tohru's Best Friends

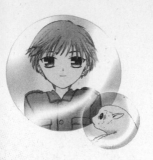

Hiro Sohma, the Ram (or sheep)

This caustic tyke is skilled at throwing verbal barbs, but he has a soft spot for Kisa.

Momiji Sohma, the Rabbit

Half-German. He's older than he looks. His mother rejected him because of the Sohma curse. His little sister, Momo, has been kept from him most of her life.

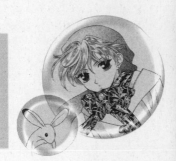

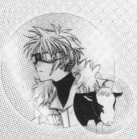

Hatsuharu Sohma, the Ox

The nicest of guys, except when he goes "Black." Then you'd better watch out. He was once in a relationship with Rin.

Kisa Sohma, the Tiger

Kisa became shy and self-conscious due to constant teasing by her classmates. Yuki, who has similar insecurities, feels particularly close to Kisa.

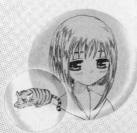

Fruits Basket Characters

Isuzu "Rin" Sohma, the Horse

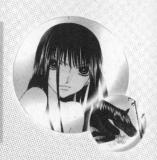

She was once in a relationship with Hatsuharu (Haru)...and Tohru leaves her rather cold. Rin is full of pride, and she can't stand the amount of deference the other Sohma family members give Akito.

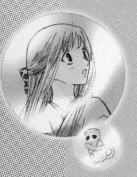

Ritsu Sohma, the Monkey

This shy kimono-wearing member of the Sohma family is gorgeous. But this "she" is really a he!! Crossdressing calms his nerves.

Akito Sohma

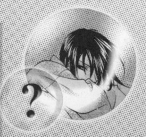

The head of the Sohma clan. A dark figure of many secrets. Treated with fear and reverence.

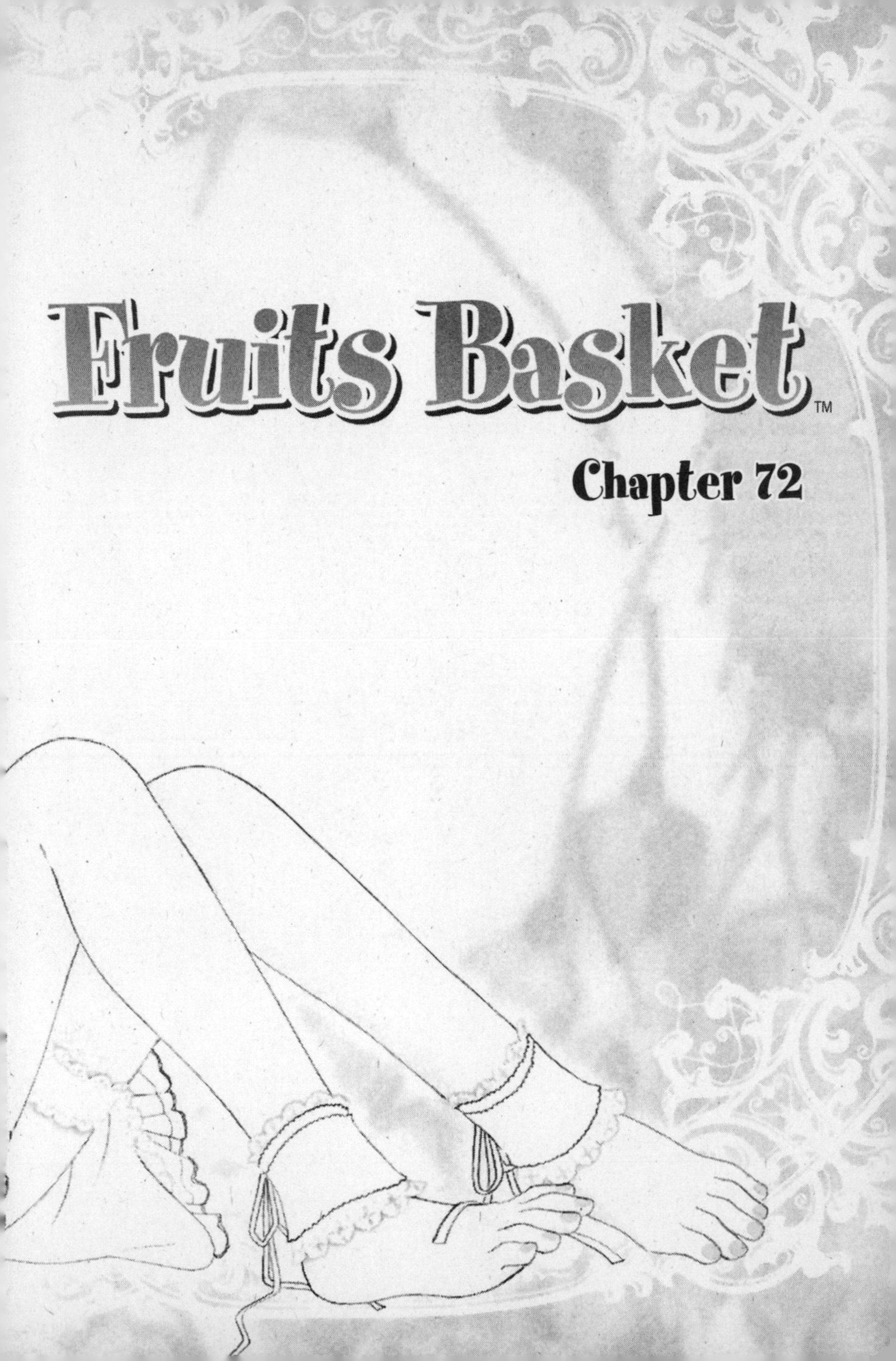
Fruits Basket™
Chapter 72

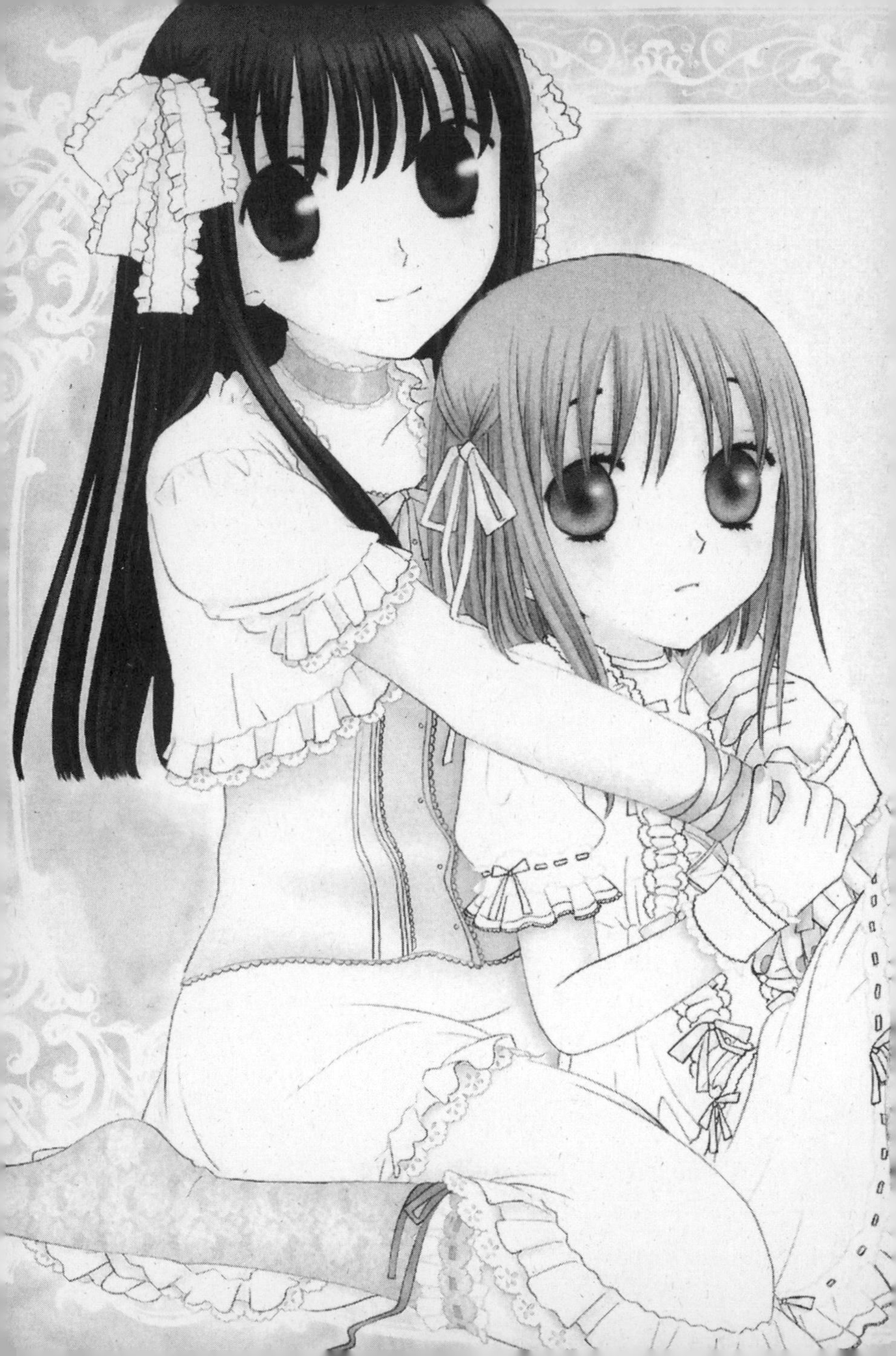

Filler Sketch

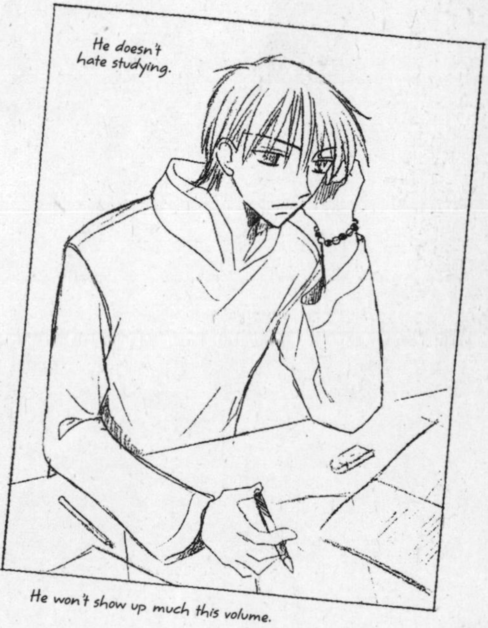
He doesn't hate studying.

He won't show up much this volume.

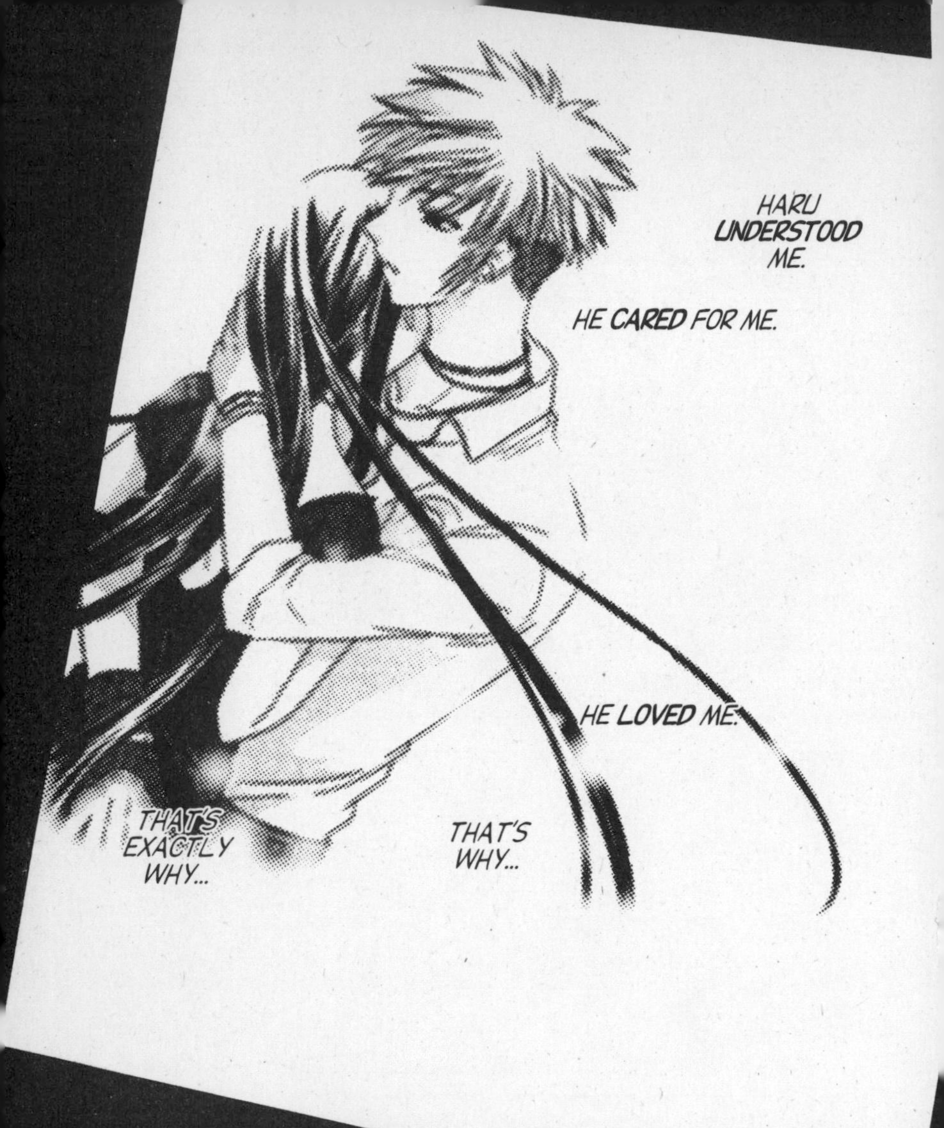

HARU UNDERSTOOD ME.
HE CARED FOR ME.
HE LOVED ME.
THAT'S WHY...
THAT'S EXACTLY WHY...

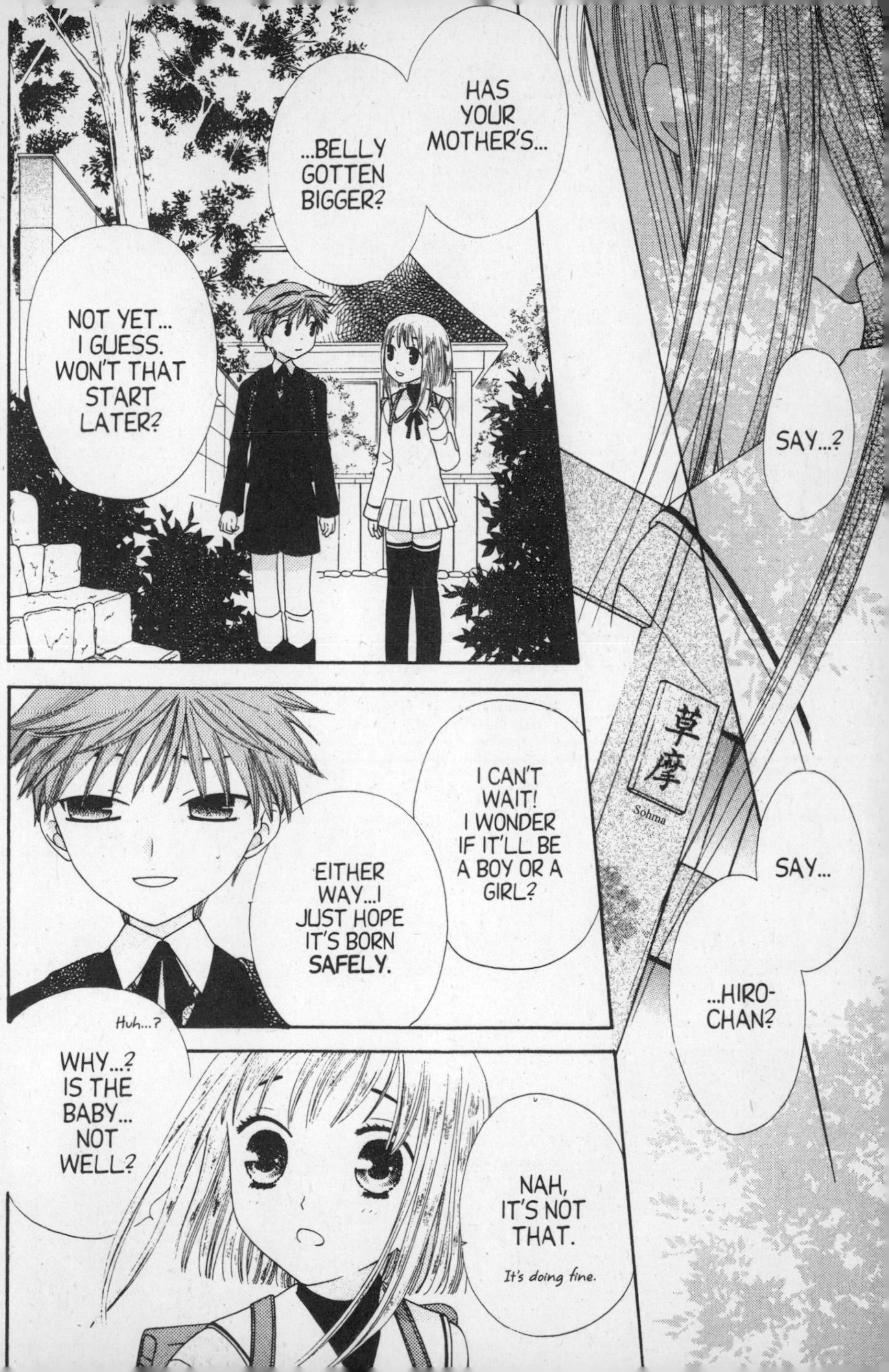
SAY...?
草摩
Sohma
SAY...
...HIRO-CHAN?
HAS YOUR MOTHER'S...
...BELLY GOTTEN BIGGER?
NOT YET... I GUESS. WON'T THAT START LATER?
I CAN'T WAIT! I WONDER IF IT'LL BE A BOY OR A GIRL?
EITHER WAY...I JUST HOPE IT'S BORN SAFELY.
Huh...?
WHY...? IS THE BABY... NOT WELL?
NAH, IT'S NOT THAT.
It's doing fine.

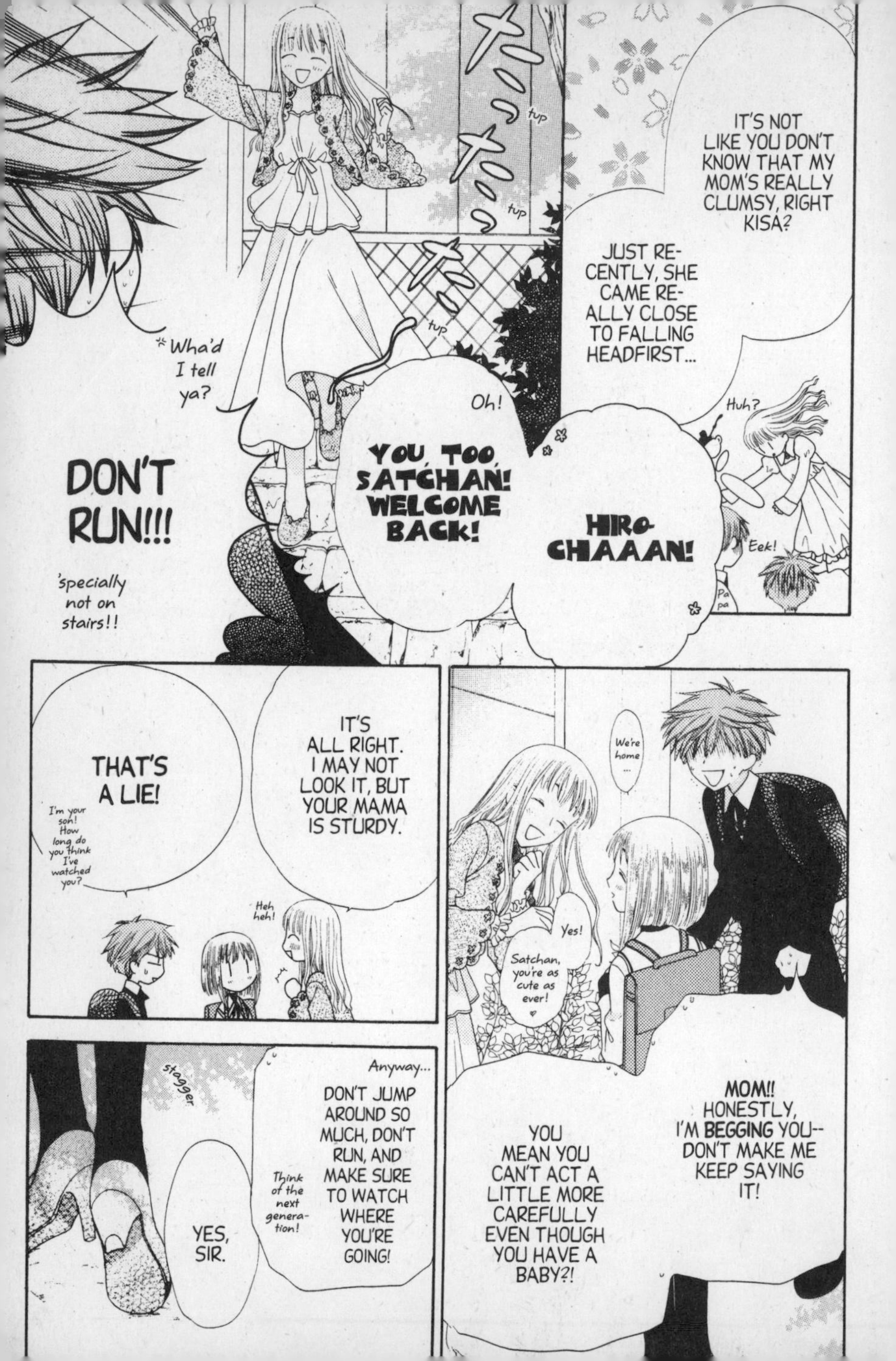
IT'S NOT LIKE YOU DON'T KNOW THAT MY MOM'S REALLY CLUMSY, RIGHT KISA?
JUST RE-CENTLY, SHE CAME RE-ALLY CLOSE TO FALLING HEADFIRST...
Huh?
HIRO-CHAAAN!
Eek!
Pa pa
Oh!
YOU, TOO, SATCHAN! WELCOME BACK!
tup
tup
tup
DON'T RUN!!!
*Wha'd I tell ya?
'specially not on stairs!!
We're home ...
Yes!
Satchan, you're as cute as ever!
IT'S ALL RIGHT. I MAY NOT LOOK IT, BUT YOUR MAMA IS STURDY.
THAT'S A LIE!
I'm your son! How long do you think I've watched you?
Heh heh!
MOM!! HONESTLY, I'M BEGGING YOU-- DON'T MAKE ME KEEP SAYING IT!
YOU MEAN YOU CAN'T ACT A LITTLE MORE CAREFULLY EVEN THOUGH YOU HAVE A BABY?!
Anyway...
DON'T JUMP AROUND SO MUCH, DON'T RUN, AND MAKE SURE TO WATCH WHERE YOU'RE GOING!
Think of the next genera-tion!
YES, SIR.
stagger

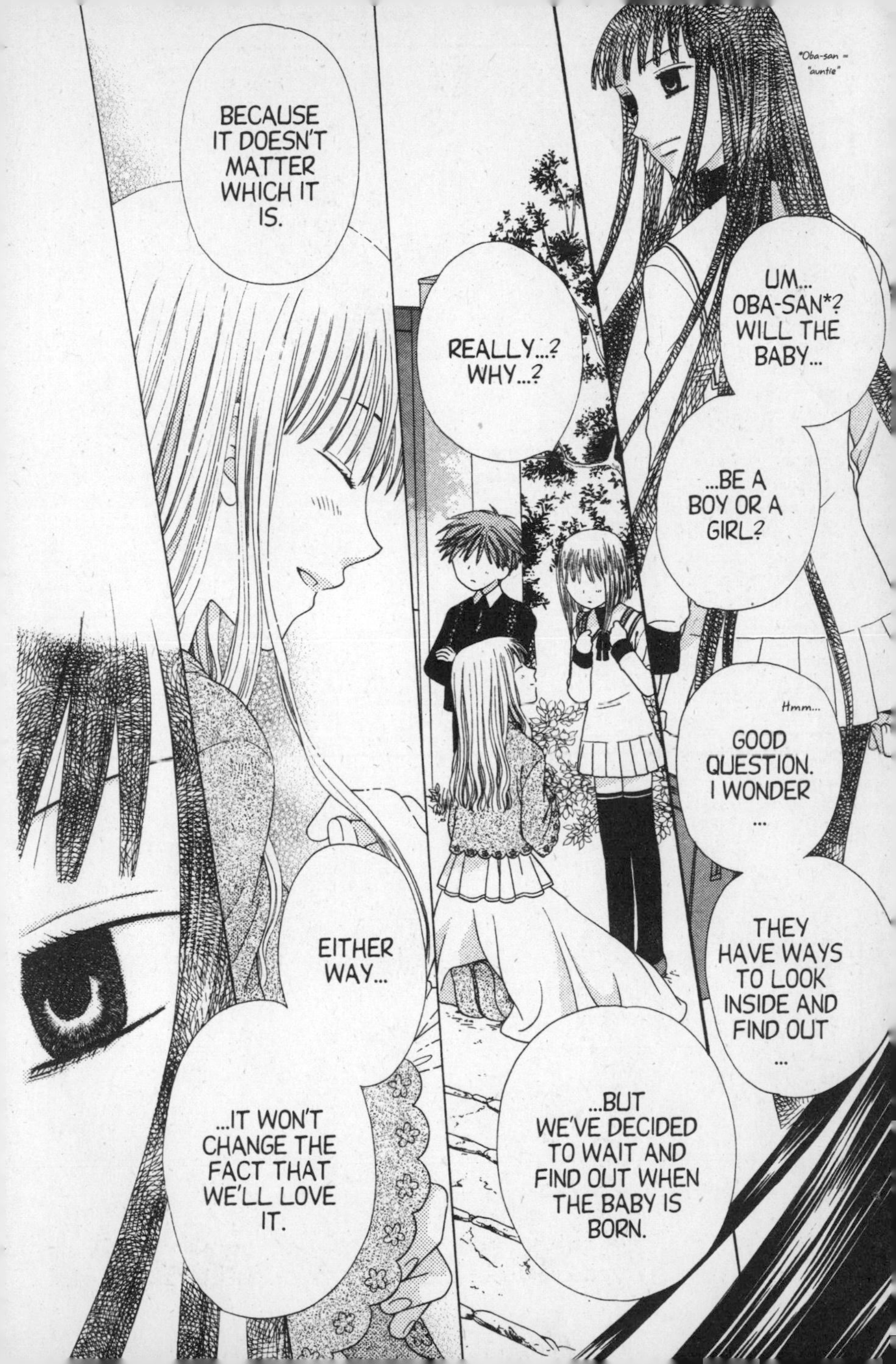
UM... OBA-SAN*? WILL THE BABY...
...BE A BOY OR A GIRL?
Hmm...
GOOD QUESTION. I WONDER ...
THEY HAVE WAYS TO LOOK INSIDE AND FIND OUT ...
...BUT WE'VE DECIDED TO WAIT AND FIND OUT WHEN THE BABY IS BORN.
REALLY...? WHY...?
BECAUSE IT DOESN'T MATTER WHICH IT IS.
EITHER WAY...
...IT WON'T CHANGE THE FACT THAT WE'LL LOVE IT.

*Oba-san = "auntie"

Fruits Basket 14

Hajimemashite and konnichiwa!

Takaya here. Volume 14 ended up with Kureno-san on the cover after all. If you go in the actual order of revelation, it should be Akito, because he was the next Sohma to reveal his identity when he said, "I'm God." (No, he didn't say it like that.)

But, you know... Since Yuki was on the cover of volume 2, it's always been members of the Zodiac, so I thought I should see it to the end. Thus, Kureno-san. He doesn't show up in this volume, though. He was told that he's no good (laugh). By Rin.

Anyway, here is volume 14. Please enjoy it!

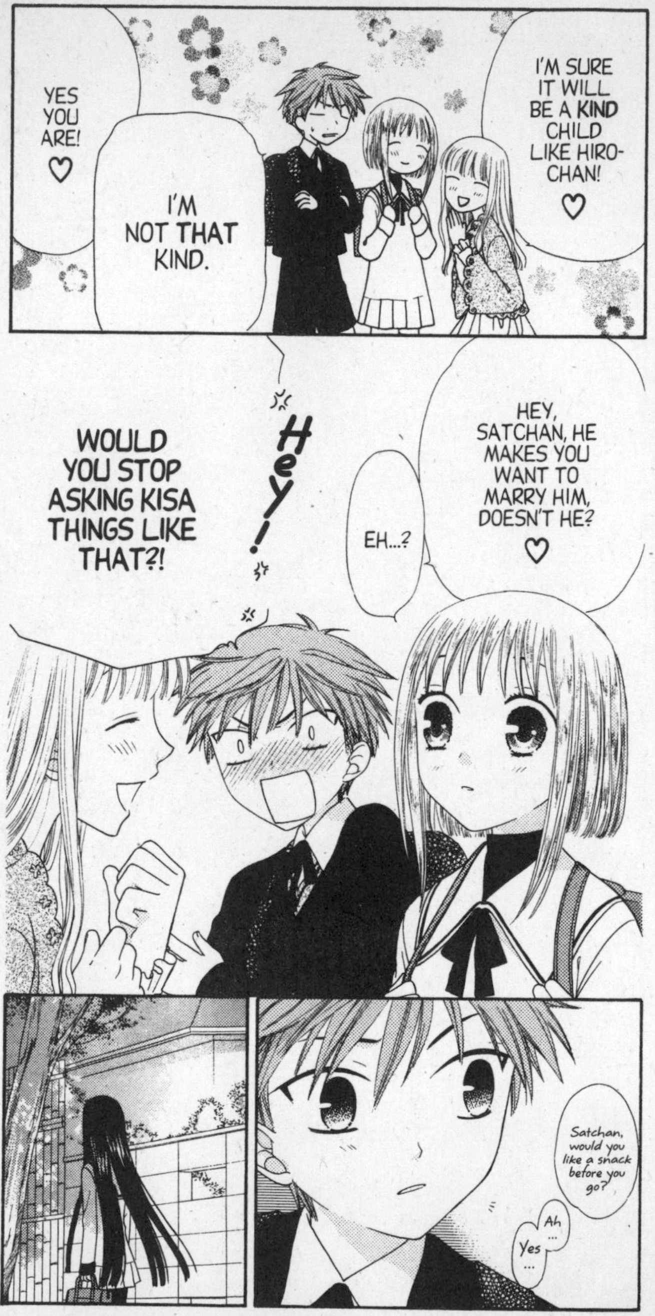
I'M SURE IT WILL BE A KIND CHILD LIKE HIRO-CHAN! ♡
I'M NOT THAT KIND.
YES YOU ARE! ♡
HEY, SATCHAN, HE MAKES YOU WANT TO MARRY HIM, DOESN'T HE? ♡
EH...?
Hey!
WOULD YOU STOP ASKING KISA THINGS LIKE THAT?!
Satchan, would you like a snack before you go?
Ah ... Yes ...

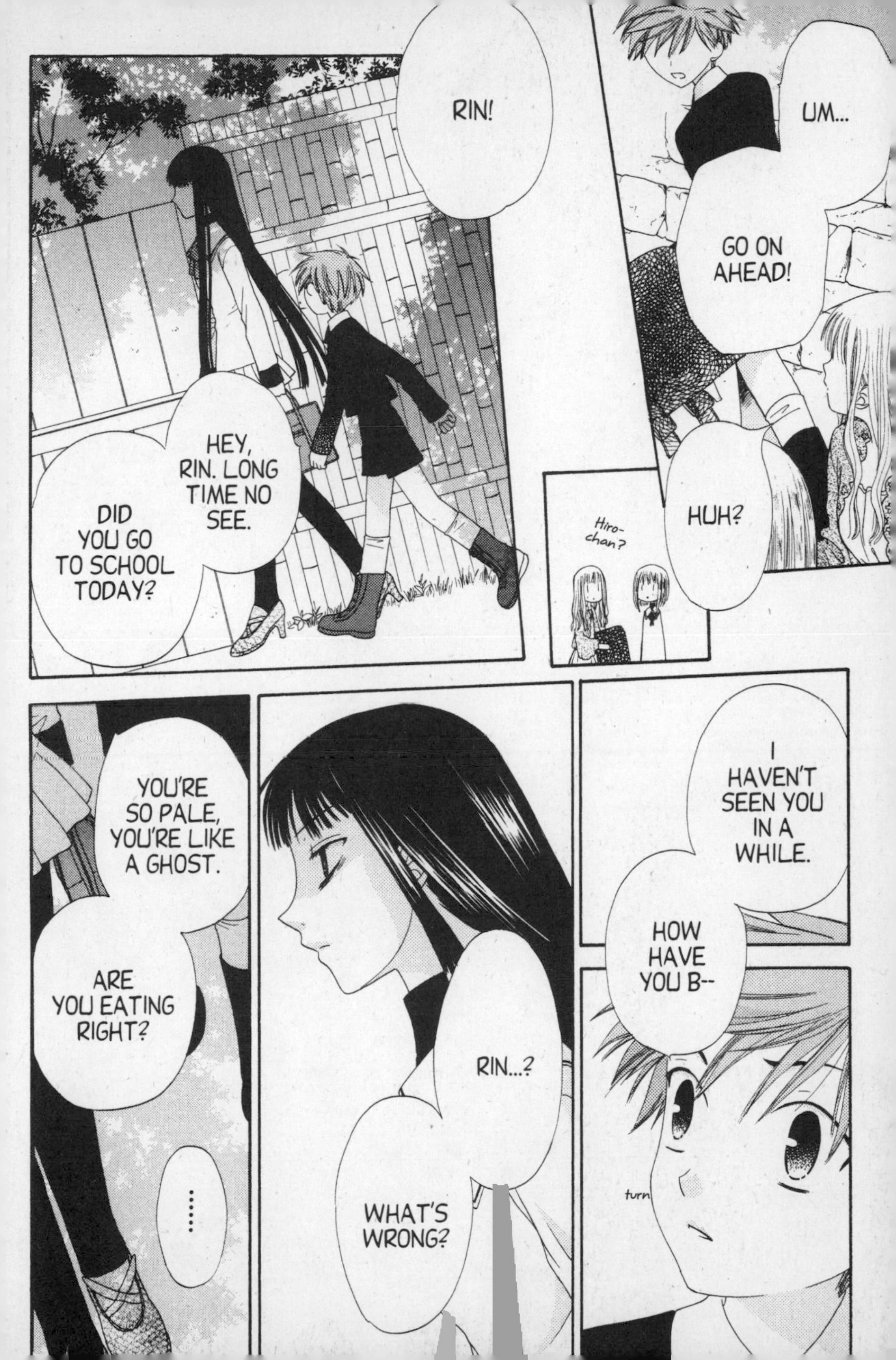
UM...
GO ON AHEAD!
HUH?
Hiro-chan?
RIN!
HEY, RIN. LONG TIME NO SEE.
DID YOU GO TO SCHOOL TODAY?
I HAVEN'T SEEN YOU IN A WHILE.
HOW HAVE YOU B--
turn
RIN...?
WHAT'S WRONG?
YOU'RE SO PALE, YOU'RE LIKE A GHOST.
ARE YOU EATING RIGHT?
......

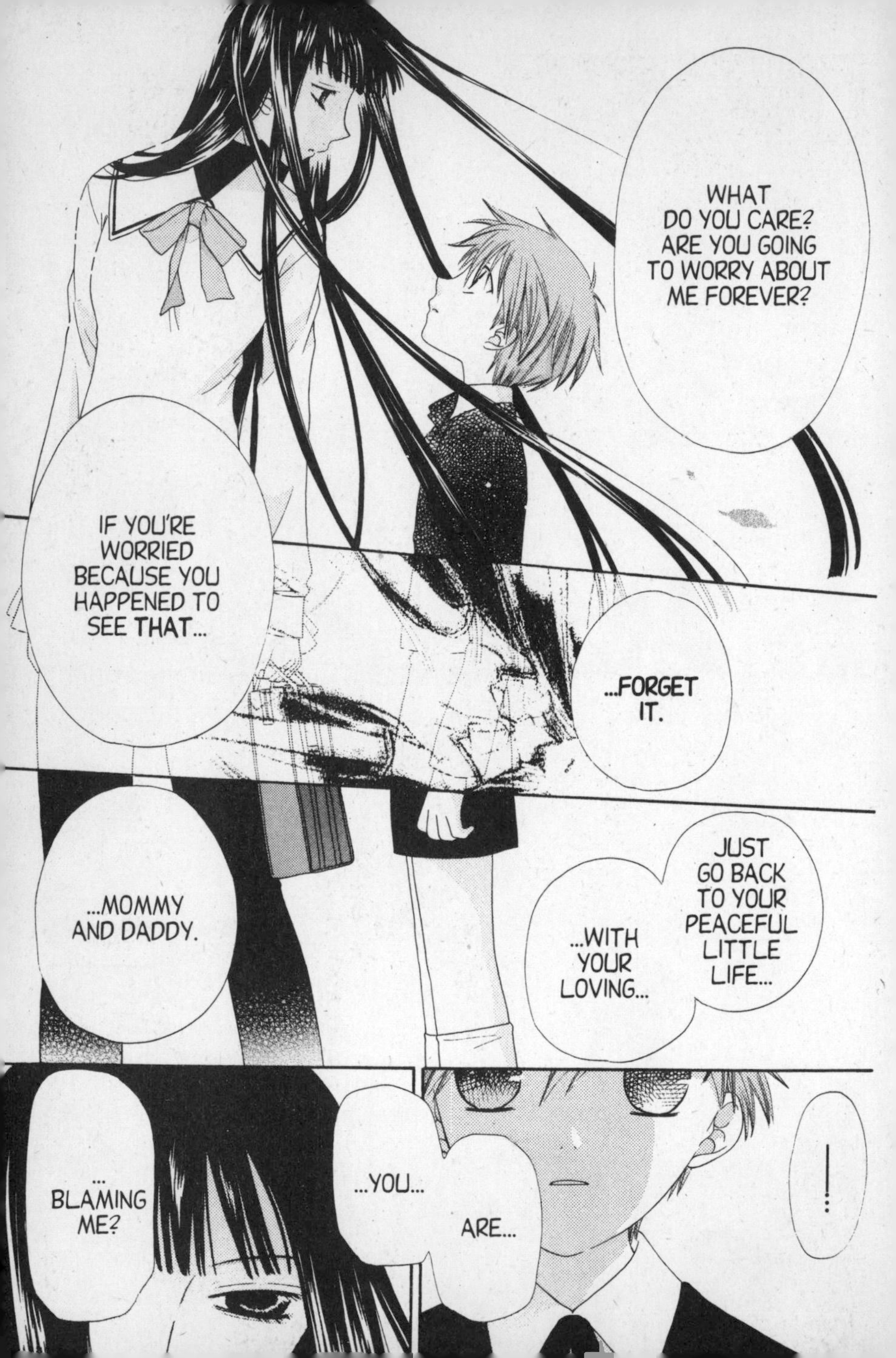
WHAT DO YOU CARE? ARE YOU GOING TO WORRY ABOUT ME FOREVER?
IF YOU'RE WORRIED BECAUSE YOU HAPPENED TO SEE THAT...
...FORGET IT.
JUST GO BACK TO YOUR PEACEFUL LITTLE LIFE...
...WITH YOUR LOVING...
...MOMMY AND DADDY.
...!
...YOU...
ARE...
...BLAMING ME?

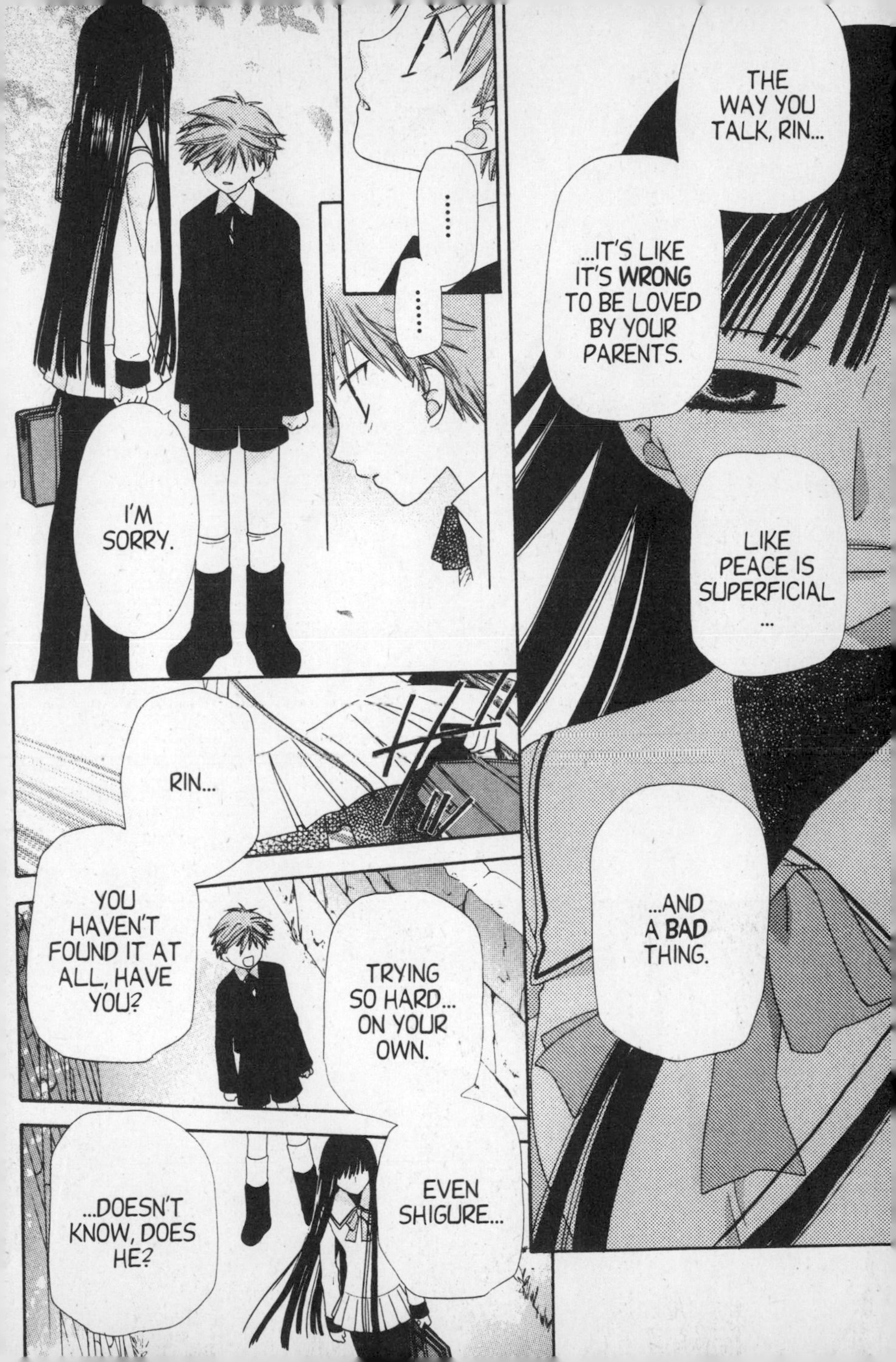
THE WAY YOU TALK, RIN...
...IT'S LIKE IT'S WRONG TO BE LOVED BY YOUR PARENTS.
LIKE PEACE IS SUPERFICIAL ...
...AND A BAD THING.
......
......
I'M SORRY.
RIN...
YOU HAVEN'T FOUND IT AT ALL, HAVE YOU?
TRYING SO HARD... ON YOUR OWN.
EVEN SHIGURE...
...DOESN'T KNOW, DOES HE?

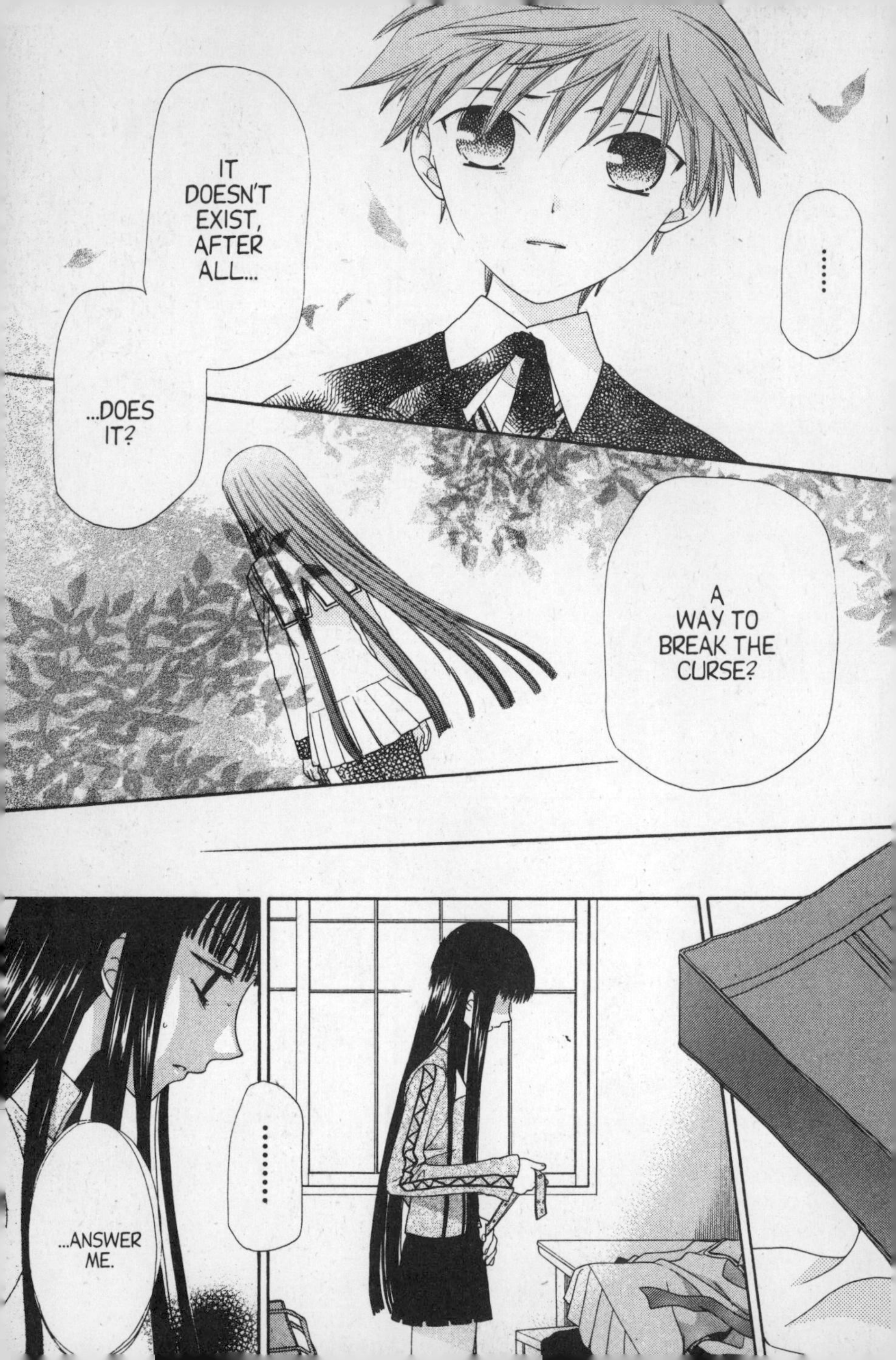
......
IT DOESN'T EXIST, AFTER ALL...
...DOES IT?
A WAY TO BREAK THE CURSE?
....
...ANSWER ME.

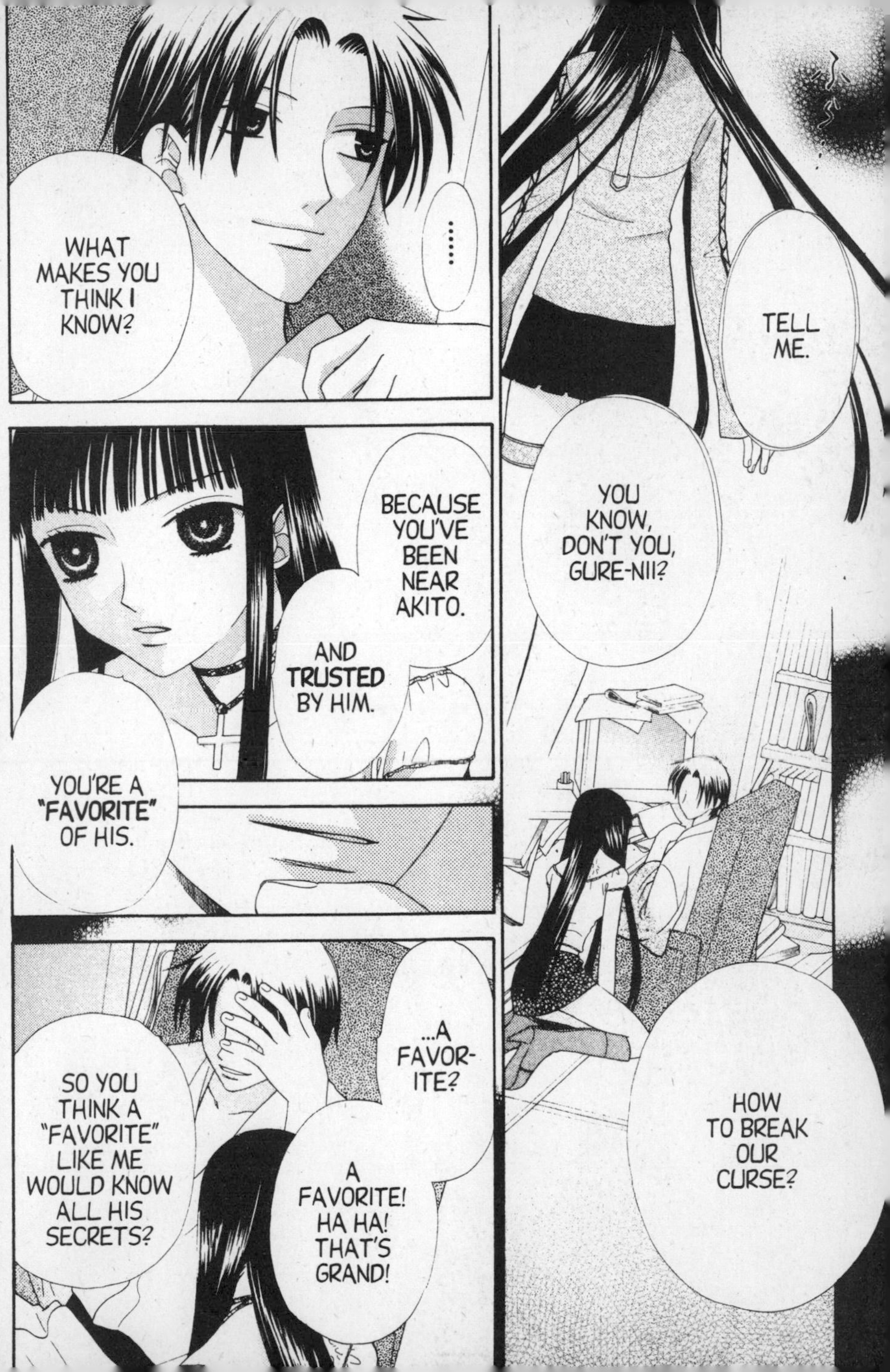
TELL ME.
YOU KNOW, DON'T YOU, GURE-NII?
HOW TO BREAK OUR CURSE?
......
WHAT MAKES YOU THINK I KNOW?
BECAUSE YOU'VE BEEN NEAR AKITO.
AND TRUSTED BY HIM.
YOU'RE A "FAVORITE" OF HIS.
...A FAVOR-ITE?
A FAVORITE! HA HA! THAT'S GRAND!
SO YOU THINK A "FAVORITE" LIKE ME WOULD KNOW ALL HIS SECRETS?

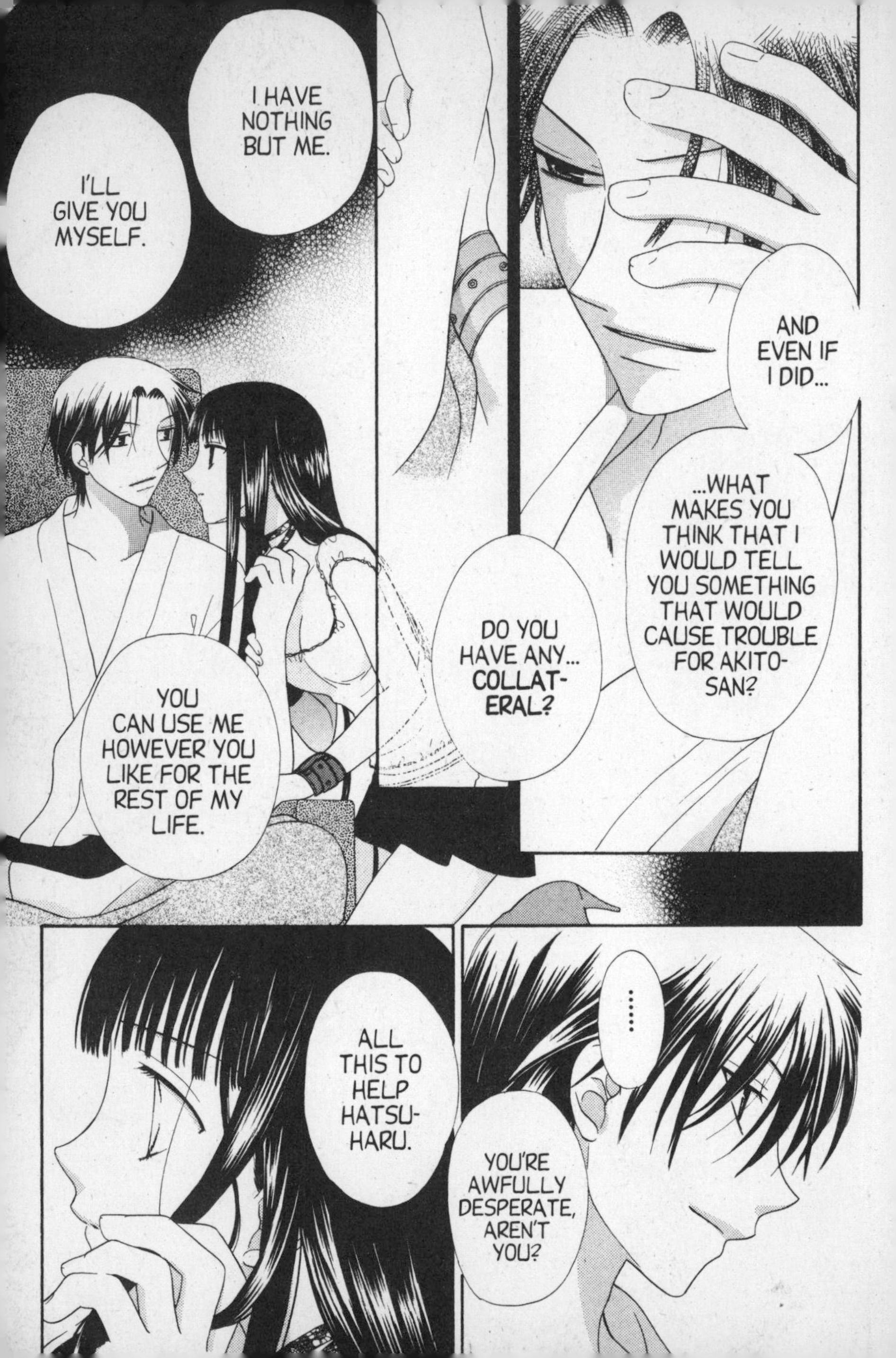
AND EVEN IF I DID...
...WHAT MAKES YOU THINK THAT I WOULD TELL YOU SOMETHING THAT WOULD CAUSE TROUBLE FOR AKITO-SAN?
DO YOU HAVE ANY... COLLATERAL?
I HAVE NOTHING BUT ME.
I'LL GIVE YOU MYSELF.
YOU CAN USE ME HOWEVER YOU LIKE FOR THE REST OF MY LIFE.
......
YOU'RE AWFULLY DESPERATE, AREN'T YOU?
ALL THIS TO HELP HATSU-HARU.

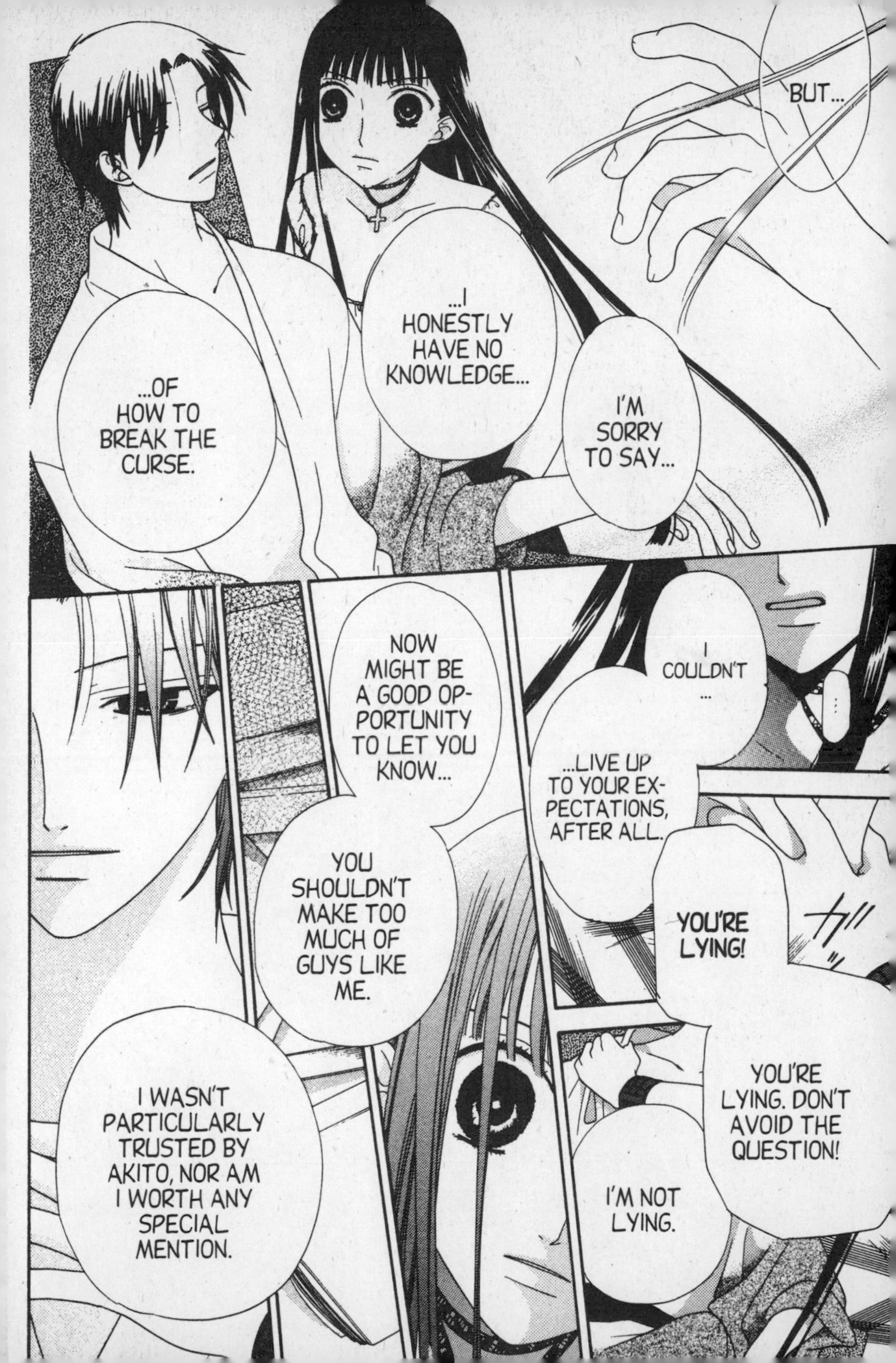
BUT...
I'M SORRY TO SAY...
...I HONESTLY HAVE NO KNOWLEDGE...
...OF HOW TO BREAK THE CURSE.
I COULDN'T ...
...LIVE UP TO YOUR EX-PECTATIONS, AFTER ALL.
NOW MIGHT BE A GOOD OP-PORTUNITY TO LET YOU KNOW...
YOU SHOULDN'T MAKE TOO MUCH OF GUYS LIKE ME.
I WASN'T PARTICULARLY TRUSTED BY AKITO, NOR AM I WORTH ANY SPECIAL MENTION.
YOU'RE LYING!
YOU'RE LYING. DON'T AVOID THE QUESTION!
I'M NOT LYING.

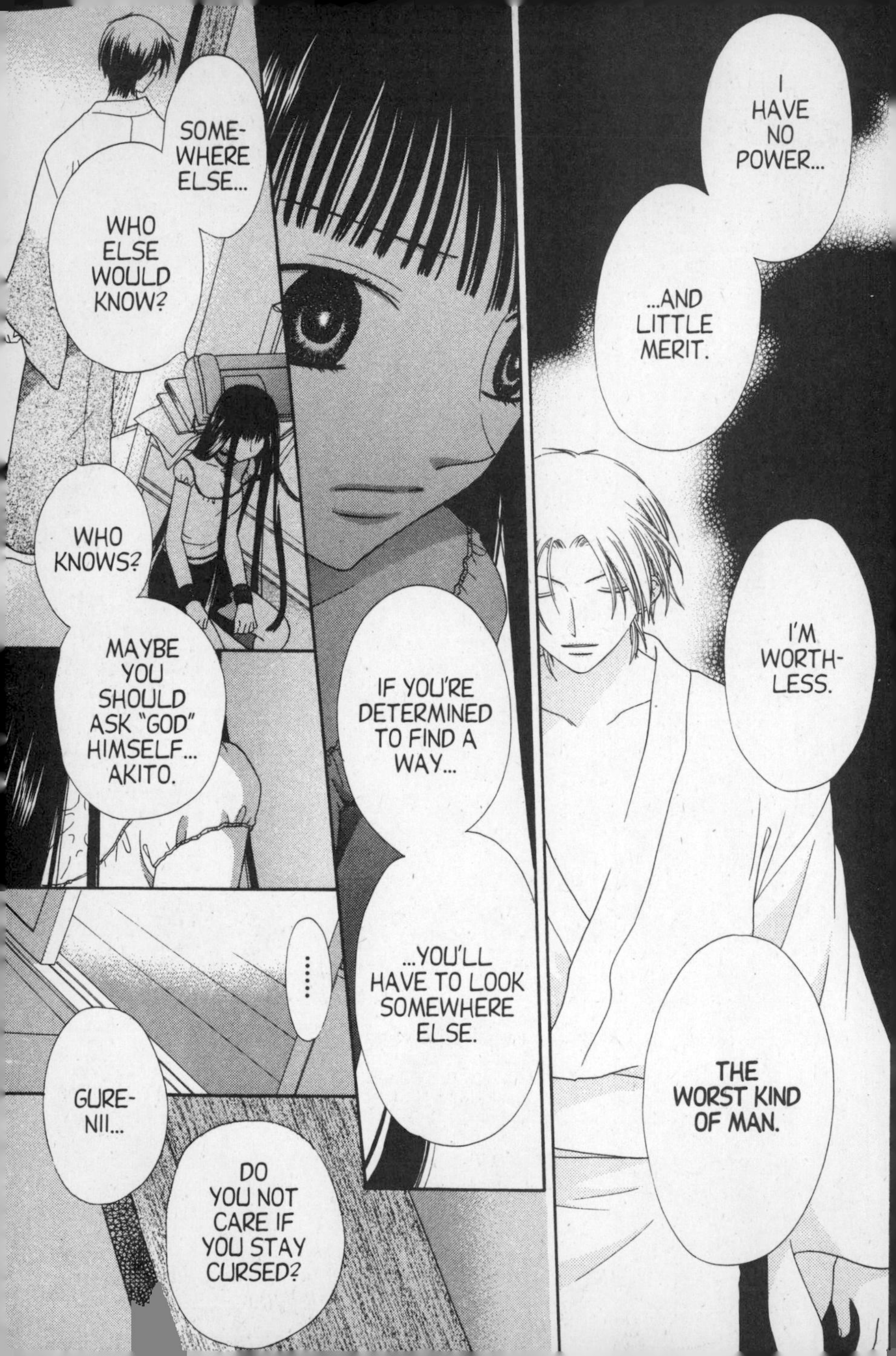
I HAVE NO POWER...
...AND LITTLE MERIT.
I'M WORTH-LESS.
THE WORST KIND OF MAN.
IF YOU'RE DETERMINED TO FIND A WAY...
...YOU'LL HAVE TO LOOK SOMEWHERE ELSE.
SOME-WHERE ELSE...
WHO ELSE WOULD KNOW?
WHO KNOWS?
MAYBE YOU SHOULD ASK "GOD" HIMSELF... AKITO.
......
GURE-NII...
DO YOU NOT CARE IF YOU STAY CURSED?

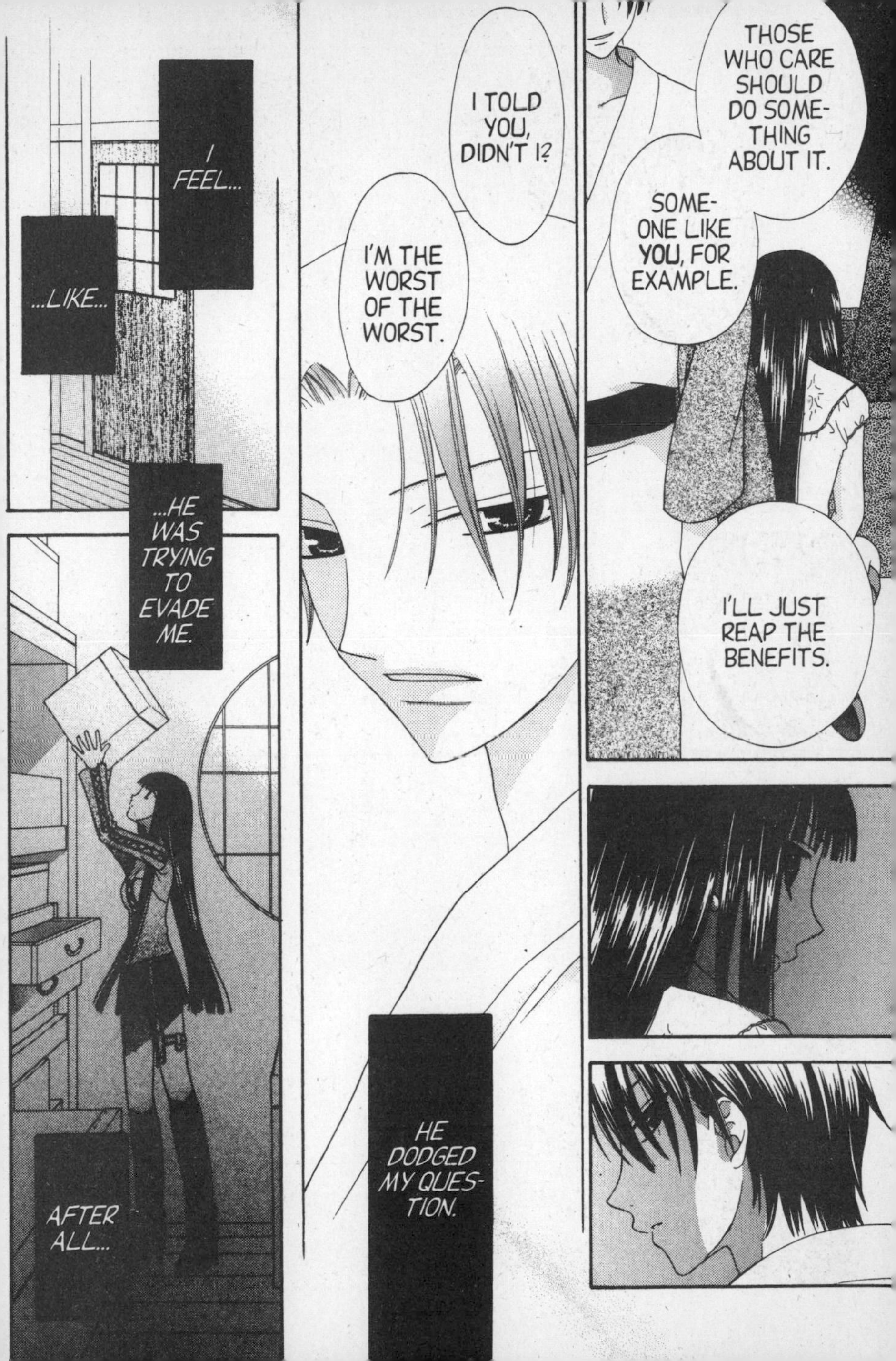
THOSE WHO CARE SHOULD DO SOME-THING ABOUT IT.
SOME-ONE LIKE YOU, FOR EXAMPLE.
I'LL JUST REAP THE BENEFITS.
I TOLD YOU, DIDN'T I?
I'M THE WORST OF THE WORST.
HE DODGED MY QUES-TION.
I FEEL...
...LIKE...
...HE WAS TRYING TO EVADE ME.
AFTER ALL...

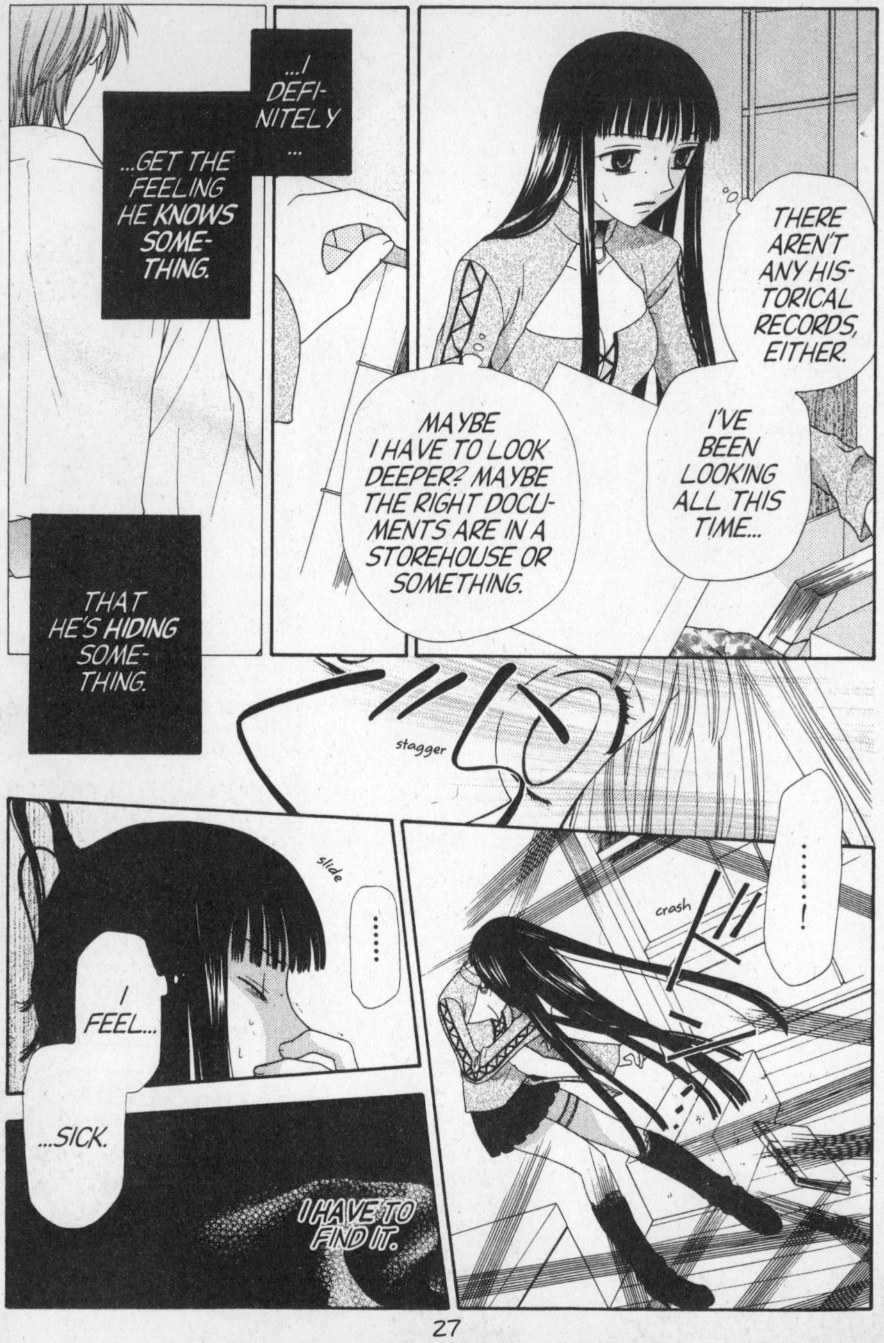
THERE AREN'T ANY HISTORICAL RECORDS, EITHER.
I'VE BEEN LOOKING ALL THIS TIME...
MAYBE I HAVE TO LOOK DEEPER? MAYBE THE RIGHT DOCUMENTS ARE IN A STOREHOUSE OR SOMETHING.
...I DEFINITELY...
...GET THE FEELING HE KNOWS SOMETHING.
THAT HE'S HIDING SOMETHING.
stagger
crash
......!
slide
......
I FEEL...
...SICK.
I HAVE TO FIND IT.

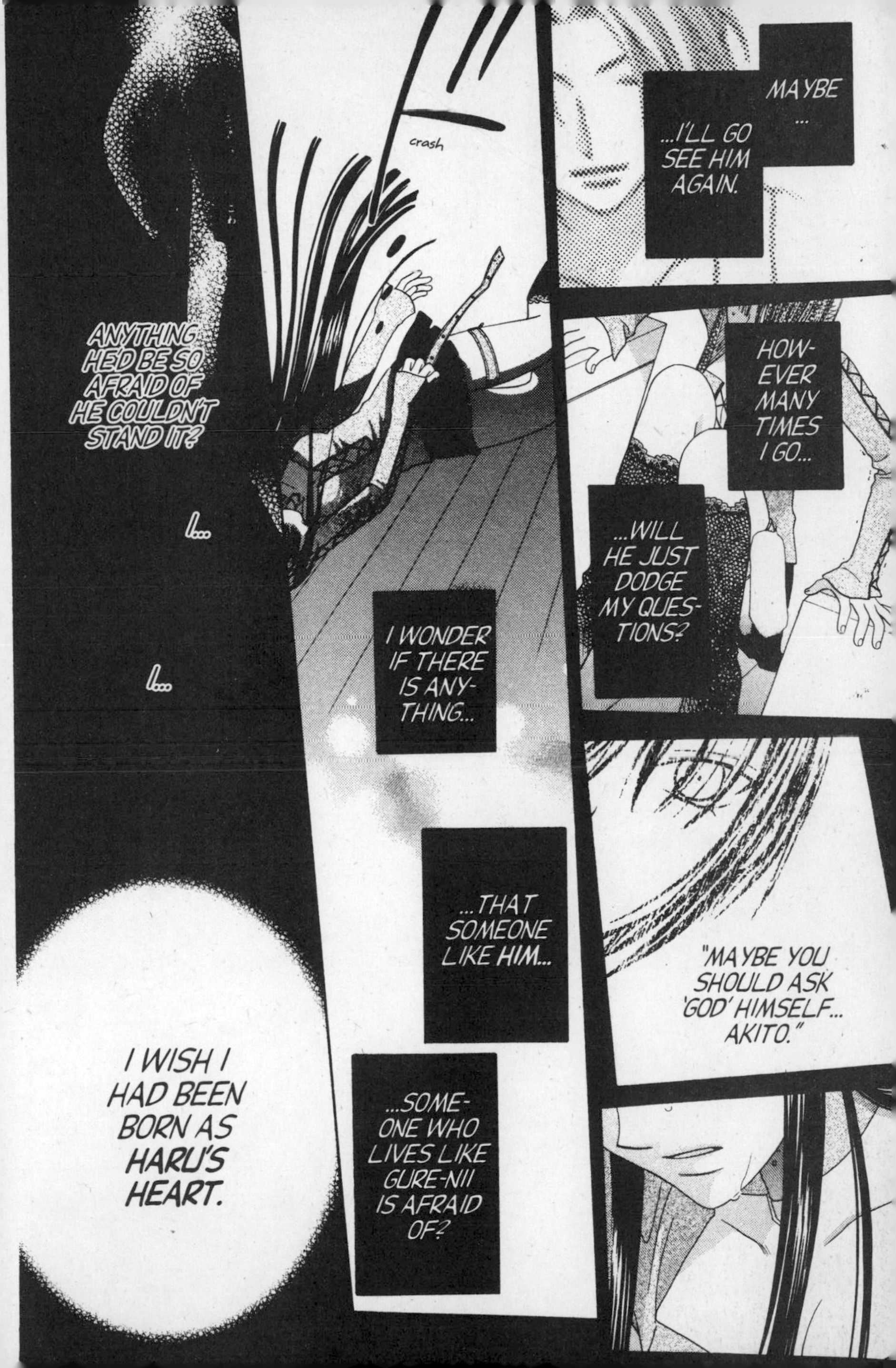
MAYBE ...
...I'LL GO SEE HIM AGAIN.
HOW-EVER MANY TIMES I GO...
...WILL HE JUST DODGE MY QUES-TIONS?
"MAYBE YOU SHOULD ASK 'GOD' HIMSELF... AKITO."
crash
I WONDER IF THERE IS ANY-THING...
...THAT SOMEONE LIKE HIM...
...SOME-ONE WHO LIVES LIKE GURE-NII IS AFRAID OF?
ANYTHING HED BE SO AFRAID OF HE COULDN'T STAND IT?
I...
I...
I WISH I HAD BEEN BORN AS HARU'S HEART.

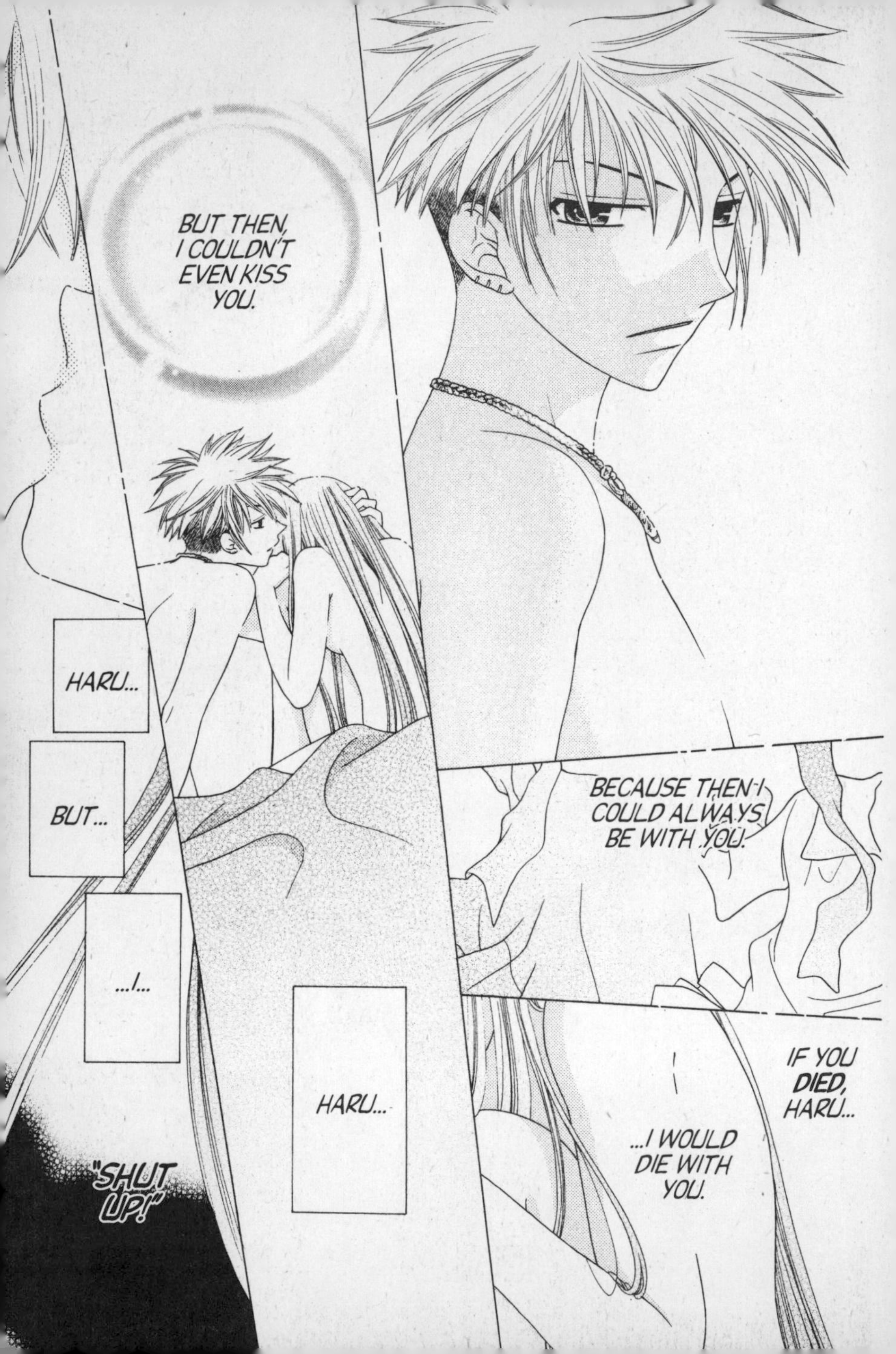
BECAUSE THEN I COULD ALWAYS BE WITH YOU.
IF YOU DIED, HARU...
...I WOULD DIE WITH YOU.
BUT THEN, I COULDN'T EVEN KISS YOU.
HARU...
HARU...
BUT...
...I...
"SHUT UP!"

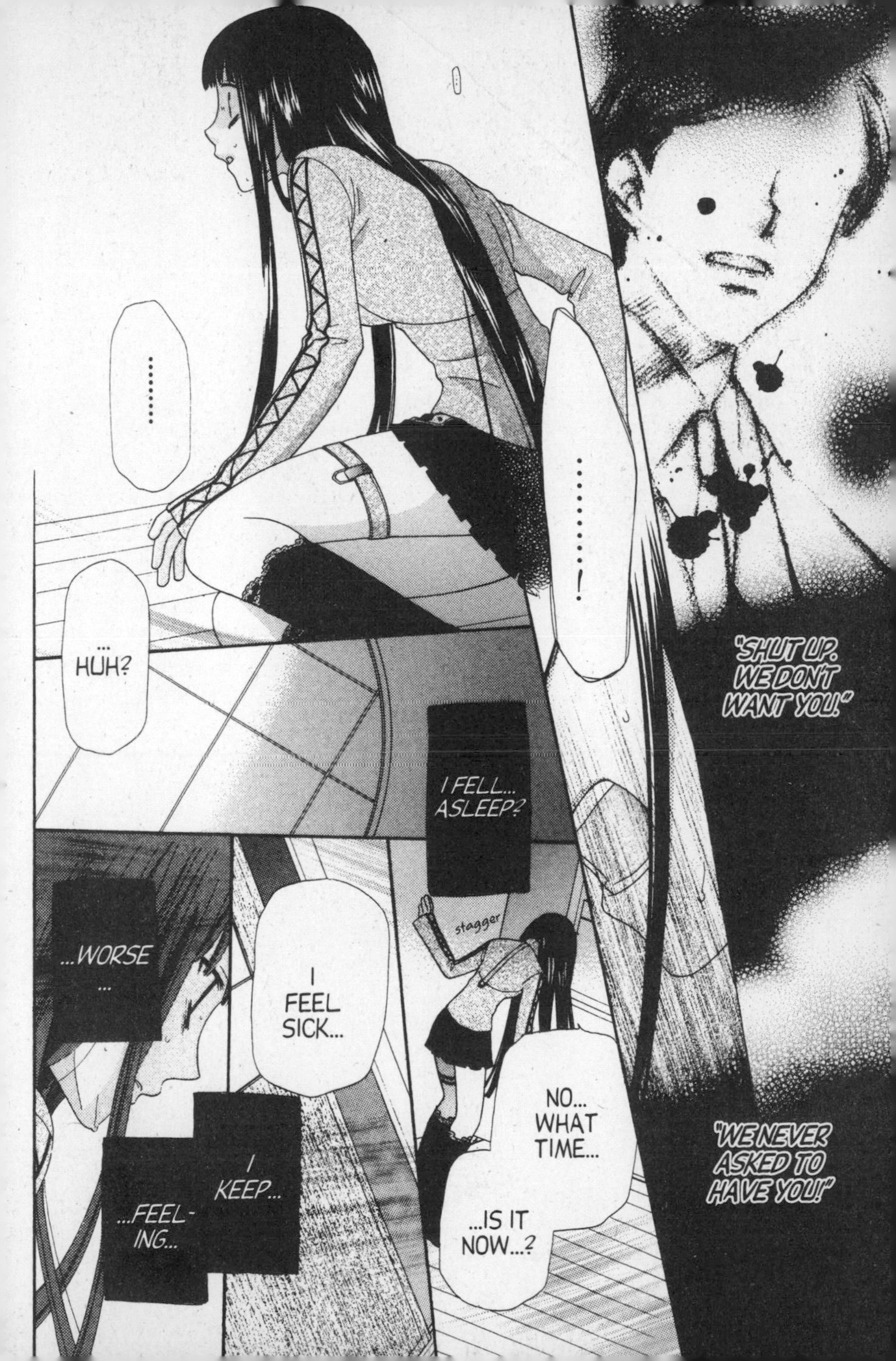
"SHUT UP. WE DON'T WANT YOU."
"WE NEVER ASKED TO HAVE YOU!"
......!
!
......
...HUH?
I FELL... ASLEEP?
stagger
I FEEL SICK...
NO... WHAT TIME...
...IS IT NOW...?
...WORSE...
I KEEP...
...FEEL-ING...

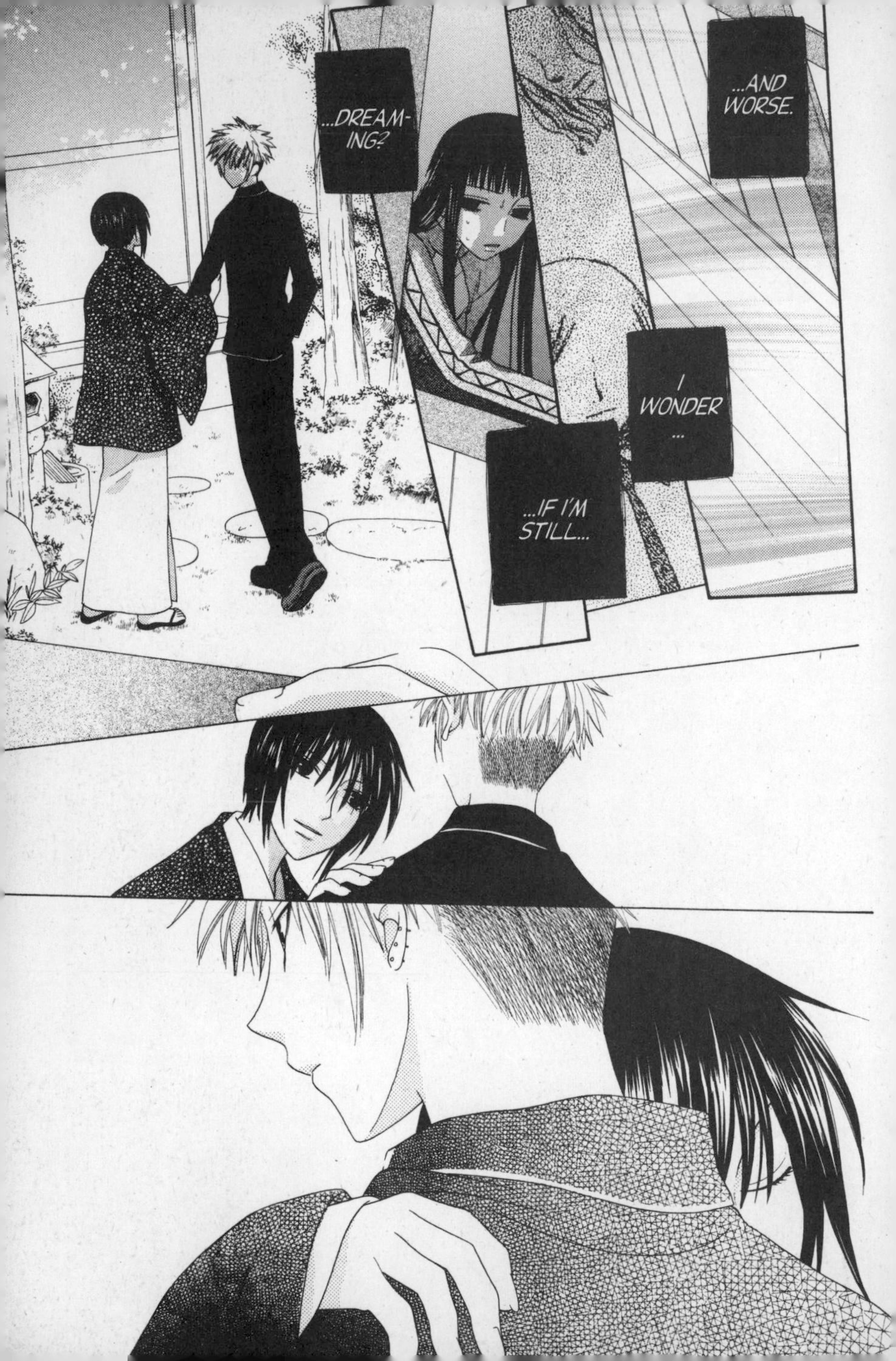
...AND WORSE.
I WONDER...
...IF I'M STILL...
...DREAMING?

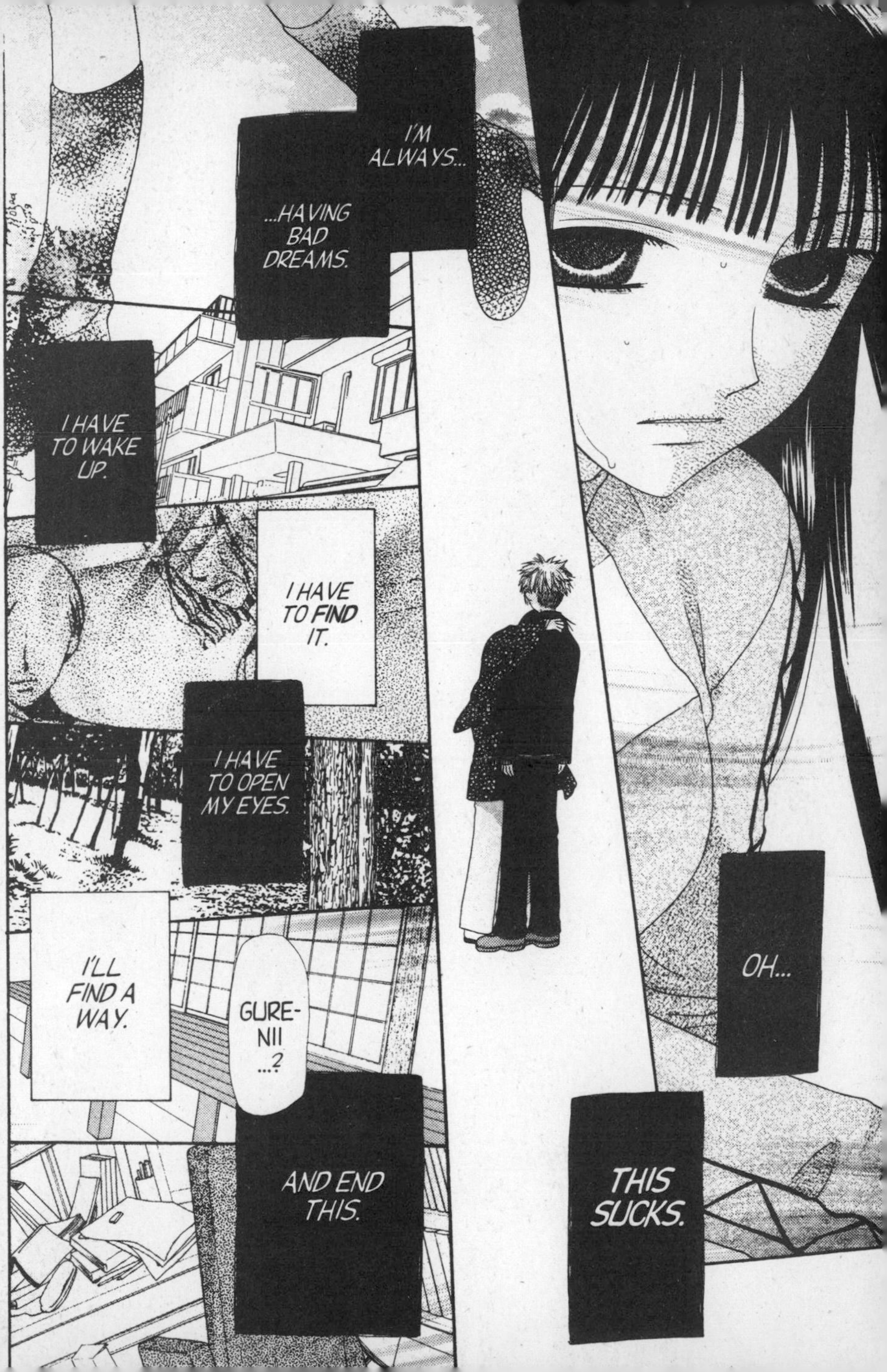

I'M ALWAYS...
...HAVING BAD DREAMS.
I HAVE TO WAKE UP.
I HAVE TO FIND IT.
I HAVE TO OPEN MY EYES.
I'LL FIND A WAY.
AND END THIS.
GURE-NII...?
OH...
THIS SUCKS.

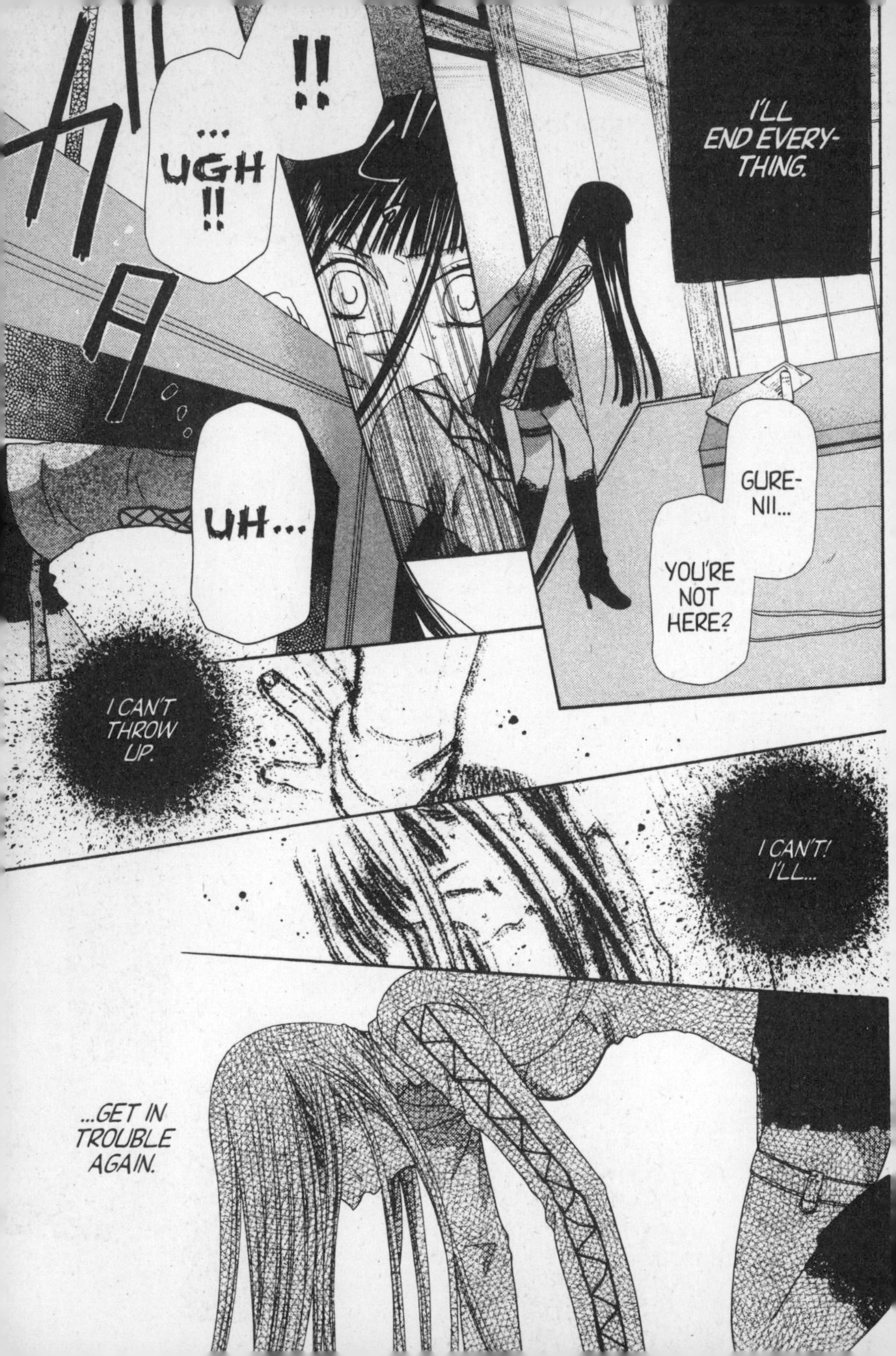
I'LL END EVERY-THING.
GURE-NII...
YOU'RE NOT HERE?
!!
...UGH!!
UH...
I CAN'T THROW UP.
I CAN'T! I'LL...
...GET IN TROUBLE AGAIN.

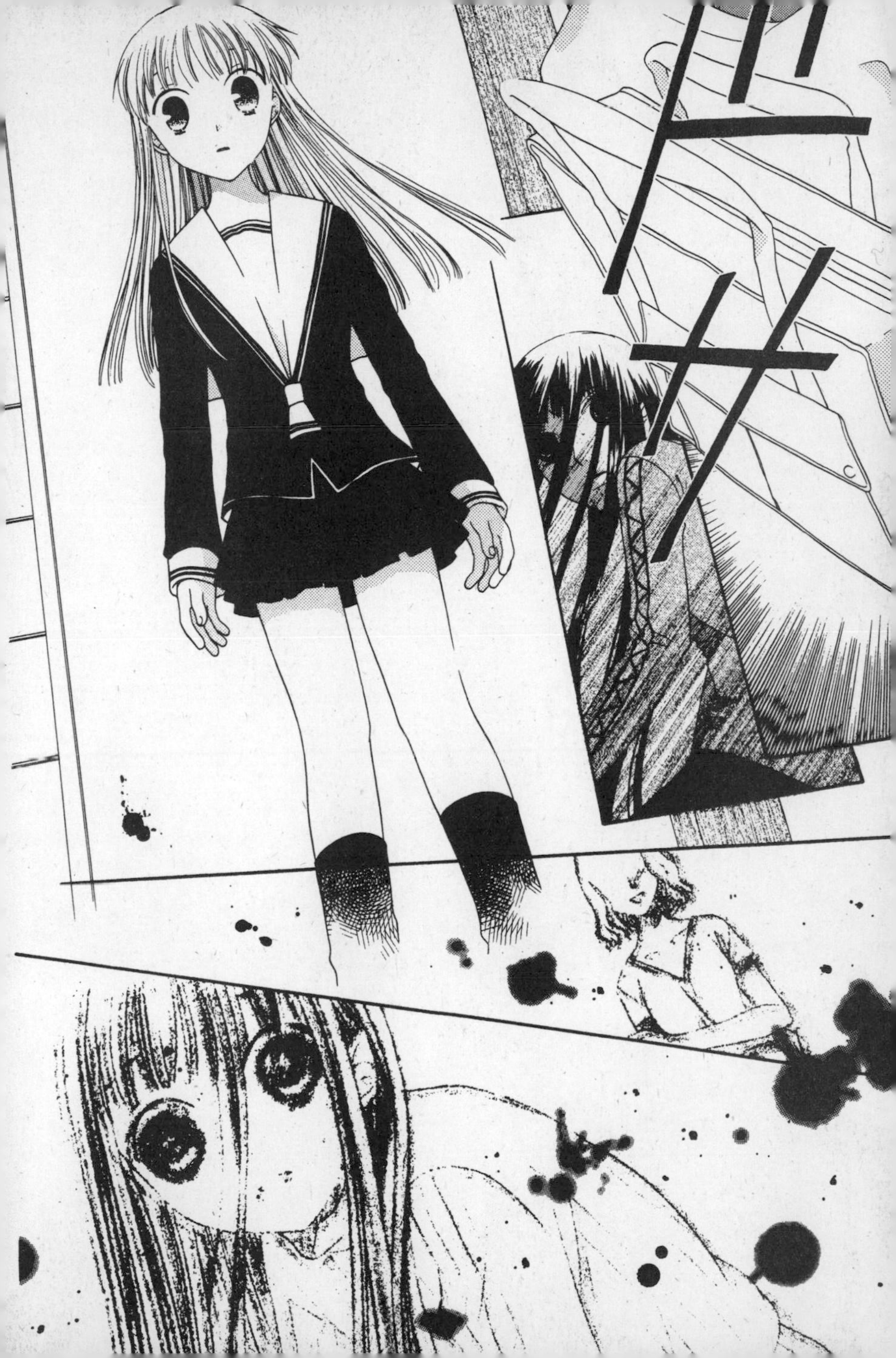

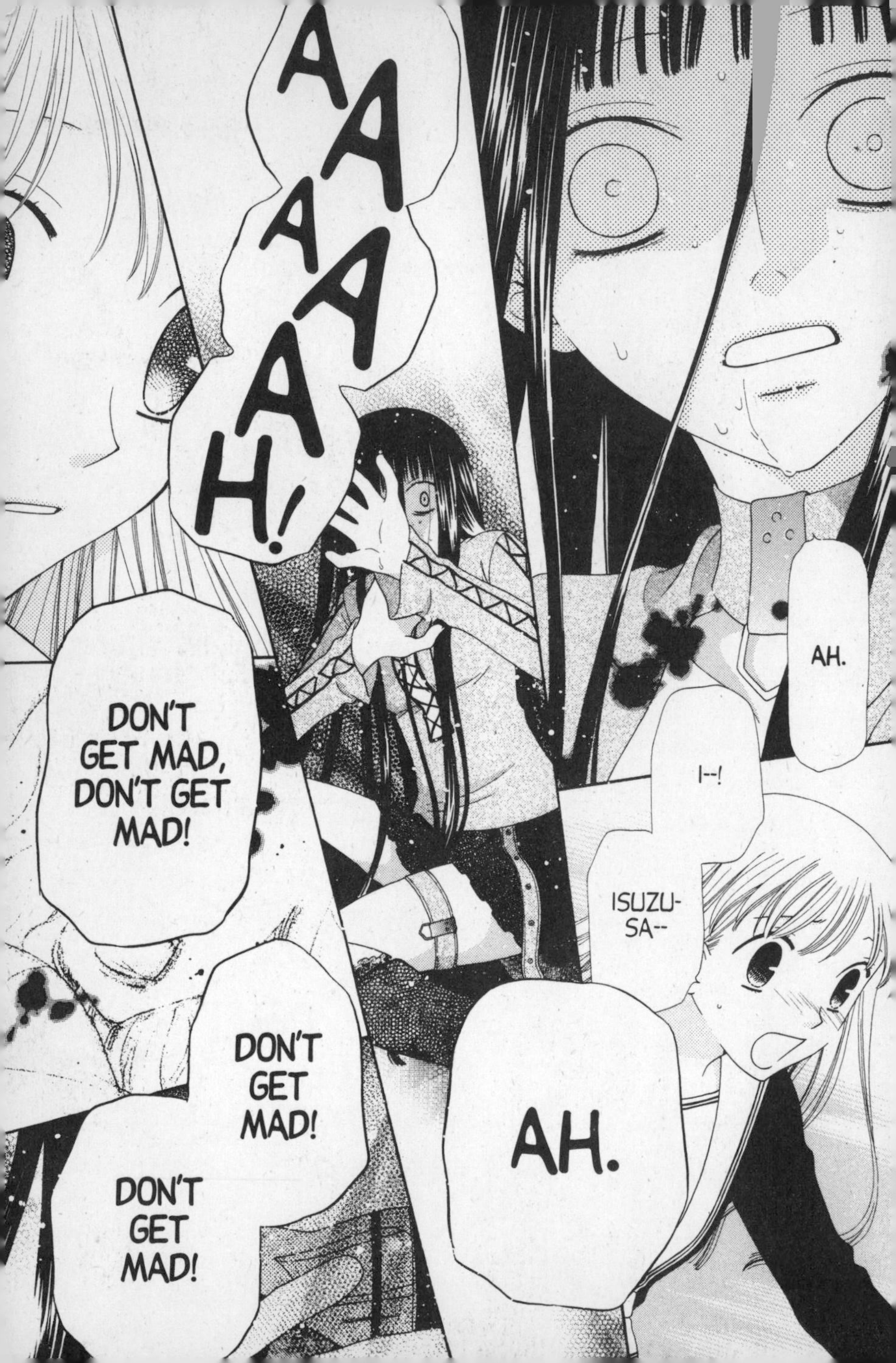
AH.
I--!
ISUZU-SA--
AH.
AAAAAH!
DON'T GET MAD, DON'T GET MAD!
DON'T GET MAD!
DON'T GET MAD!

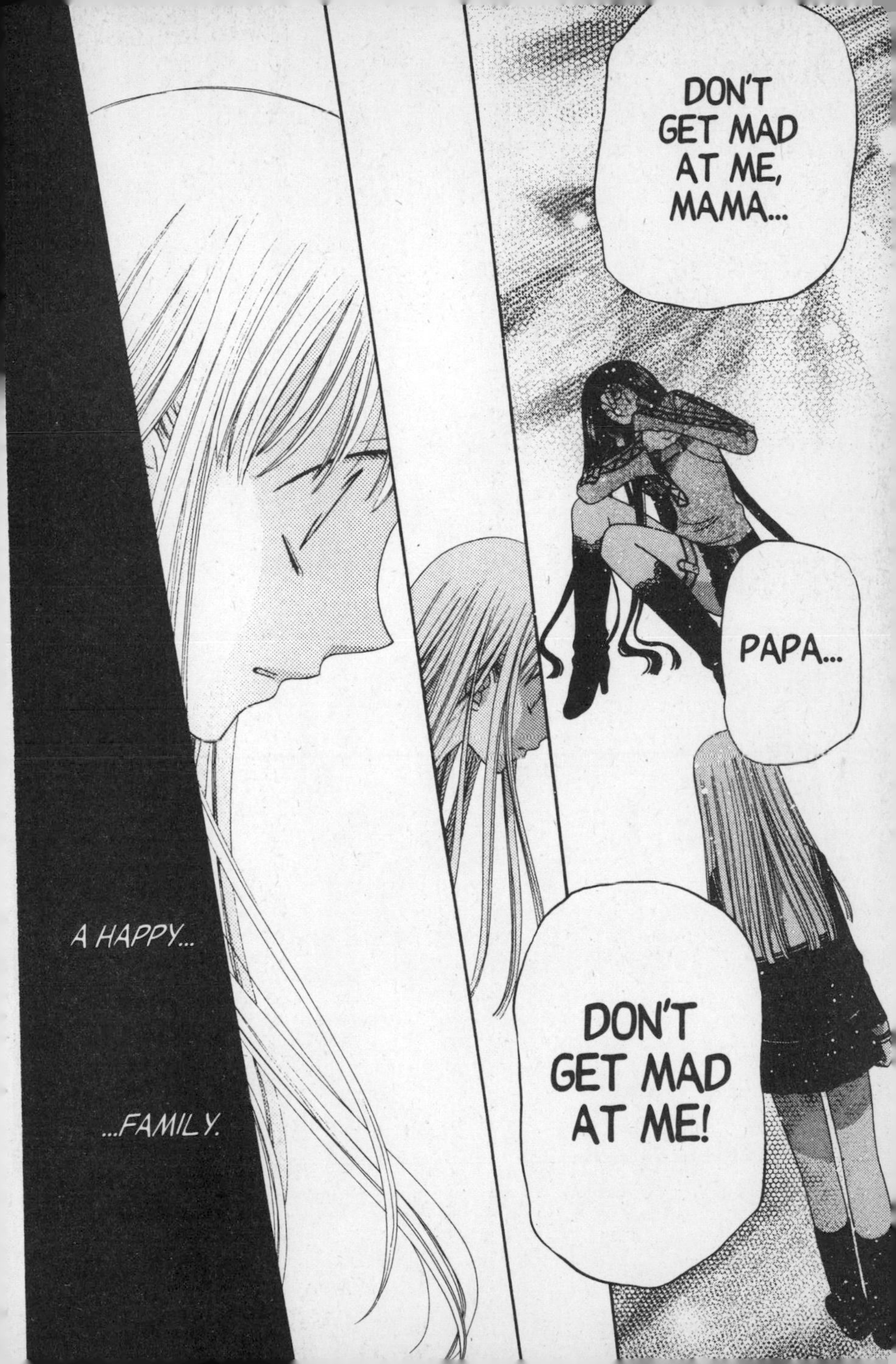
DON'T GET MAD AT ME, MAMA...
PAPA...
DON'T GET MAD AT ME!
A HAPPY...
...FAMILY.

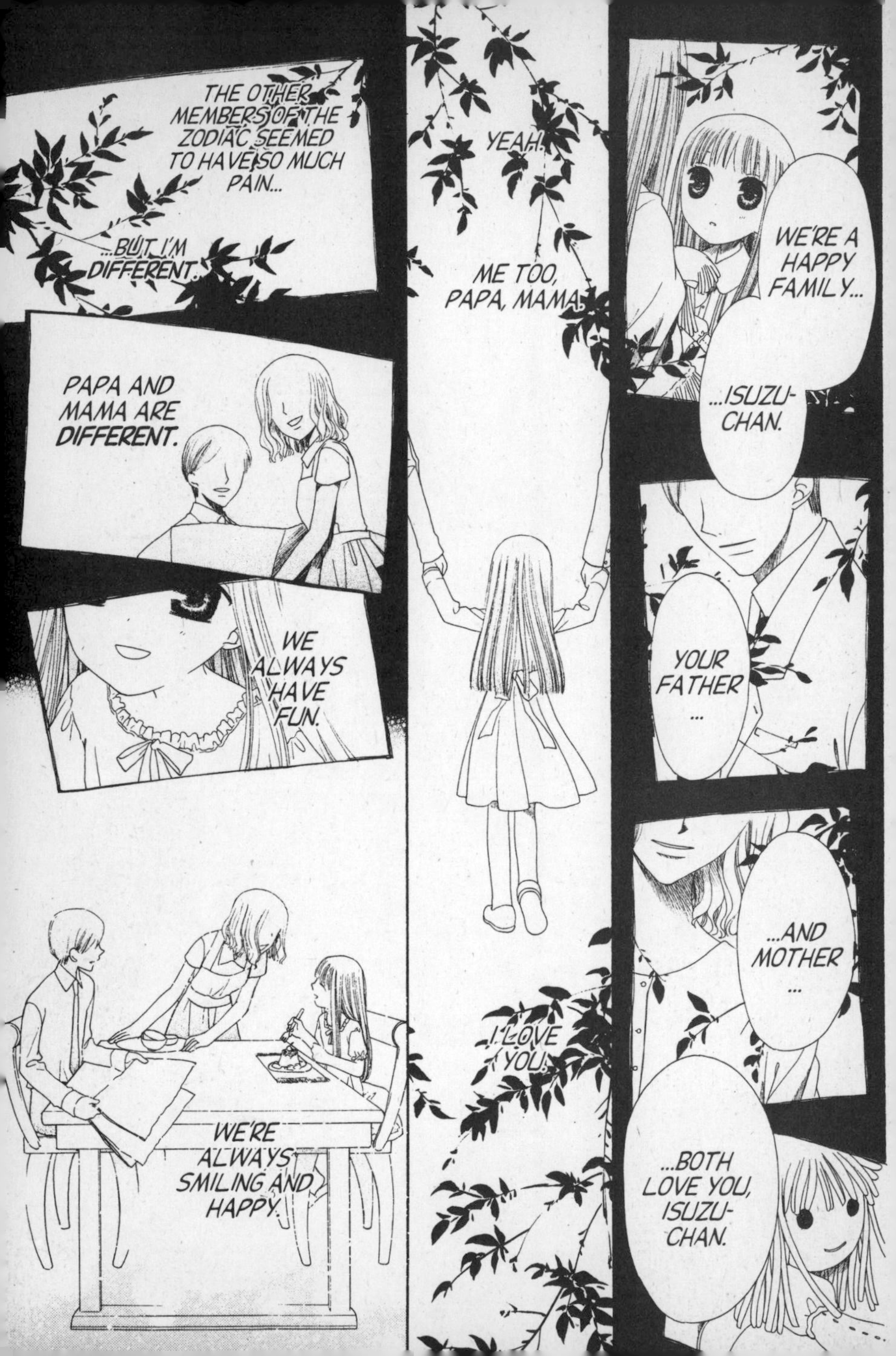

WE'RE A HAPPY FAMILY...
...ISUZU-CHAN.
YOUR FATHER ...
...AND MOTHER ...
...BOTH LOVE YOU, ISUZU-CHAN.
YEAH.
ME TOO, PAPA, MAMA.
I LOVE YOU.
THE OTHER MEMBERS OF THE ZODIAC SEEMED TO HAVE SO MUCH PAIN...
...BUT I'M DIFFERENT.
PAPA AND MAMA ARE DIFFERENT.
WE ALWAYS HAVE FUN.
WE'RE ALWAYS SMILING AND HAPPY.

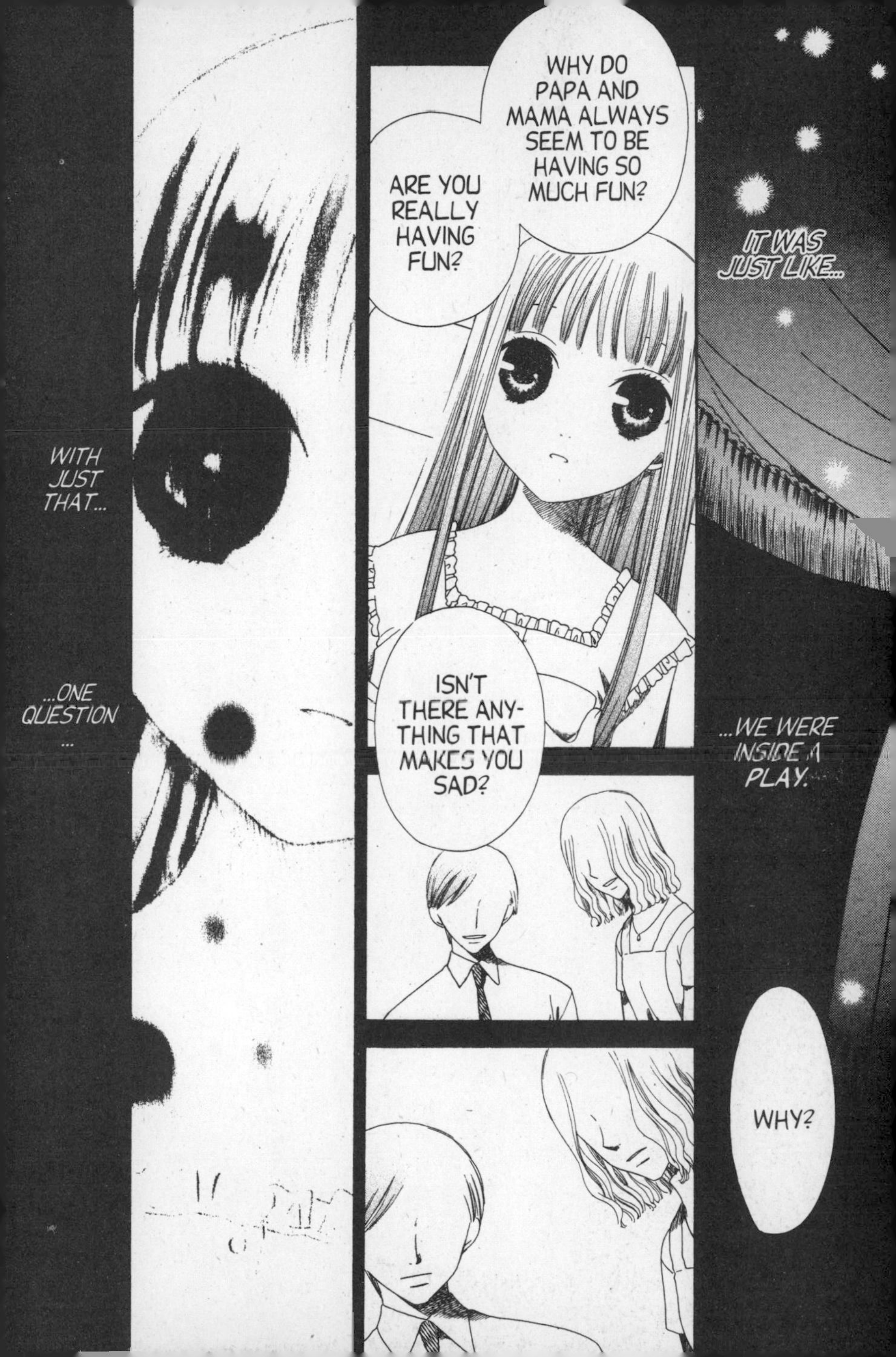
IT WAS JUST LIKE...
...WE WERE INSIDE A PLAY.
WHY DO PAPA AND MAMA ALWAYS SEEM TO BE HAVING SO MUCH FUN?
ARE YOU REALLY HAVING FUN?
ISN'T THERE ANY-THING THAT MAKES YOU SAD?
WHY?
WITH JUST THAT...
...ONE QUESTION ...

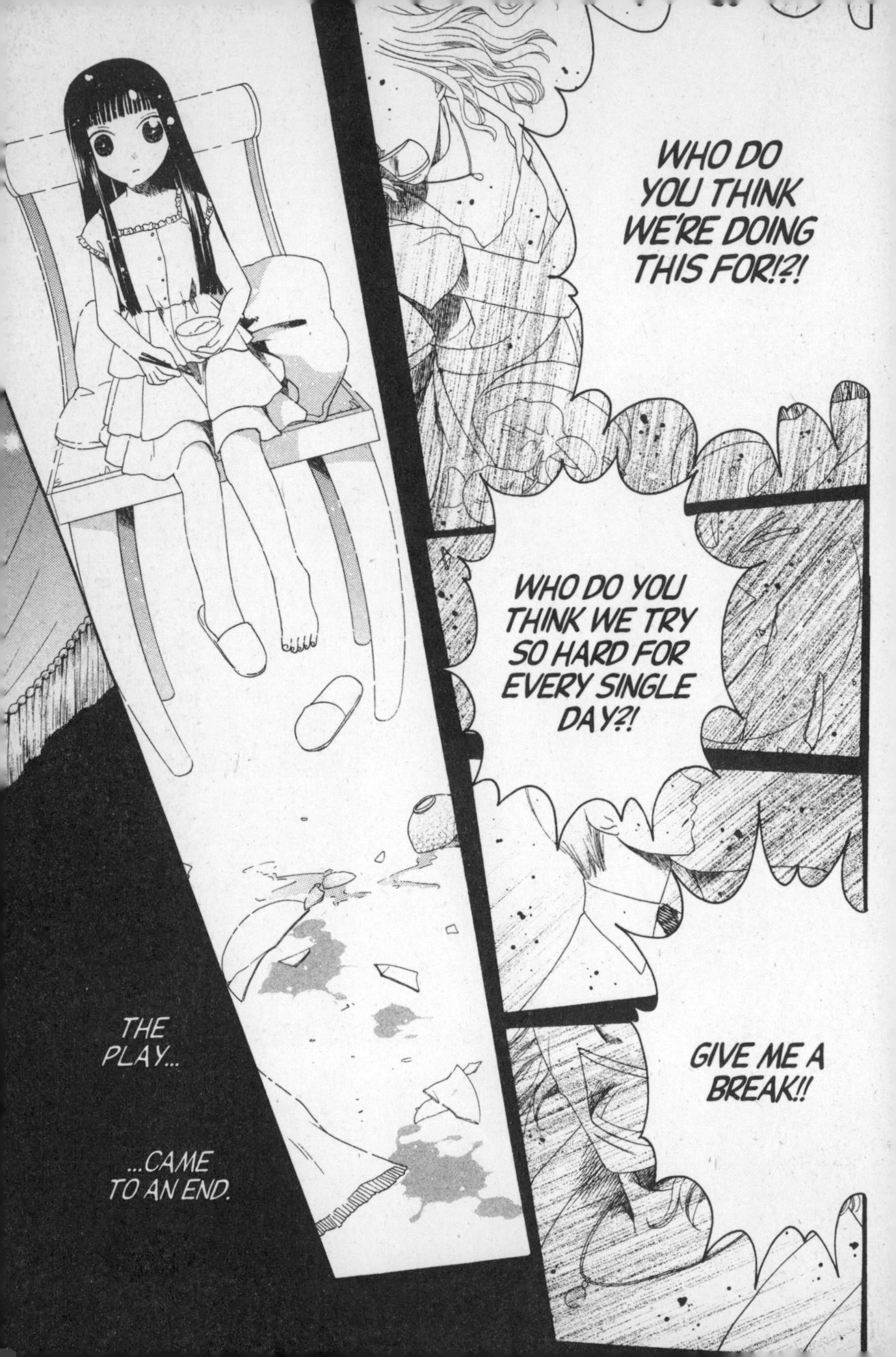
WHO DO YOU THINK WE'RE DOING THIS FOR!?!
WHO DO YOU THINK WE TRY SO HARD FOR EVERY SINGLE DAY?!
GIVE ME A BREAK!!
THE PLAY...
...CAME TO AN END.

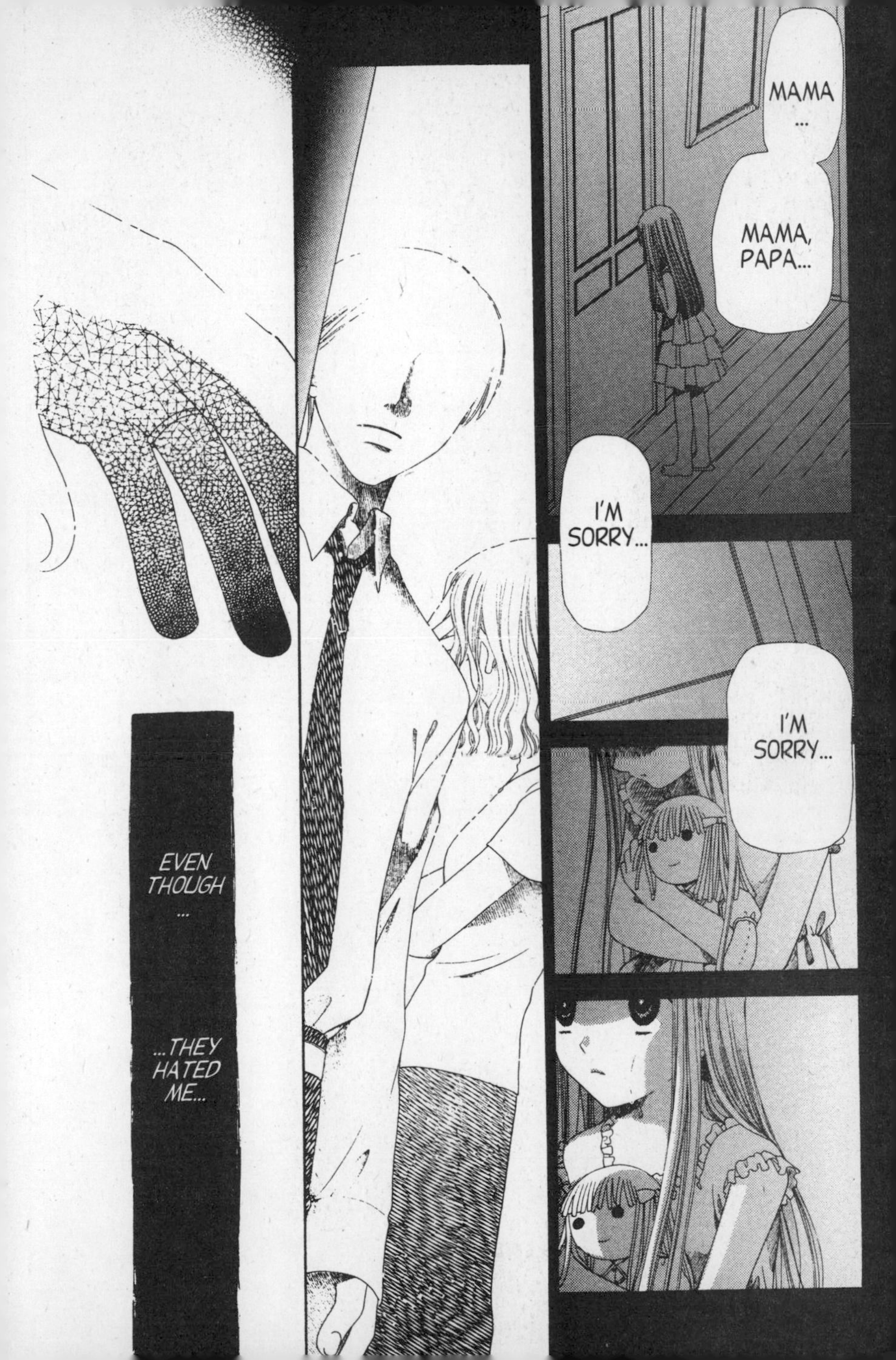
MAMA ...
MAMA, PAPA...
I'M SORRY...
I'M SORRY...
EVEN THOUGH ...
...THEY HATED ME...

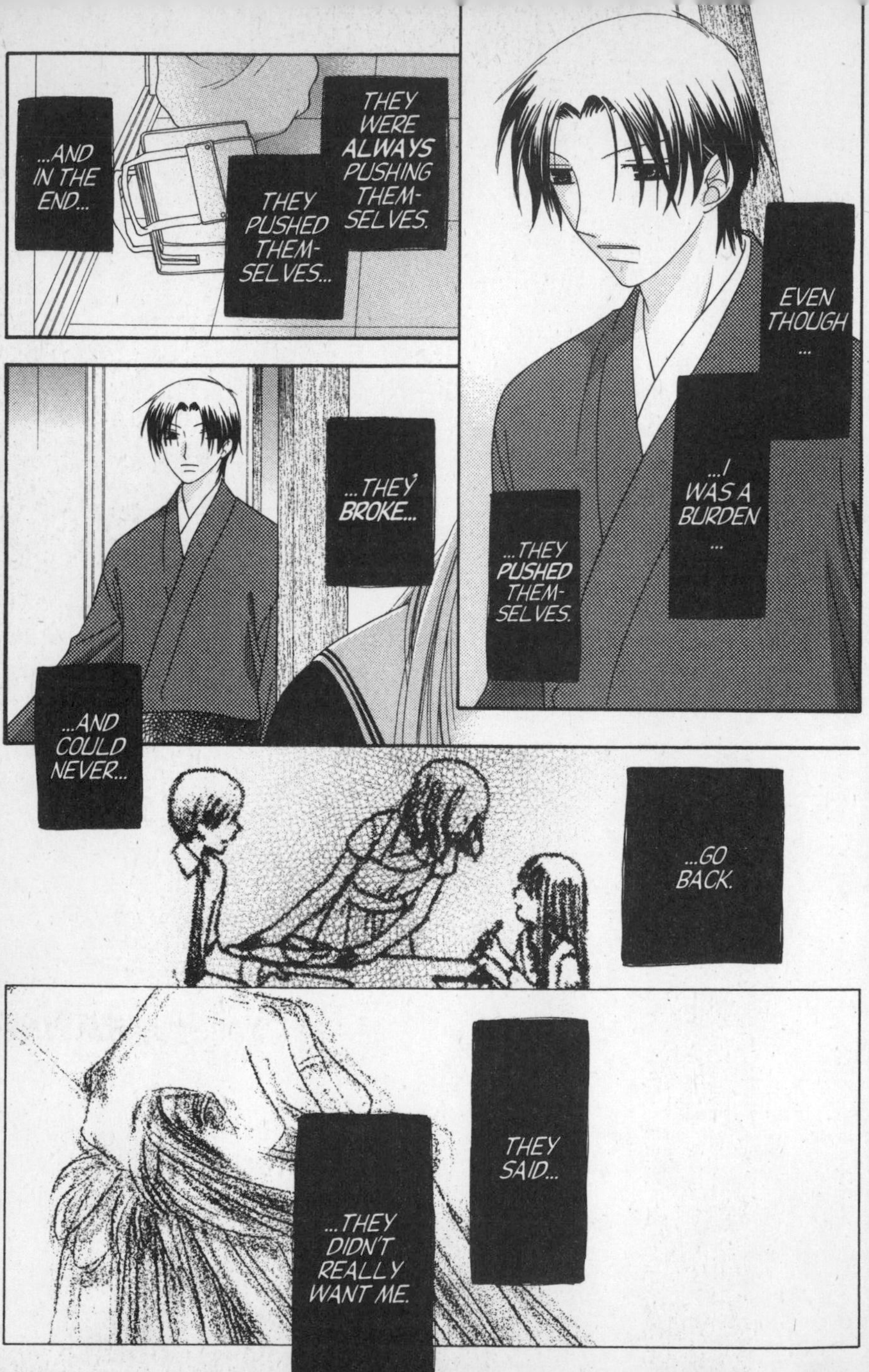
EVEN THOUGH...
...I WAS A BURDEN...
...THEY PUSHED THEMSELVES.
THEY WERE ALWAYS PUSHING THEMSELVES.
THEY PUSHED THEMSELVES...
...AND IN THE END...
...THEY BROKE...
...AND COULD NEVER...
...GO BACK.
THEY SAID...
...THEY DIDN'T REALLY WANT ME.

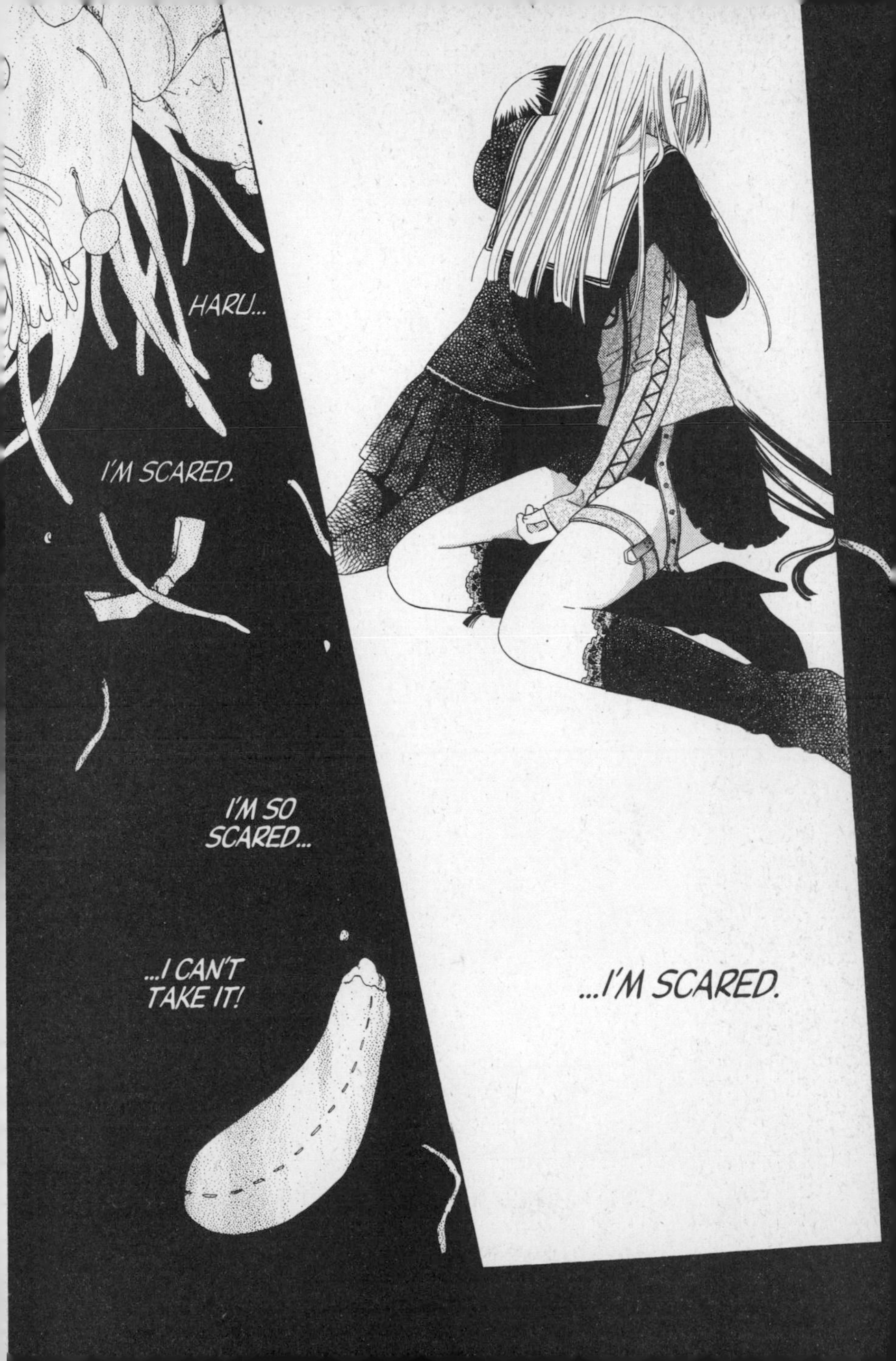
HARU...
I'M SCARED.
I'M SO SCARED...
...I CAN'T TAKE IT!
...I'M SCARED.

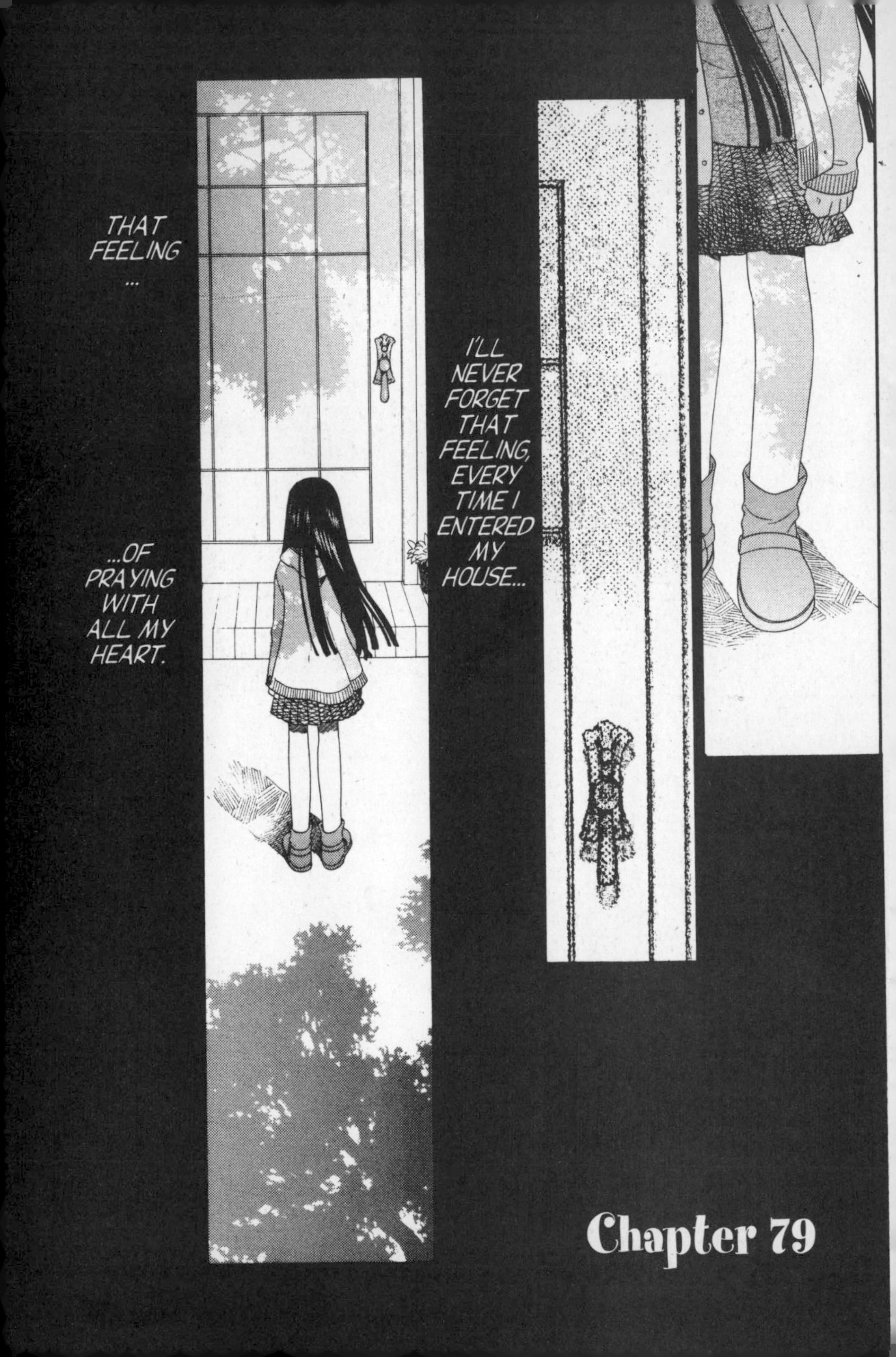
I'LL NEVER FORGET THAT FEELING, EVERY TIME I ENTERED MY HOUSE...
THAT FEELING ...
...OF PRAYING WITH ALL MY HEART.
Chapter 79

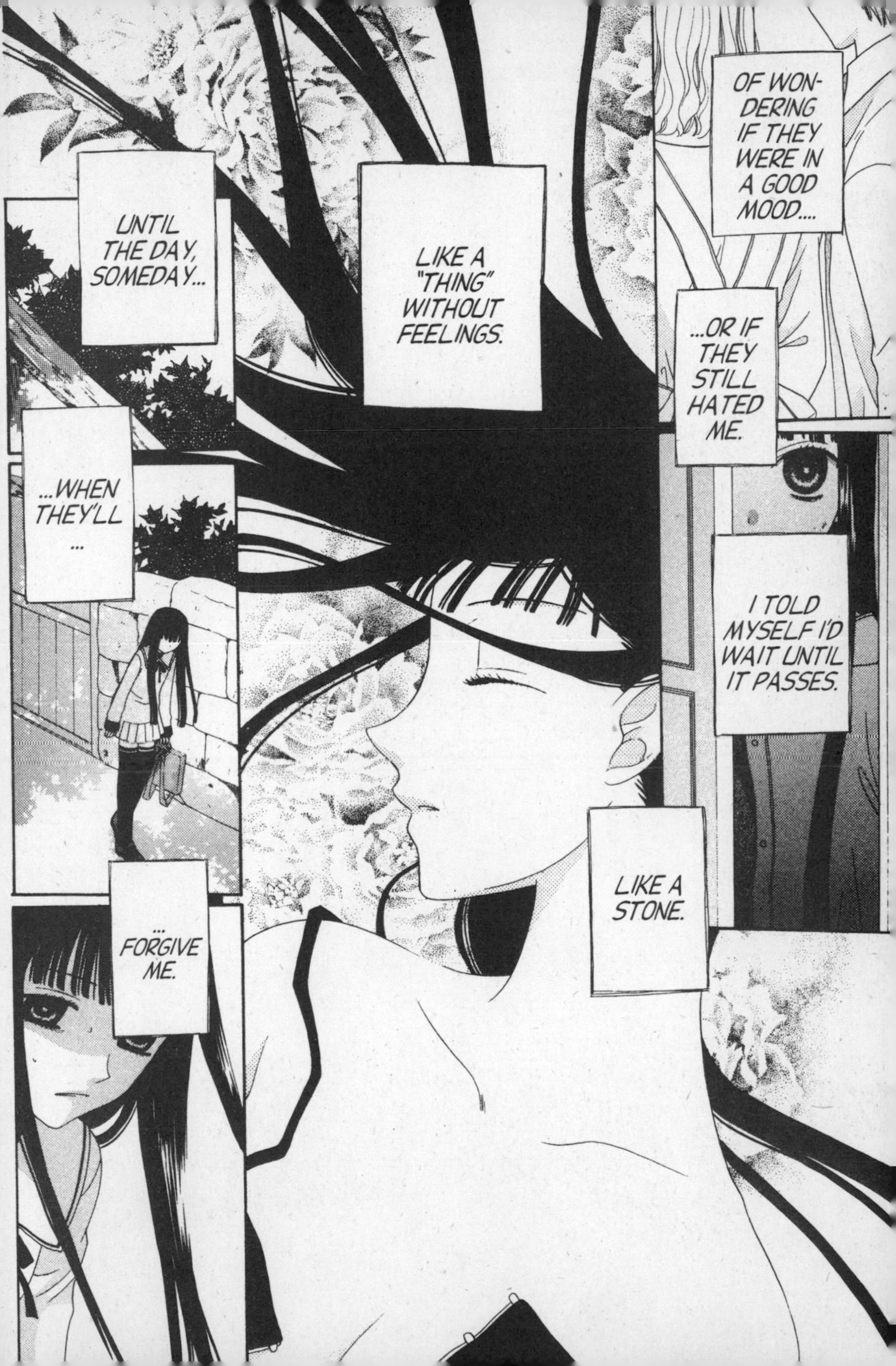
OF WONDERING IF THEY WERE IN A GOOD MOOD....
...OR IF THEY STILL HATED ME.
I TOLD MYSELF I'D WAIT UNTIL IT PASSES.
LIKE A "THING" WITHOUT FEELINGS.
LIKE A STONE.
UNTIL THE DAY, SOMEDAY...
...WHEN THEY'LL ...
... FORGIVE ME.

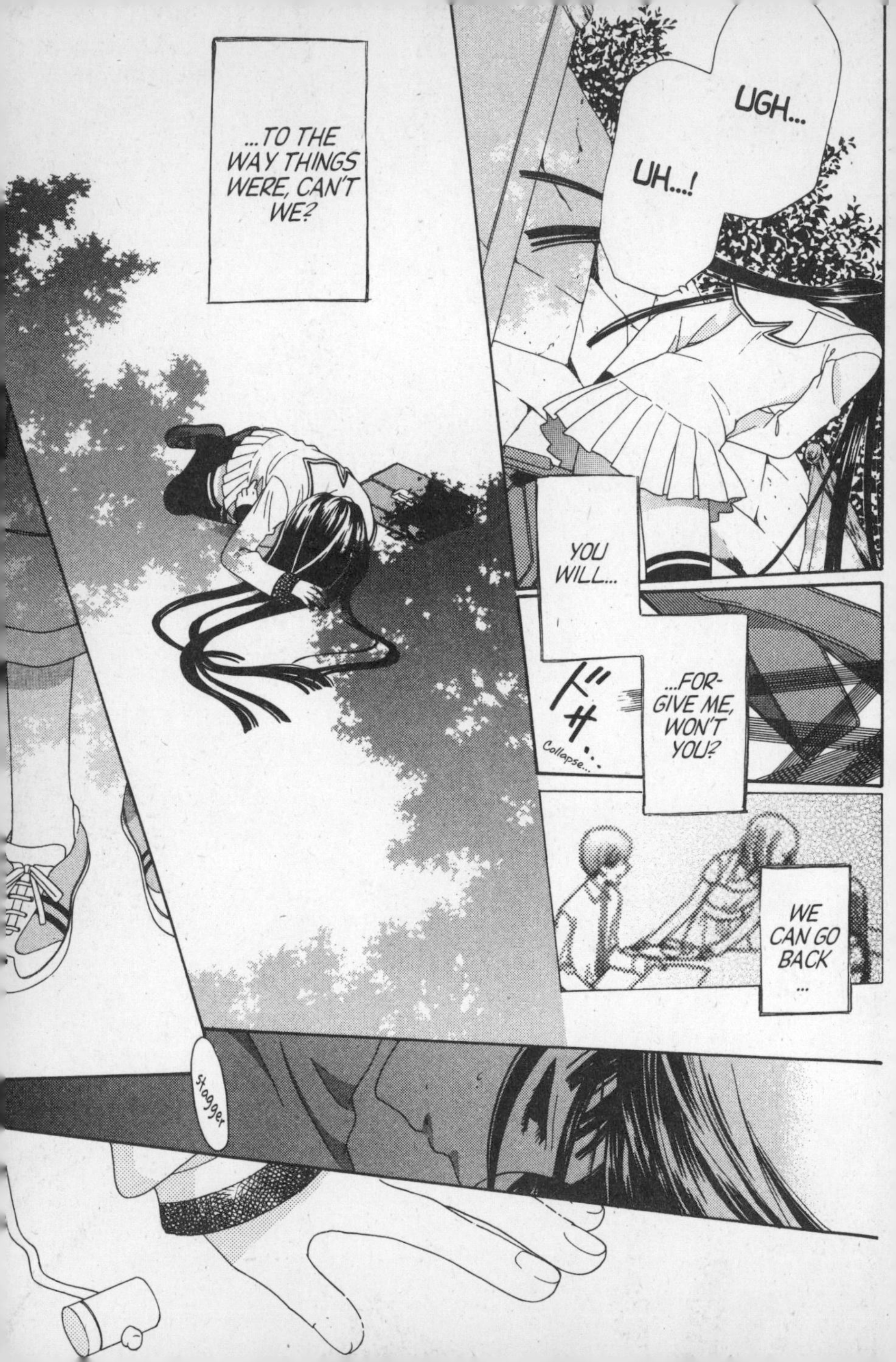
UGH...
UH...!
YOU WILL...
...FOR-GIVE ME, WON'T YOU?
ドサ
Collapse...
WE CAN GO BACK ...
...TO THE WAY THINGS WERE, CAN'T WE?
stagger

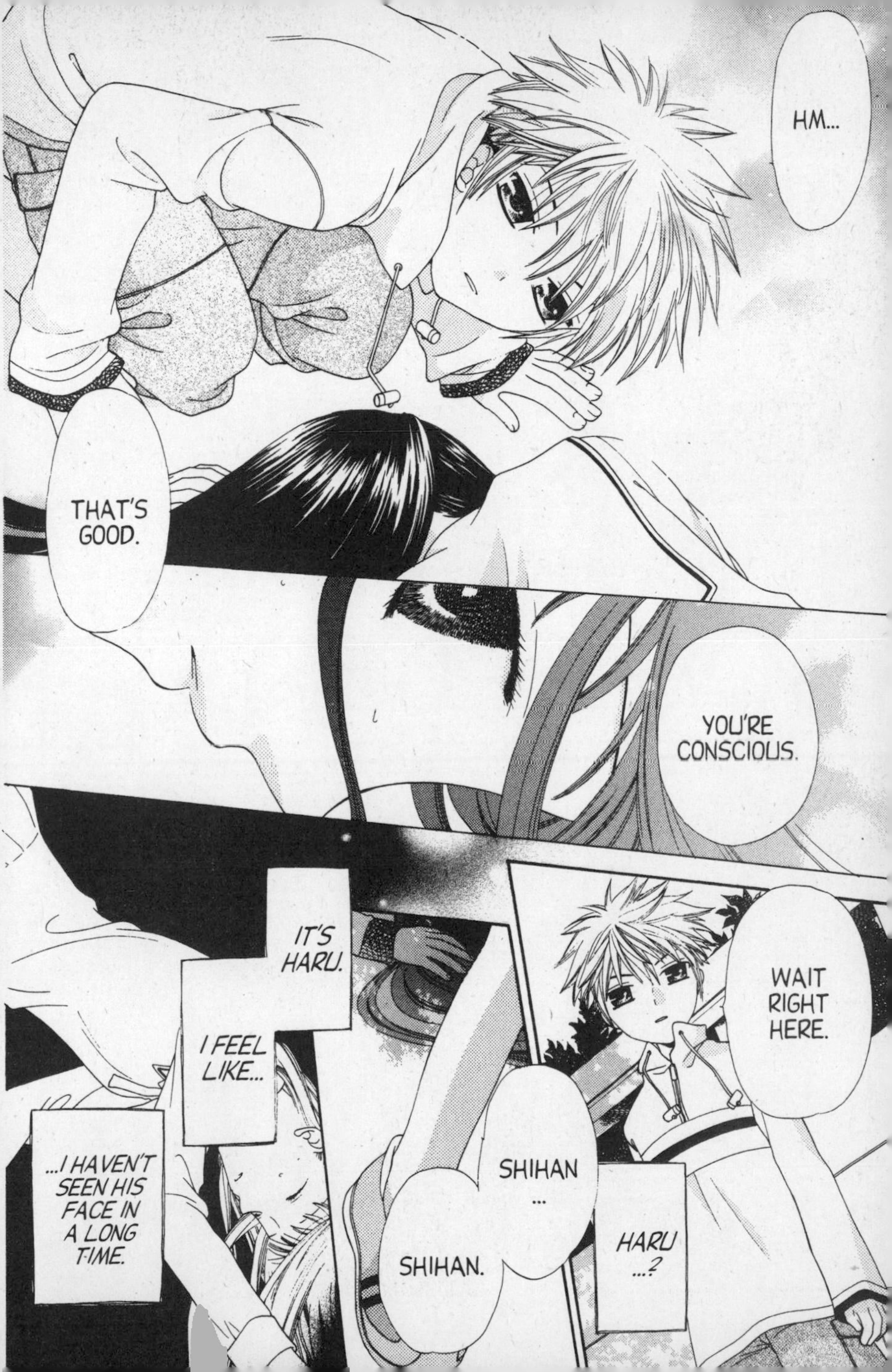
HM...
THAT'S GOOD.
YOU'RE CONSCIOUS.
WAIT RIGHT HERE.
HARU ...?
SHIHAN ...
SHIHAN.
IT'S HARU.
I FEEL LIKE...
...I HAVEN'T SEEN HIS FACE IN A LONG TIME.

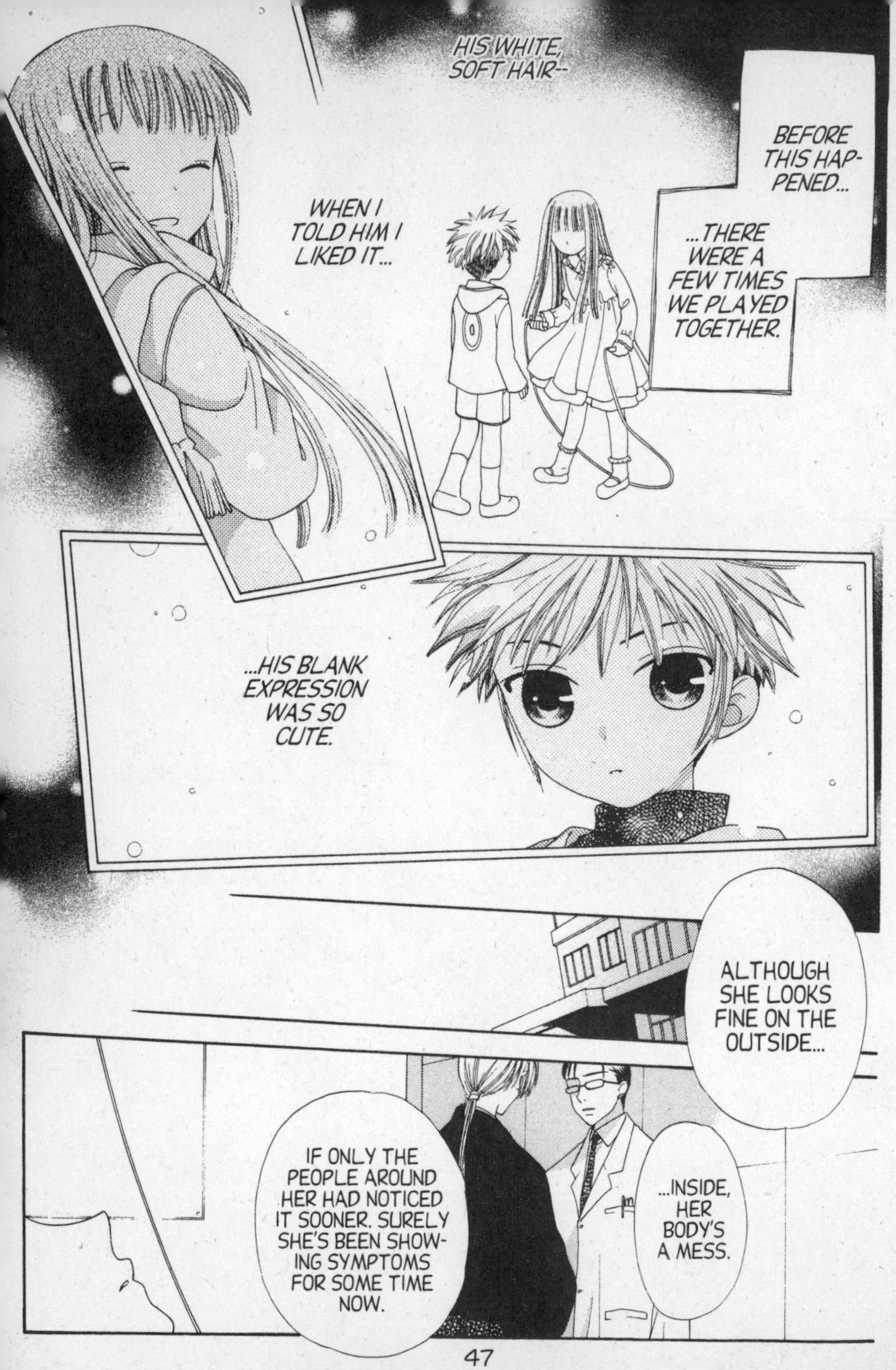
BEFORE THIS HAPPENED...
...THERE WERE A FEW TIMES WE PLAYED TOGETHER.
HIS WHITE, SOFT HAIR--
WHEN I TOLD HIM I LIKED IT...
...HIS BLANK EXPRESSION WAS SO CUTE.
ALTHOUGH SHE LOOKS FINE ON THE OUTSIDE...
...INSIDE, HER BODY'S A MESS.
IF ONLY THE PEOPLE AROUND HER HAD NOTICED IT SOONER. SURELY SHE'S BEEN SHOWING SYMPTOMS FOR SOME TIME NOW.

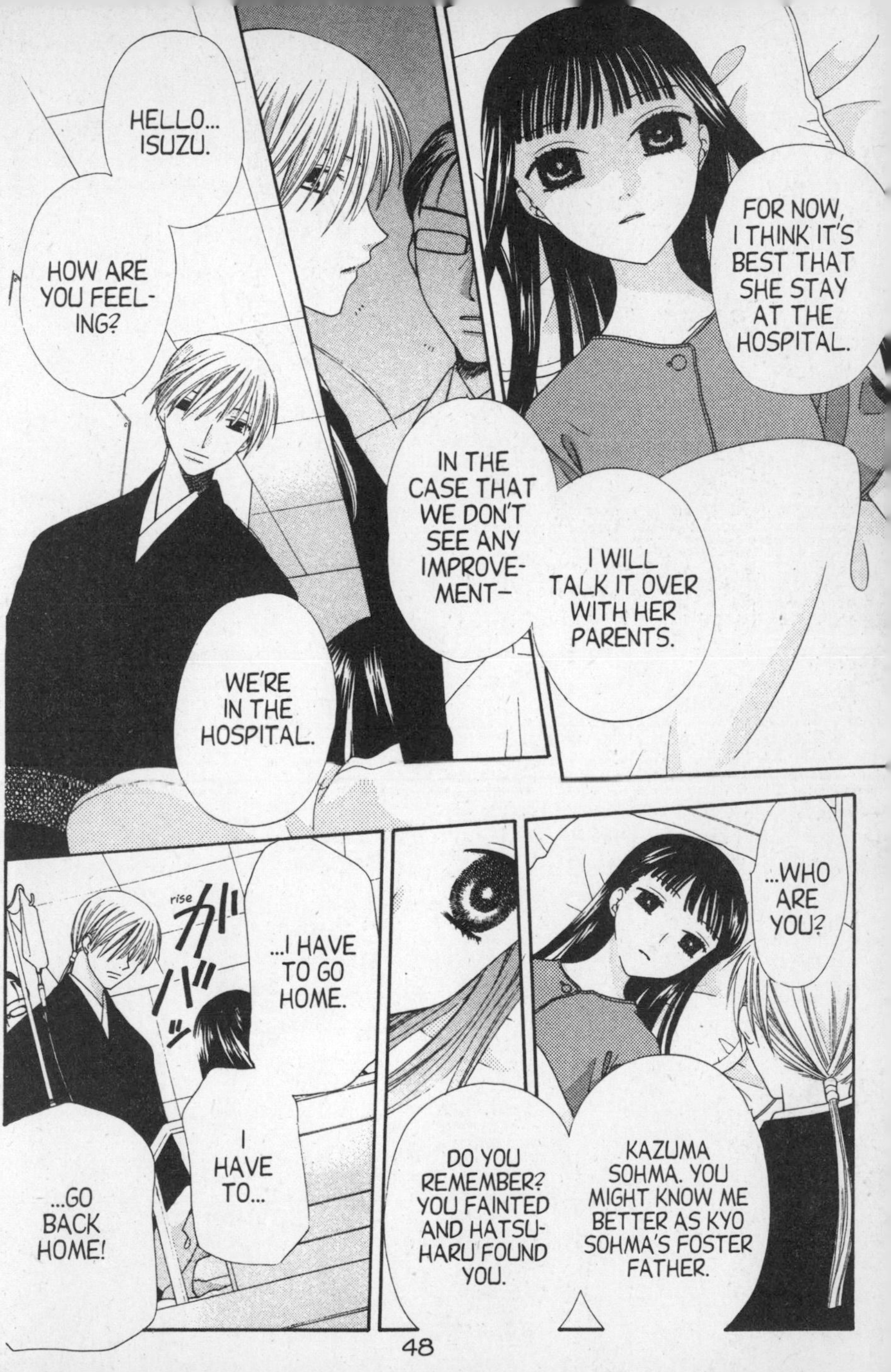
FOR NOW, I THINK IT'S BEST THAT SHE STAY AT THE HOSPITAL.
IN THE CASE THAT WE DON'T SEE ANY IMPROVEMENT—
I WILL TALK IT OVER WITH HER PARENTS.
HELLO... ISUZU.
HOW ARE YOU FEEL-ING?
WE'RE IN THE HOSPITAL.
...WHO ARE YOU?
KAZUMA SOHMA. YOU MIGHT KNOW ME BETTER AS KYO SOHMA'S FOSTER FATHER.
DO YOU REMEMBER? YOU FAINTED AND HATSU-HARU FOUND YOU.
rise ガバッ
...I HAVE TO GO HOME.
I HAVE TO...
...GO BACK HOME!

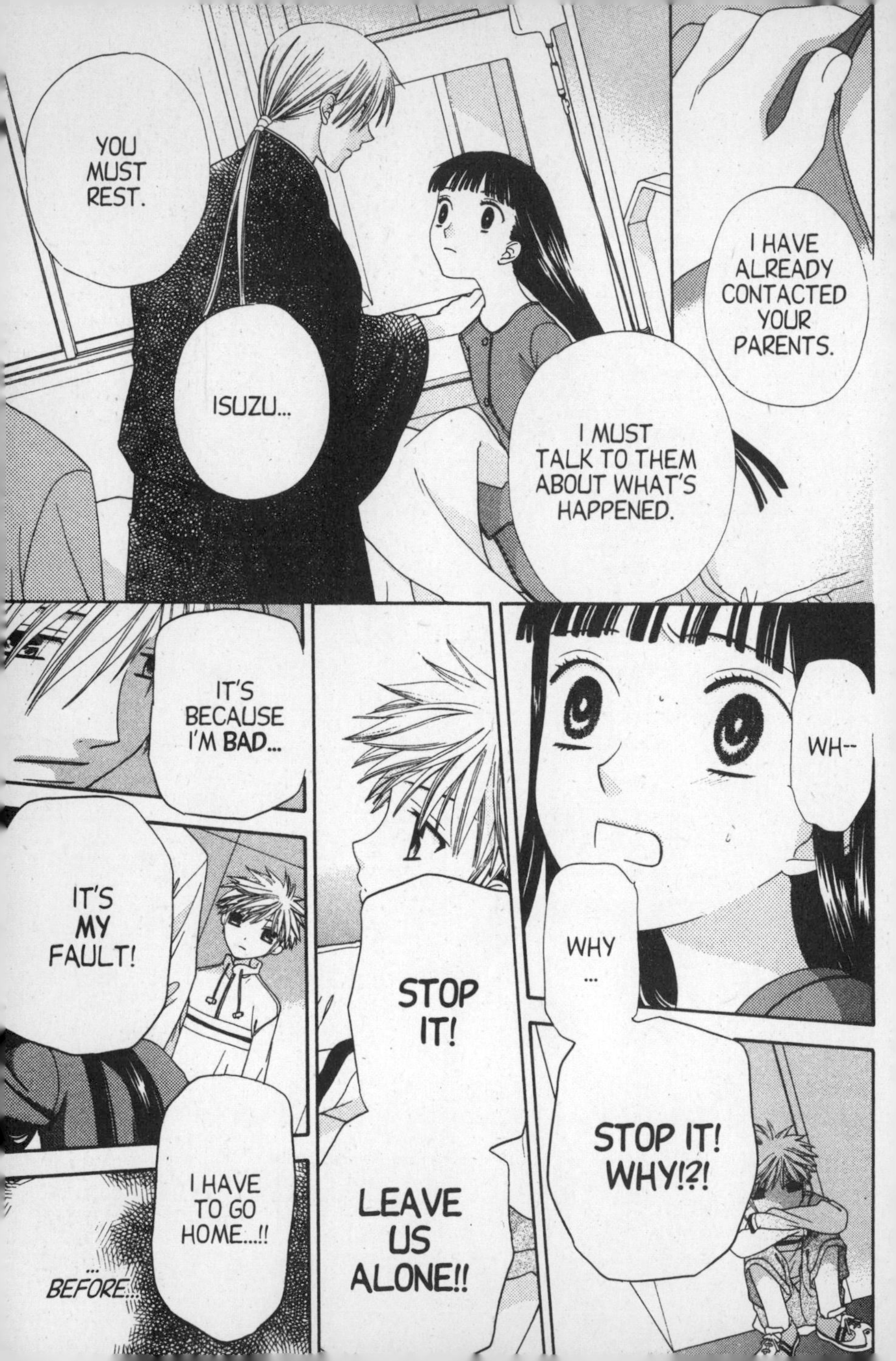
I HAVE ALREADY CONTACTED YOUR PARENTS.
I MUST TALK TO THEM ABOUT WHAT'S HAPPENED.
YOU MUST REST.
ISUZU...
WH--
WHY ...
STOP IT! WHY!?!
STOP IT!
LEAVE US ALONE!!
IT'S BECAUSE I'M **BAD**...
IT'S MY FAULT!
I HAVE TO GO HOME...!!
... *BEFORE...*

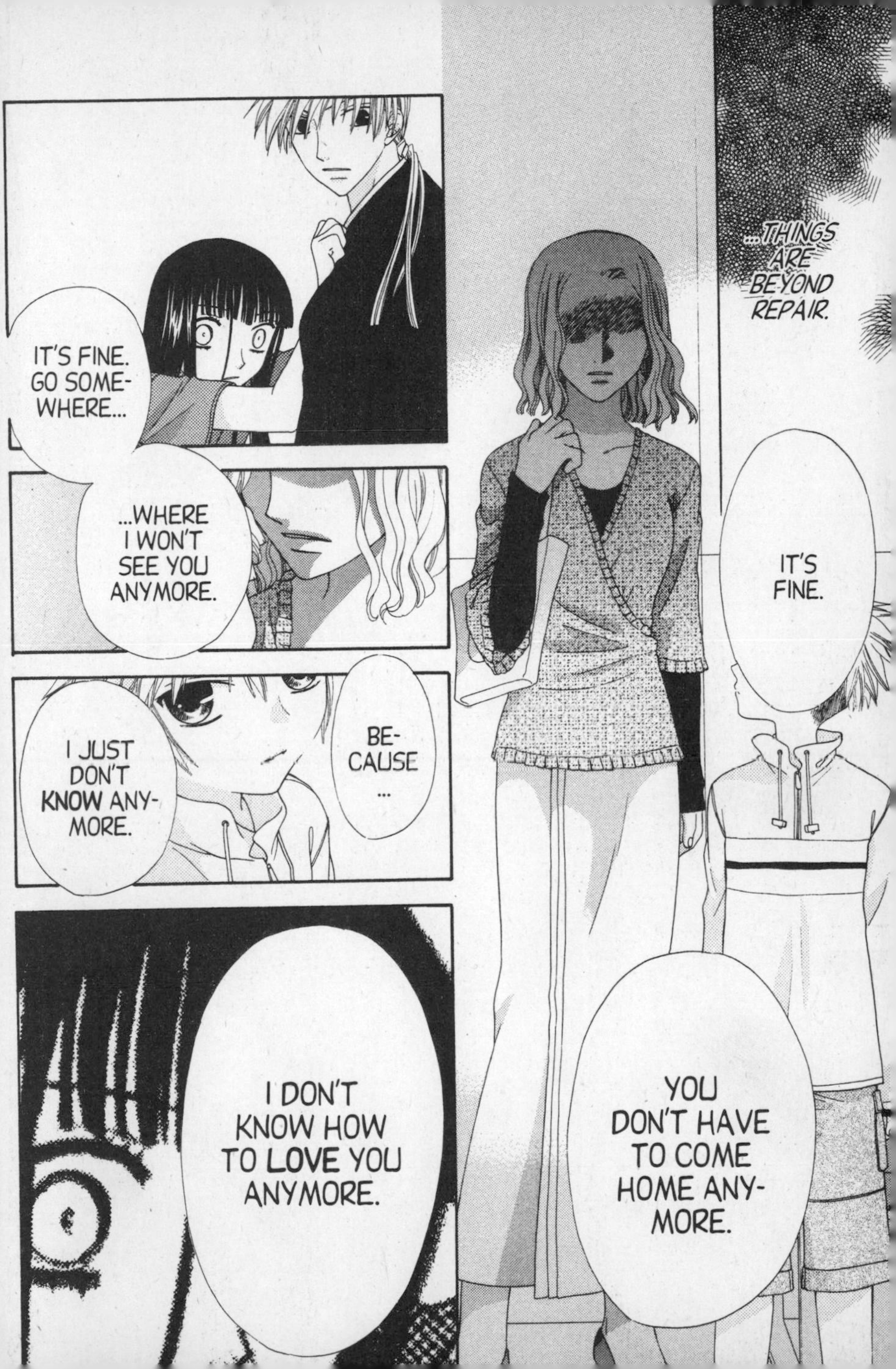
...THINGS ARE BEYOND REPAIR.
IT'S FINE.
YOU DON'T HAVE TO COME HOME ANY-MORE.
IT'S FINE. GO SOME-WHERE...
...WHERE I WON'T SEE YOU ANYMORE.
BE-CAUSE ...
I JUST DON'T KNOW ANY-MORE.
I DON'T KNOW HOW TO LOVE YOU ANYMORE.

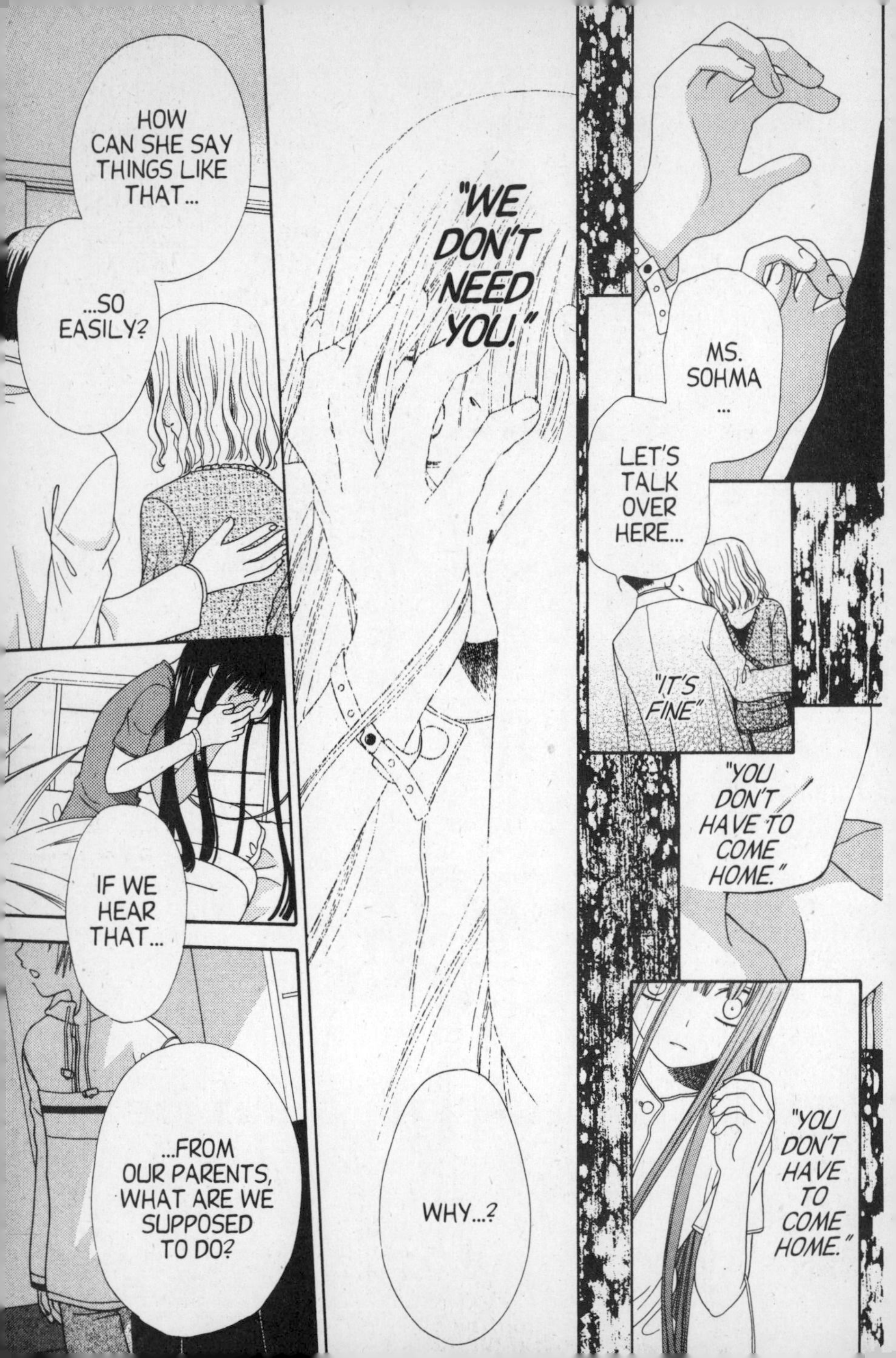
MS. SOHMA ...
LET'S TALK OVER HERE...
"IT'S FINE"
"YOU DON'T HAVE TO COME HOME."
"YOU DON'T HAVE TO COME HOME."
"WE DON'T NEED YOU."
WHY...?
HOW CAN SHE SAY THINGS LIKE THAT...
...SO EASILY?
IF WE HEAR THAT...
...FROM OUR PARENTS, WHAT ARE WE SUPPOSED TO DO?

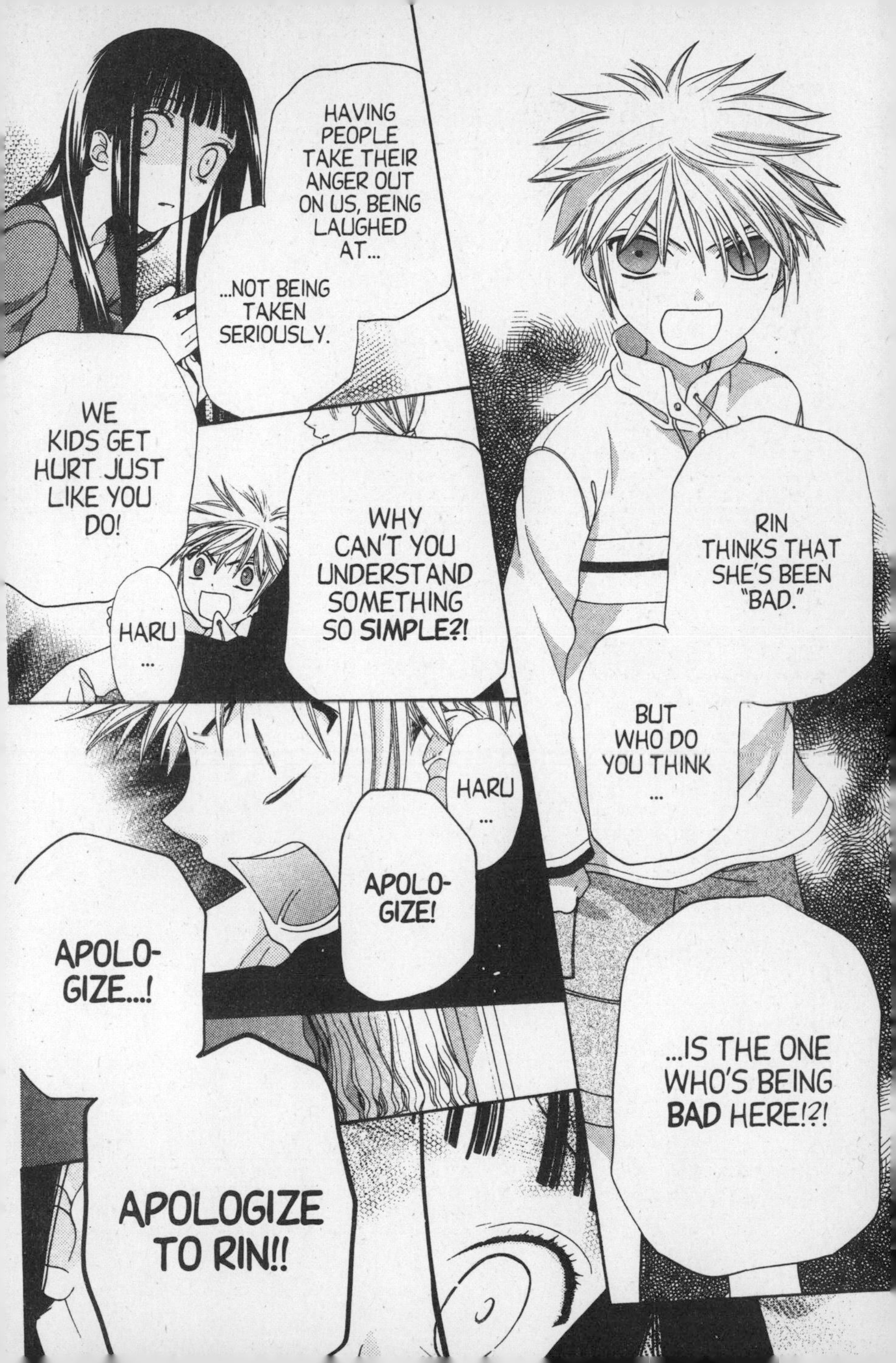
RIN THINKS THAT SHE'S BEEN "BAD."
BUT WHO DO YOU THINK ...
...IS THE ONE WHO'S BEING BAD HERE!?!
HAVING PEOPLE TAKE THEIR ANGER OUT ON US, BEING LAUGHED AT...
...NOT BEING TAKEN SERIOUSLY.
WE KIDS GET HURT JUST LIKE YOU DO!
WHY CAN'T YOU UNDERSTAND SOMETHING SO SIMPLE?!
HARU ...
HARU ...
APOLO-GIZE!
APOLO-GIZE...!
APOLOGIZE TO RIN!!

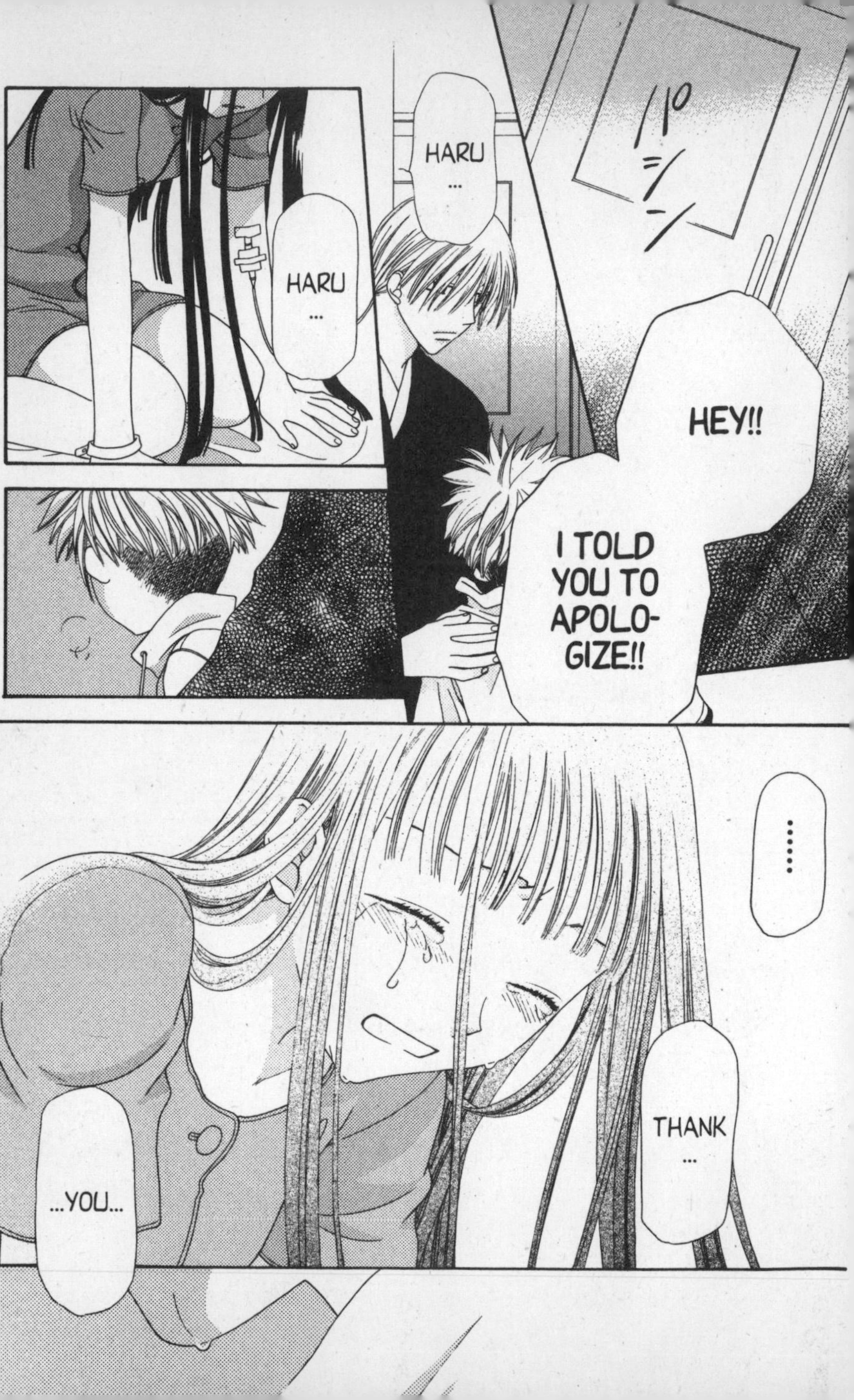
HEY!!
I TOLD YOU TO APOLO-GIZE!!
HARU ...
HARU ...
......
THANK ...
...YOU...

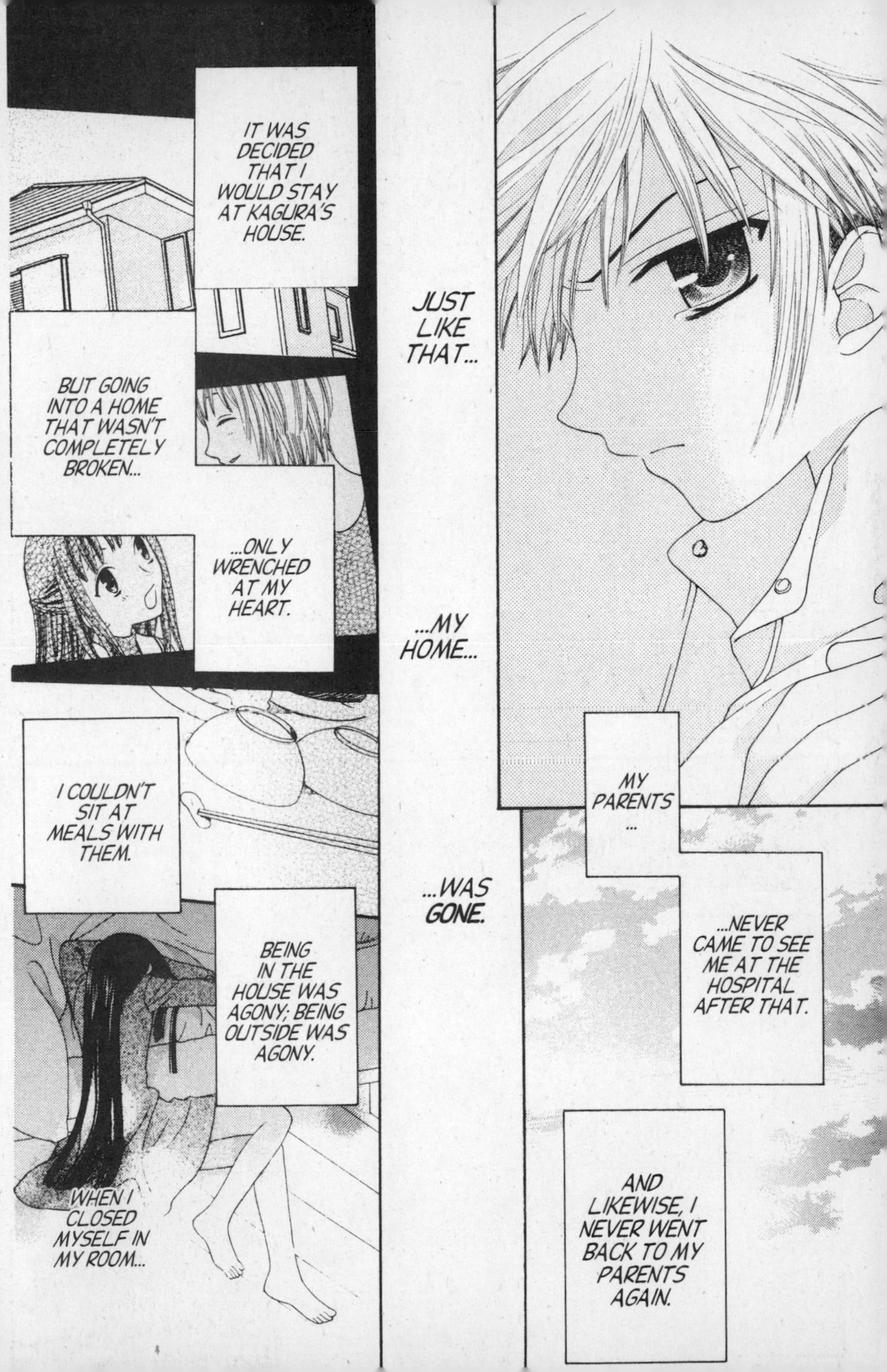
JUST LIKE THAT...
...MY HOME...
...WAS GONE.
MY PARENTS...
...NEVER CAME TO SEE ME AT THE HOSPITAL AFTER THAT.
AND LIKEWISE, I NEVER WENT BACK TO MY PARENTS AGAIN.
IT WAS DECIDED THAT I WOULD STAY AT KAGURA'S HOUSE.
BUT GOING INTO A HOME THAT WASN'T COMPLETELY BROKEN...
...ONLY WRENCHED AT MY HEART.
I COULDN'T SIT AT MEALS WITH THEM.
BEING IN THE HOUSE WAS AGONY; BEING OUTSIDE WAS AGONY.
WHEN I CLOSED MYSELF IN MY ROOM...

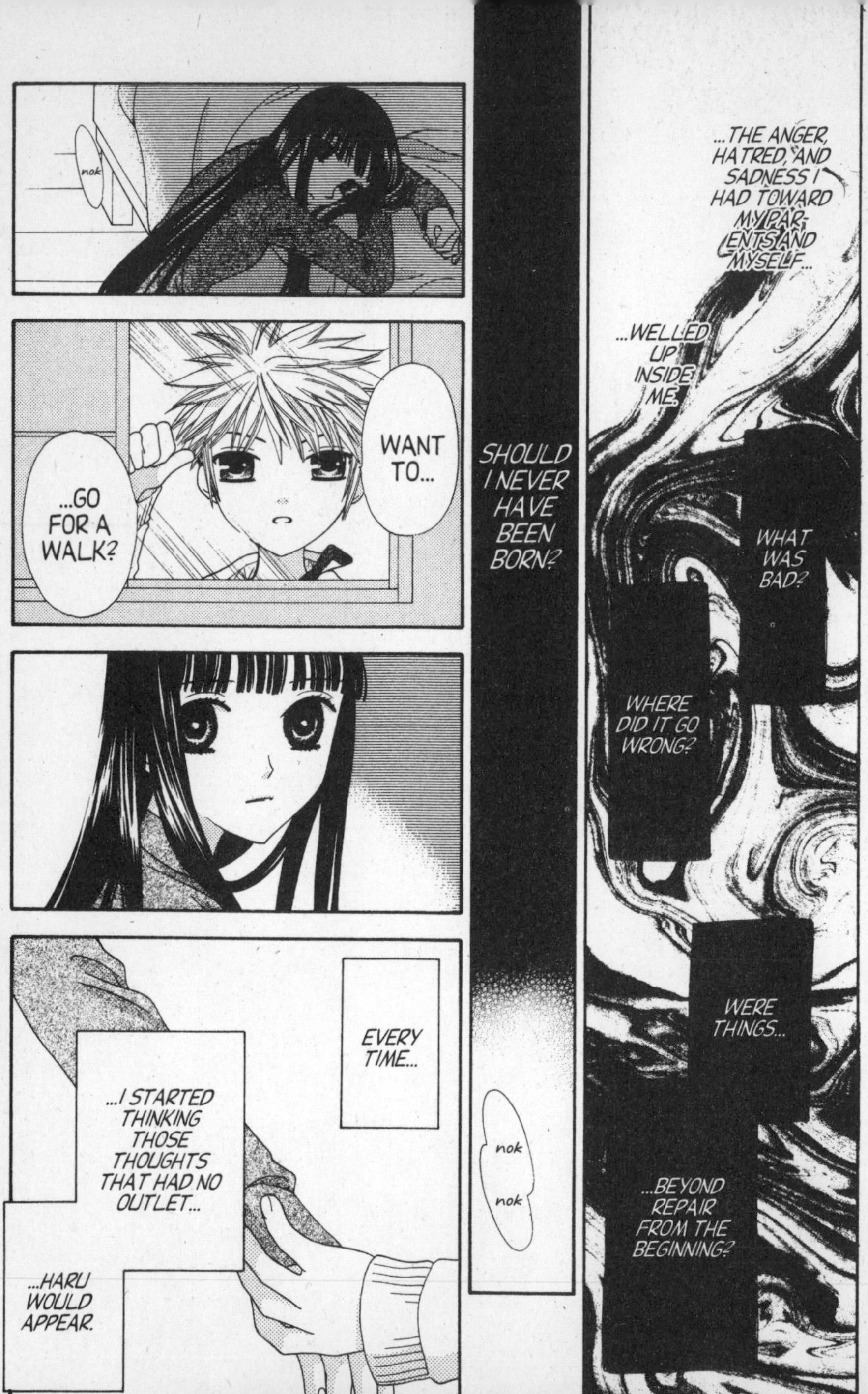

...THE ANGER, HATRED, AND SADNESS I HAD TOWARD MY PARENTS AND MYSELF...
...WELLED UP INSIDE ME.
WHAT WAS BAD?
WHERE DID IT GO WRONG?
WERE THINGS...
...BEYOND REPAIR FROM THE BEGINNING?
SHOULD I NEVER HAVE BEEN BORN?
nok nok
nok
WANT TO...
...GO FOR A WALK?
EVERY TIME...
...I STARTED THINKING THOSE THOUGHTS THAT HAD NO OUTLET...
...HARU WOULD APPEAR.

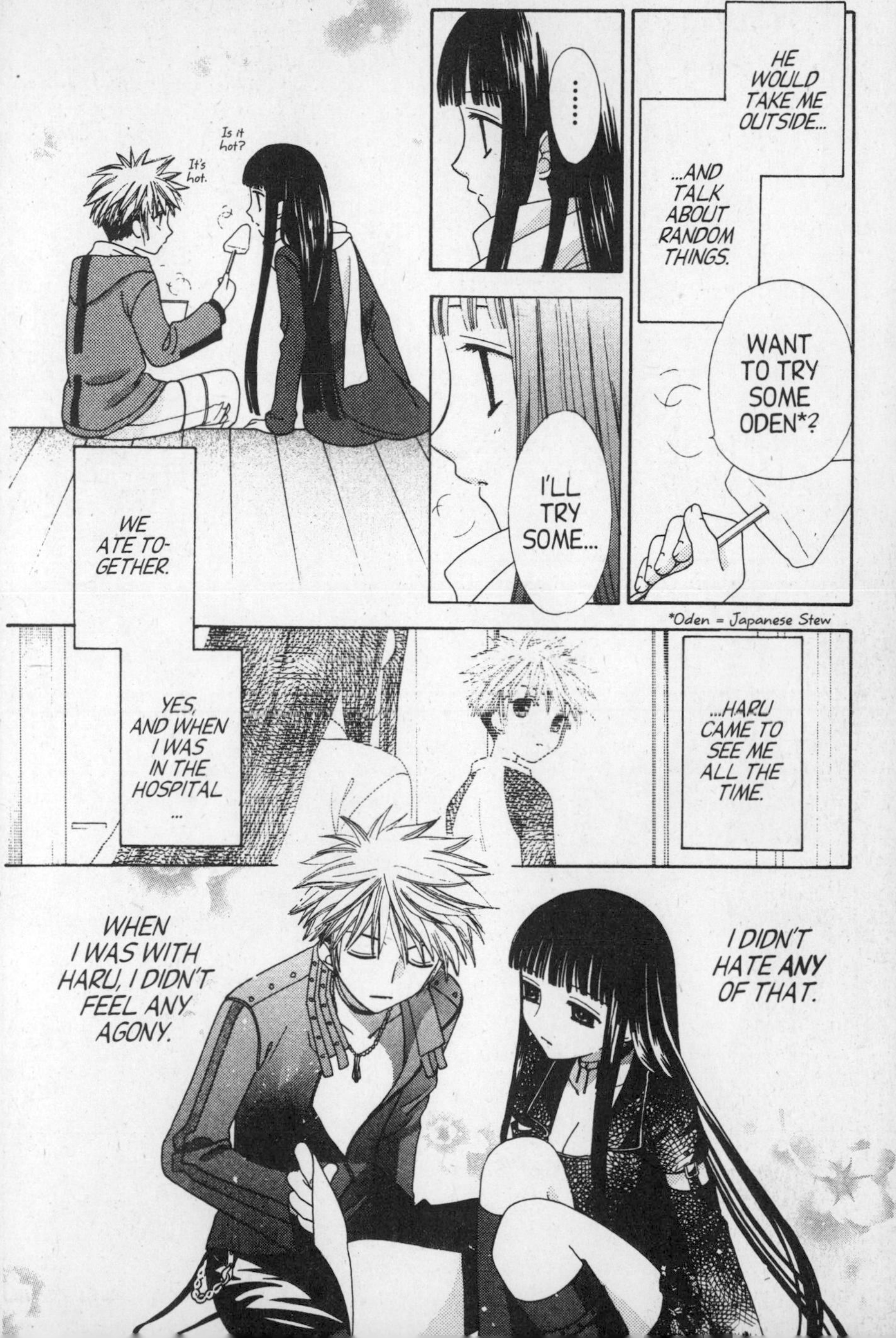
HE WOULD TAKE ME OUTSIDE...
...AND TALK ABOUT RANDOM THINGS.
WANT TO TRY SOME ODEN*?
......
I'LL TRY SOME...
Is it hot?
It's hot.
WE ATE TO-GETHER.
YES, AND WHEN I WAS IN THE HOSPITAL ...
...HARU CAME TO SEE ME ALL THE TIME.
I DIDN'T HATE ANY OF THAT.
WHEN I WAS WITH HARU, I DIDN'T FEEL ANY AGONY.
*Oden = Japanese Stew

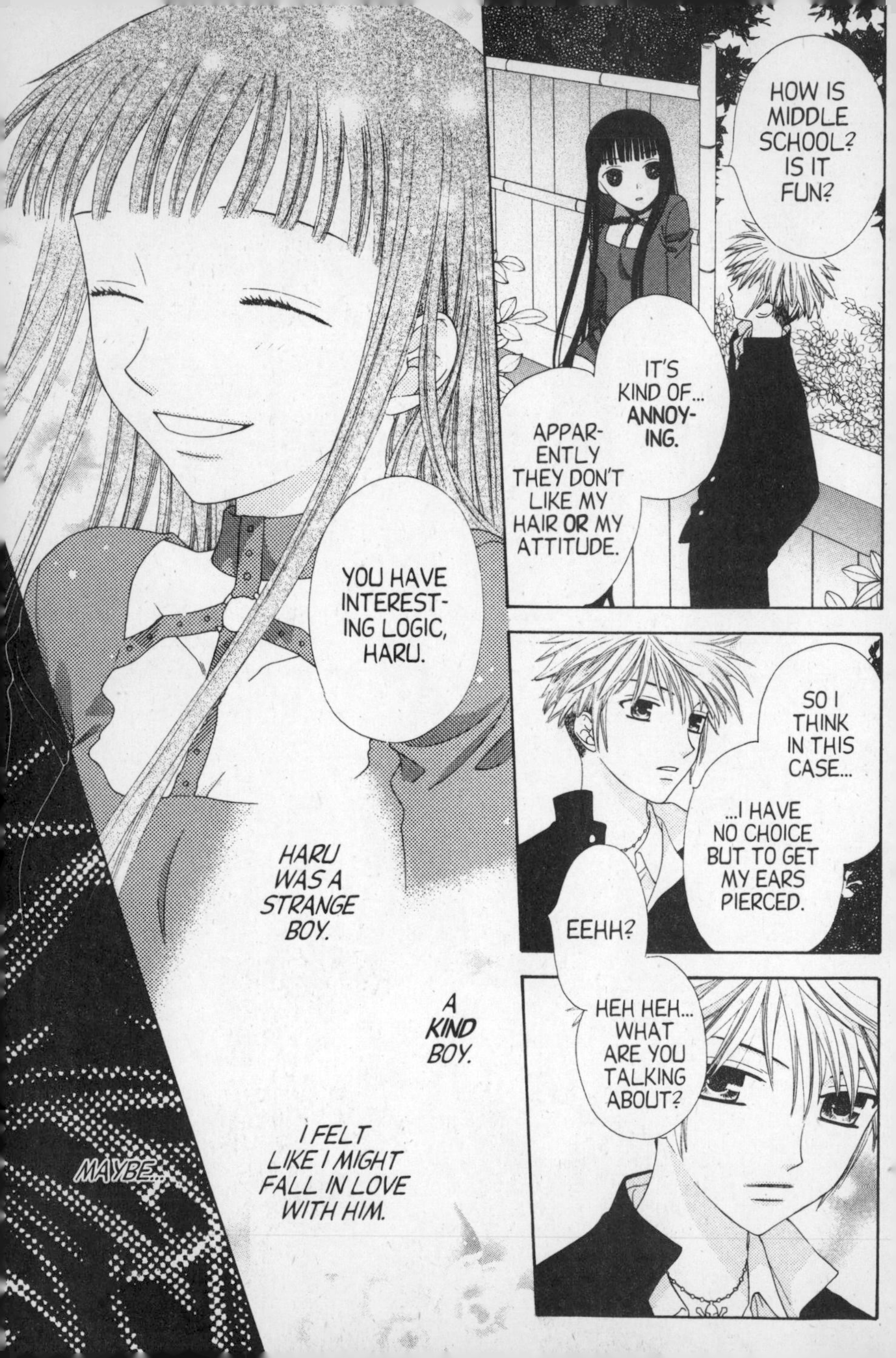
HOW IS MIDDLE SCHOOL? IS IT FUN?
IT'S KIND OF... ANNOYING.
APPARENTLY THEY DON'T LIKE MY HAIR OR MY ATTITUDE.
SO I THINK IN THIS CASE...
...I HAVE NO CHOICE BUT TO GET MY EARS PIERCED.
EEHH?
HEH HEH... WHAT ARE YOU TALKING ABOUT?
YOU HAVE INTERESTING LOGIC, HARU.
HARU WAS A STRANGE BOY.
A KIND BOY.
I FELT LIKE I MIGHT FALL IN LOVE WITH HIM.
MAYBE...

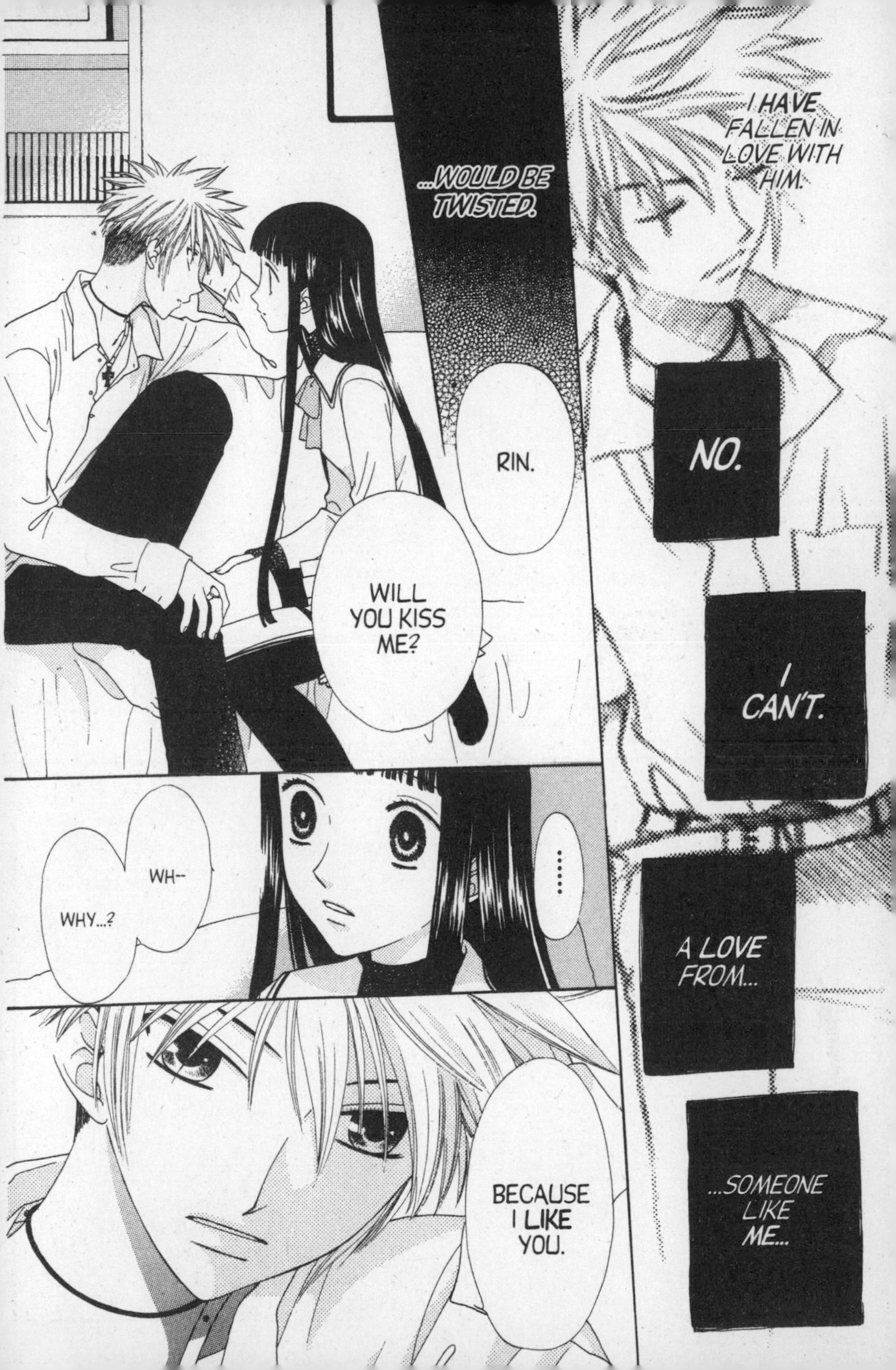

I HAVE FALLEN IN LOVE WITH HIM.
NO.
I CAN'T.
A LOVE FROM...
...SOMEONE LIKE ME...
...WOULD BE TWISTED.
RIN.
WILL YOU KISS ME?
......
WH--
WHY...?
BECAUSE I LIKE YOU.

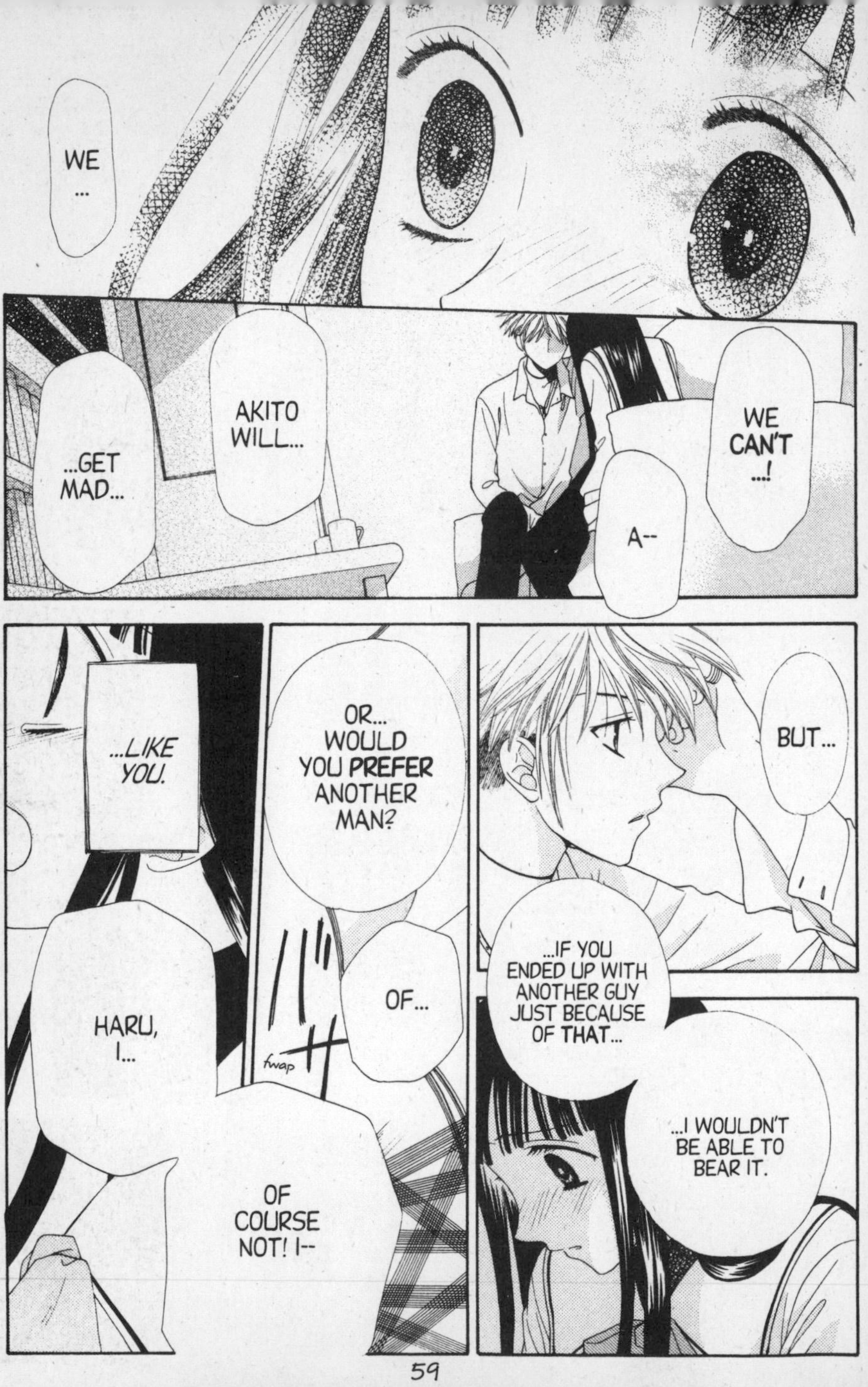
WE ...
WE CAN'T ...!
A--
AKITO WILL...
...GET MAD...
BUT...
...IF YOU ENDED UP WITH ANOTHER GUY JUST BECAUSE OF THAT...
...I WOULDN'T BE ABLE TO BEAR IT.
OR... WOULD YOU PREFER ANOTHER MAN?
OF...
fwap
OF COURSE NOT! I--
HARU, I...
...LIKE YOU.

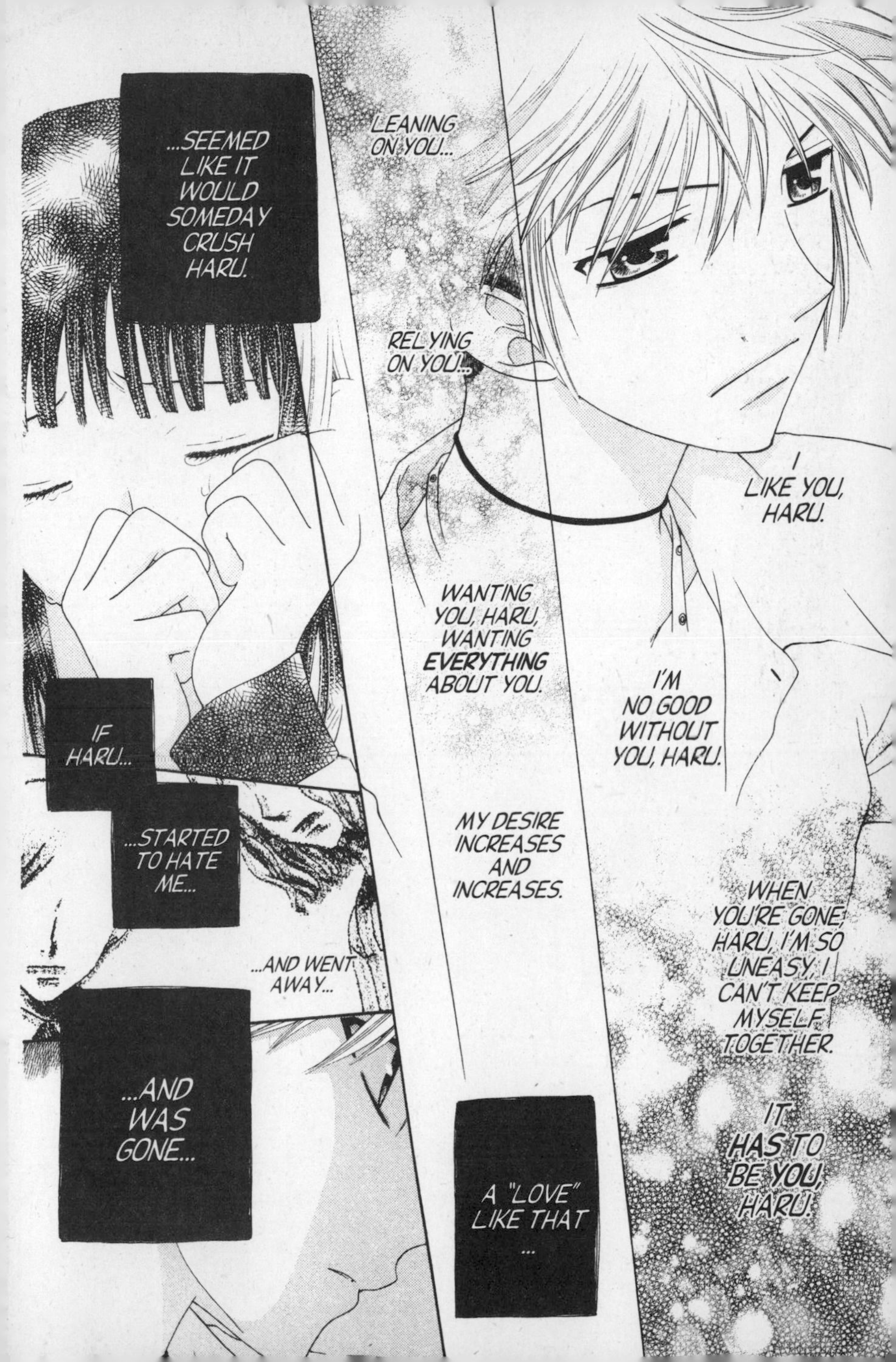
I LIKE YOU, HARU.
I'M NO GOOD WITHOUT YOU, HARU.
WHEN YOU'RE GONE, HARU, I'M SO UNEASY, I CAN'T KEEP MYSELF TOGETHER.
IT HAS TO BE YOU, HARU.
LEANING ON YOU...
RELYING ON YOU...
WANTING YOU, HARU, WANTING EVERYTHING ABOUT YOU.
MY DESIRE INCREASES AND INCREASES.
A "LOVE" LIKE THAT ...
...SEEMED LIKE IT WOULD SOMEDAY CRUSH HARU.
IF HARU...
...STARTED TO HATE ME...
...AND WENT AWAY...
...AND WAS GONE...

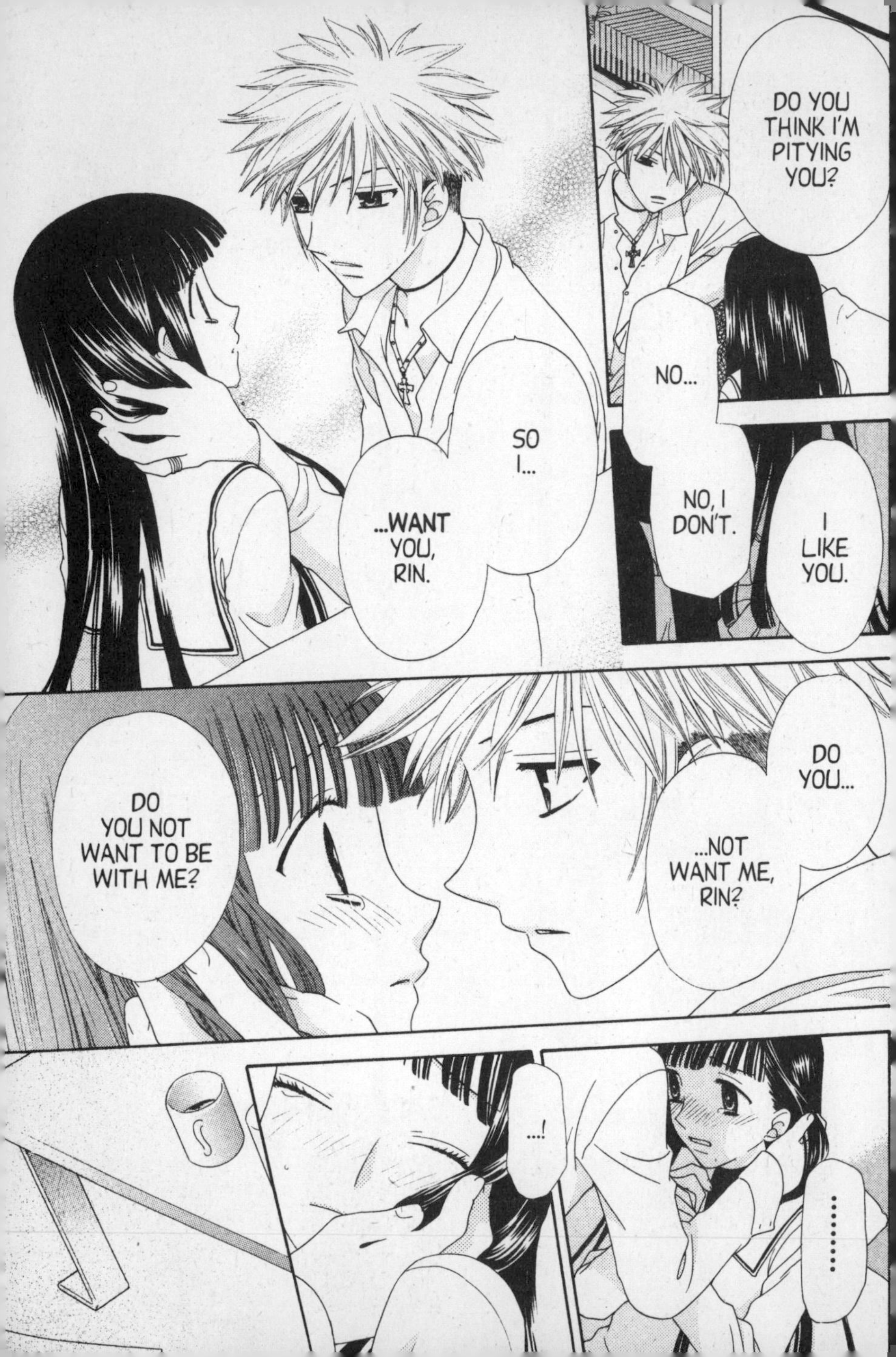

DO YOU THINK I'M PITYING YOU?
NO...
NO, I DON'T.
I LIKE YOU.
SO I...
...WANT YOU, RIN.
DO YOU...
...NOT WANT ME, RIN?
DO YOU NOT WANT TO BE WITH ME?
....
...!

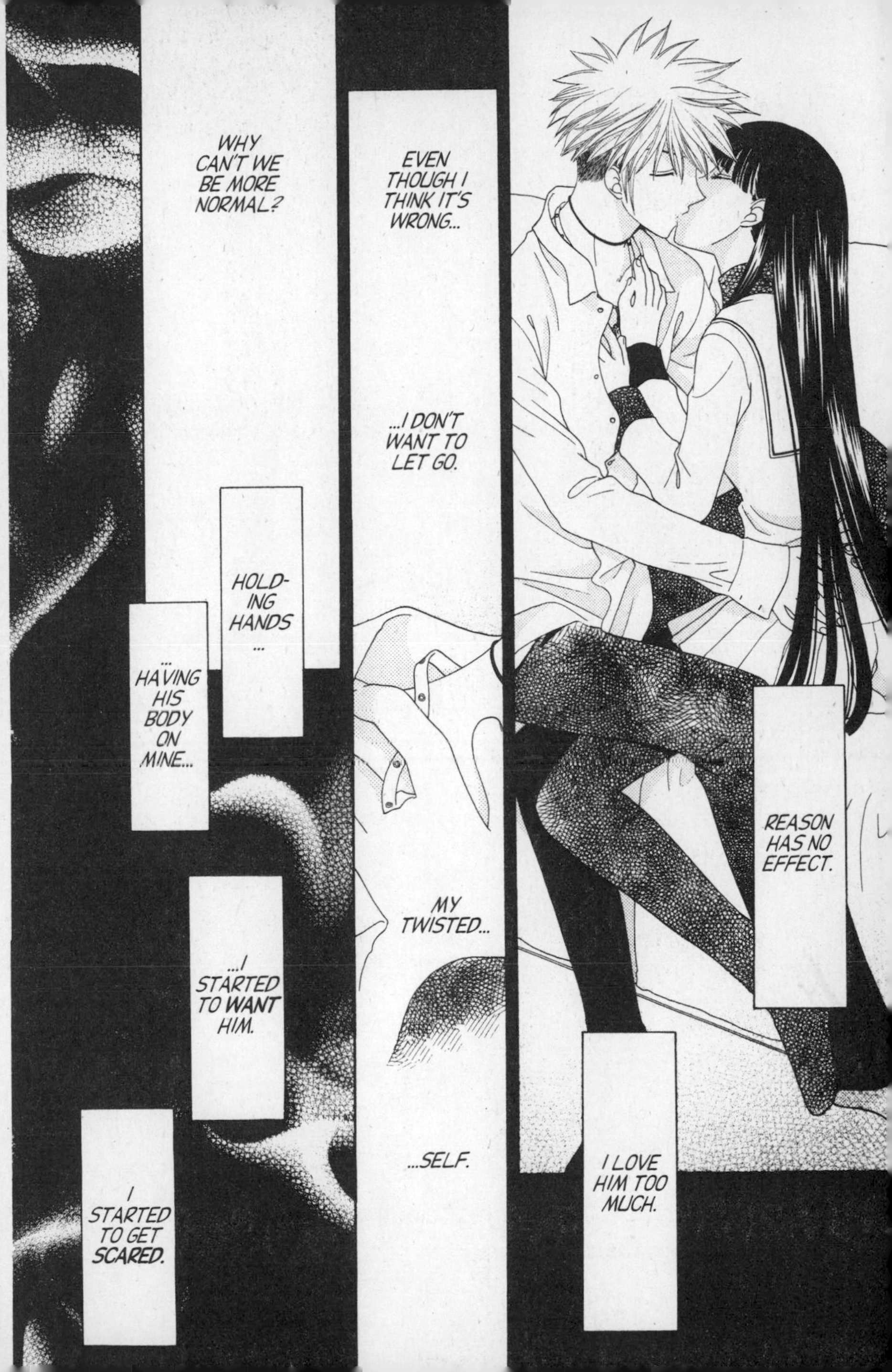
REASON HAS NO EFFECT.
I LOVE HIM TOO MUCH.
EVEN THOUGH I THINK IT'S WRONG...
...I DON'T WANT TO LET GO.
MY TWISTED...
...SELF.
WHY CAN'T WE BE MORE NORMAL?
HOLD-ING HANDS...
...HAVING HIS BODY ON MINE...
...I STARTED TO WANT HIM.
I STARTED TO GET SCARED.

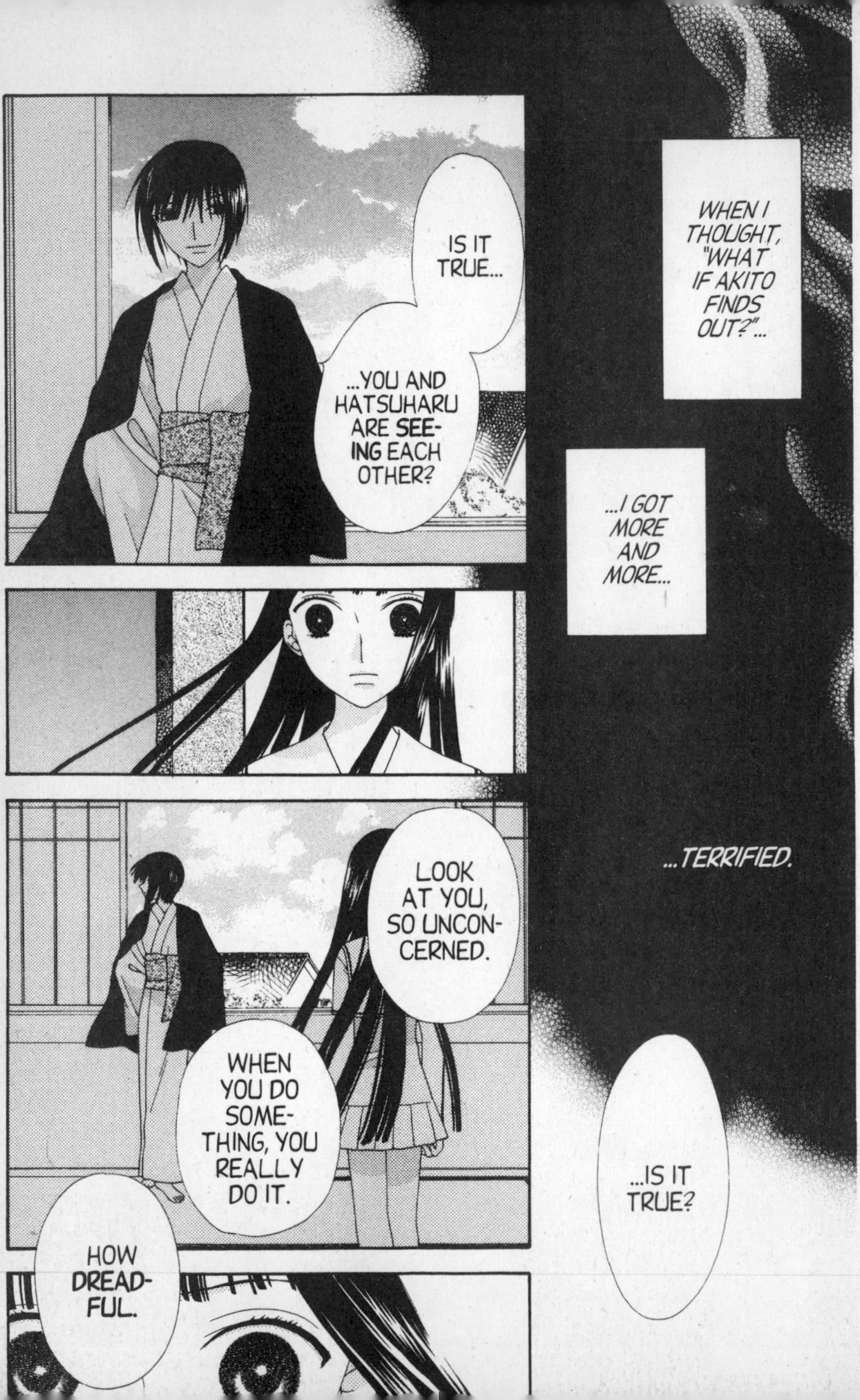
WHEN I THOUGHT, "WHAT IF AKITO FINDS OUT?"...
...I GOT MORE AND MORE...
...TERRIFIED.
...IS IT TRUE?
IS IT TRUE...
...YOU AND HATSUHARU ARE SEEING EACH OTHER?
LOOK AT YOU, SO UNCONCERNED.
WHEN YOU DO SOMETHING, YOU REALLY DO IT.
HOW DREADFUL.

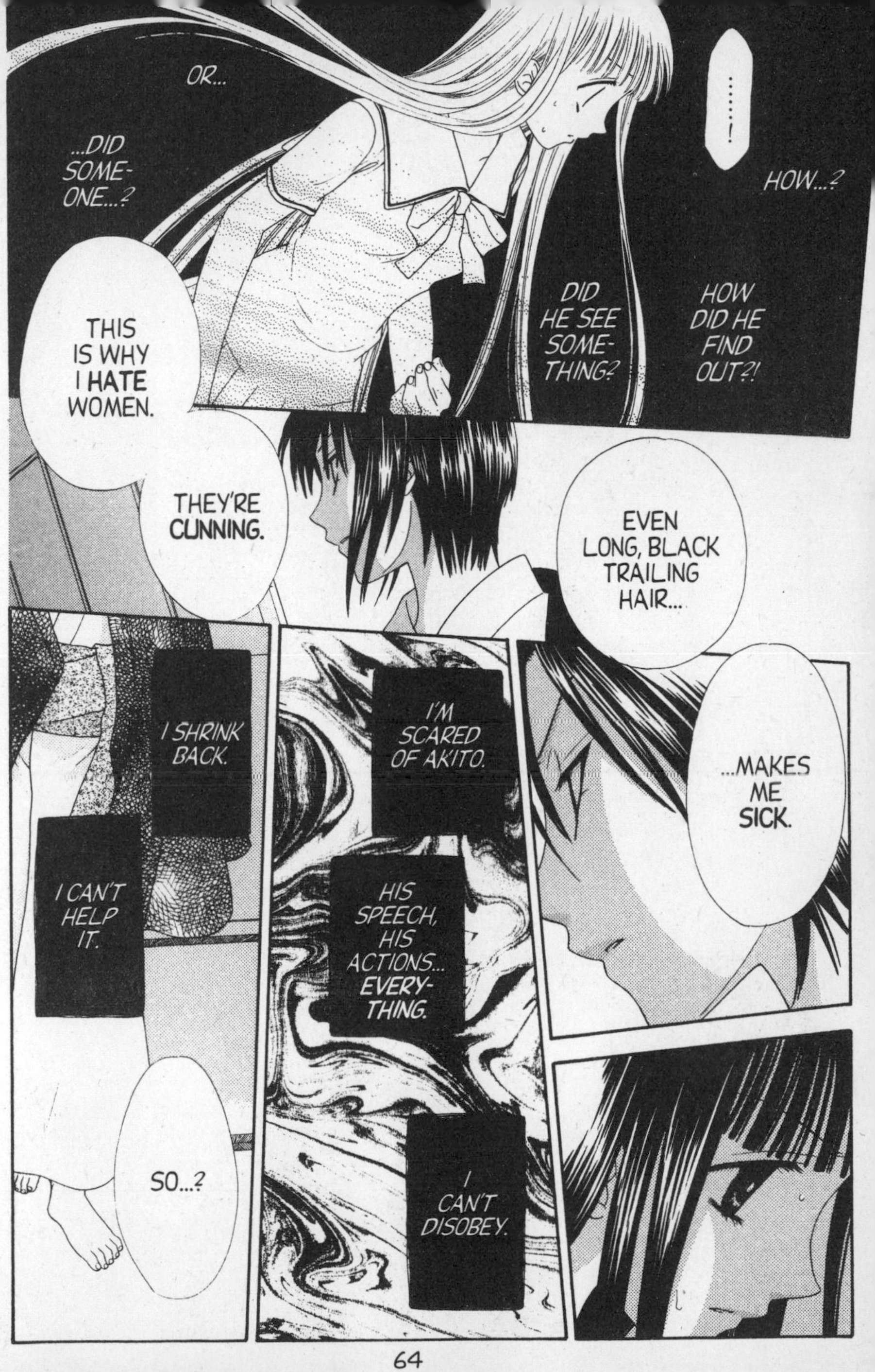
......!
HOW...?
HOW DID HE FIND OUT?!
DID HE SEE SOME-THING?
OR...
...DID SOME-ONE...?
THIS IS WHY I HATE WOMEN.
THEY'RE CUNNING.
EVEN LONG, BLACK TRAILING HAIR...
...MAKES ME SICK.
I'M SCARED OF AKITO.
HIS SPEECH, HIS ACTIONS... EVERY-THING.
I CAN'T DISOBEY.
I SHRINK BACK.
I CAN'T HELP IT.
SO...?

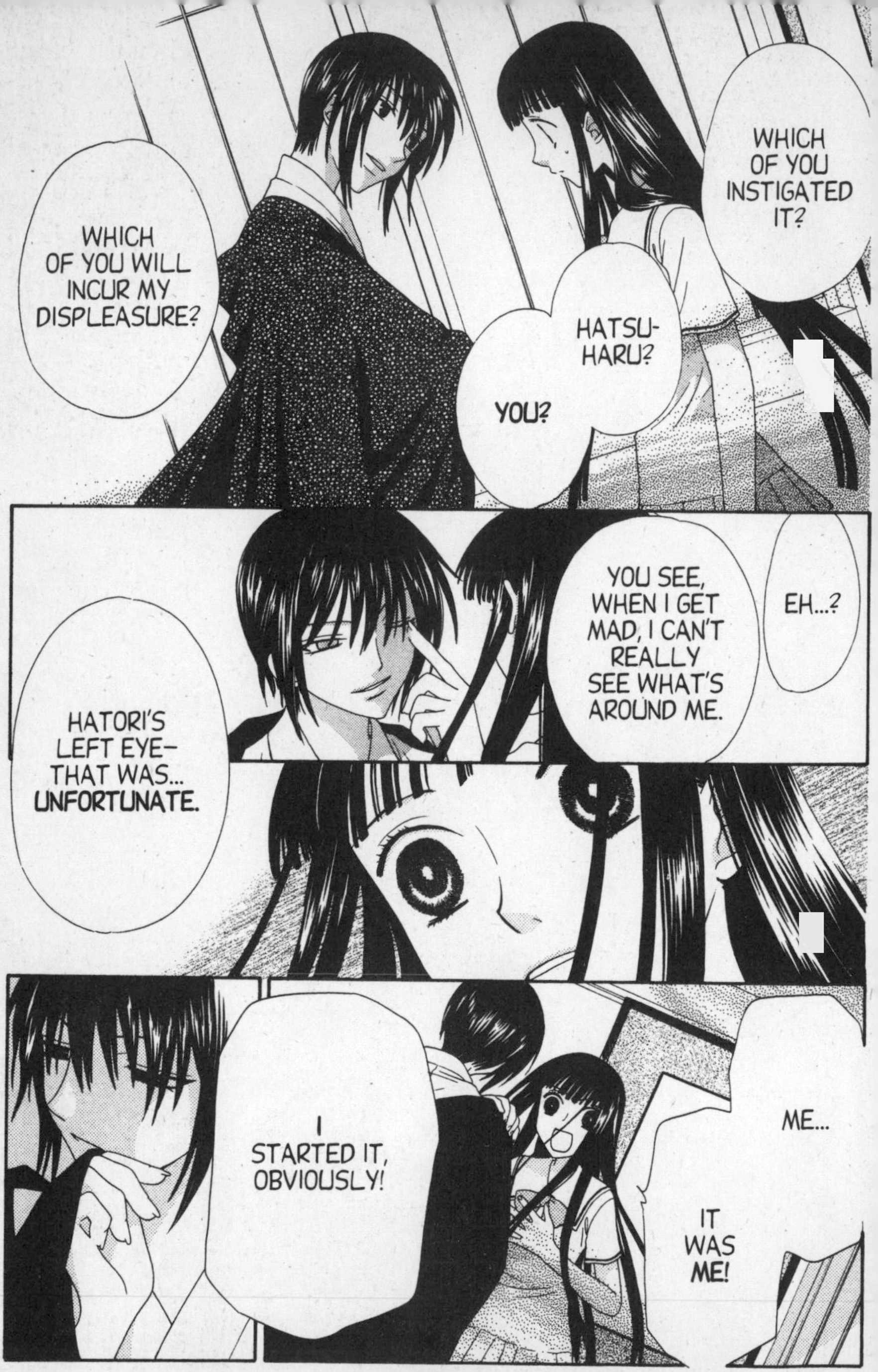
WHICH OF YOU INSTIGATED IT?
HATSU-HARU?
YOU?
WHICH OF YOU WILL INCUR MY DISPLEASURE?
EH...?
YOU SEE, WHEN I GET MAD, I CAN'T REALLY SEE WHAT'S AROUND ME.
HATORI'S LEFT EYE— THAT WAS... **UNFORTUNATE.**
ME...
IT WAS **ME!**
I STARTED IT, OBVIOUSLY!

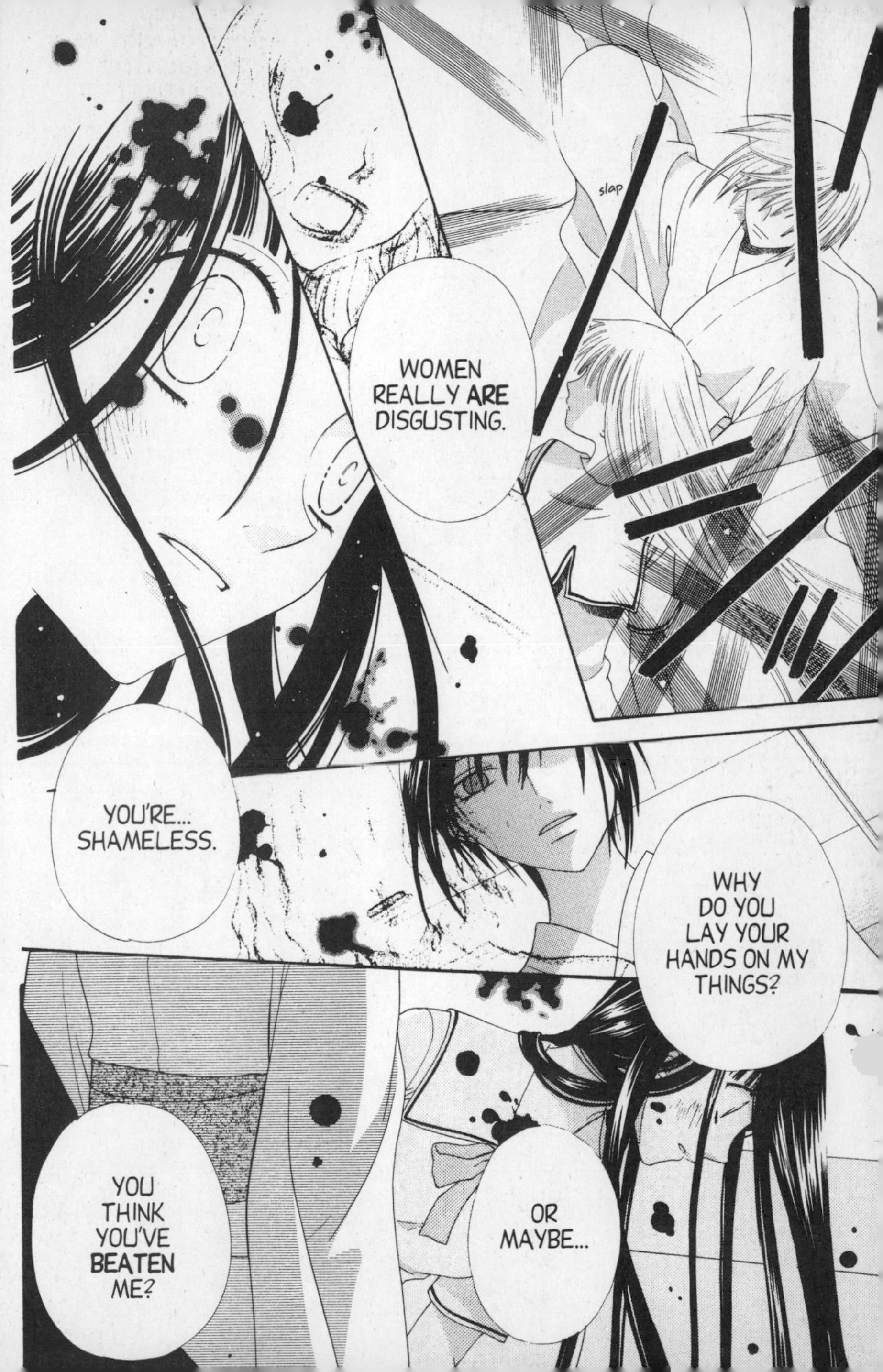
slap
WOMEN REALLY ARE DISGUSTING.
YOU'RE... SHAMELESS.
WHY DO YOU LAY YOUR HANDS ON MY THINGS?
OR MAYBE...
YOU THINK YOU'VE BEATEN ME?

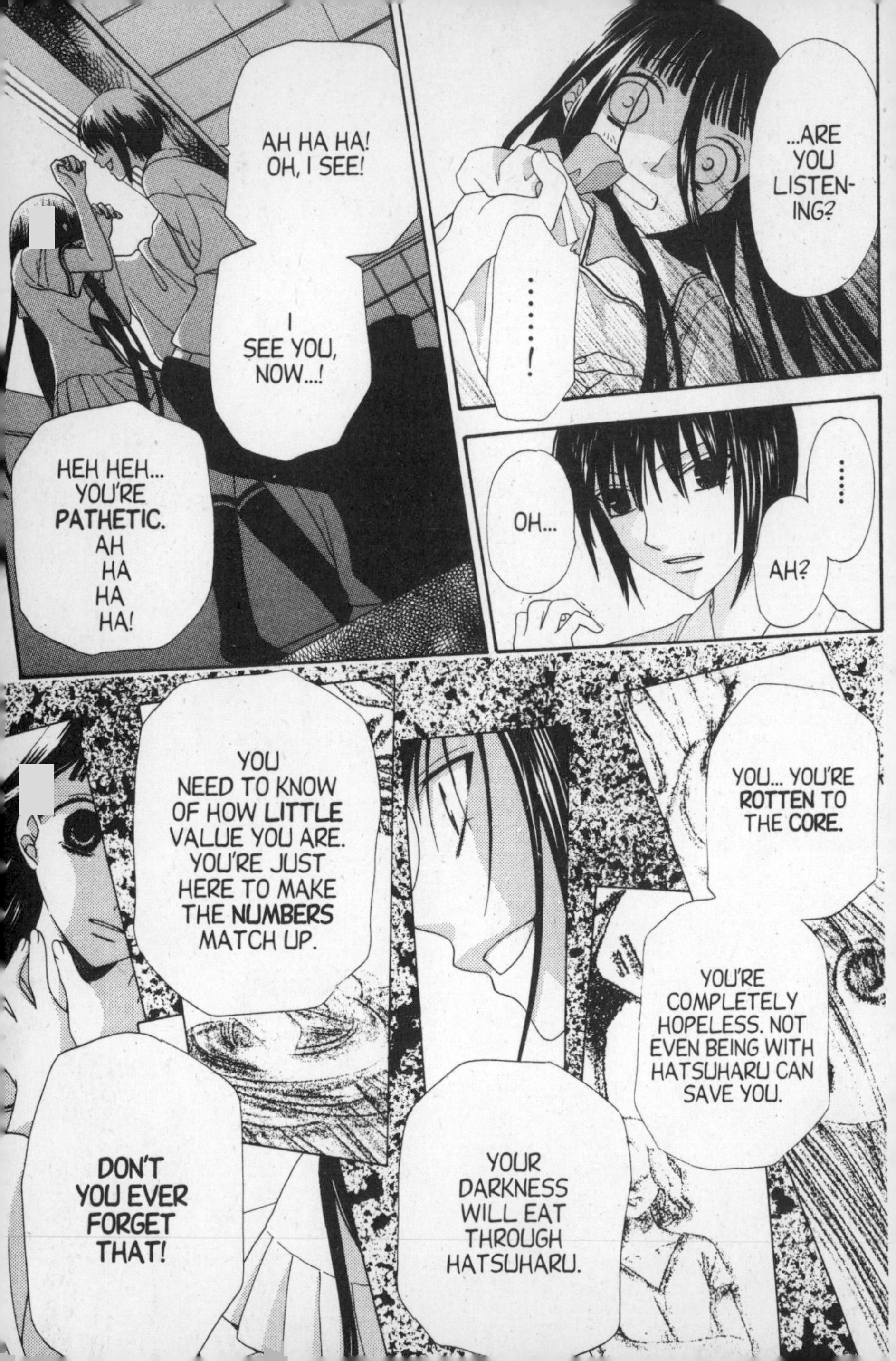

...ARE YOU LISTENING?
......!
......
AH?
OH...
AH HA HA! OH, I SEE!
I SEE YOU, NOW...!
HEH HEH... YOU'RE **PATHETIC.** AH HA HA HA!
YOU... YOU'RE **ROTTEN** TO THE **CORE.**
YOU'RE COMPLETELY HOPELESS. NOT EVEN BEING WITH HATSUHARU CAN SAVE YOU.
YOUR DARKNESS WILL EAT THROUGH HATSUHARU.
YOU NEED TO KNOW OF HOW **LITTLE** VALUE YOU ARE. YOU'RE JUST HERE TO MAKE THE **NUMBERS** MATCH UP.
DON'T YOU EVER FORGET THAT!

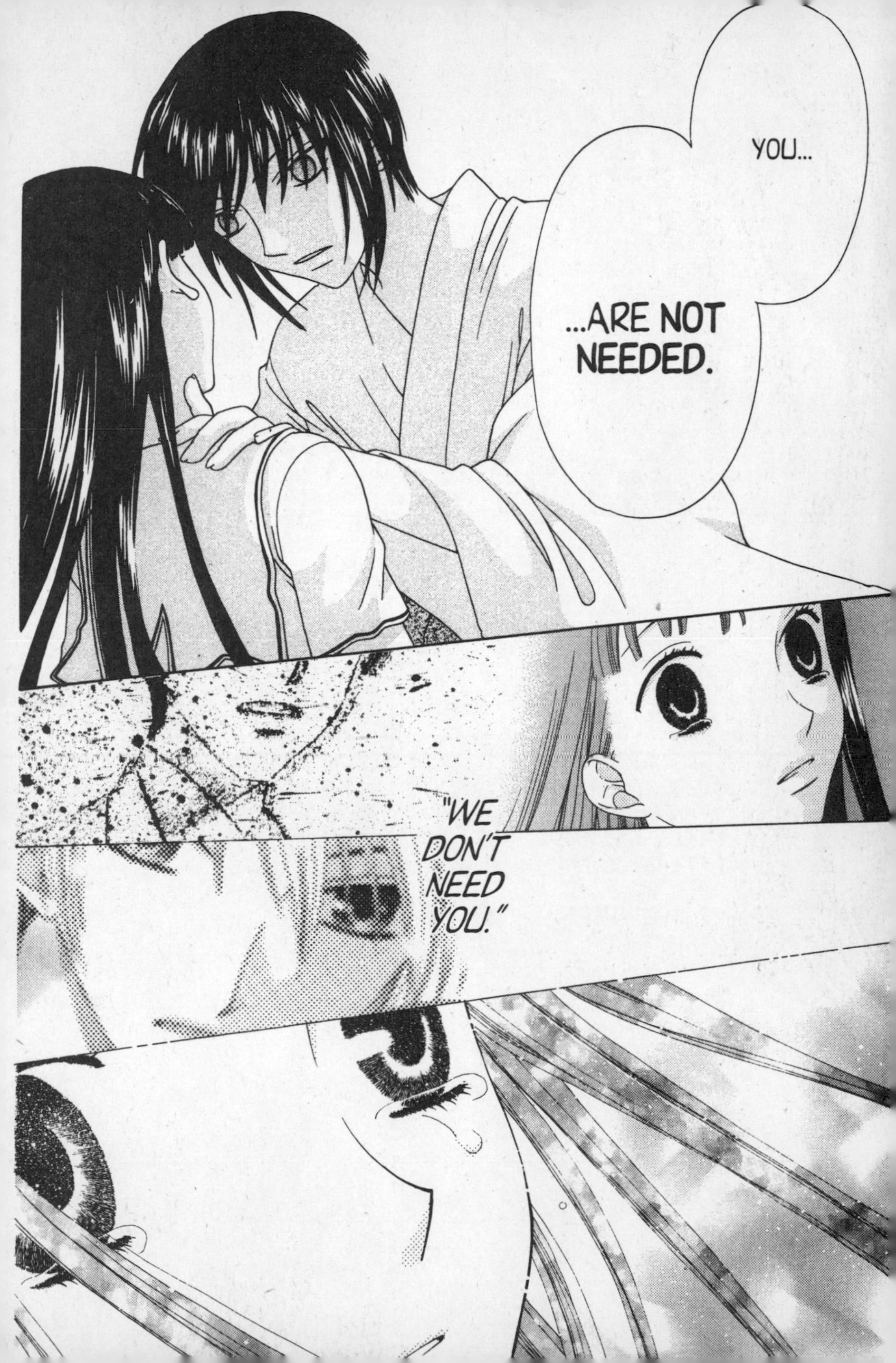
YOU...
...ARE NOT NEEDED.
"WE DON'T NEED YOU."

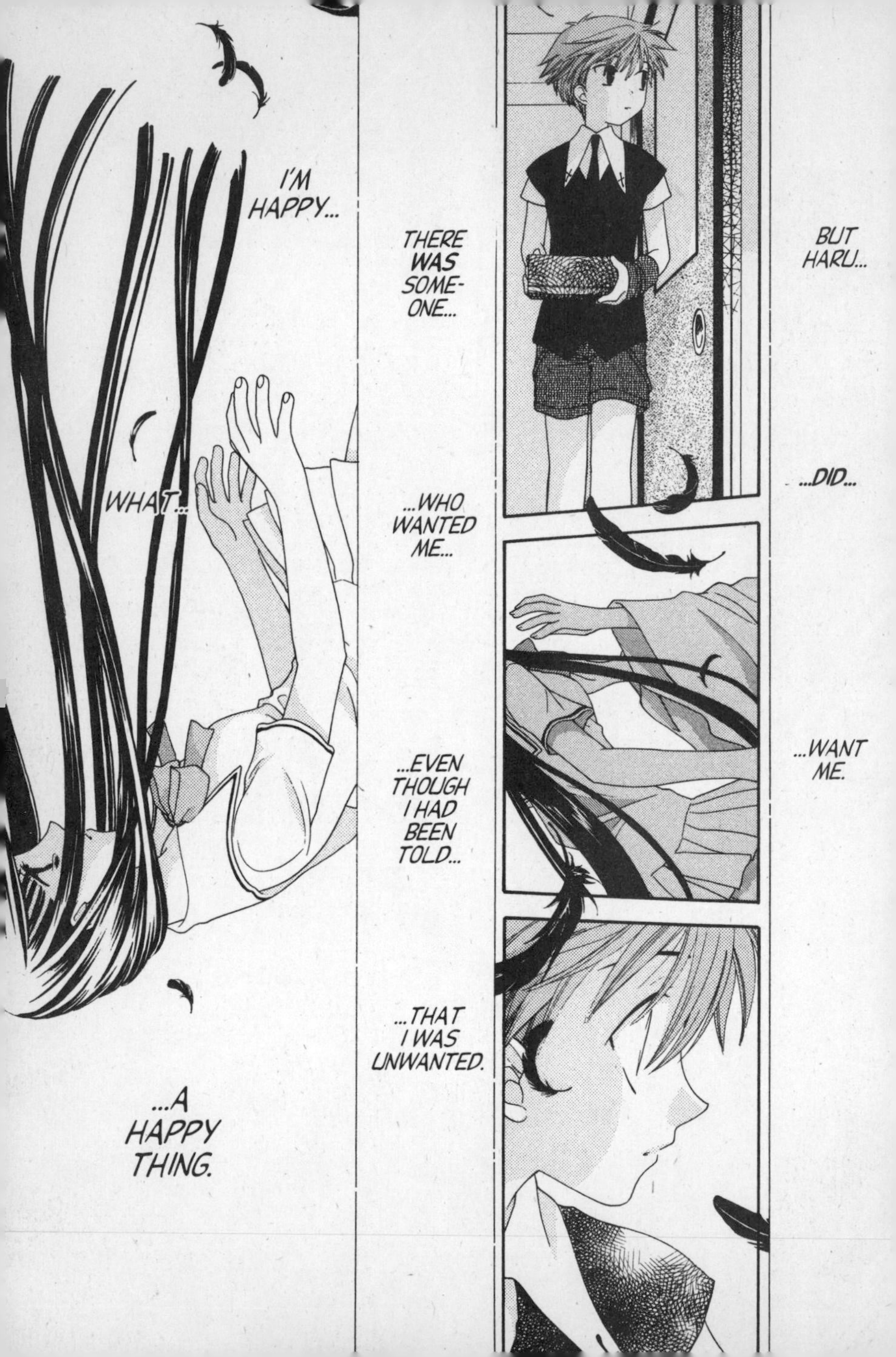
BUT HARU...
...DID...
...WANT ME.
THERE WAS SOME-ONE...
...WHO WANTED ME...
...EVEN THOUGH I HAD BEEN TOLD...
...THAT I WAS UNWANTED.
I'M HAPPY...
WHAT...
...A HAPPY THING.

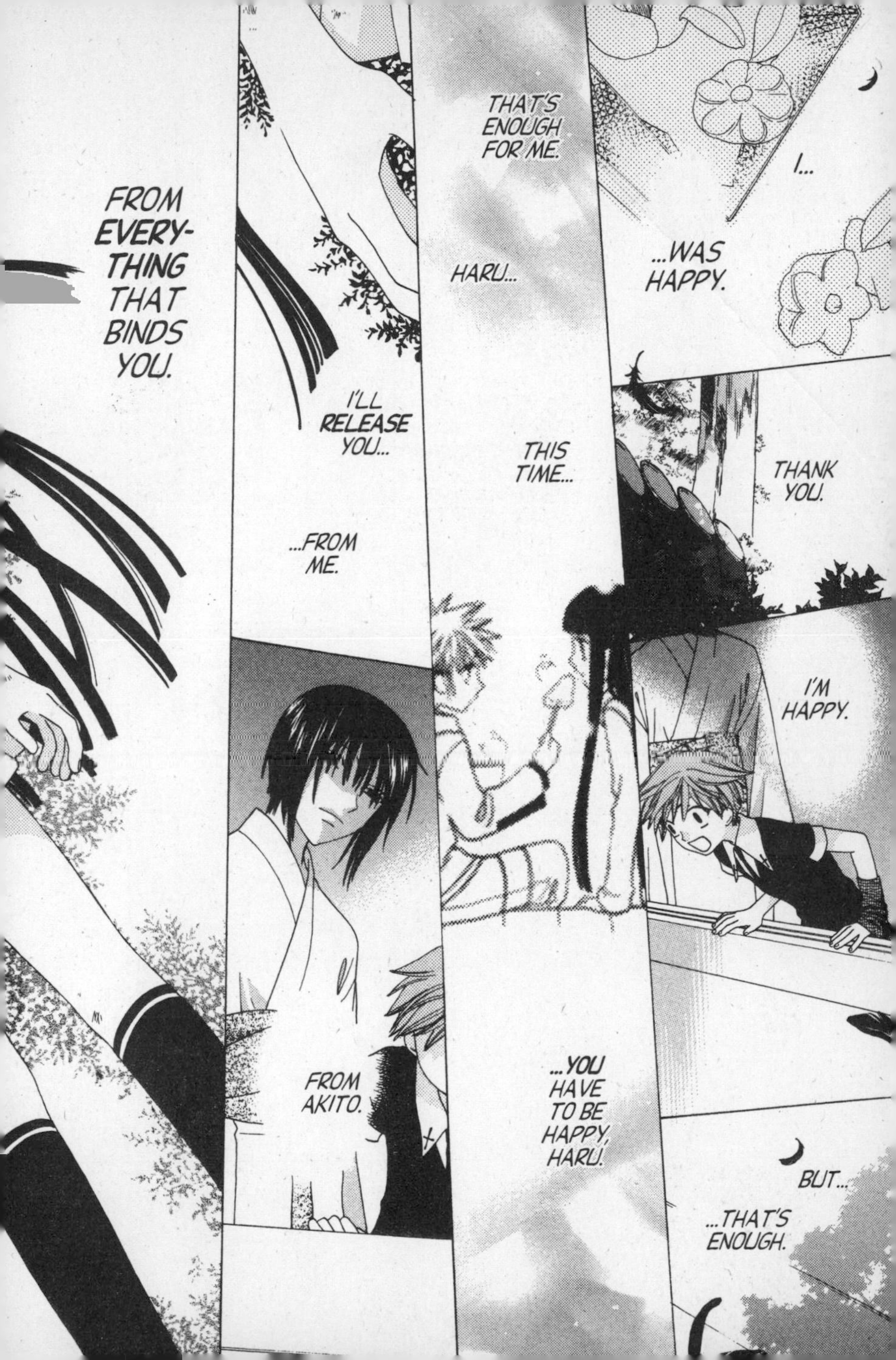
I...
...WAS HAPPY.
THANK YOU.
I'M HAPPY.
BUT...
...THAT'S ENOUGH.
THAT'S ENOUGH FOR ME.
HARU...
THIS TIME...
...YOU HAVE TO BE HAPPY, HARU.
I'LL RELEASE YOU...
...FROM ME.
FROM AKITO.
FROM EVERY-THING THAT BINDS YOU.

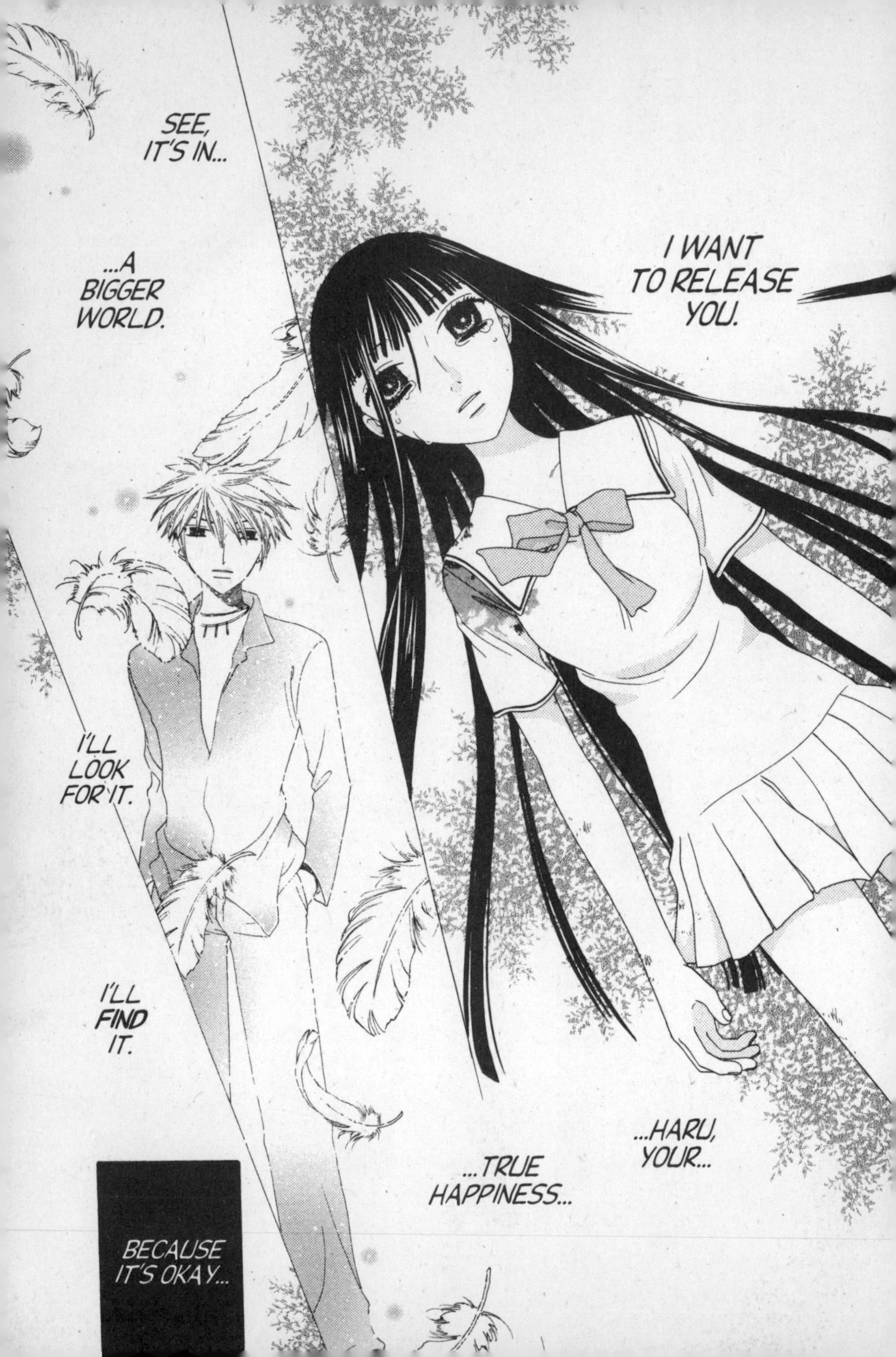
I WANT TO RELEASE YOU.
...HARU, YOUR...
...TRUE HAPPINESS...
SEE, IT'S IN...
...A BIGGER WORLD.
I'LL LOOK FOR IT.
I'LL FIND IT.
BECAUSE IT'S OKAY...

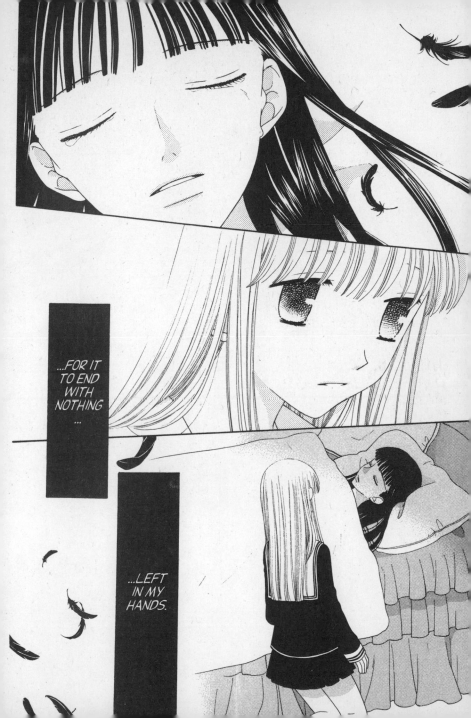

...FOR IT TO END WITH NOTHING...

...LEFT IN MY HANDS.

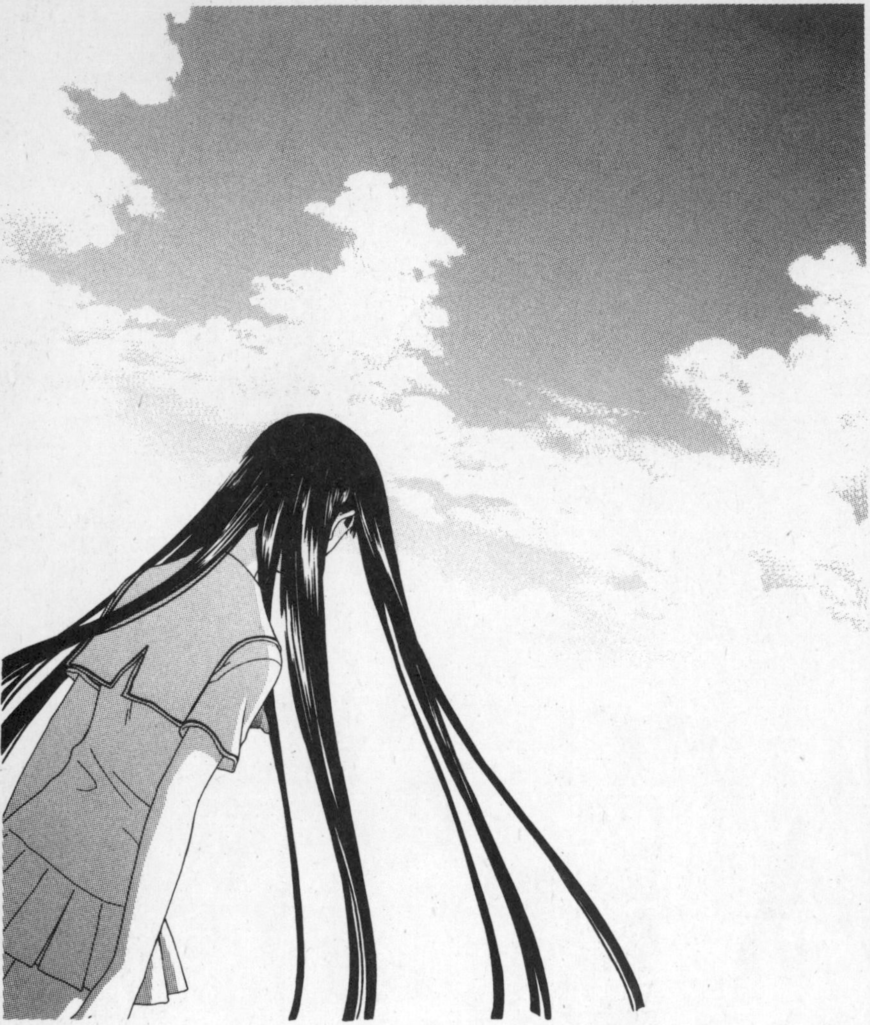

Chapter 80

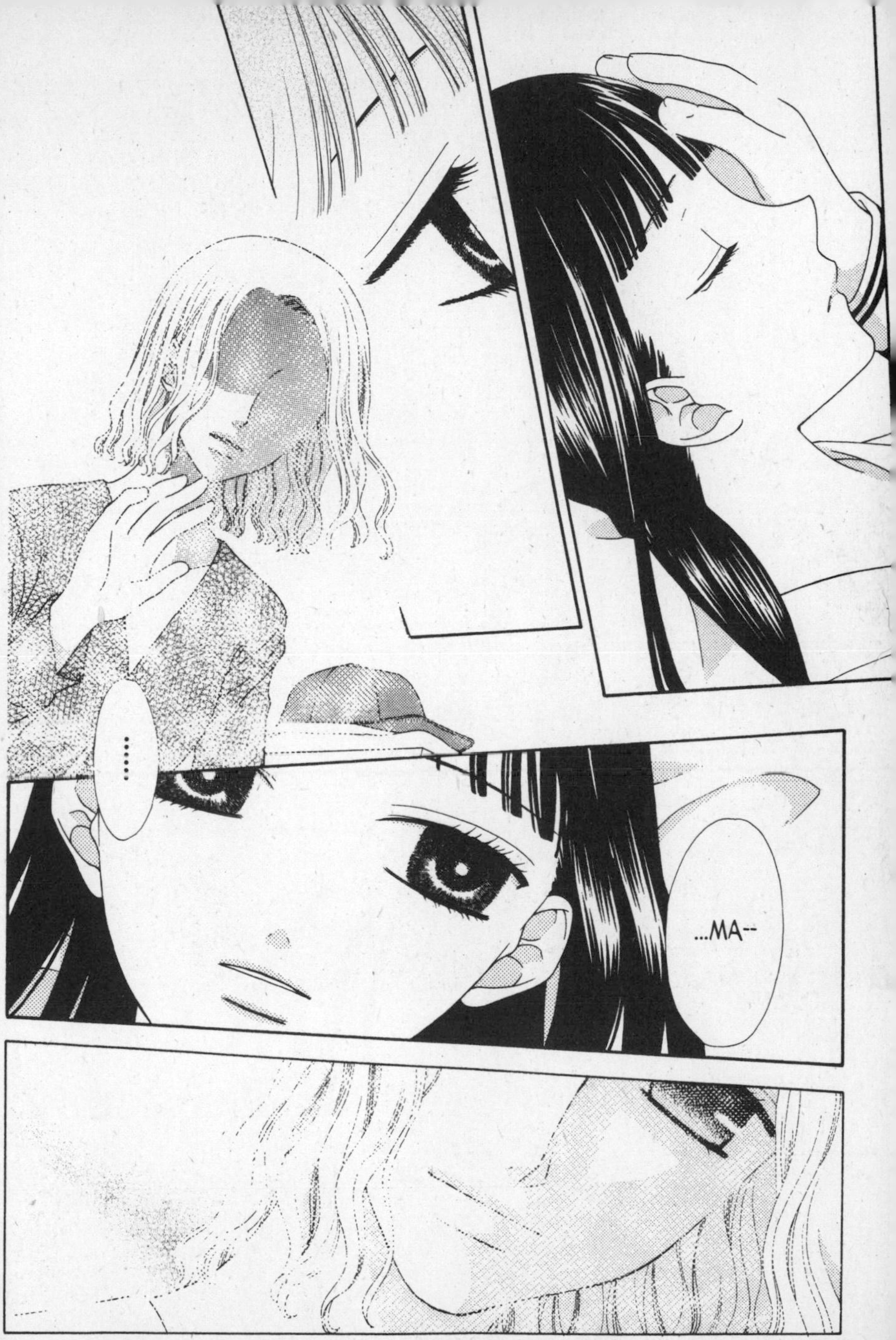
......
...MA--

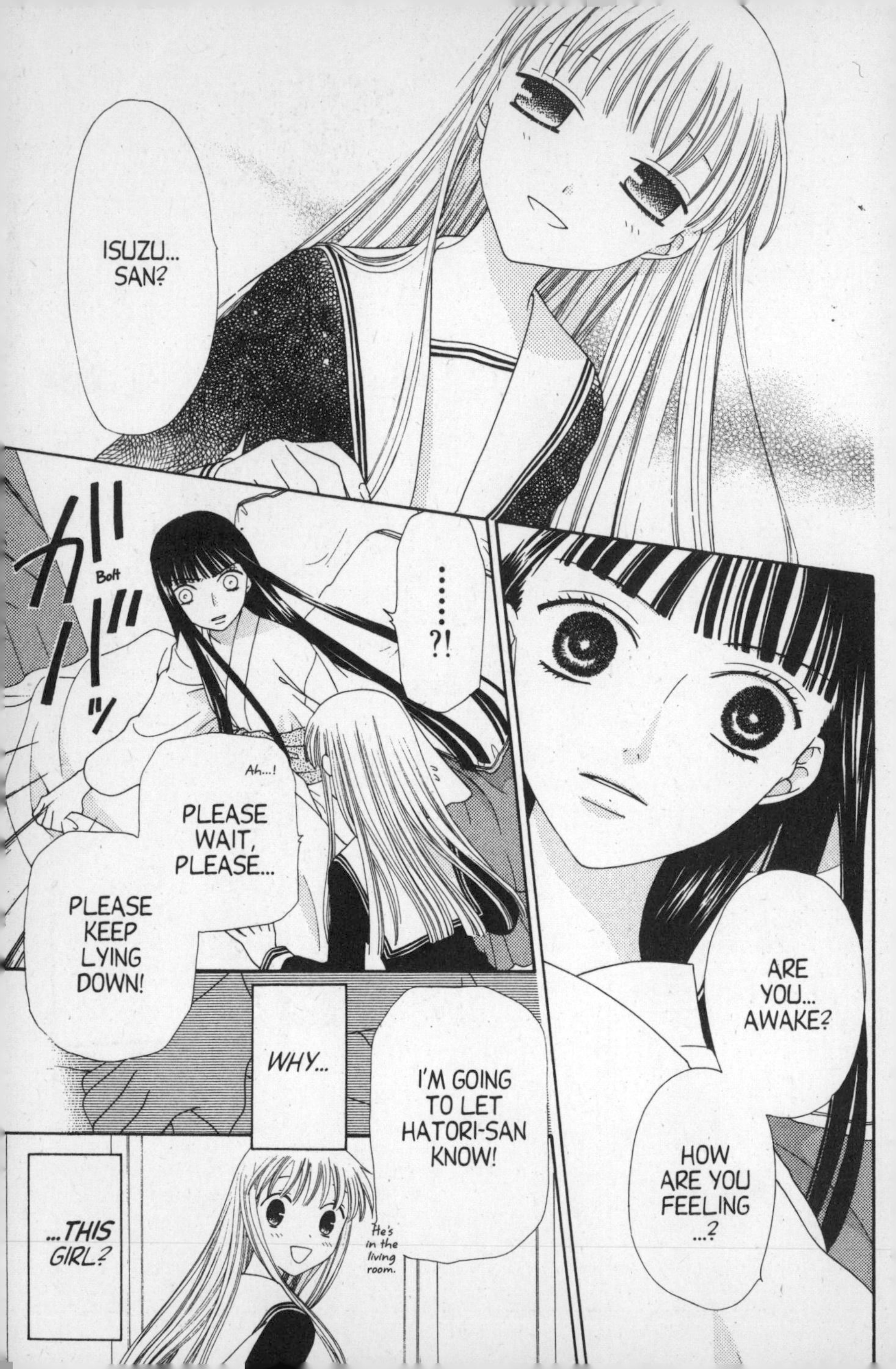
ISUZU... SAN?
ARE YOU... AWAKE?
HOW ARE YOU FEELING ...?
ガバーッ
Bolt
....?!
Ah...!
PLEASE WAIT, PLEASE...
PLEASE KEEP LYING DOWN!
I'M GOING TO LET HATORI-SAN KNOW!
He's in the living room.
WHY...
...THIS GIRL?

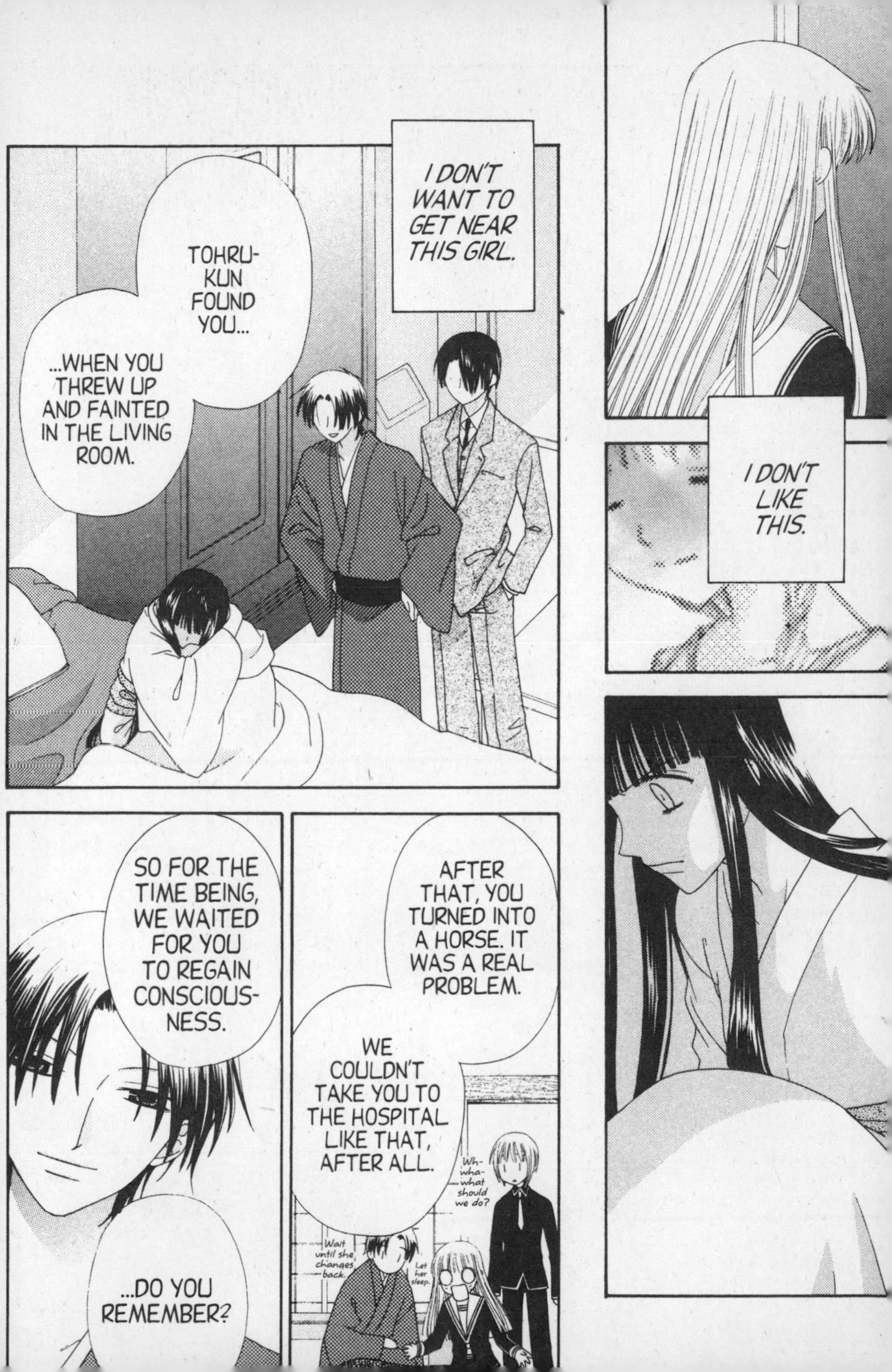
I DON'T WANT TO GET NEAR THIS GIRL.
I DON'T LIKE THIS.
TOHRU-KUN FOUND YOU...
...WHEN YOU THREW UP AND FAINTED IN THE LIVING ROOM.
AFTER THAT, YOU TURNED INTO A HORSE. IT WAS A REAL PROBLEM.
WE COULDN'T TAKE YOU TO THE HOSPITAL LIKE THAT, AFTER ALL.
Wh-wha-what should we do?
Let her sleep.
Wait until she changes back.
SO FOR THE TIME BEING, WE WAITED FOR YOU TO REGAIN CONSCIOUS-NESS.
...DO YOU REMEMBER?

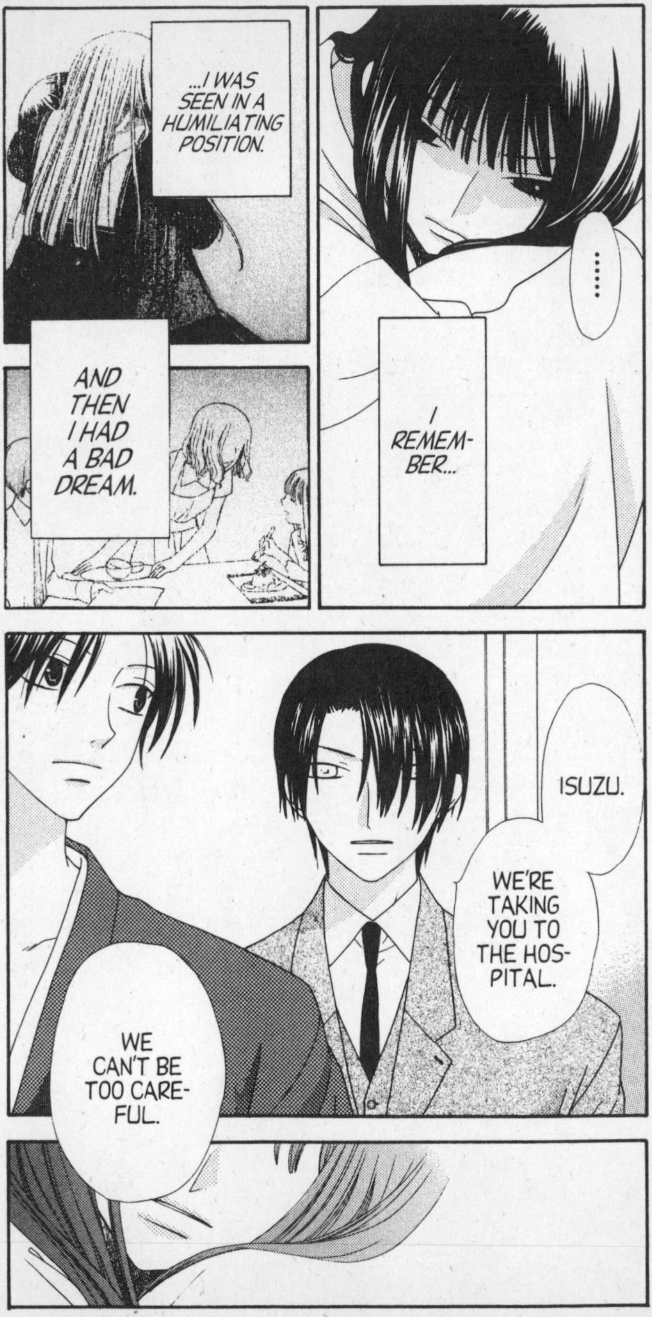
......
I REMEMBER...
...I WAS SEEN IN A HUMILIATING POSITION.
AND THEN I HAD A BAD DREAM.
ISUZU.
WE'RE TAKING YOU TO THE HOSPITAL.
WE CAN'T BE TOO CAREFUL.

Now then.

Now that all the members of the Zodiac have been revealed, I can finally tell you that all of their names were taken from names of the months. I think there are some people who have already realized this, though.

The reason I kept quiet about it until now is that if I said it, it would be a huge spoiler in that you would be able to figure out which Zodiac each character was by their name. (Figure that out before you name them!)

There's no real meaning behind my naming them after the months. Not really. I was just playing with sounds.

[Currently, in Japan, the months are known as "First month," "Second month," etc. But they all have many, many other names, some of which will be listed later. They're based on the lunar calendar, so they don't necessarily match up with the months of the Western calendar. In addition to there being "the month of the Rat," "the month of the Ox," etc., the hours of the day were designated in the same way. –ed.]

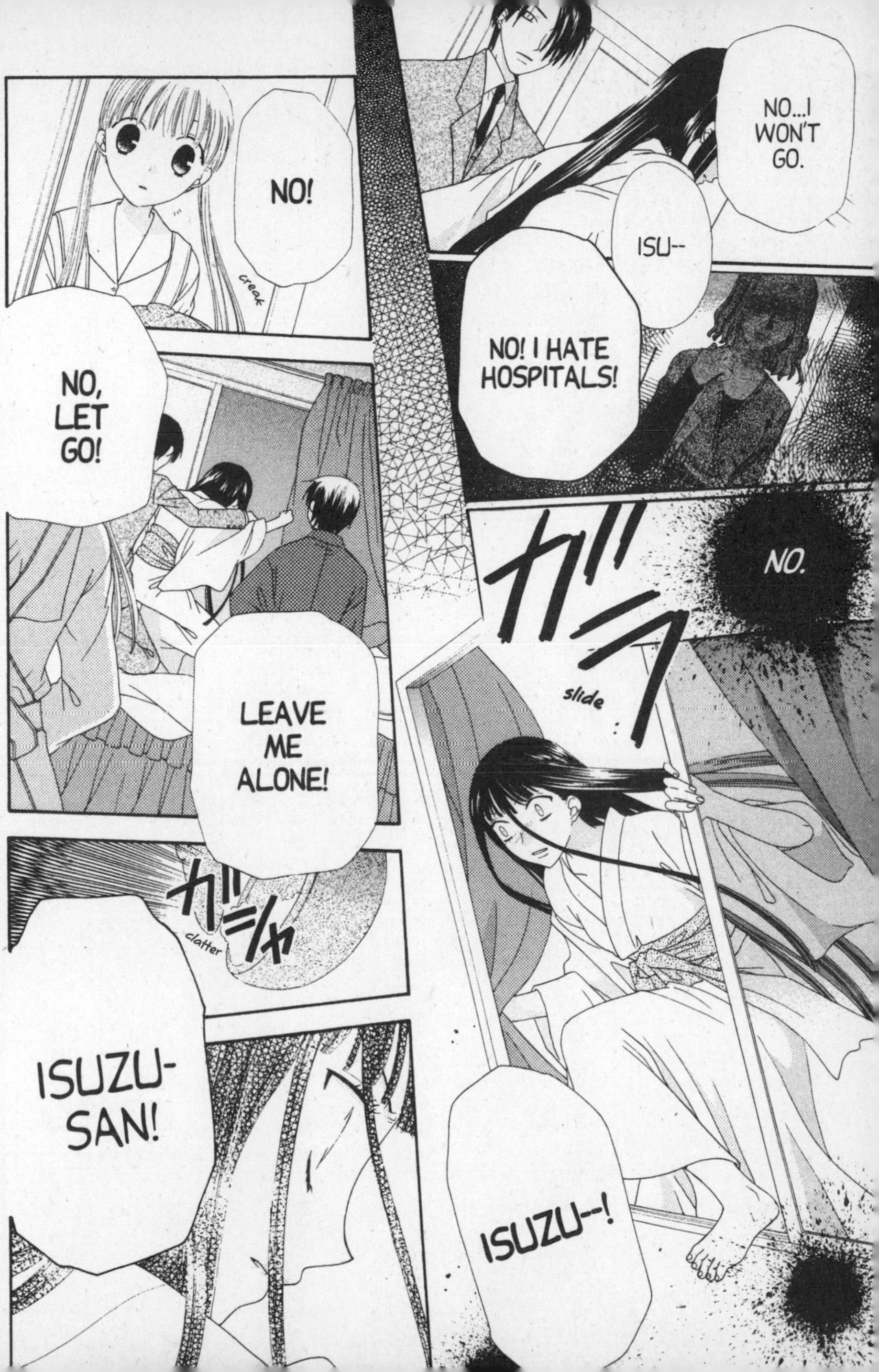
NO...I WON'T GO.
ISU--
NO! I HATE HOSPITALS!
ガラ
NO.
slide
ISUZU--!
NO!
creak
NO, LET GO!
LEAVE ME ALONE!
ガシャ
clatter
ISUZU-SAN!

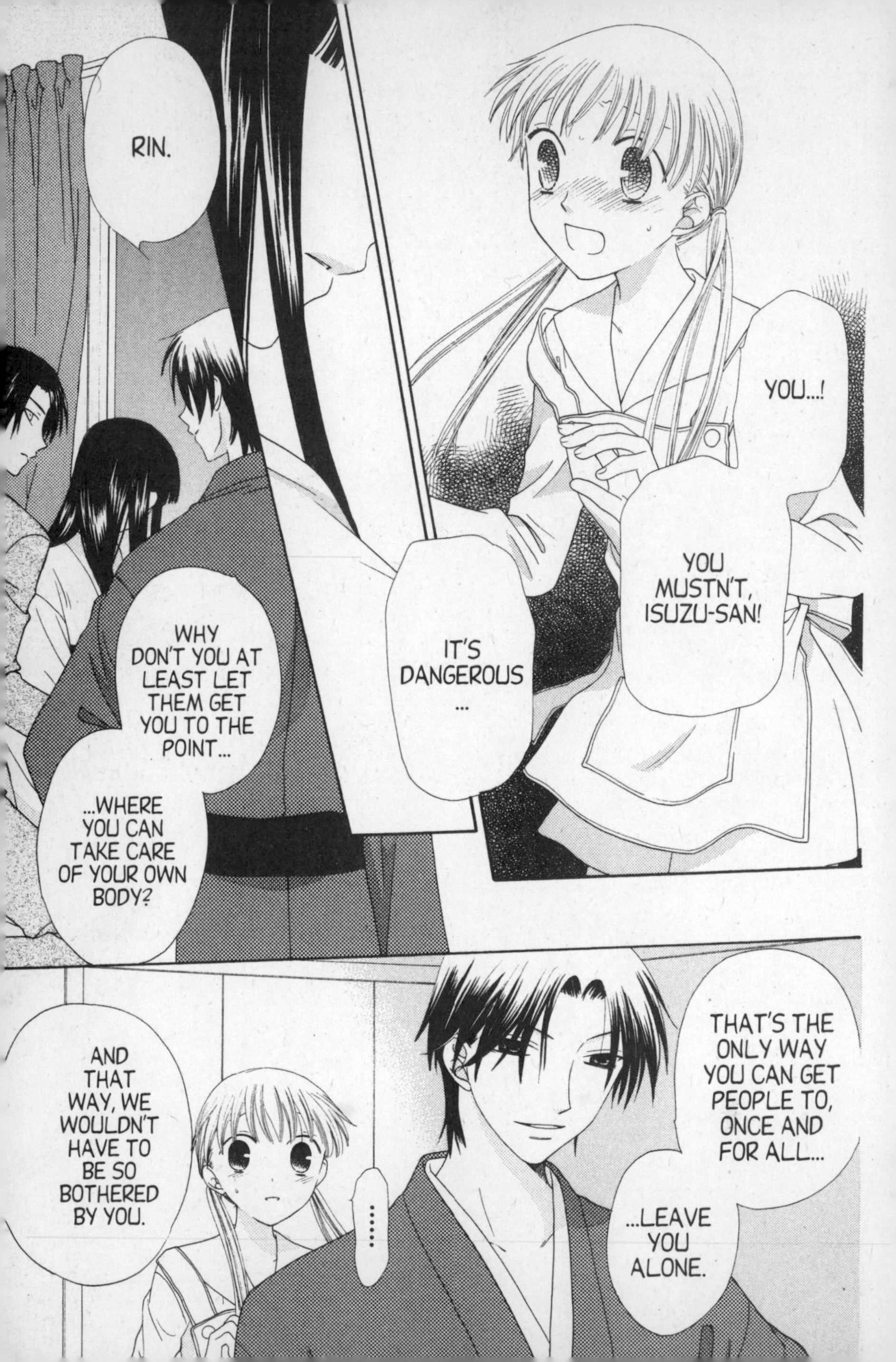
YOU...!
YOU MUSTN'T, ISUZU-SAN!
IT'S DANGEROUS ...
RIN.
WHY DON'T YOU AT LEAST LET THEM GET YOU TO THE POINT...
...WHERE YOU CAN TAKE CARE OF YOUR OWN BODY?
THAT'S THE ONLY WAY YOU CAN GET PEOPLE TO, ONCE AND FOR ALL...
...LEAVE YOU ALONE.
......
AND THAT WAY, WE WOULDN'T HAVE TO BE SO BOTHERED BY YOU.

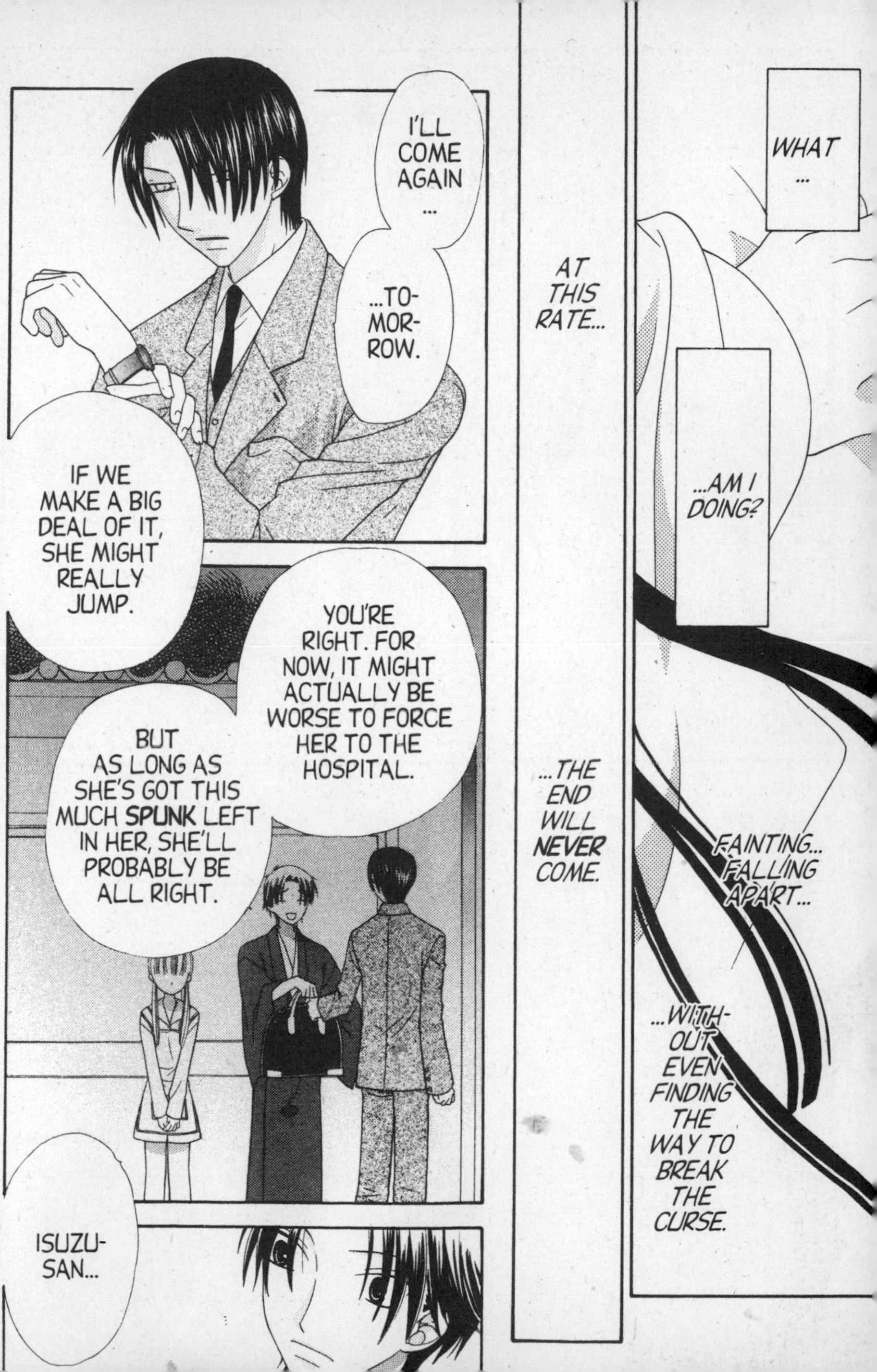

WHAT ...
...AM I DOING?
FAINTING... FALLING APART...
...WITH-OUT EVEN FINDING THE WAY TO BREAK THE CURSE.
AT THIS RATE...
...THE END WILL NEVER COME.
I'LL COME AGAIN ...
...TO-MOR-ROW.
IF WE MAKE A BIG DEAL OF IT, SHE MIGHT REALLY JUMP.
YOU'RE RIGHT. FOR NOW, IT MIGHT ACTUALLY BE WORSE TO FORCE HER TO THE HOSPITAL.
BUT AS LONG AS SHE'S GOT THIS MUCH SPUNK LEFT IN HER, SHE'LL PROBABLY BE ALL RIGHT.
ISUZU-SAN...

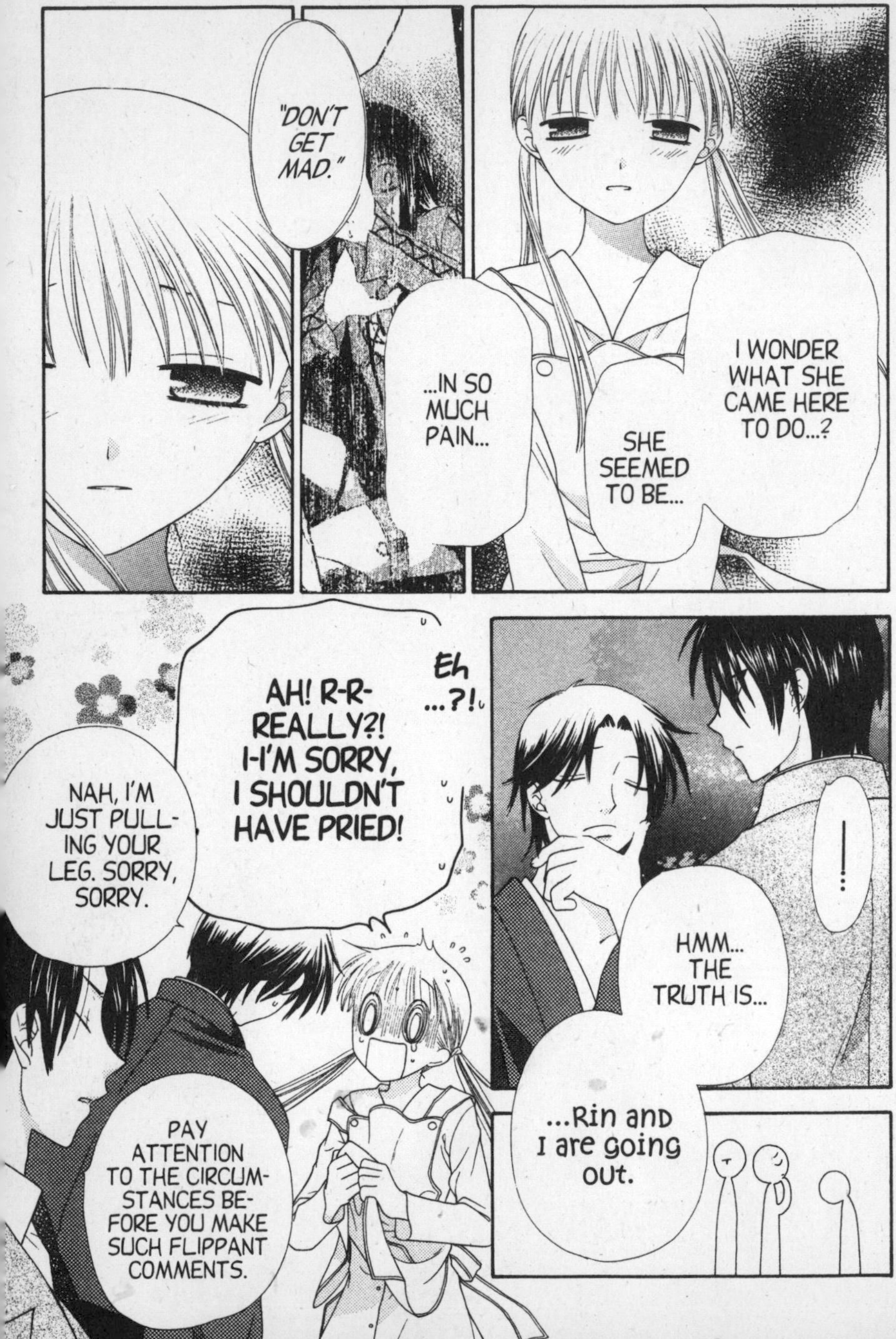
I WONDER WHAT SHE CAME HERE TO DO...?
SHE SEEMED TO BE...
...IN SO MUCH PAIN...
"DON'T GET MAD."
...!
HMM... THE TRUTH IS...
...Rin and I are going out.
Eh ...?!
AH! R-R-REALLY?! I-I'M SORRY, I SHOULDN'T HAVE PRIED!
NAH, I'M JUST PULLING YOUR LEG. SORRY, SORRY.
PAY ATTENTION TO THE CIRCUMSTANCES BEFORE YOU MAKE SUCH FLIPPANT COMMENTS.

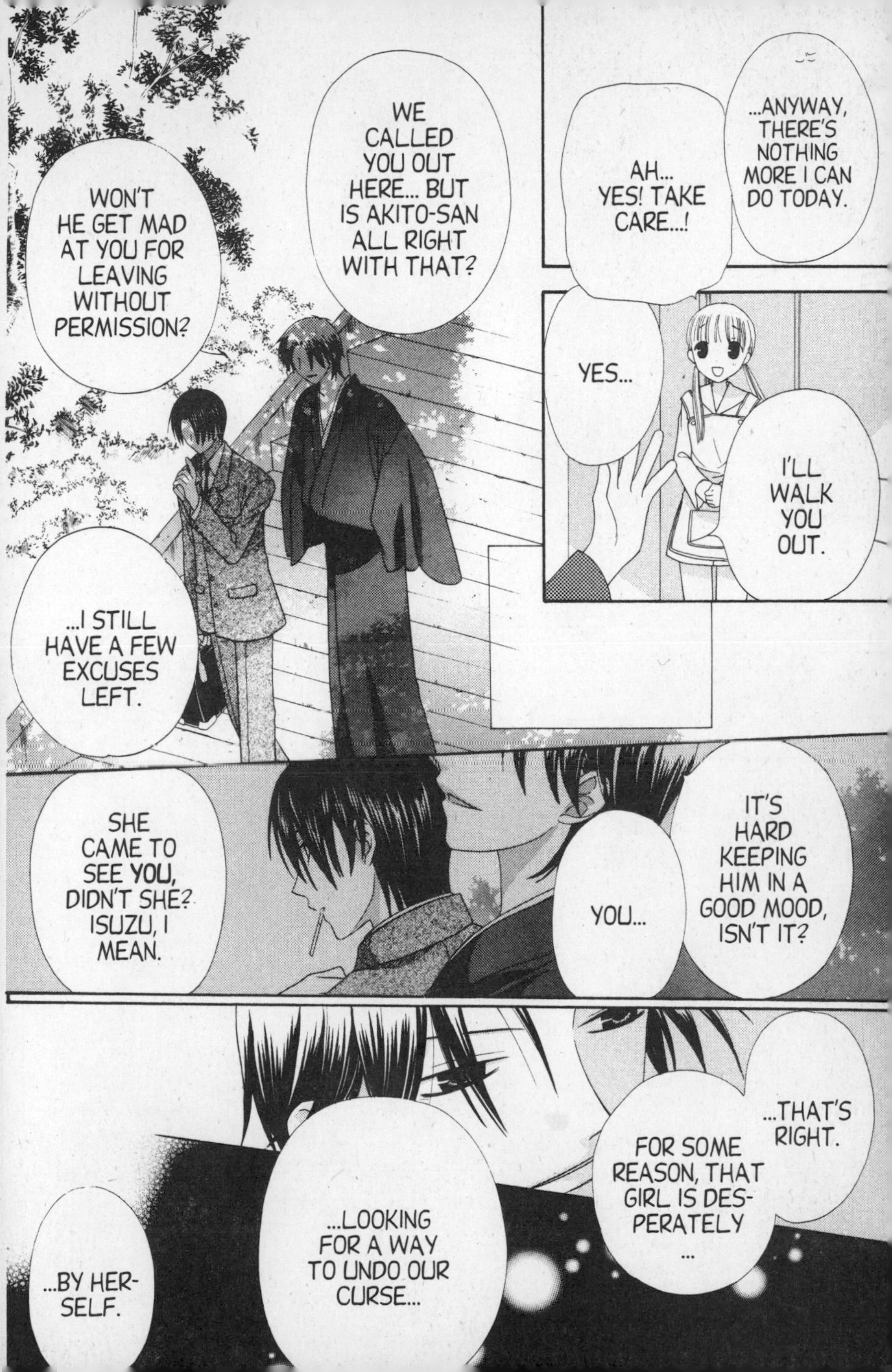
...ANYWAY, THERE'S NOTHING MORE I CAN DO TODAY.
AH... YES! TAKE CARE...!
I'LL WALK YOU OUT.
YES...
WE CALLED YOU OUT HERE... BUT IS AKITO-SAN ALL RIGHT WITH THAT?
WON'T HE GET MAD AT YOU FOR LEAVING WITHOUT PERMISSION?
...I STILL HAVE A FEW EXCUSES LEFT.
IT'S HARD KEEPING HIM IN A GOOD MOOD, ISN'T IT?
YOU...
SHE CAME TO SEE YOU, DIDN'T SHE? ISUZU, I MEAN.
...THAT'S RIGHT.
FOR SOME REASON, THAT GIRL IS DES-PERATELY ...
...LOOKING FOR A WAY TO UNDO OUR CURSE...
...BY HER-SELF.

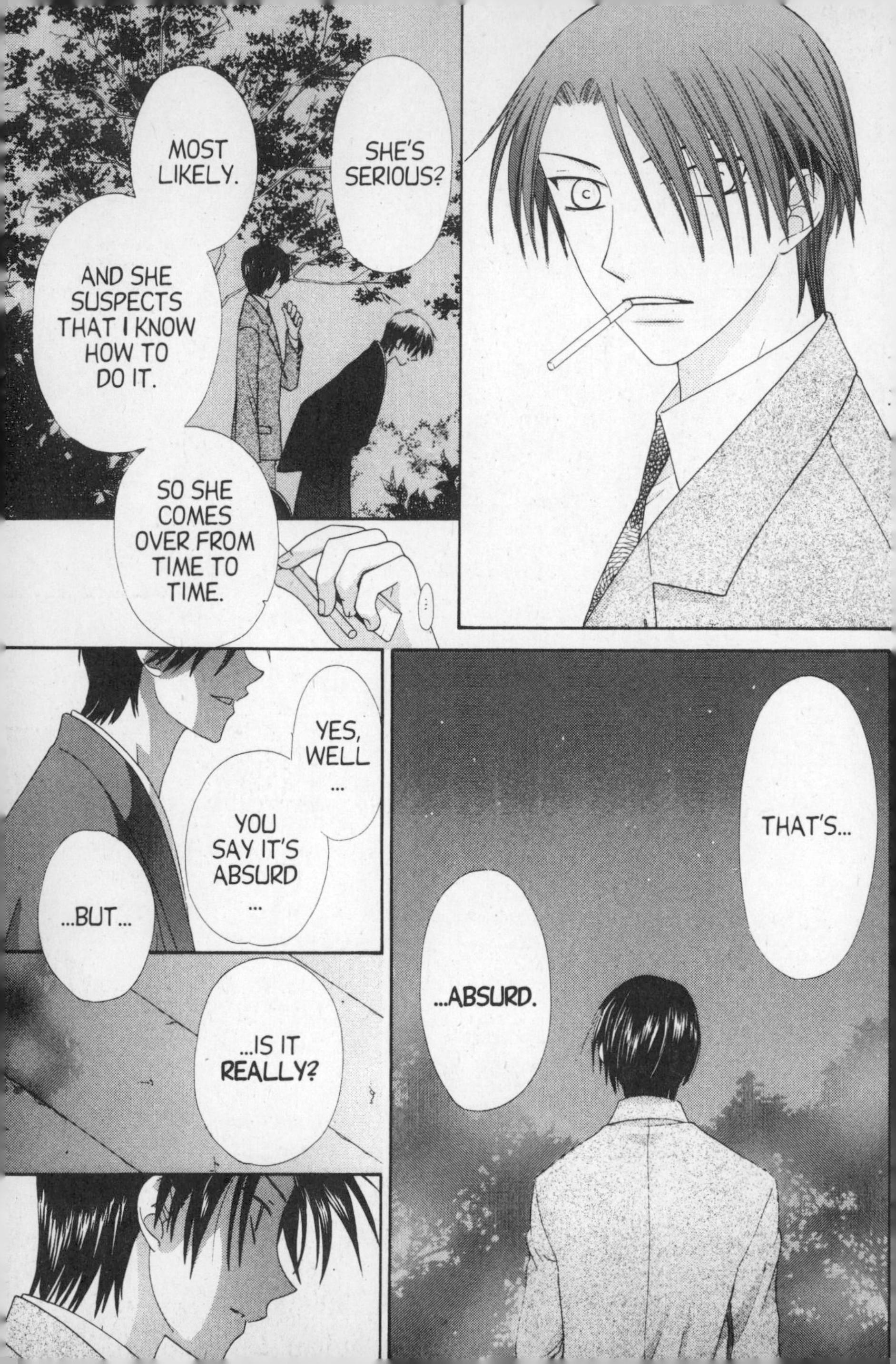
SHE'S SERIOUS?
MOST LIKELY.
AND SHE SUSPECTS THAT I KNOW HOW TO DO IT.
SO SHE COMES OVER FROM TIME TO TIME.
...
THAT'S...
...ABSURD.
YES, WELL ...
YOU SAY IT'S ABSURD ...
...BUT...
...IS IT REALLY?

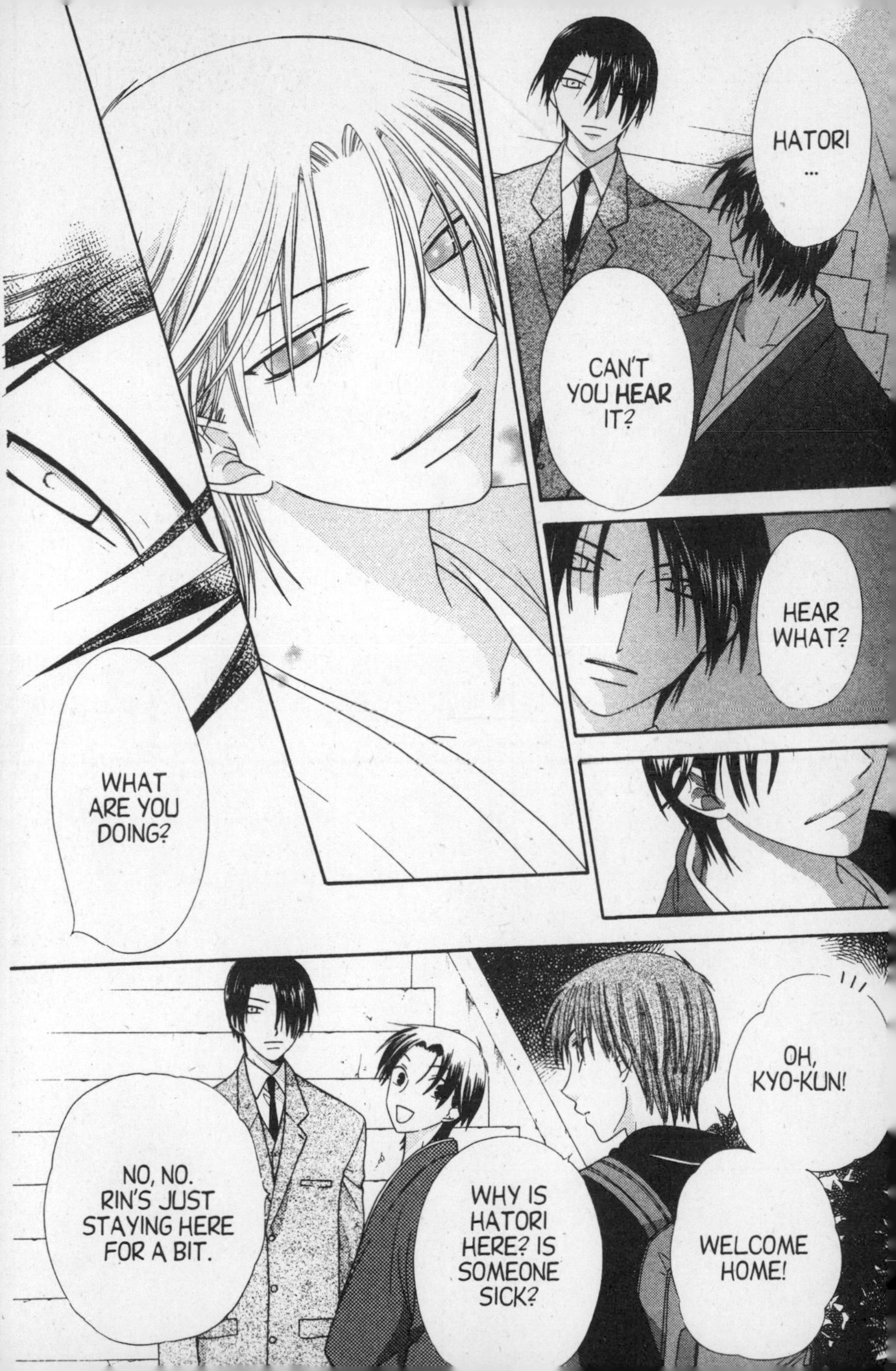
HATORI ...
CAN'T YOU HEAR IT?
HEAR WHAT?
WHAT ARE YOU DOING?
OH, KYO-KUN!
WELCOME HOME!
WHY IS HATORI HERE? IS SOMEONE SICK?
NO, NO. RIN'S JUST STAYING HERE FOR A BIT.

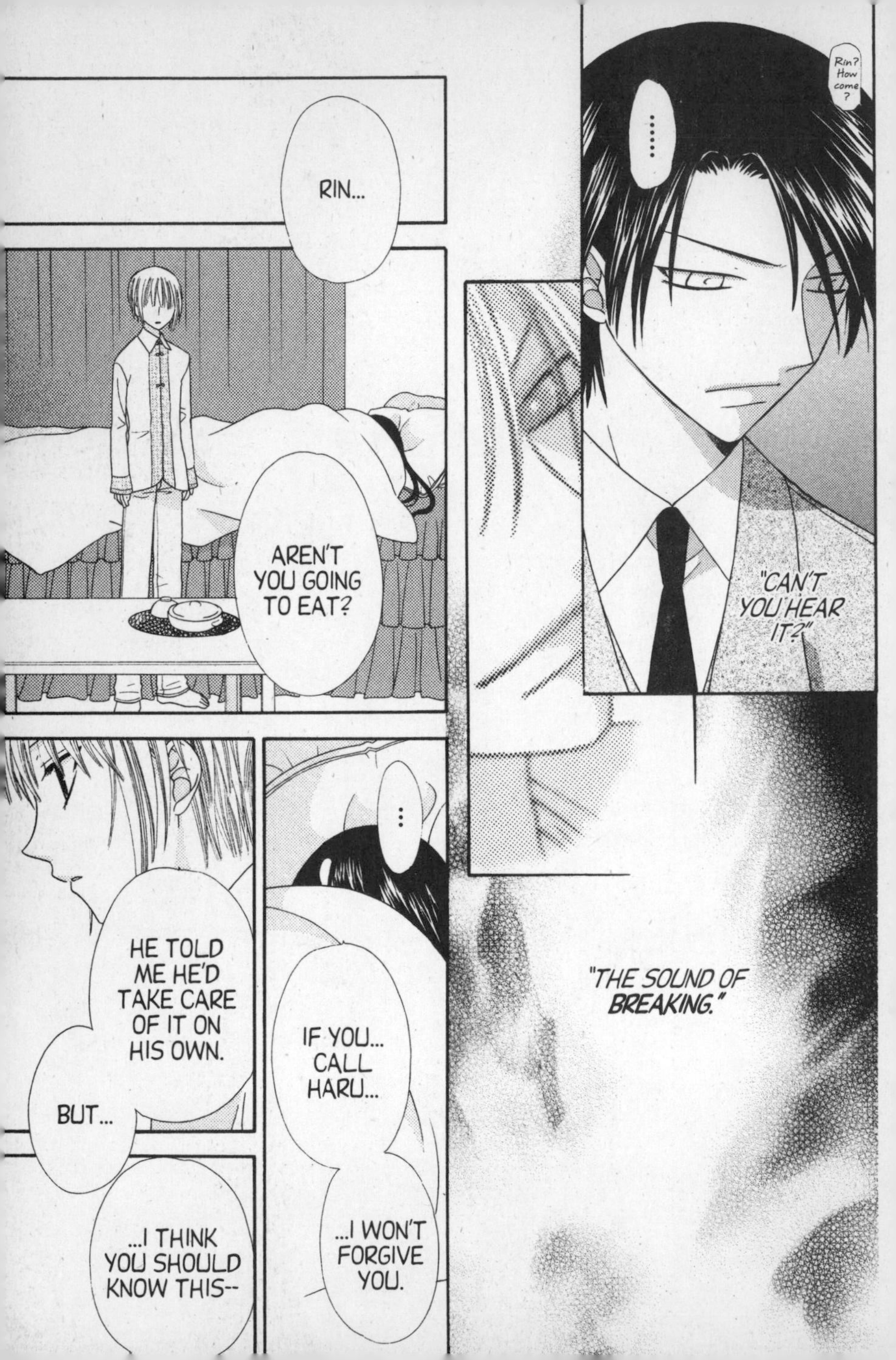
Rin? How come?
......
"CAN'T YOU HEAR IT?"
"THE SOUND OF BREAKING."
RIN...
AREN'T YOU GOING TO EAT?
...
IF YOU... CALL HARU...
...I WON'T FORGIVE YOU.
HE TOLD ME HE'D TAKE CARE OF IT ON HIS OWN.
BUT...
...I THINK YOU SHOULD KNOW THIS--

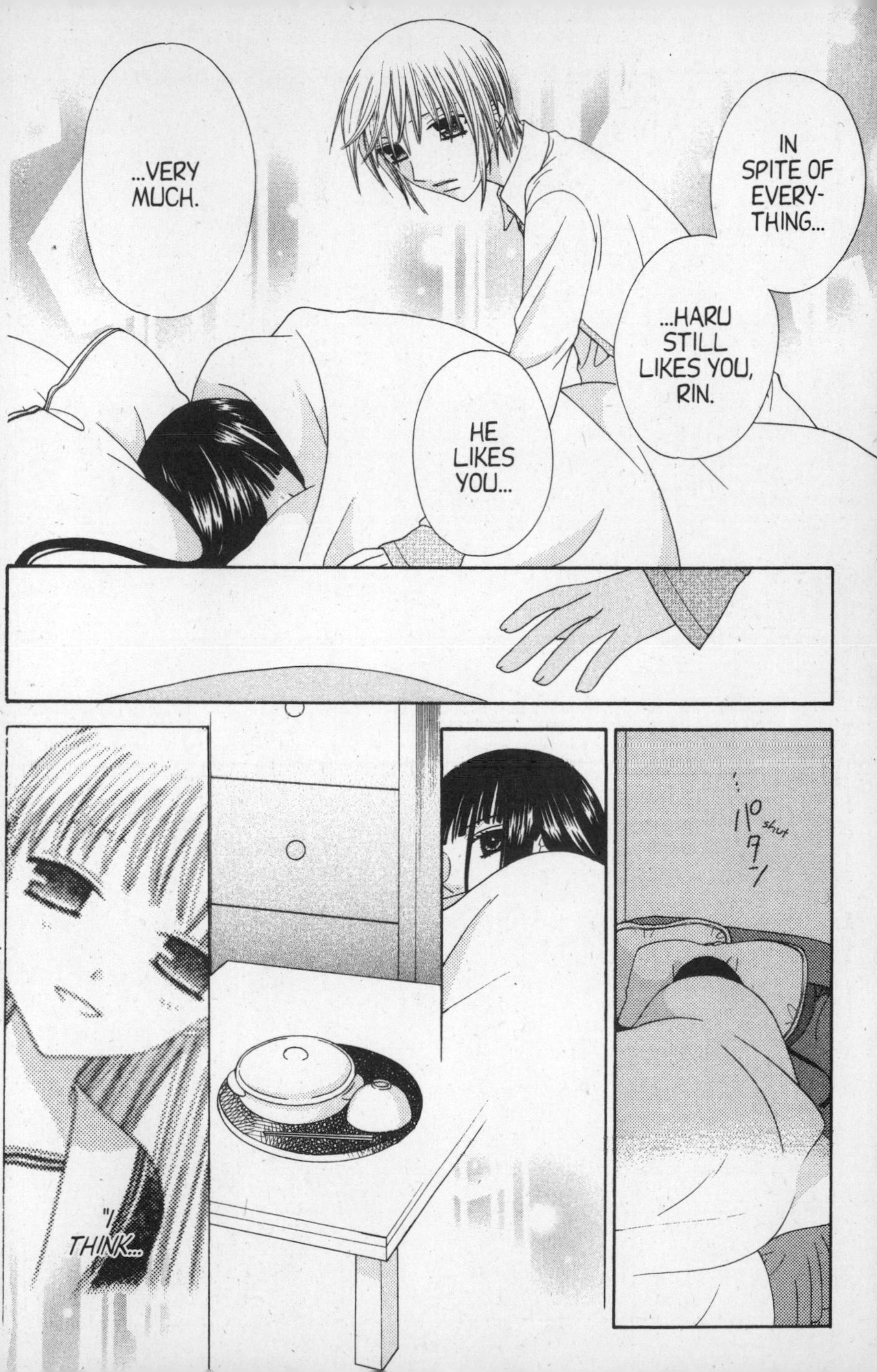
IN SPITE OF EVERY-THING...
...HARU STILL LIKES YOU, RIN.
HE LIKES YOU...
...VERY MUCH.
shut
"I THINK...

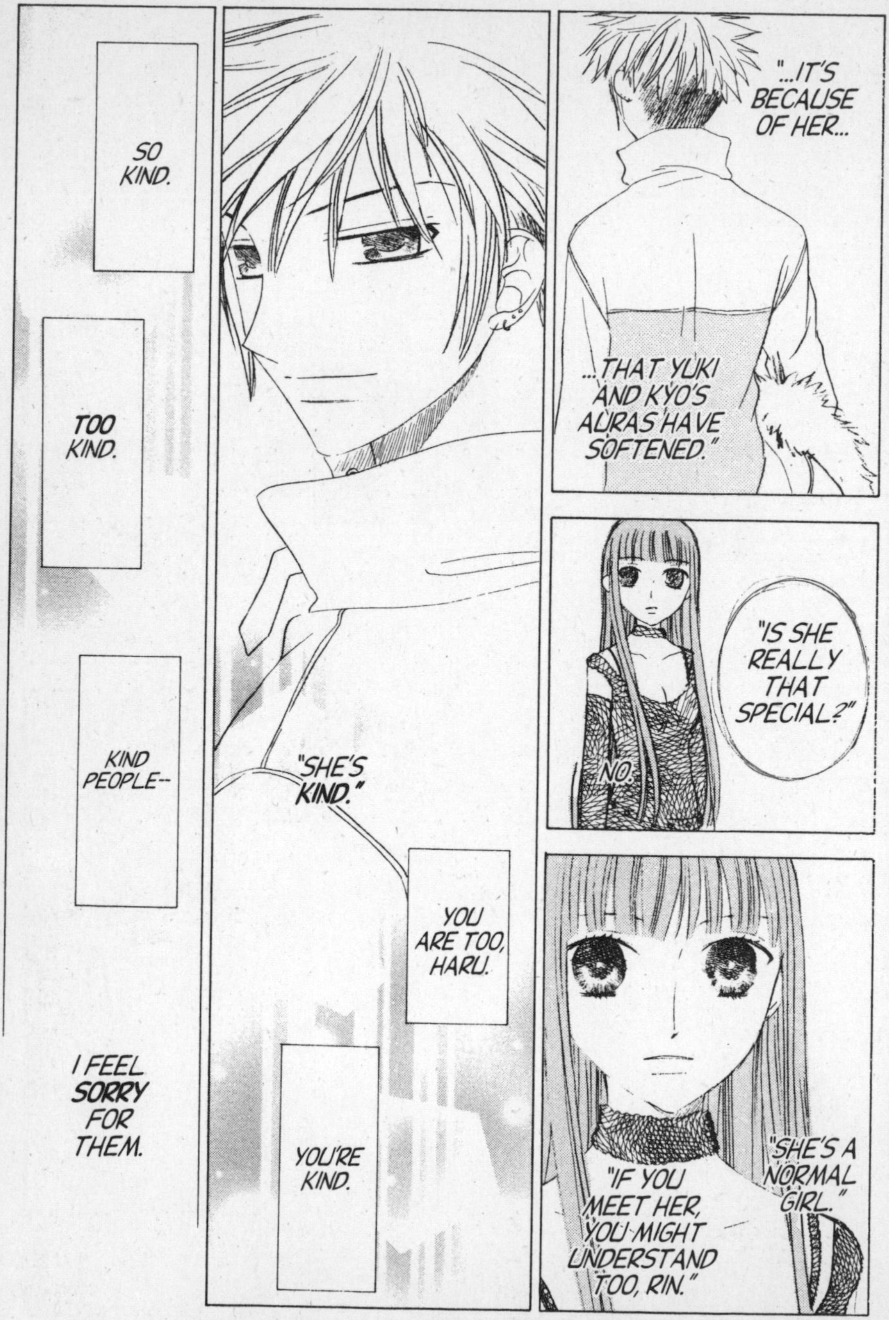
"...IT'S BECAUSE OF HER...
...THAT YUKI AND KYO'S AURAS HAVE SOFTENED."
"IS SHE REALLY THAT SPECIAL?"
NO.
"SHE'S A NORMAL GIRL."
"IF YOU MEET HER, YOU MIGHT UNDERSTAND TOO, RIN."
"SHE'S KIND."
YOU ARE TOO, HARU.
YOU'RE KIND.
SO KIND.
TOO KIND.
KIND PEOPLE--
I FEEL SORRY FOR THEM.

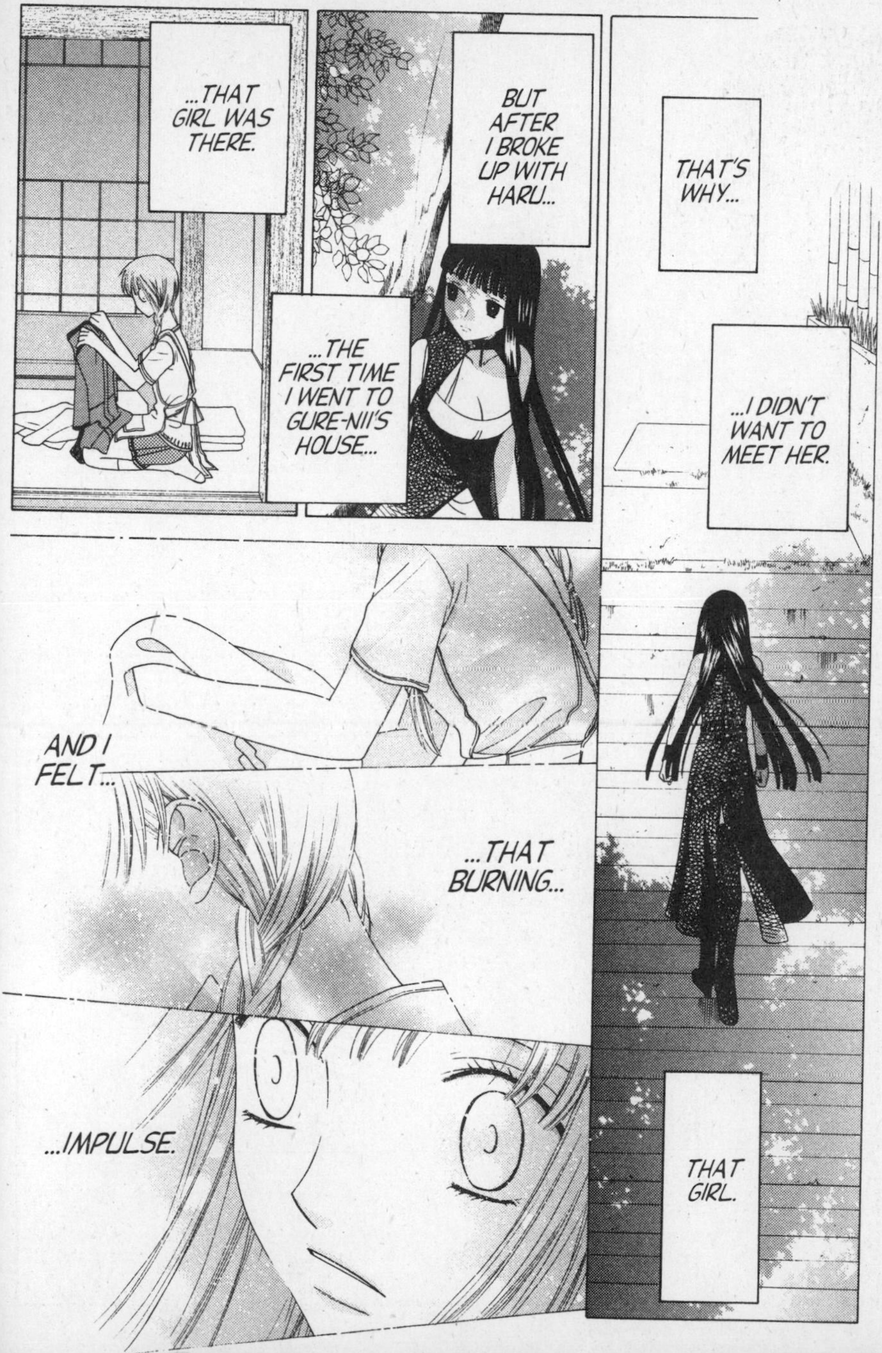
THAT'S WHY...
...I DIDN'T WANT TO MEET HER.
BUT AFTER I BROKE UP WITH HARU...
...THE FIRST TIME I WENT TO GURE-NII'S HOUSE...
...THAT GIRL WAS THERE.
THAT GIRL.
AND I FELT...
...THAT BURNING...
...IMPULSE.

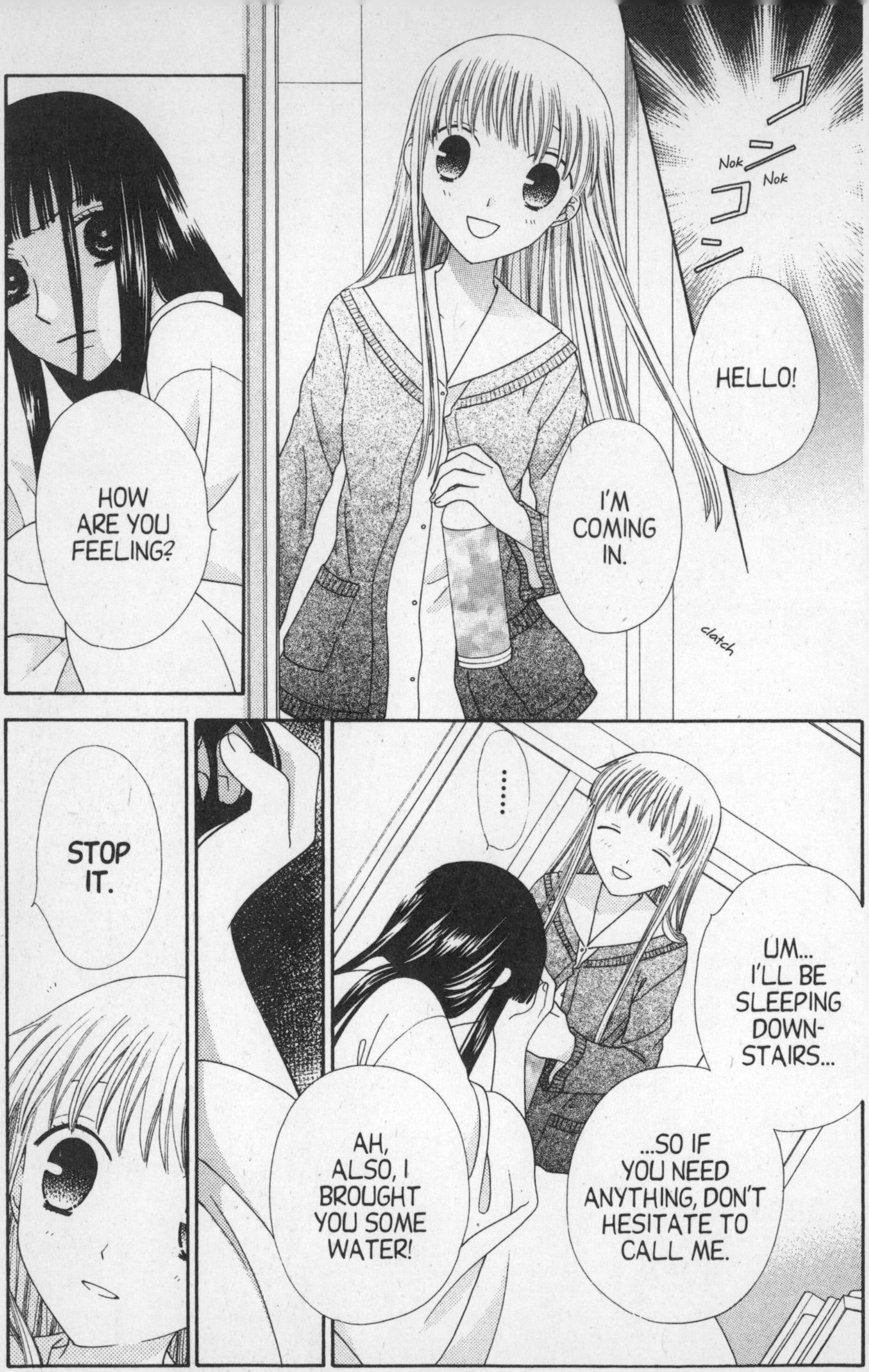
Nok
Nok
HELLO!
I'M COMING IN.
clatch
HOW ARE YOU FEELING?
......
UM... I'LL BE SLEEPING DOWN-STAIRS...
...SO IF YOU NEED ANYTHING, DON'T HESITATE TO CALL ME.
AH, ALSO, I BROUGHT YOU SOME WATER!
STOP IT.

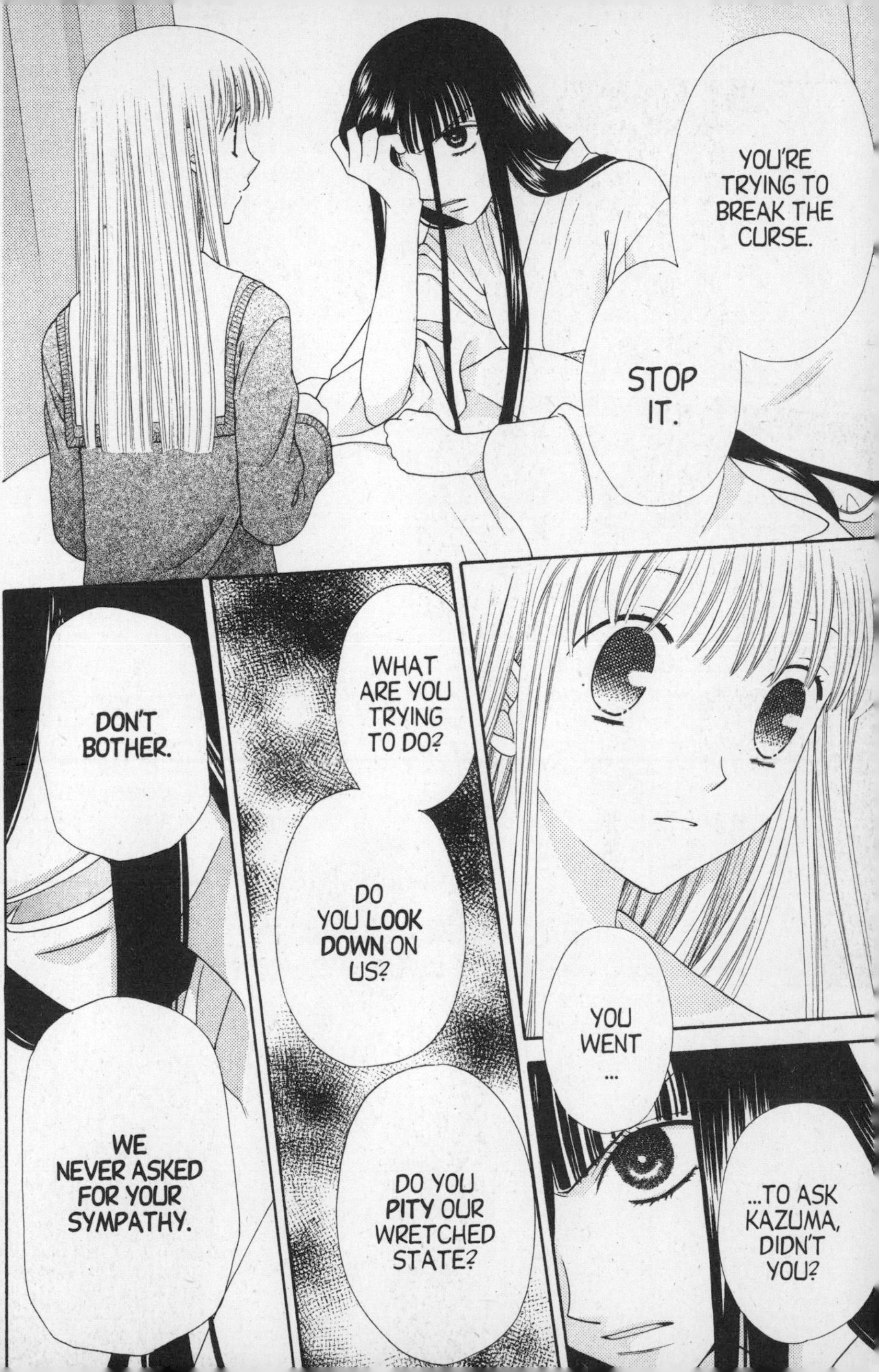
YOU'RE TRYING TO BREAK THE CURSE.
STOP IT.
YOU WENT ...
...TO ASK KAZUMA, DIDN'T YOU?
WHAT ARE YOU TRYING TO DO?
DO YOU LOOK DOWN ON US?
DO YOU PITY OUR WRETCHED STATE?
DON'T BOTHER.
WE NEVER ASKED FOR YOUR SYMPATHY.

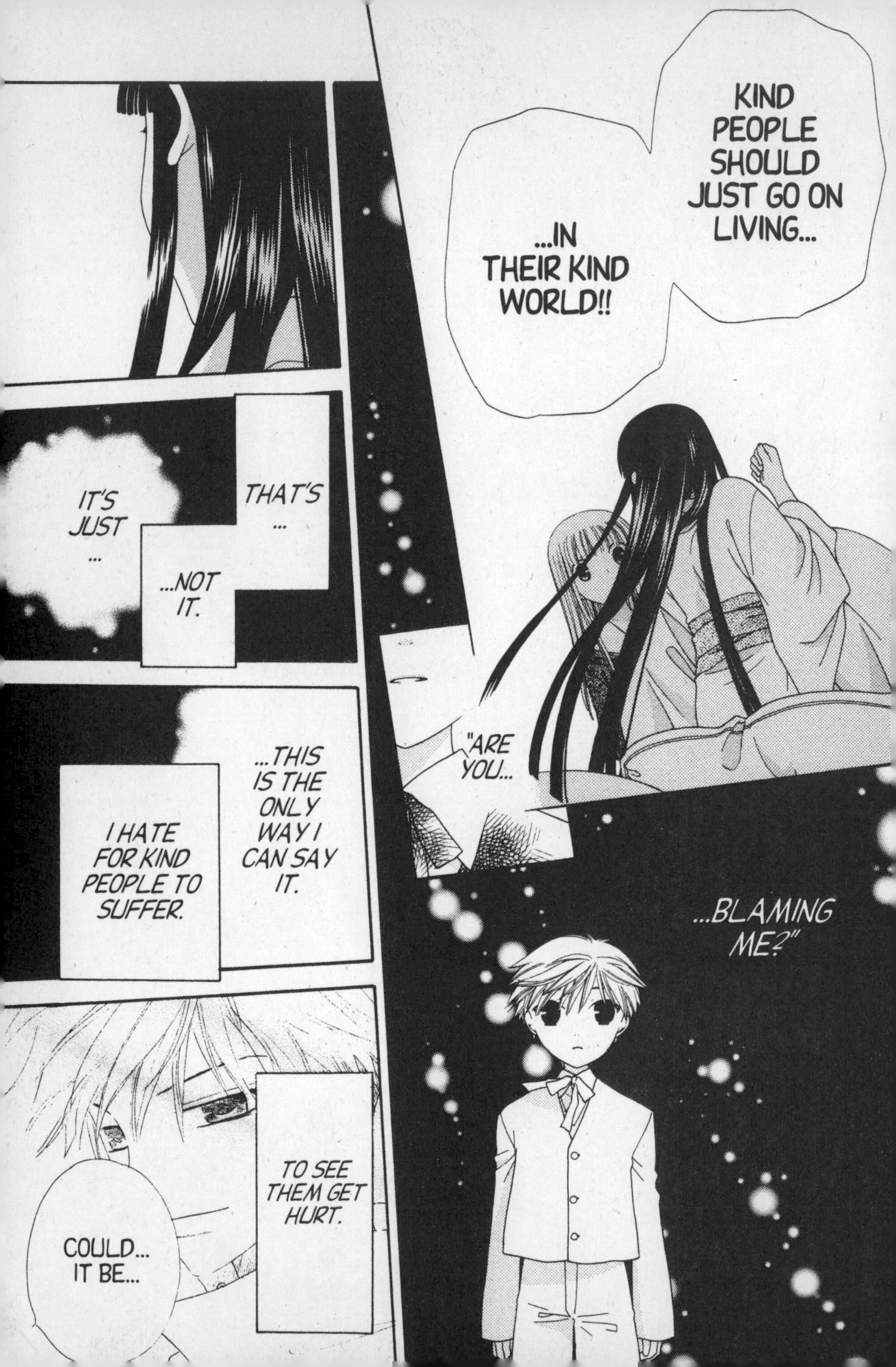
KIND PEOPLE SHOULD JUST GO ON LIVING...
...IN THEIR KIND WORLD!!
"ARE YOU...
...BLAMING ME?"
THAT'S...
IT'S JUST...
...NOT IT.
...THIS IS THE ONLY WAY I CAN SAY IT.
I HATE FOR KIND PEOPLE TO SUFFER.
TO SEE THEM GET HURT.
COULD... IT BE...

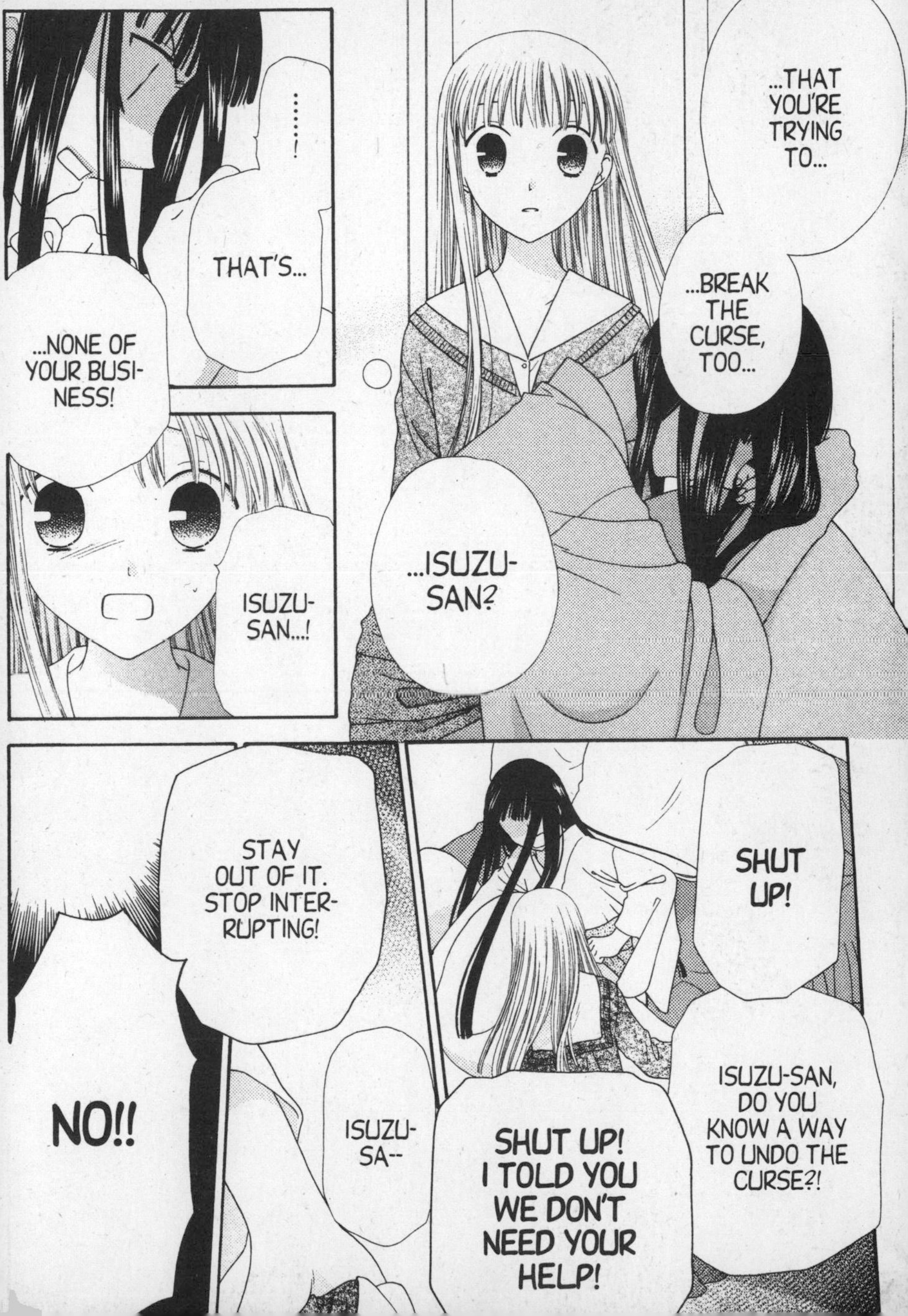
...THAT YOU'RE TRYING TO...
...BREAK THE CURSE, TOO...
...ISUZU-SAN?
......!
THAT'S...
...NONE OF YOUR BUSI-NESS!
ISUZU-SAN...!
SHUT UP!
ISUZU-SAN, DO YOU KNOW A WAY TO UNDO THE CURSE?!
SHUT UP! I TOLD YOU WE DON'T NEED YOUR HELP!
ISUZU-SA--
STAY OUT OF IT. STOP INTER-RUPTING!
NO!!

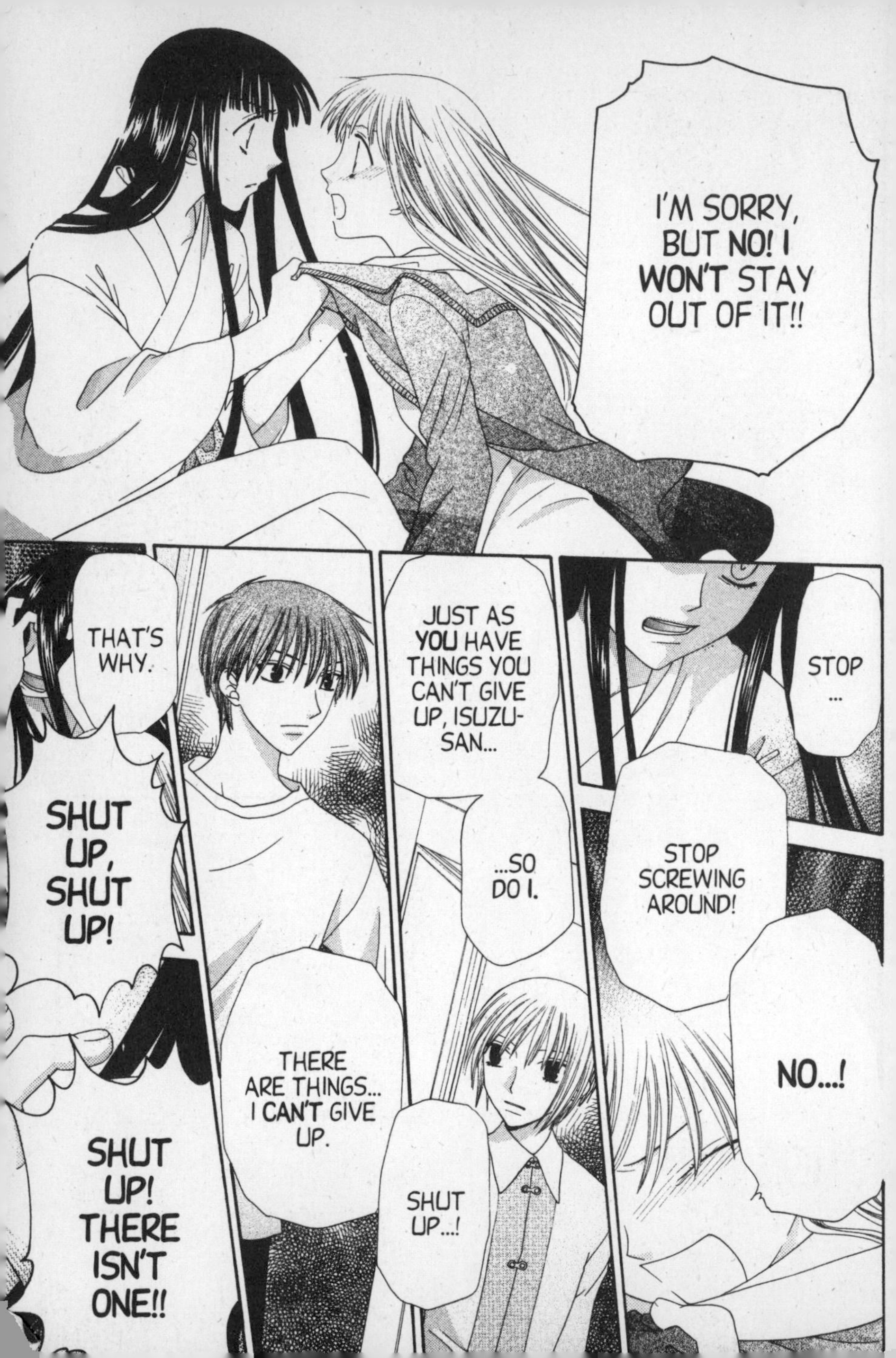
I'M SORRY, BUT NO! I WON'T STAY OUT OF IT!!
STOP ...
STOP SCREWING AROUND!
NO...!
JUST AS YOU HAVE THINGS YOU CAN'T GIVE UP, ISUZU-SAN...
...SO DO I.
SHUT UP...!
THERE ARE THINGS... I CAN'T GIVE UP.
THAT'S WHY.
SHUT UP, SHUT UP, SHUT UP!
SHUT UP! THERE ISN'T ONE!!

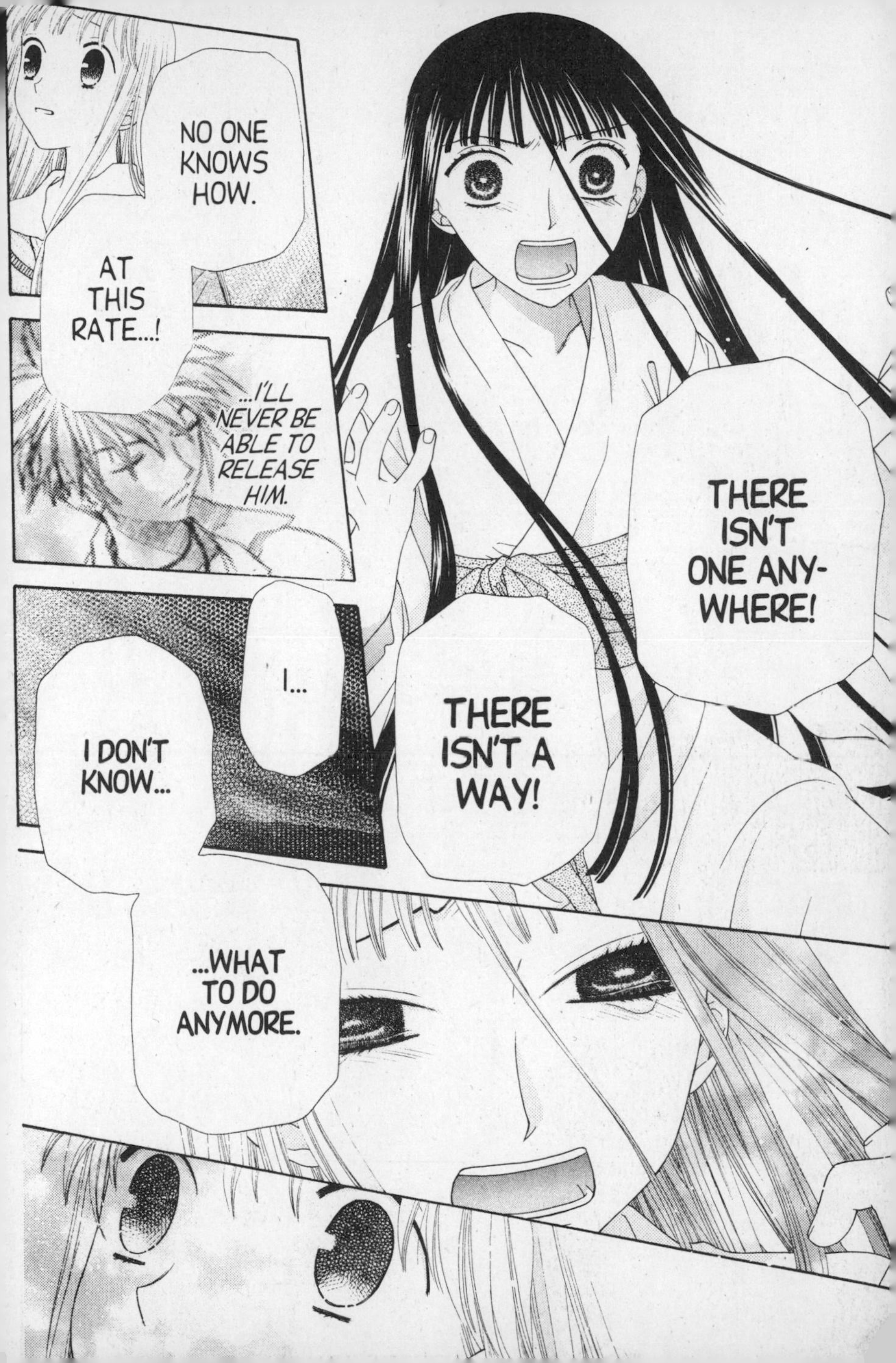
THERE ISN'T ONE ANY-WHERE!
THERE ISN'T A WAY!
NO ONE KNOWS HOW.
AT THIS RATE...!
...I'LL NEVER BE ABLE TO RELEASE HIM.
I...
I DON'T KNOW...
...WHAT TO DO ANYMORE.

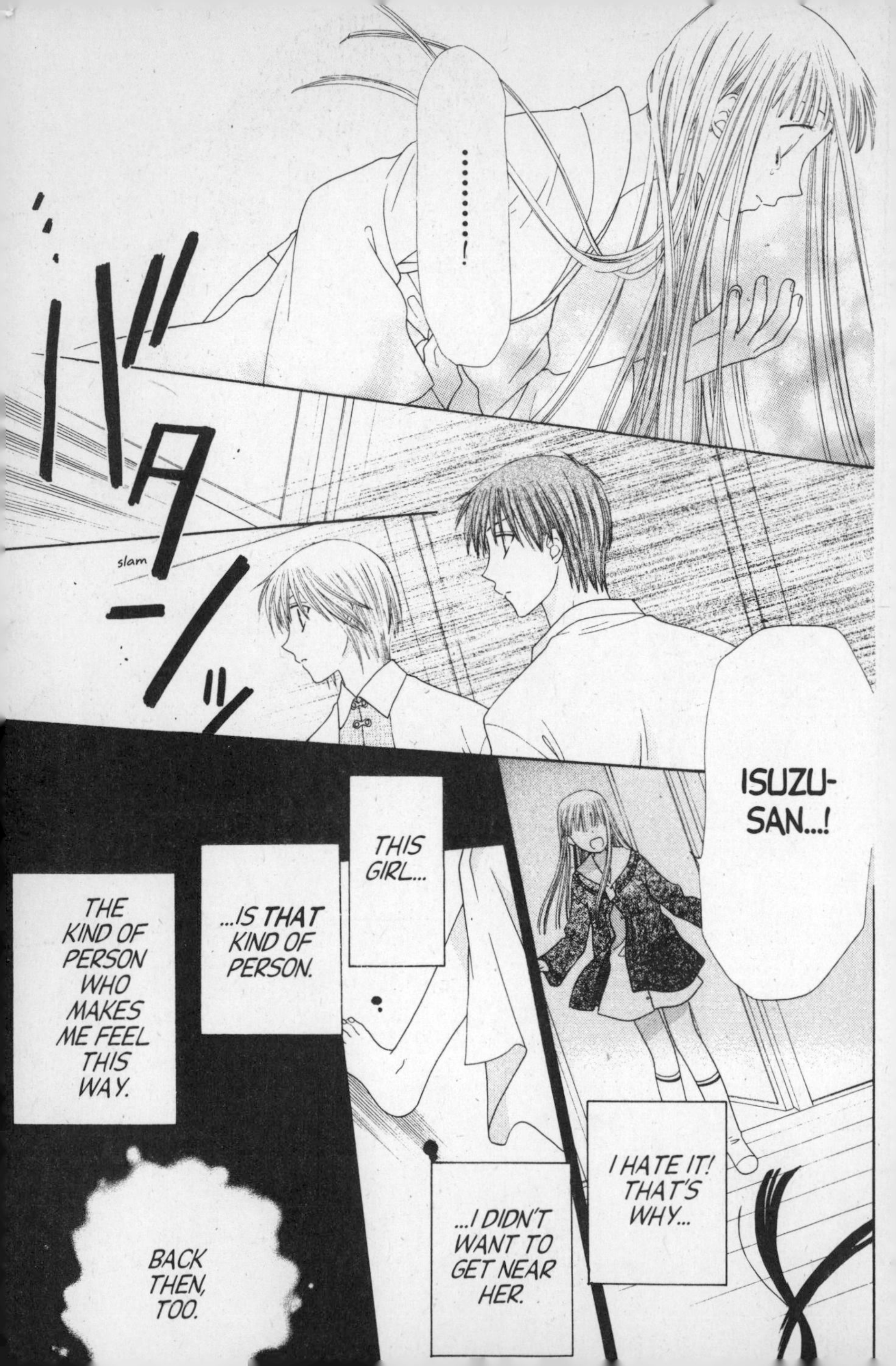
......!
slam
ISUZU-SAN...!
I HATE IT! THAT'S WHY...
...I DIDN'T WANT TO GET NEAR HER.
THIS GIRL...
...IS THAT KIND OF PERSON.
THE KIND OF PERSON WHO MAKES ME FEEL THIS WAY.
BACK THEN, TOO.

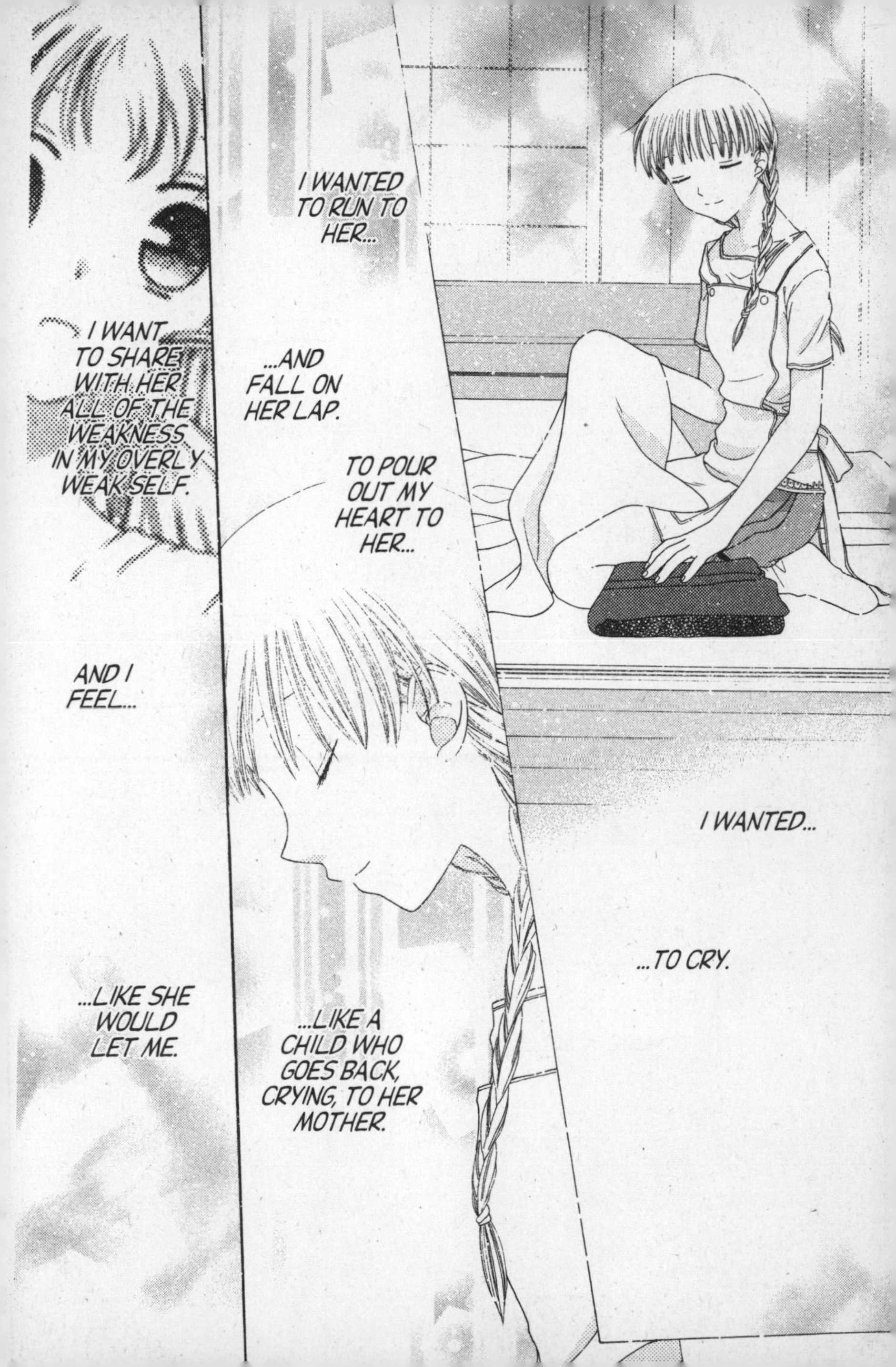
I WANTED...
...TO CRY.
I WANTED TO RUN TO HER...
...AND FALL ON HER LAP.
TO POUR OUT MY HEART TO HER...
...LIKE A CHILD WHO GOES BACK, CRYING, TO HER MOTHER.
I WANT TO SHARE WITH HER ALL OF THE WEAKNESS IN MY OVERLY WEAK SELF.
AND I FEEL...
...LIKE SHE WOULD LET ME.

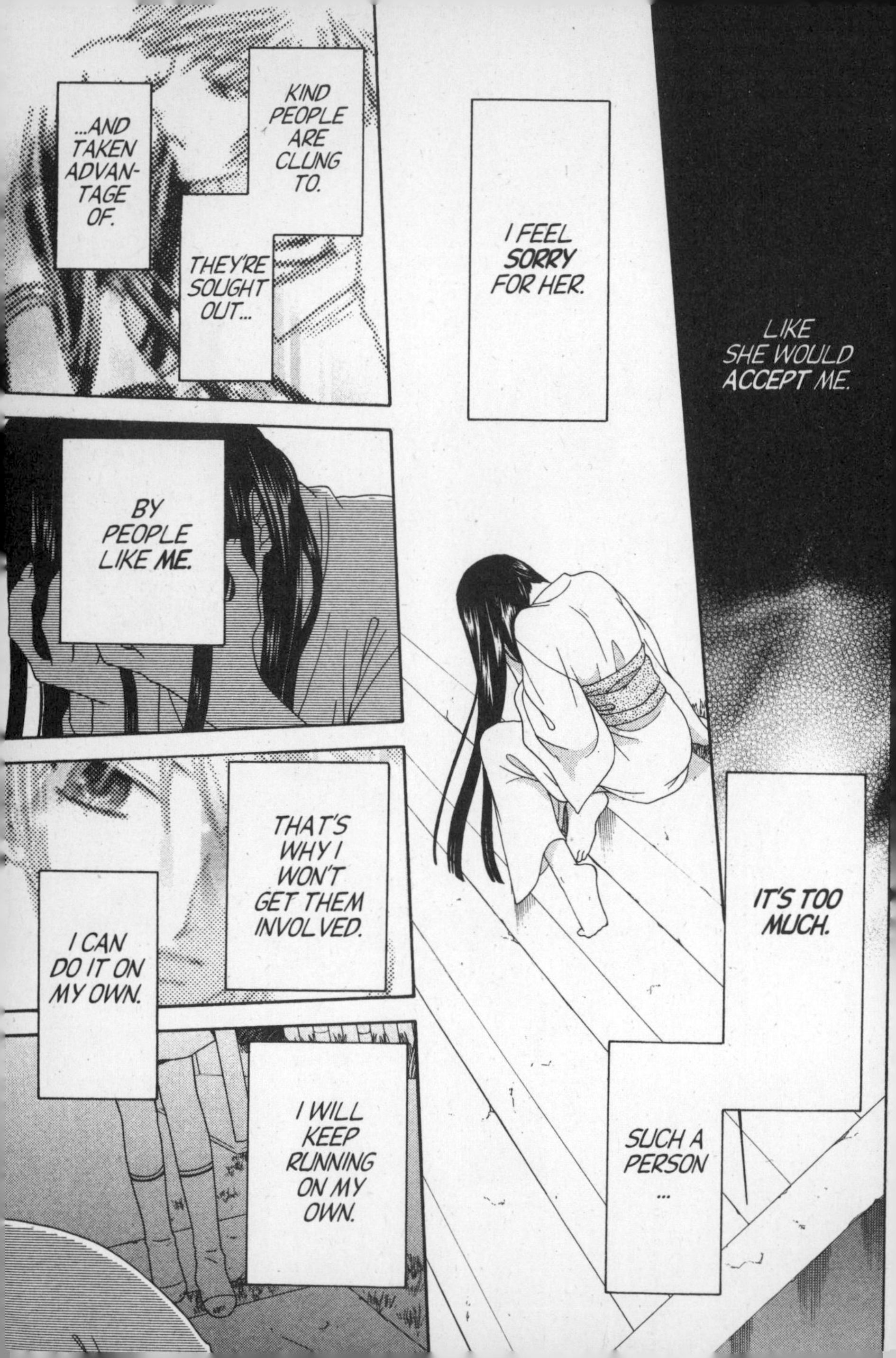
LIKE SHE WOULD ACCEPT ME.
IT'S TOO MUCH.
SUCH A PERSON ...
I FEEL SORRY FOR HER.
KIND PEOPLE ARE CLUNG TO.
THEY'RE SOUGHT OUT...
...AND TAKEN ADVANTAGE OF.
BY PEOPLE LIKE ME.
THAT'S WHY I WON'T GET THEM INVOLVED.
I CAN DO IT ON MY OWN.
I WILL KEEP RUNNING ON MY OWN.

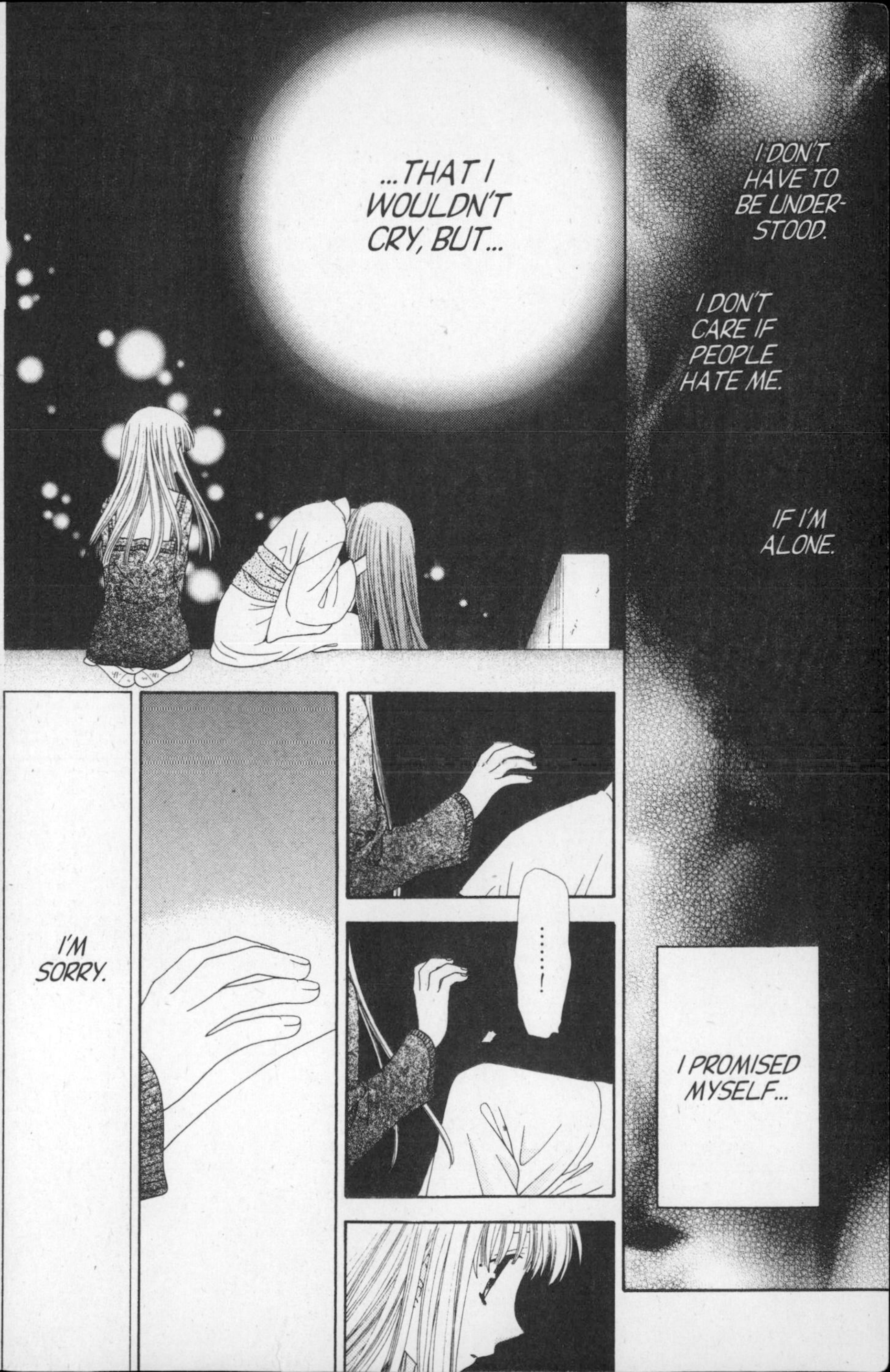
I DON'T HAVE TO BE UNDER-STOOD.
I DON'T CARE IF PEOPLE HATE ME.
IF I'M ALONE.
I PROMISED MYSELF...
...THAT I WOULDN'T CRY, BUT...
......!
I'M SORRY.

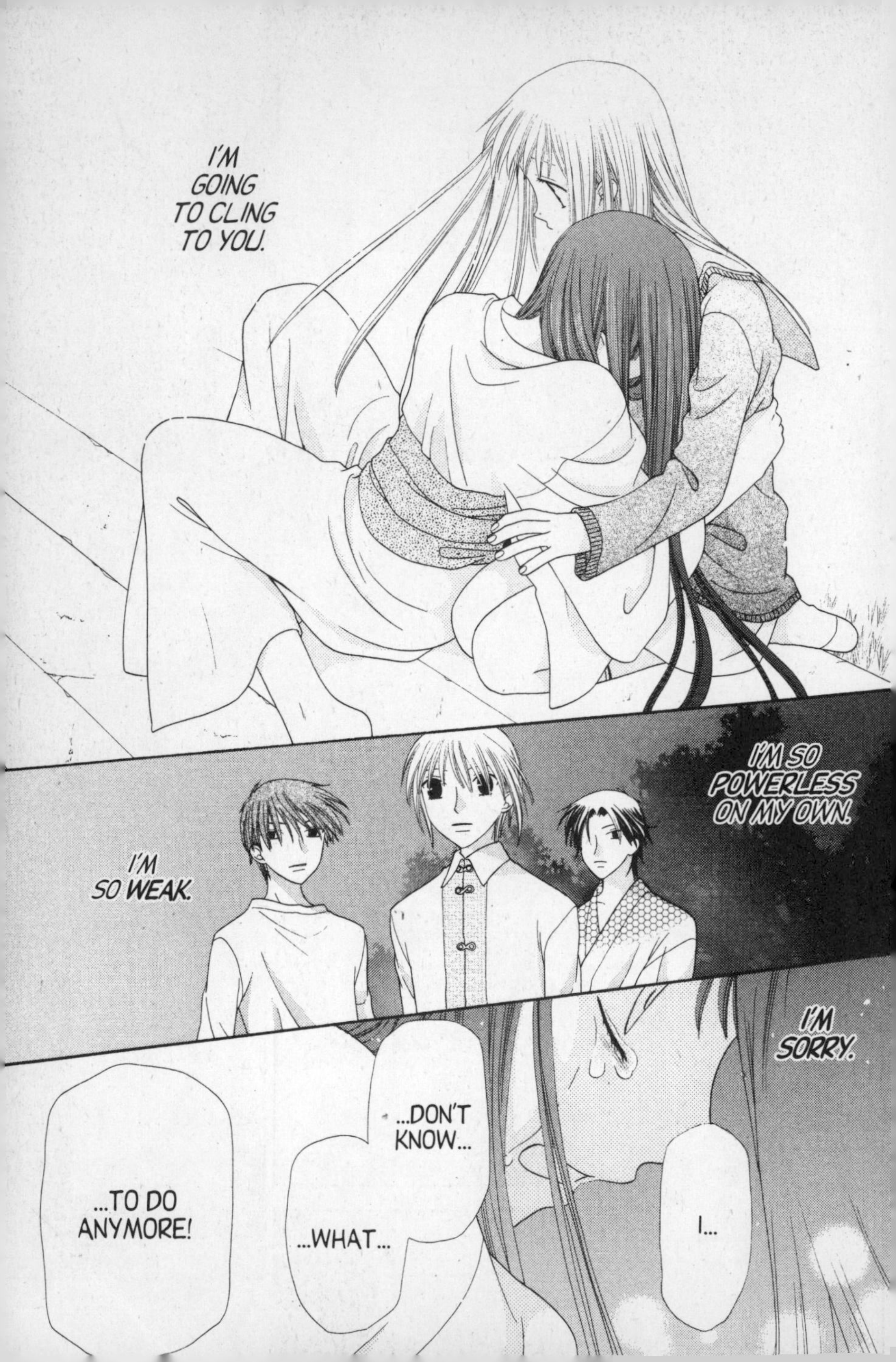
I'M GOING TO CLING TO YOU.
I'M SO POWERLESS ON MY OWN.
I'M SO WEAK.
I'M SORRY.
I...
...DON'T KNOW...
...WHAT...
...TO DO ANYMORE!

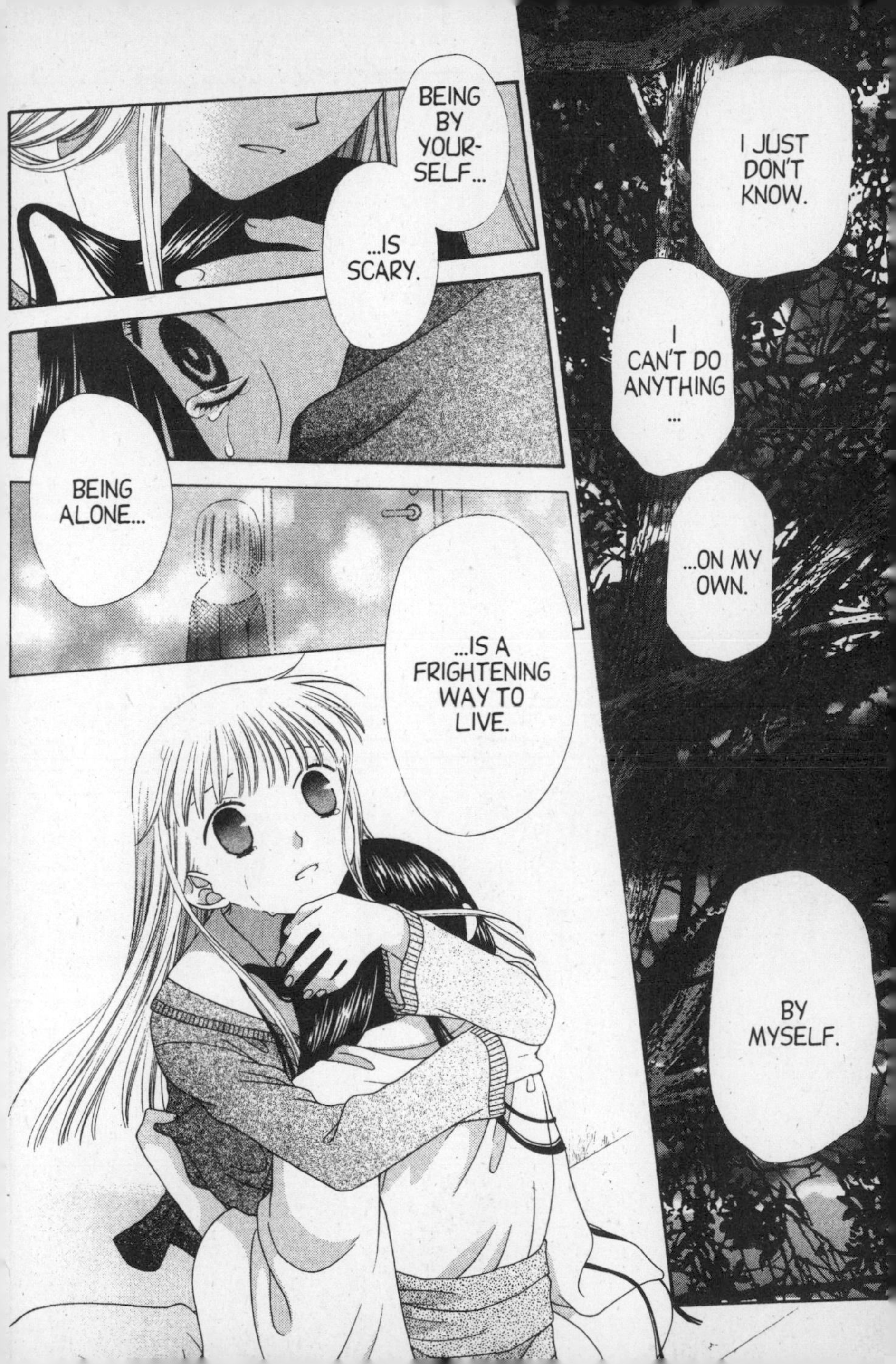
I JUST DON'T KNOW.
I CAN'T DO ANYTHING...
...ON MY OWN.
BY MYSELF.
BEING BY YOUR-SELF...
...IS SCARY.
BEING ALONE...
...IS A FRIGHTENING WAY TO LIVE.

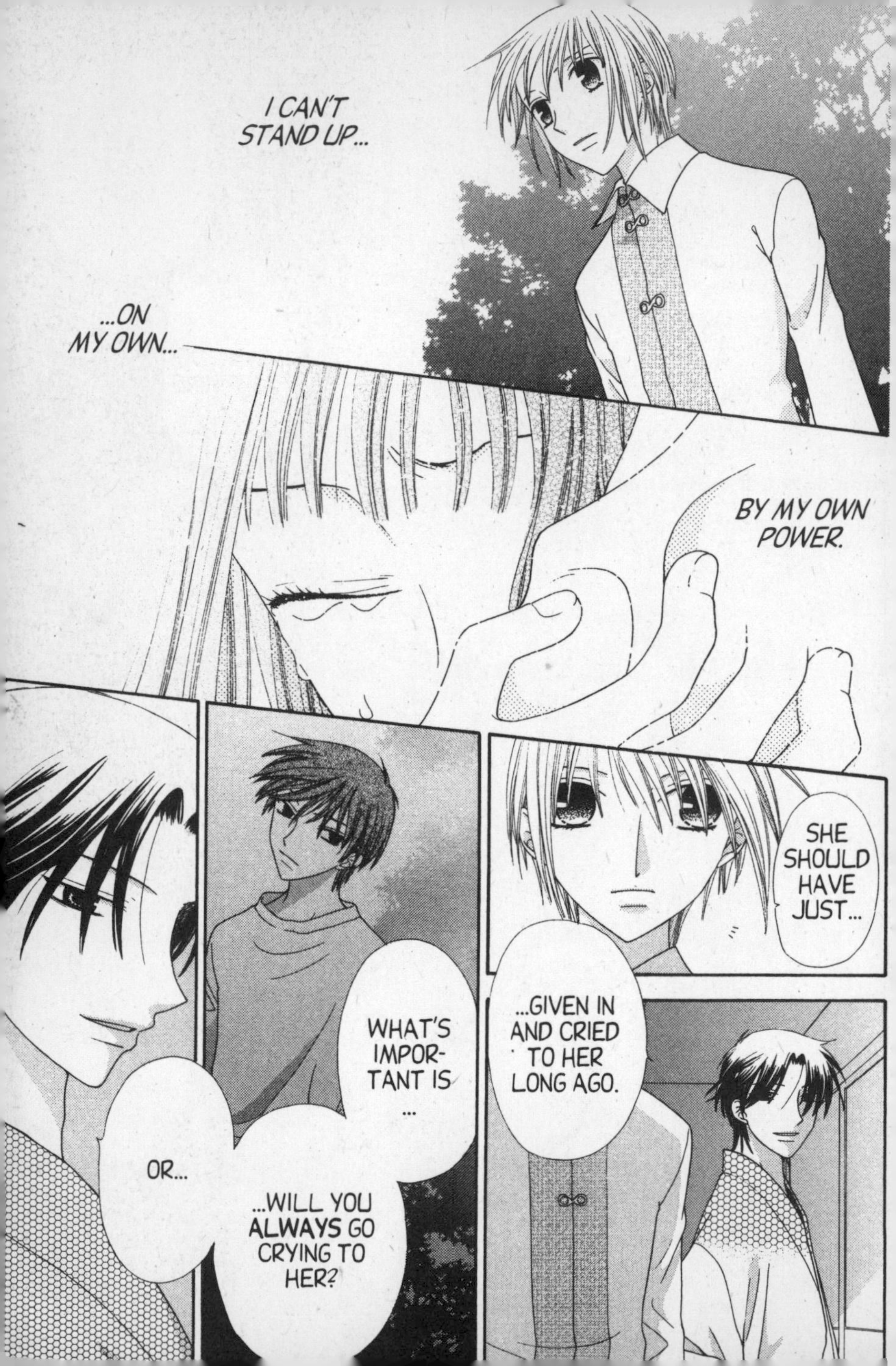
I CAN'T STAND UP...
...ON MY OWN...
BY MY OWN POWER.
SHE SHOULD HAVE JUST...
...GIVEN IN AND CRIED TO HER LONG AGO.
WHAT'S IMPOR-TANT IS ...
OR...
...WILL YOU ALWAYS GO CRYING TO HER?

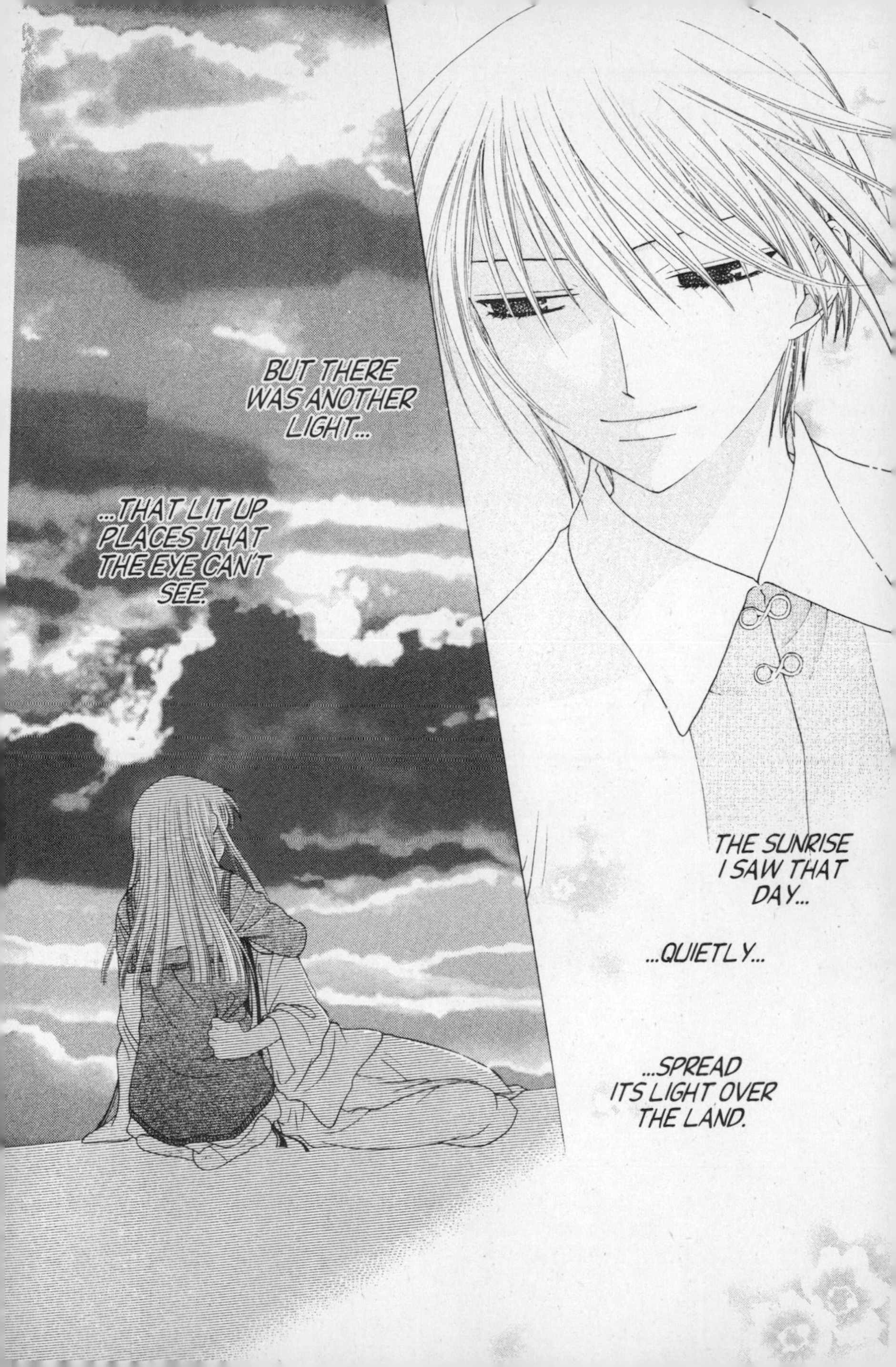
THE SUNRISE I SAW THAT DAY...
...QUIETLY...
...SPREAD ITS LIGHT OVER THE LAND.
BUT THERE WAS ANOTHER LIGHT...
...THAT LIT UP PLACES THAT THE EYE CAN'T SEE.

Filler Sketch

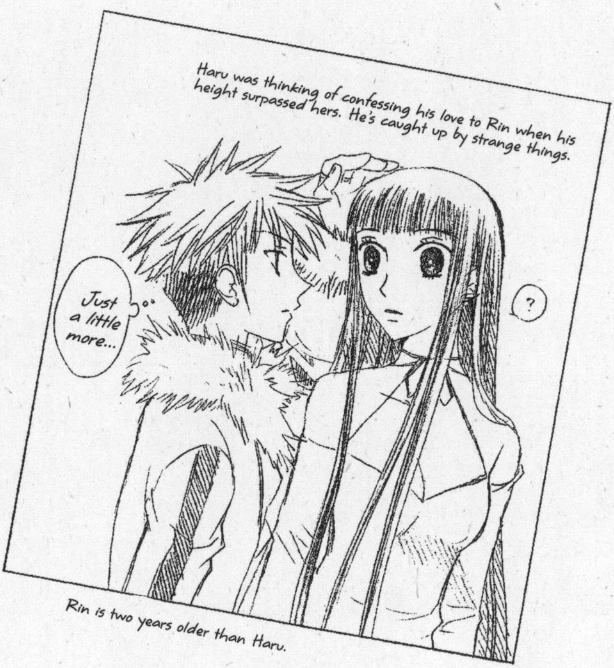
Haru was thinking of confessing his love to Rin when his height surpassed hers. He's caught up by strange things.
?
Just a little more...

Rin is two years older than Haru.

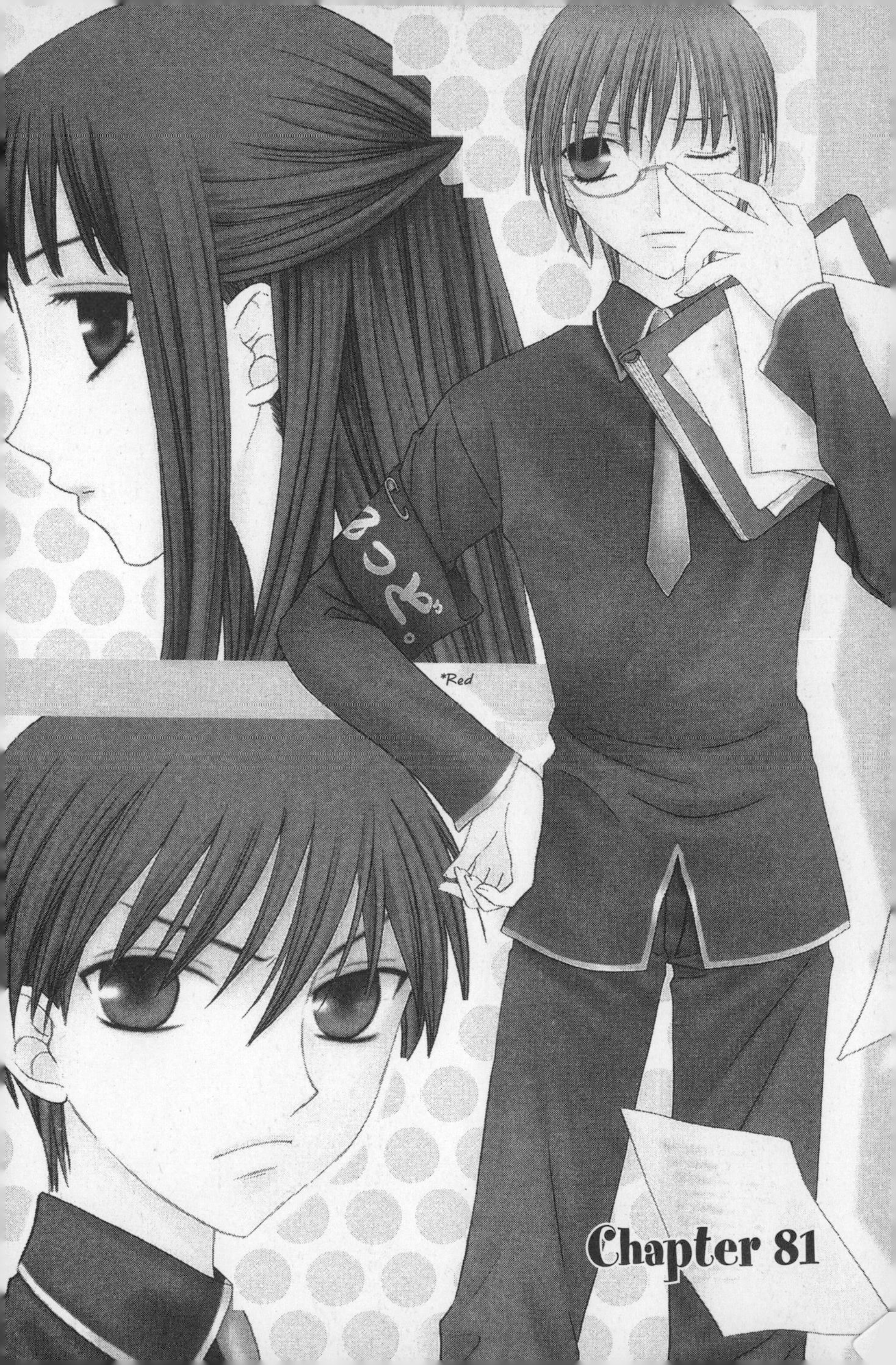
*Red
Chapter 81

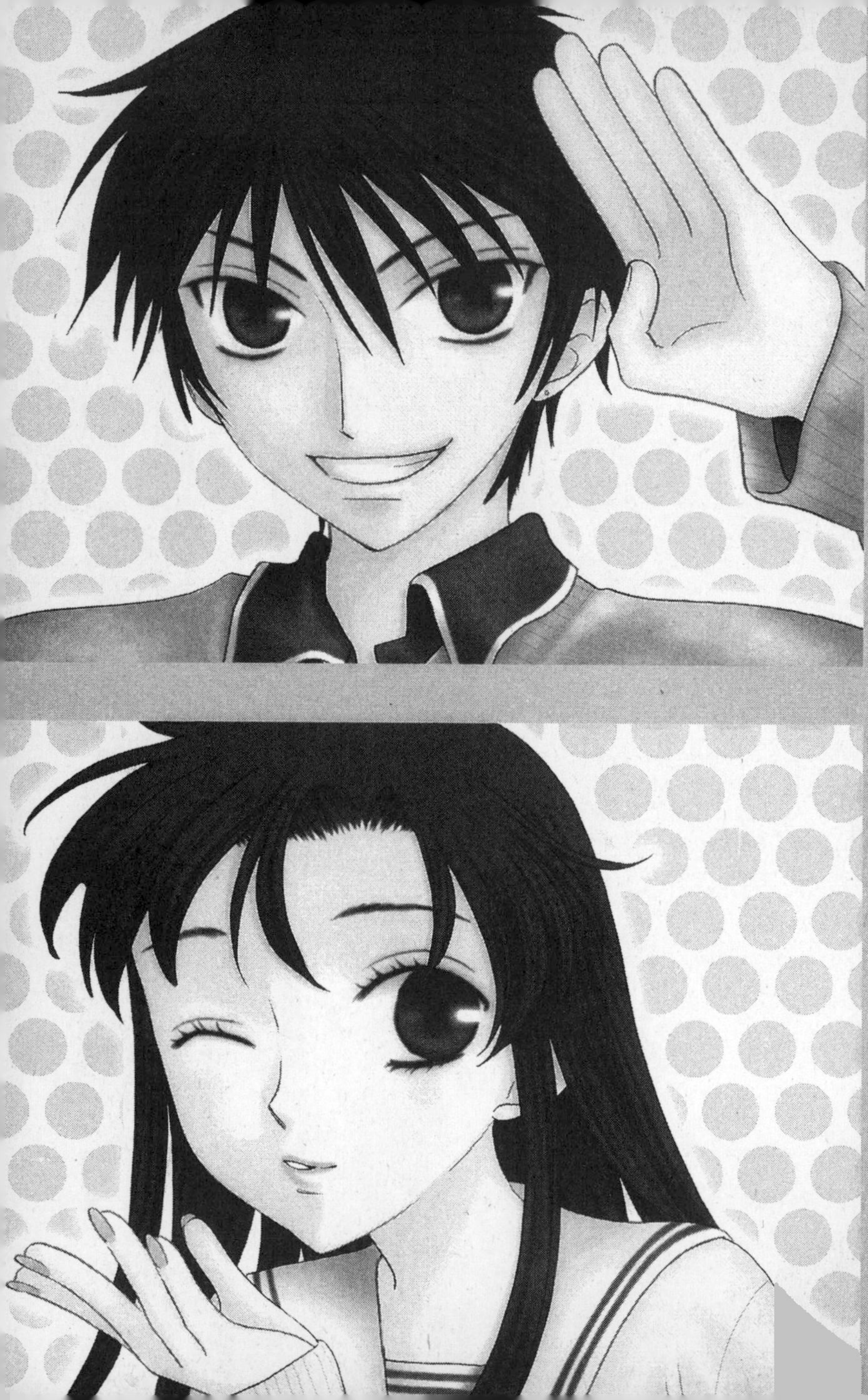

I feel so grateful!

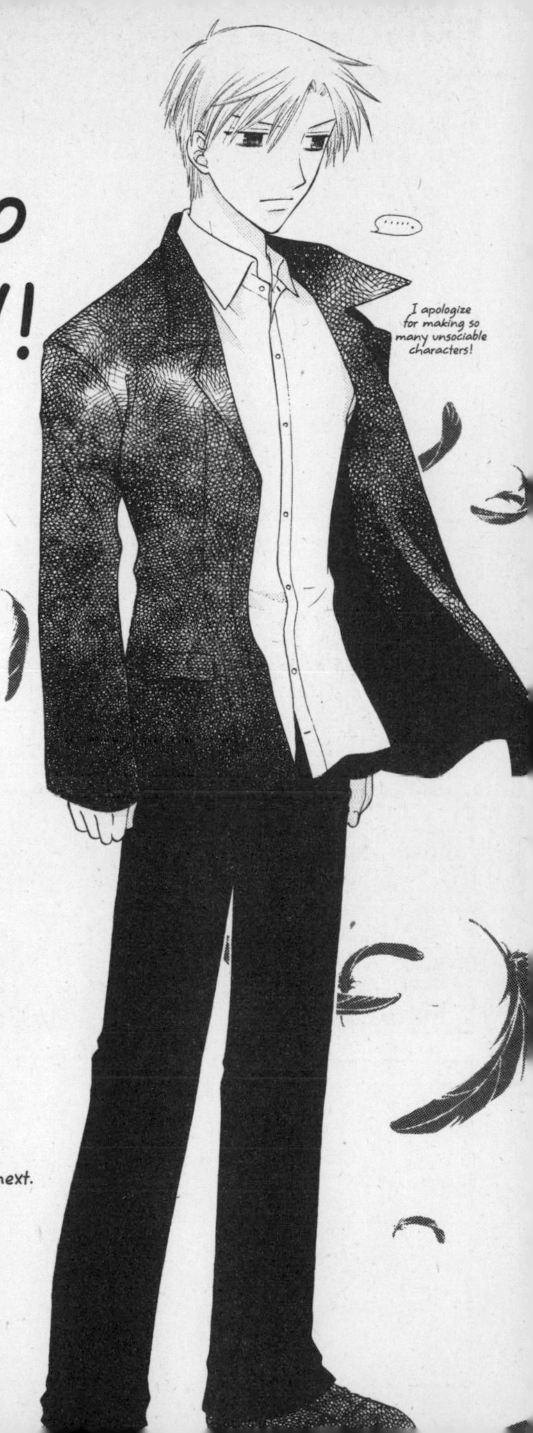
......
I apologize for making so many unsociable characters!

Harada-sama, Araki-sama, Mom, Dad, and everyone who reads and supports this manga... Thank you so much for your support!

The honorable head of the family is next.

–Natsuki Takaya

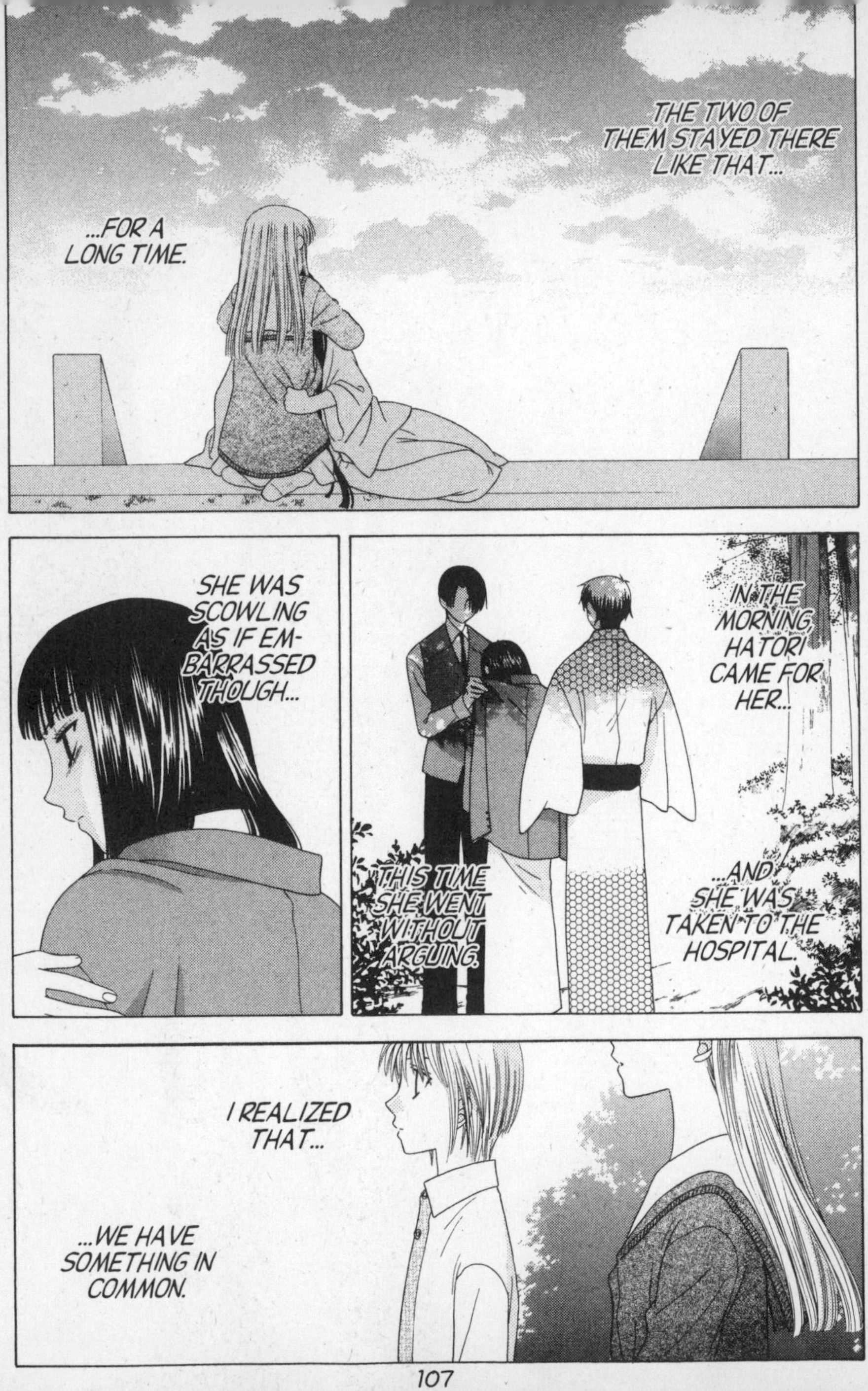
THE TWO OF THEM STAYED THERE LIKE THAT...
...FOR A LONG TIME.
IN THE MORNING, HATORI CAME FOR HER...
...AND SHE WAS TAKEN TO THE HOSPITAL.
THIS TIME SHE WENT WITHOUT ARGUING.
SHE WAS SCOWLING AS IF EM-BARRASSED THOUGH...
I REALIZED THAT...
...WE HAVE SOMETHING IN COMMON.

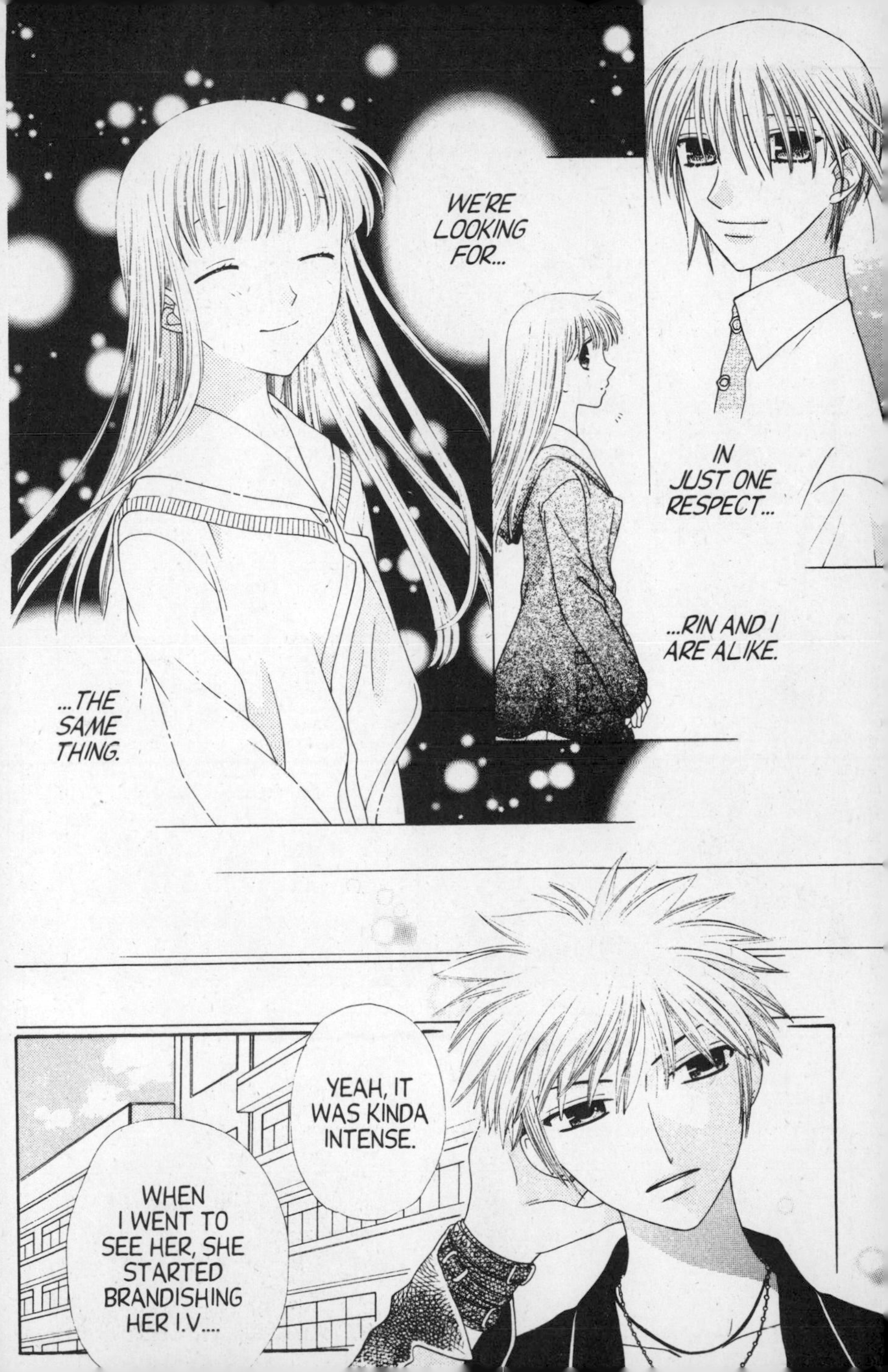
IN JUST ONE RESPECT...
...RIN AND I ARE ALIKE.
WE'RE LOOKING FOR...
...THE SAME THING.
YEAH, IT WAS KINDA INTENSE.
WHEN I WENT TO SEE HER, SHE STARTED BRANDISHING HER I.V....

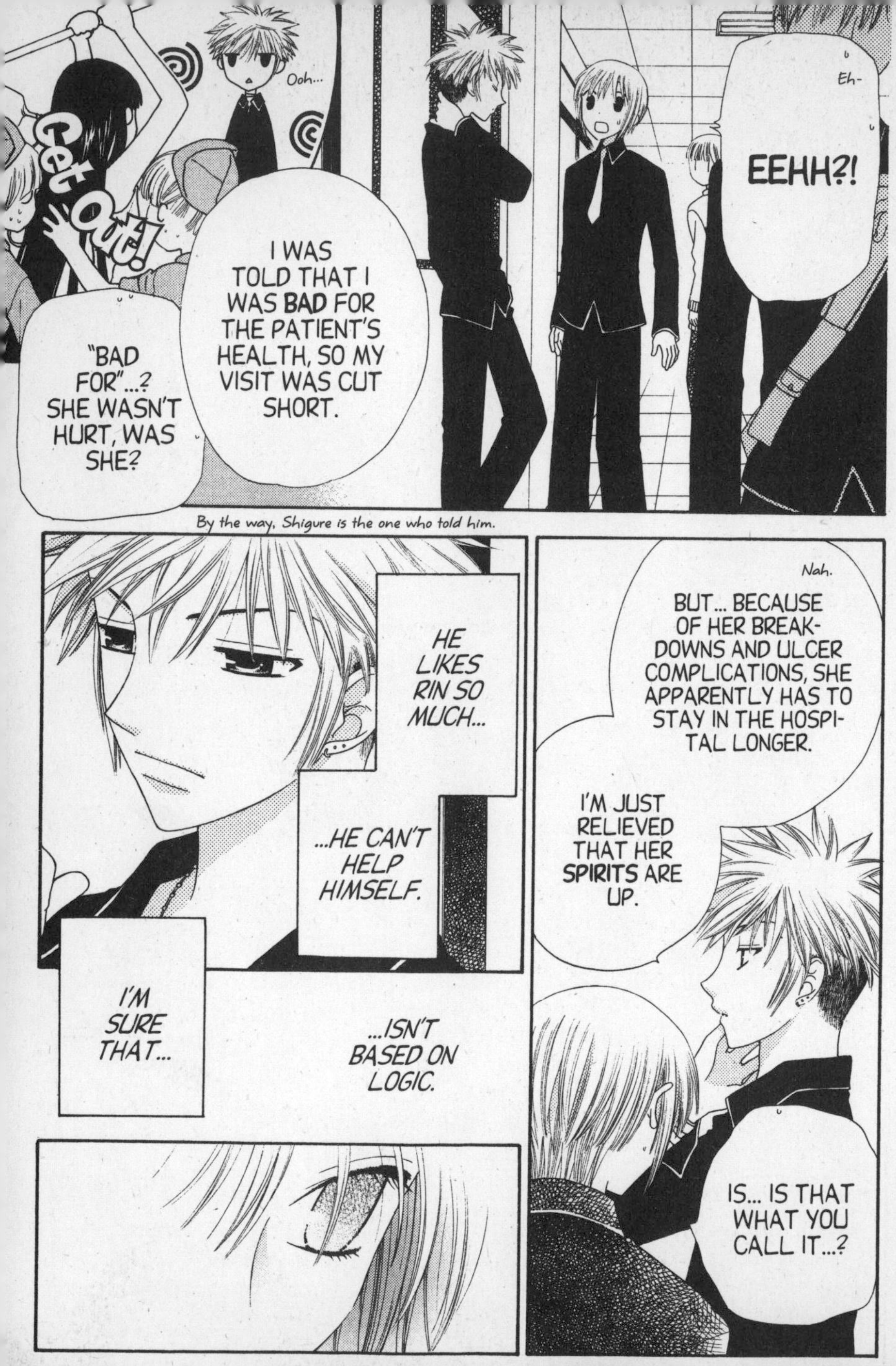
Eh-
EEHH?!
I WAS TOLD THAT I WAS BAD FOR THE PATIENT'S HEALTH, SO MY VISIT WAS CUT SHORT.
Ooh...
Get Out!
"BAD FOR"...? SHE WASN'T HURT, WAS SHE?
By the way, Shigure is the one who told him.
Nah.
BUT... BECAUSE OF HER BREAK-DOWNS AND ULCER COMPLICATIONS, SHE APPARENTLY HAS TO STAY IN THE HOSPI-TAL LONGER.
I'M JUST RELIEVED THAT HER SPIRITS ARE UP.
IS... IS THAT WHAT YOU CALL IT...?
HE LIKES RIN SO MUCH...
...HE CAN'T HELP HIMSELF.
I'M SURE THAT...
...ISN'T BASED ON LOGIC.

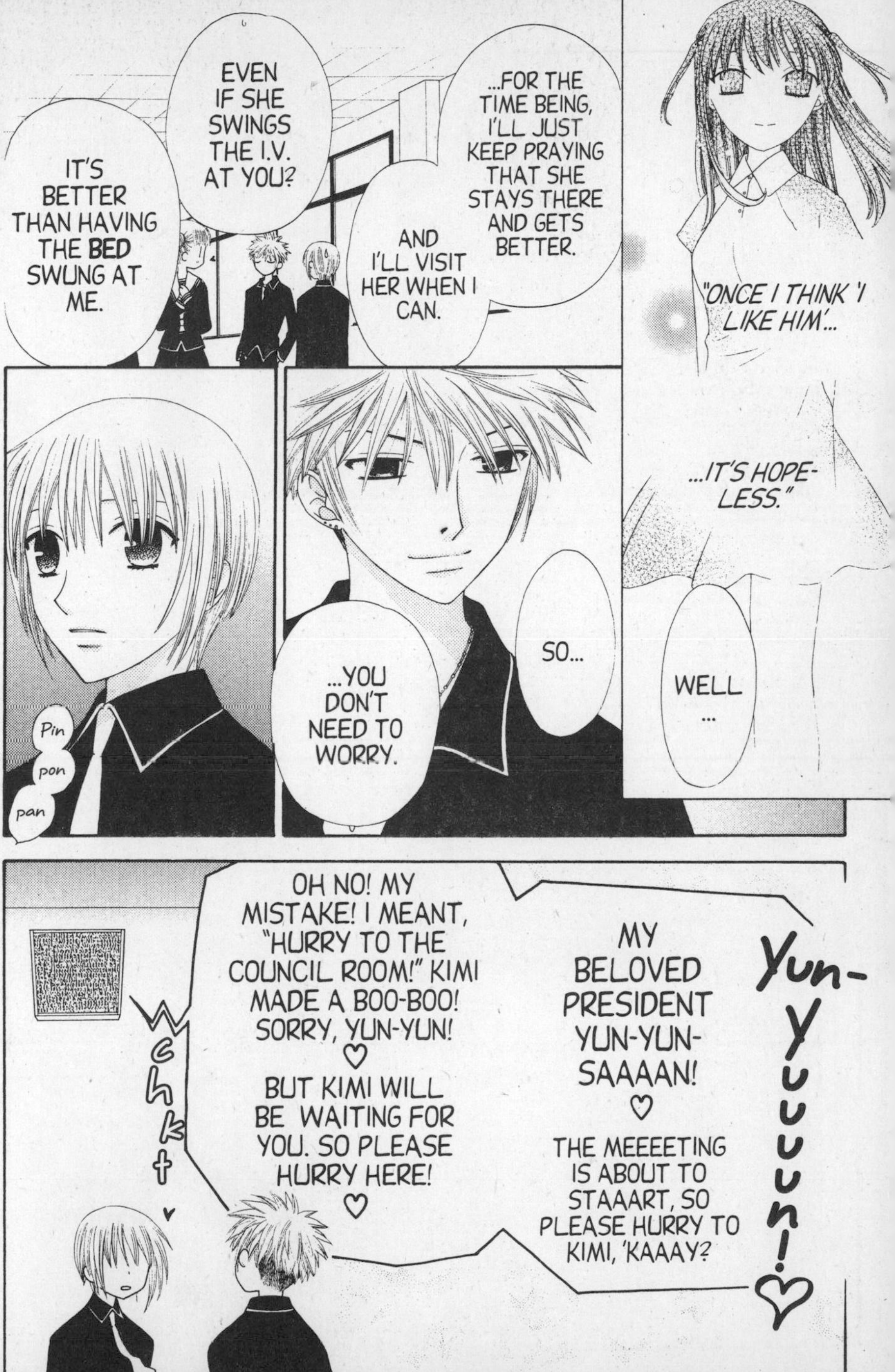
"ONCE I THINK 'I LIKE HIM'...
...IT'S HOPE-LESS."
WELL...
...FOR THE TIME BEING, I'LL JUST KEEP PRAYING THAT SHE STAYS THERE AND GETS BETTER.
AND I'LL VISIT HER WHEN I CAN.
EVEN IF SHE SWINGS THE I.V. AT YOU?
IT'S BETTER THAN HAVING THE **BED** SWUNG AT ME.
SO...
...YOU DON'T NEED TO WORRY.
Pin
pon
pan
Yun-Yuuuuun! ♡
MY BELOVED PRESIDENT YUN-YUN-SAAAAN! ♡
THE MEEEETING IS ABOUT TO STAAART, SO PLEASE HURRY TO KIMI, 'KAAAY?
OH NO! MY MISTAKE! I MEANT, "HURRY TO THE COUNCIL ROOM!" KIMI MADE A BOO-BOO! SORRY, YUN-YUN! ♡
BUT KIMI WILL BE WAITING FOR YOU. SO PLEASE HURRY HERE! ♡
Wchkt

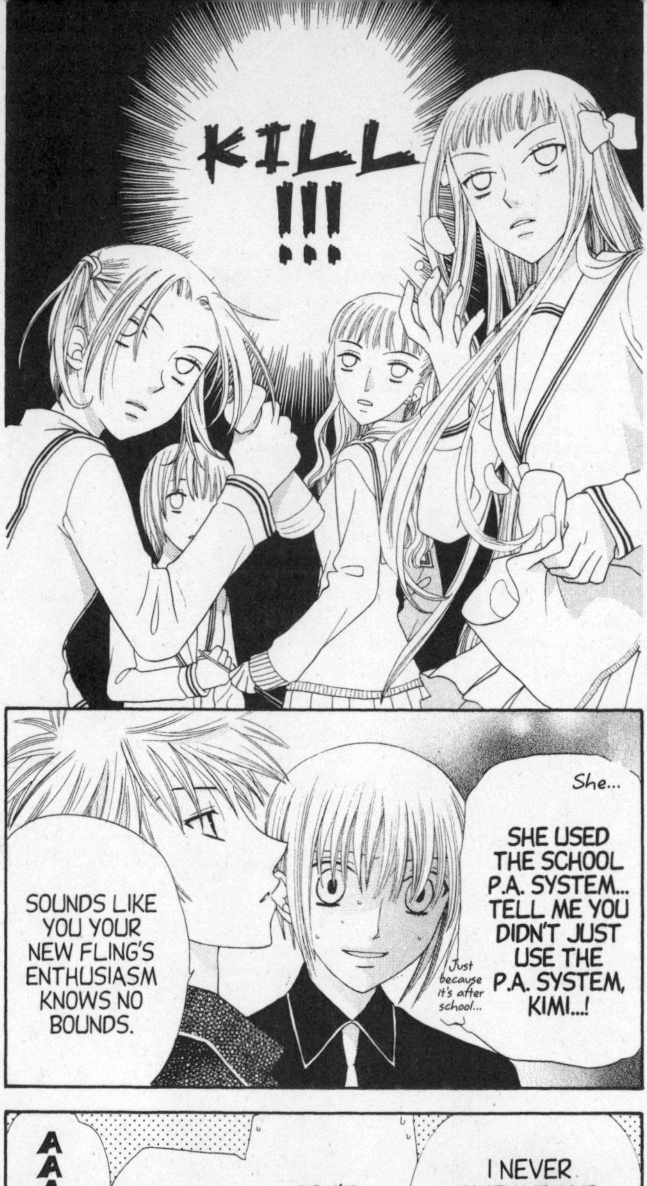
KILL!!!
She...
SHE USED THE SCHOOL P.A. SYSTEM... TELL ME YOU DIDN'T JUST USE THE P.A. SYSTEM, KIMI...!
Just because it's after school...
SOUNDS LIKE YOU YOUR NEW FLING'S ENTHUSIASM KNOWS NO BOUNDS.
I NEVER KNEW THAT KIND OF GIRL WAS YOUR TYPE... YUN-YUN.
DON'T CALL ME YUN-YUN!
AND SHE'S NOT MY TYPE!
Kimi is always like that.
AAAHH!

Basically, it's like this.

Twelfth month (in lunar calendar, or January) (0): Yuki ...He's the very first one, but Yuki is the exception. He doesn't have the name of a month. Nothing really sounded good, and the sound "Yuki" came into my head.

First month: Hatsuharu, from Hatsuharu ("Early spring")

Second month: Kisa, from Kisaragi ("changing clothes month")

Third month: Kureno, from Kurenoharu ("Late Spring")

Fourth month: Hatori, from Konohatorizuki ("Month of Taking Leaves" [to silkworms])

Fifth month: Ayame, from Ayamezuki (Month of Irises)

To be continued...

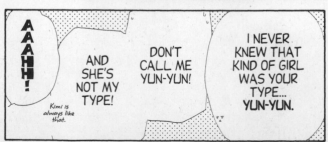

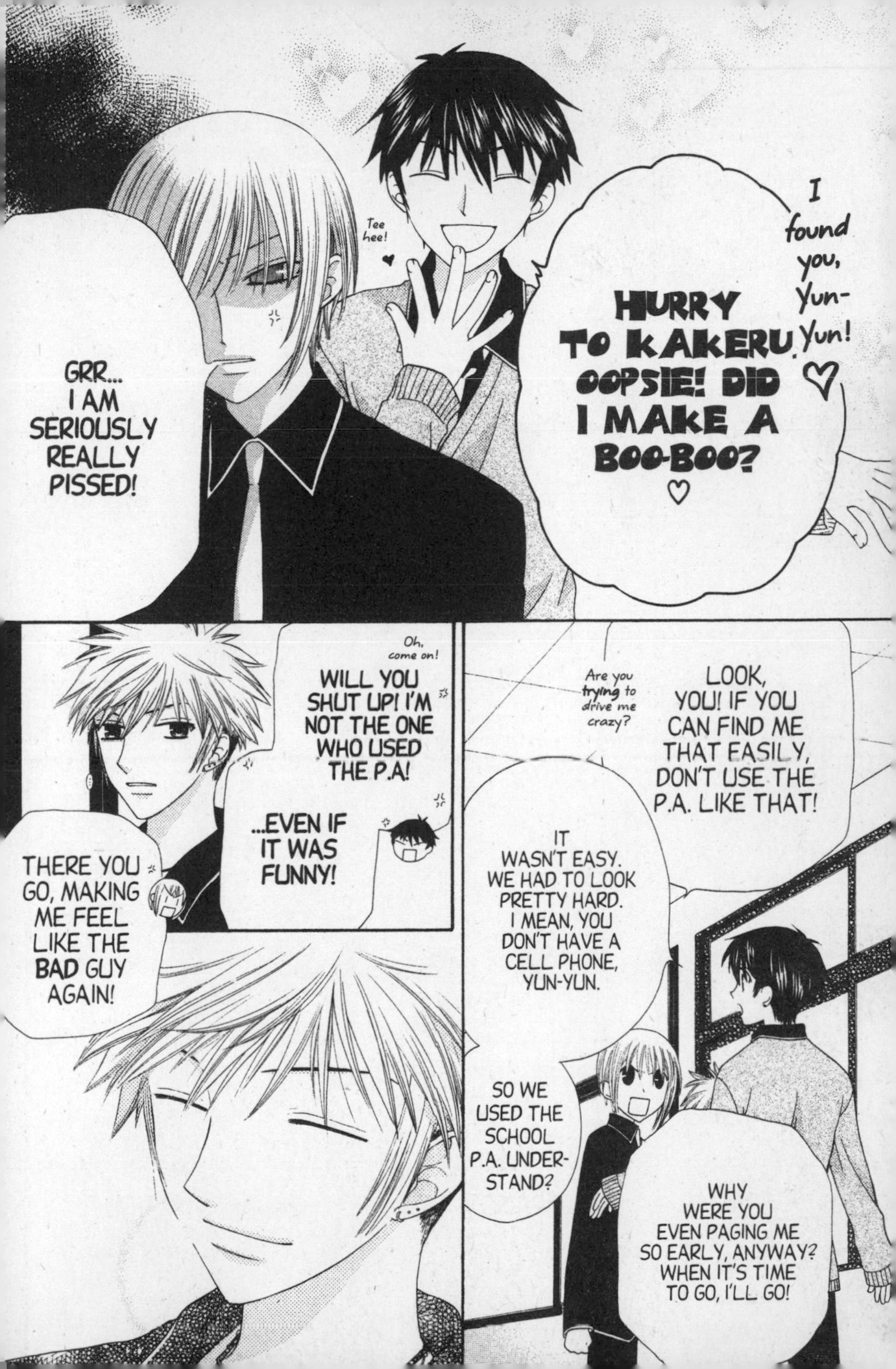
I found you, Yun-Yun! ♥
HURRY TO KAKERU. OOPSIE! DID I MAKE A BOO-BOO? ♡
Tee hee! ♥
GRR... I AM SERIOUSLY REALLY PISSED!
LOOK, YOU! IF YOU CAN FIND ME THAT EASILY, DON'T USE THE P.A. LIKE THAT!
Are you trying to drive me crazy?
IT WASN'T EASY. WE HAD TO LOOK PRETTY HARD. I MEAN, YOU DON'T HAVE A CELL PHONE, YUN-YUN.
WHY WERE YOU EVEN PAGING ME SO EARLY, ANYWAY? WHEN IT'S TIME TO GO, I'LL GO!
SO WE USED THE SCHOOL P.A. UNDER-STAND?
Oh, come on!
WILL YOU SHUT UP! I'M NOT THE ONE WHO USED THE P.A!
...EVEN IF IT WAS FUNNY!
THERE YOU GO, MAKING ME FEEL LIKE THE BAD GUY AGAIN!

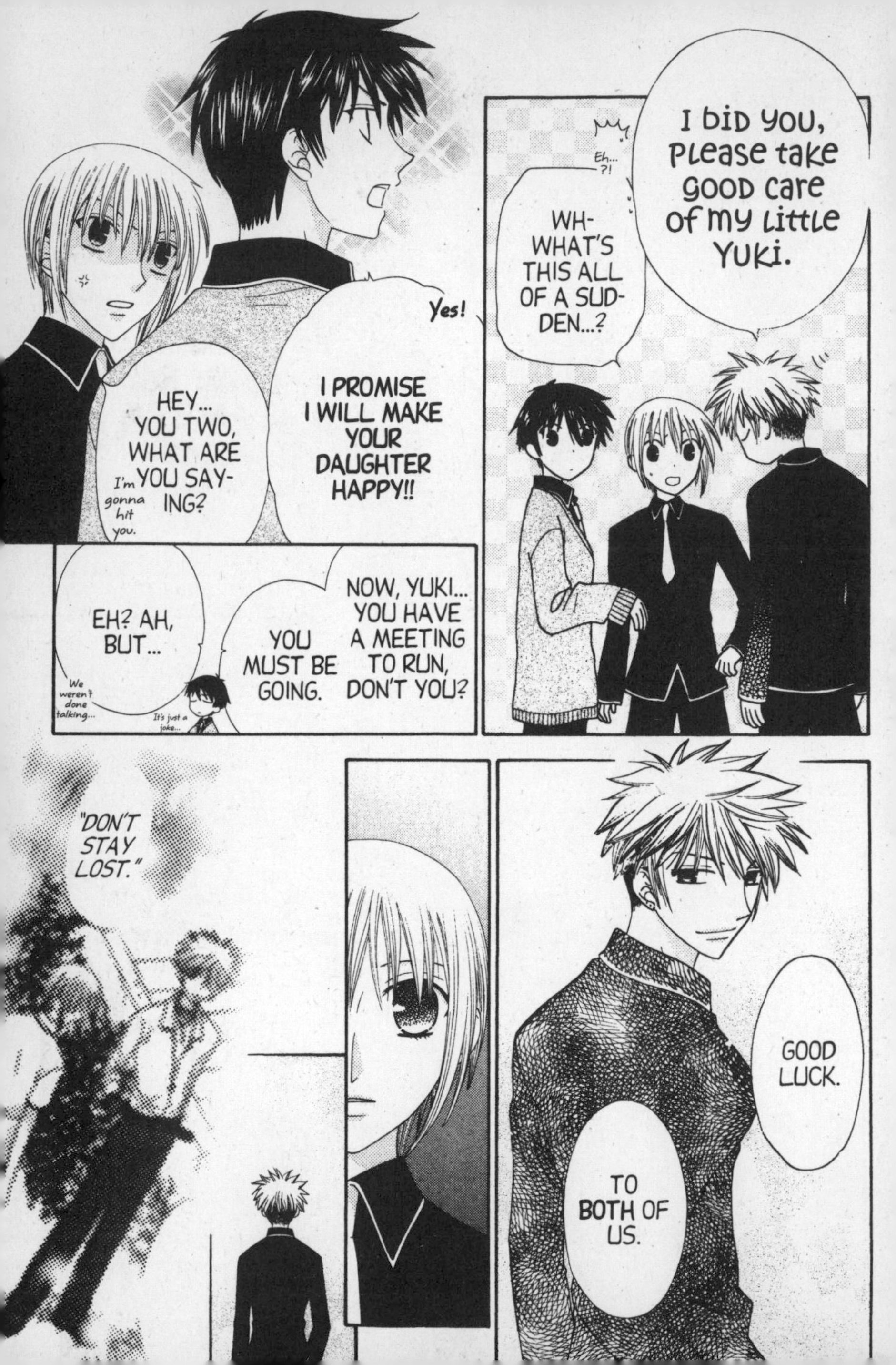

I bid you, please take good care of my little Yuki.
Eh...?!
WH-WHAT'S THIS ALL OF A SUDDEN...?
Yes!
I PROMISE I WILL MAKE YOUR DAUGHTER HAPPY!!
HEY... YOU TWO, WHAT ARE YOU SAYING?
I'm gonna hit you.
NOW, YUKI... YOU HAVE A MEETING TO RUN, DON'T YOU?
YOU MUST BE GOING.
It's just a joke...
EH? AH, BUT...
We weren't done talking...
GOOD LUCK.
TO BOTH OF US.
"DON'T STAY LOST."

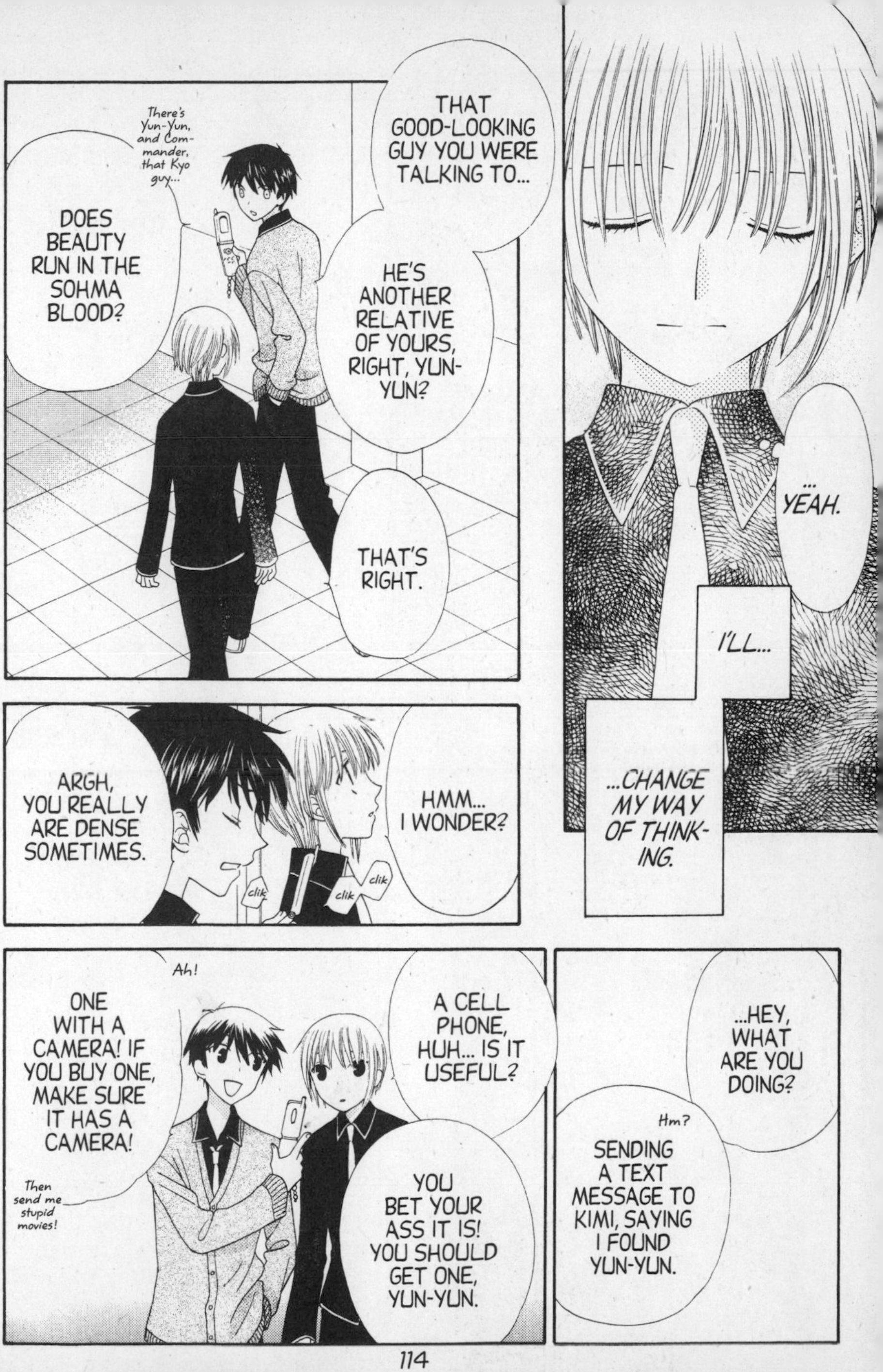
...YEAH.
I'LL...
...CHANGE MY WAY OF THINKING.
THAT GOOD-LOOKING GUY YOU WERE TALKING TO...
HE'S ANOTHER RELATIVE OF YOURS, RIGHT, YUN-YUN?
THAT'S RIGHT.
There's Yun-Yun, and Commander, that Kyo guy...
DOES BEAUTY RUN IN THE SOHMA BLOOD?
HMM... I WONDER?
clik
clik
clik
ARGH, YOU REALLY ARE DENSE SOMETIMES.
...HEY, WHAT ARE YOU DOING?
Hm?
SENDING A TEXT MESSAGE TO KIMI, SAYING I FOUND YUN-YUN.
A CELL PHONE, HUH... IS IT USEFUL?
YOU BET YOUR ASS IT IS! YOU SHOULD GET ONE, YUN-YUN.
Ah!
ONE WITH A CAMERA! IF YOU BUY ONE, MAKE SURE IT HAS A CAMERA!
Then send me stupid movies!

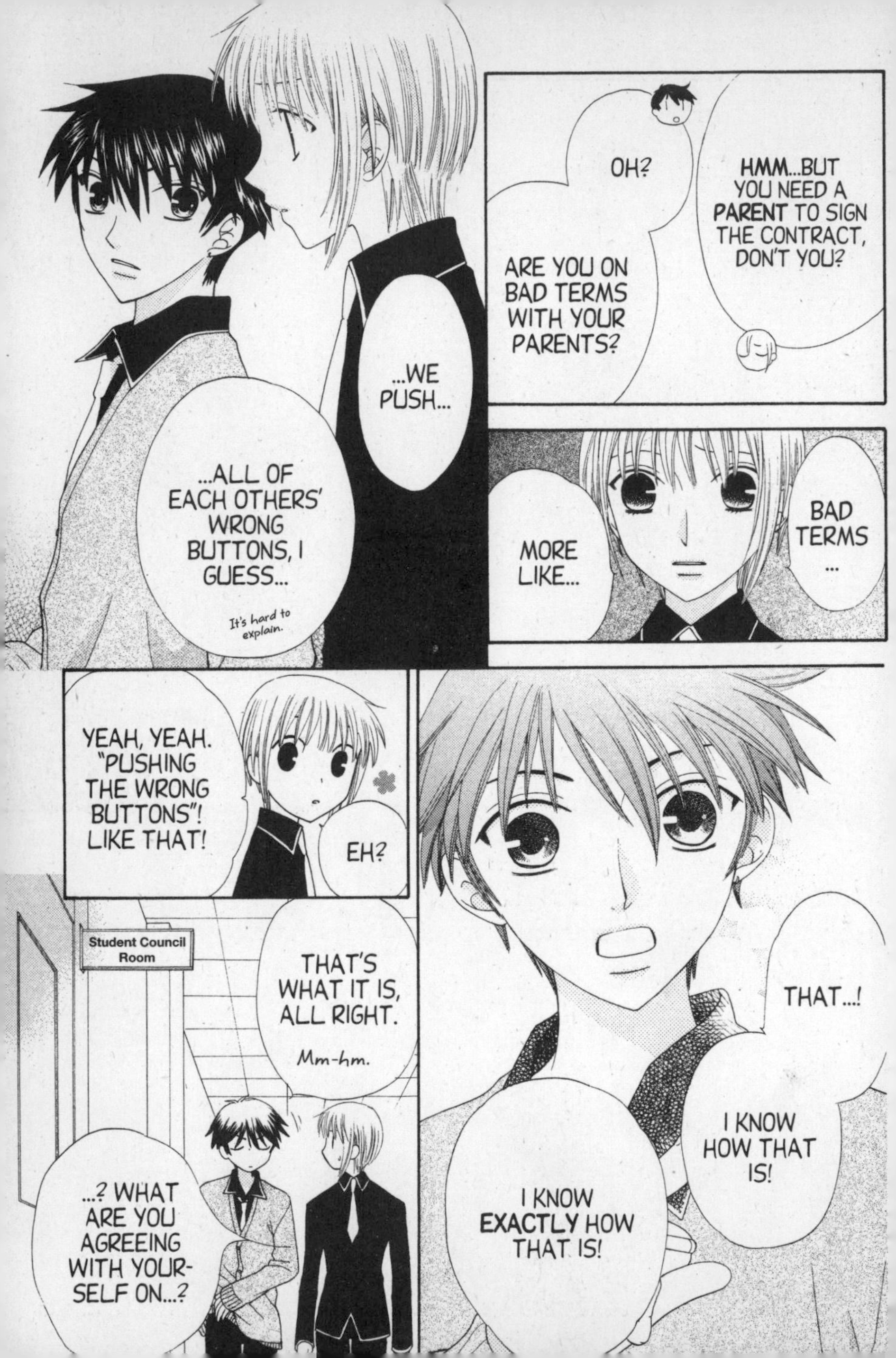
HMM...BUT YOU NEED A PARENT TO SIGN THE CONTRACT, DON'T YOU?
OH?
ARE YOU ON BAD TERMS WITH YOUR PARENTS?
BAD TERMS ...
MORE LIKE...
...WE PUSH...
...ALL OF EACH OTHERS' WRONG BUTTONS, I GUESS...
It's hard to explain.
THAT...!
I KNOW HOW THAT IS!
I KNOW EXACTLY HOW THAT IS!
YEAH, YEAH. "PUSHING THE WRONG BUTTONS"! LIKE THAT!
EH?
Student Council Room
THAT'S WHAT IT IS, ALL RIGHT.
Mm-hm.
...? WHAT ARE YOU AGREEING WITH YOUR-SELF ON...?

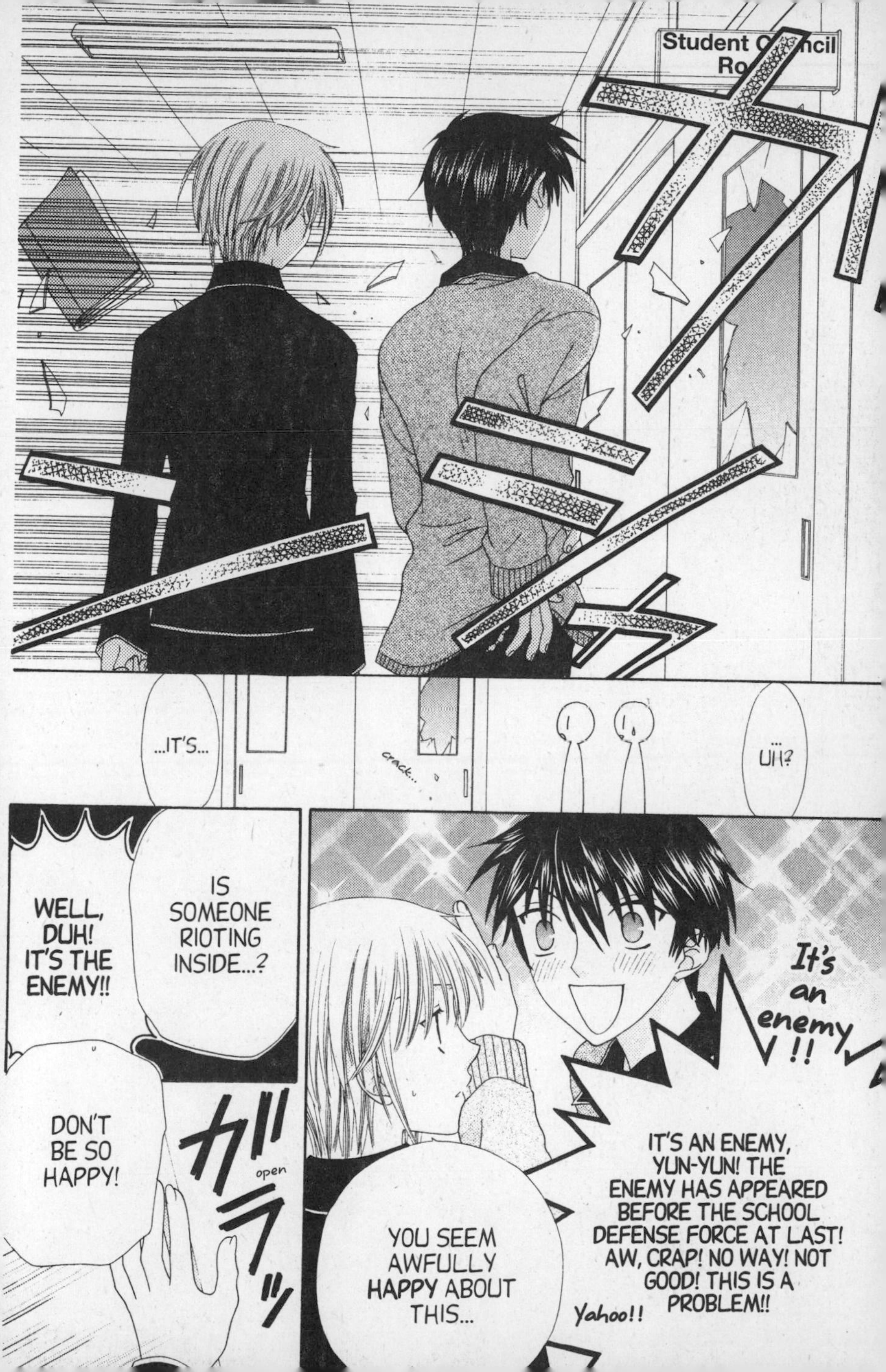
Student C ncil
Ro
...UH?
...IT'S...
crack...
It's an enemy!!
IT'S AN ENEMY, YUN-YUN! THE ENEMY HAS APPEARED BEFORE THE SCHOOL DEFENSE FORCE AT LAST! AW, CRAP! NO WAY! NOT GOOD! THIS IS A PROBLEM!!
Yahoo!!
YOU SEEM AWFULLY HAPPY ABOUT THIS...
IS SOMEONE RIOTING INSIDE...?
WELL, DUH! IT'S THE ENEMY!!
DON'T BE SO HAPPY!
open

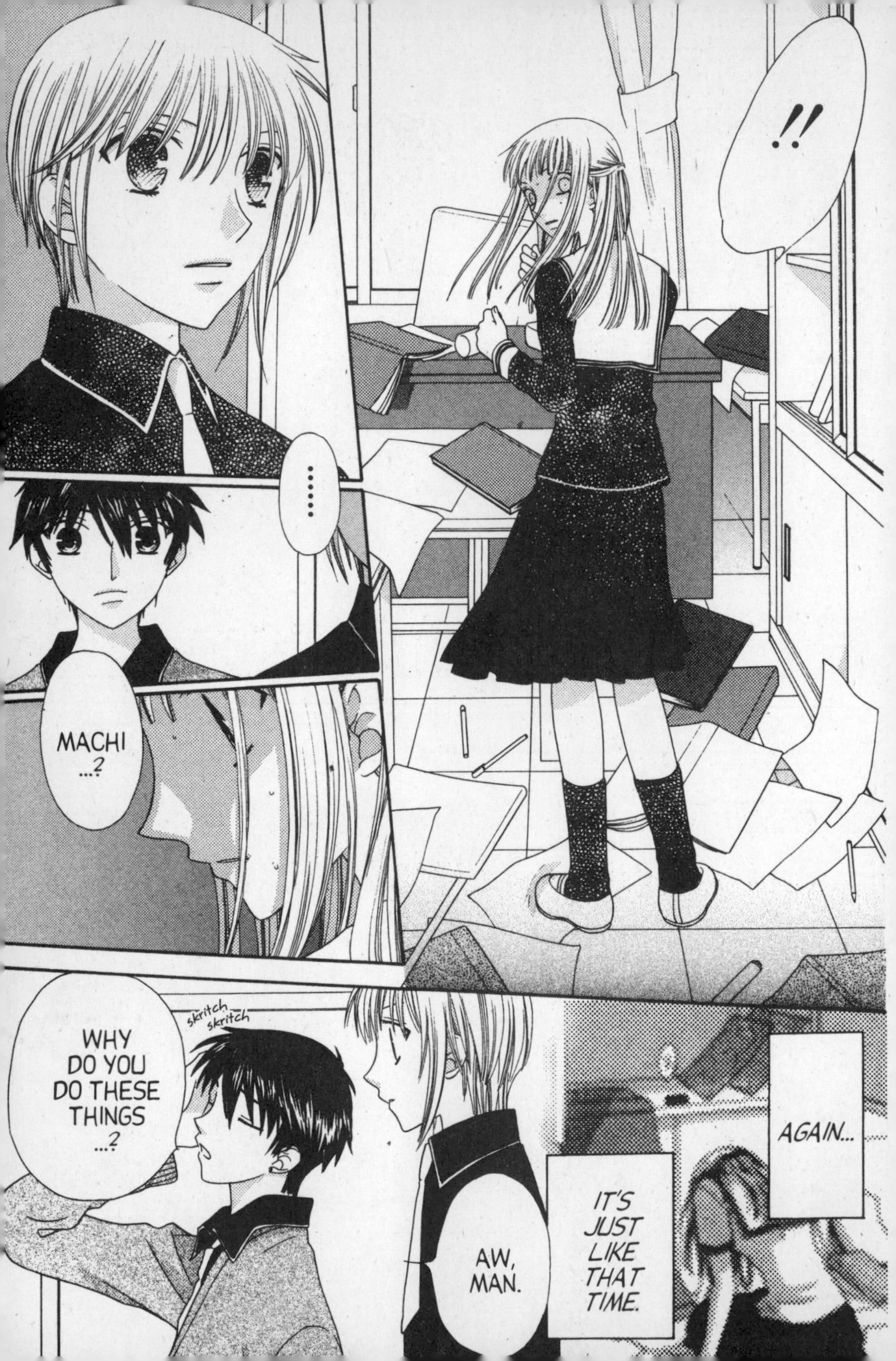
!!
......
MACHI ...?
AGAIN...
IT'S JUST LIKE THAT TIME.
AW, MAN.
skritch skritch
WHY DO YOU DO THESE THINGS ...?

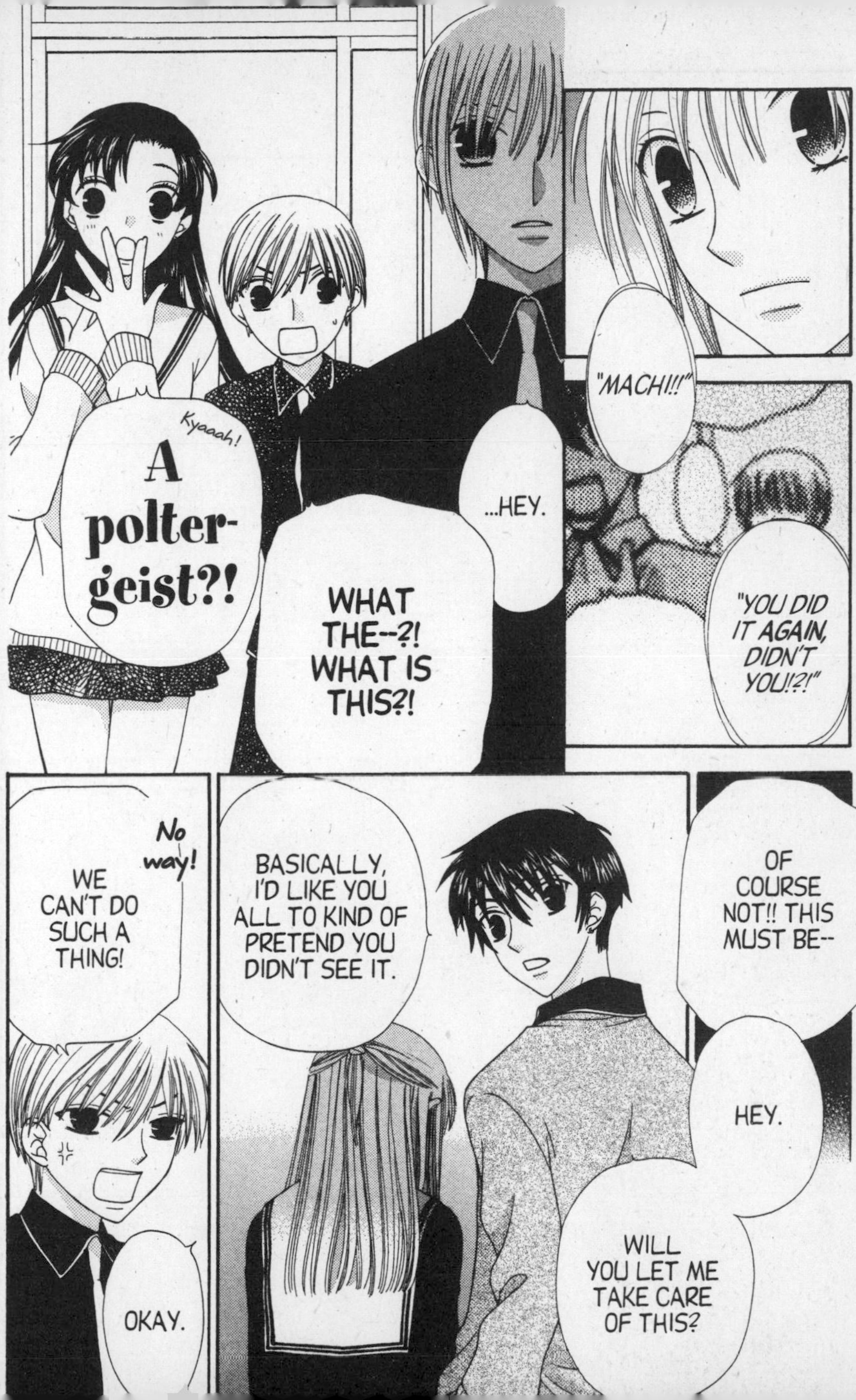
"MACHI!!"
"YOU DID IT AGAIN, DIDN'T YOU!?!"
...HEY.
WHAT THE--?! WHAT IS THIS?!
Kyaaah!
A polter-geist?!
OF COURSE NOT!! THIS MUST BE--
HEY.
WILL YOU LET ME TAKE CARE OF THIS?
BASICALLY, I'D LIKE YOU ALL TO KIND OF PRETEND YOU DIDN'T SEE IT.
No way!
WE CAN'T DO SUCH A THING!
OKAY.

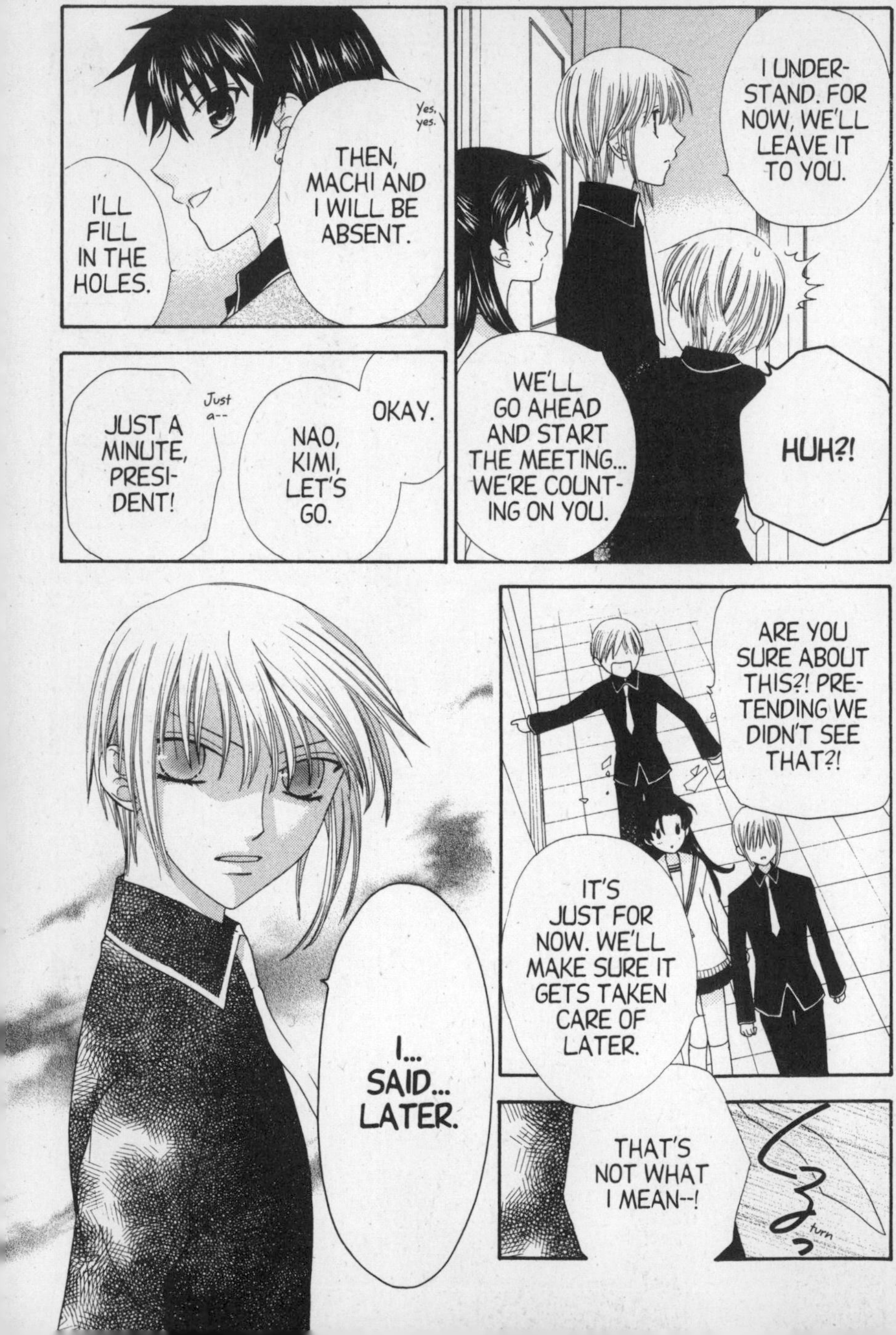
I UNDER-STAND. FOR NOW, WE'LL LEAVE IT TO YOU.
HUH?!
WE'LL GO AHEAD AND START THE MEETING... WE'RE COUNTING ON YOU.
Yes, yes.
THEN, MACHI AND I WILL BE ABSENT.
I'LL FILL IN THE HOLES.
OKAY.
NAO, KIMI, LET'S GO.
Just a--
JUST A MINUTE, PRESI-DENT!
ARE YOU SURE ABOUT THIS?! PRE-TENDING WE DIDN'T SEE THAT?!
IT'S JUST FOR NOW. WE'LL MAKE SURE IT GETS TAKEN CARE OF LATER.
THAT'S NOT WHAT I MEAN--!
turn
I... SAID... LATER.

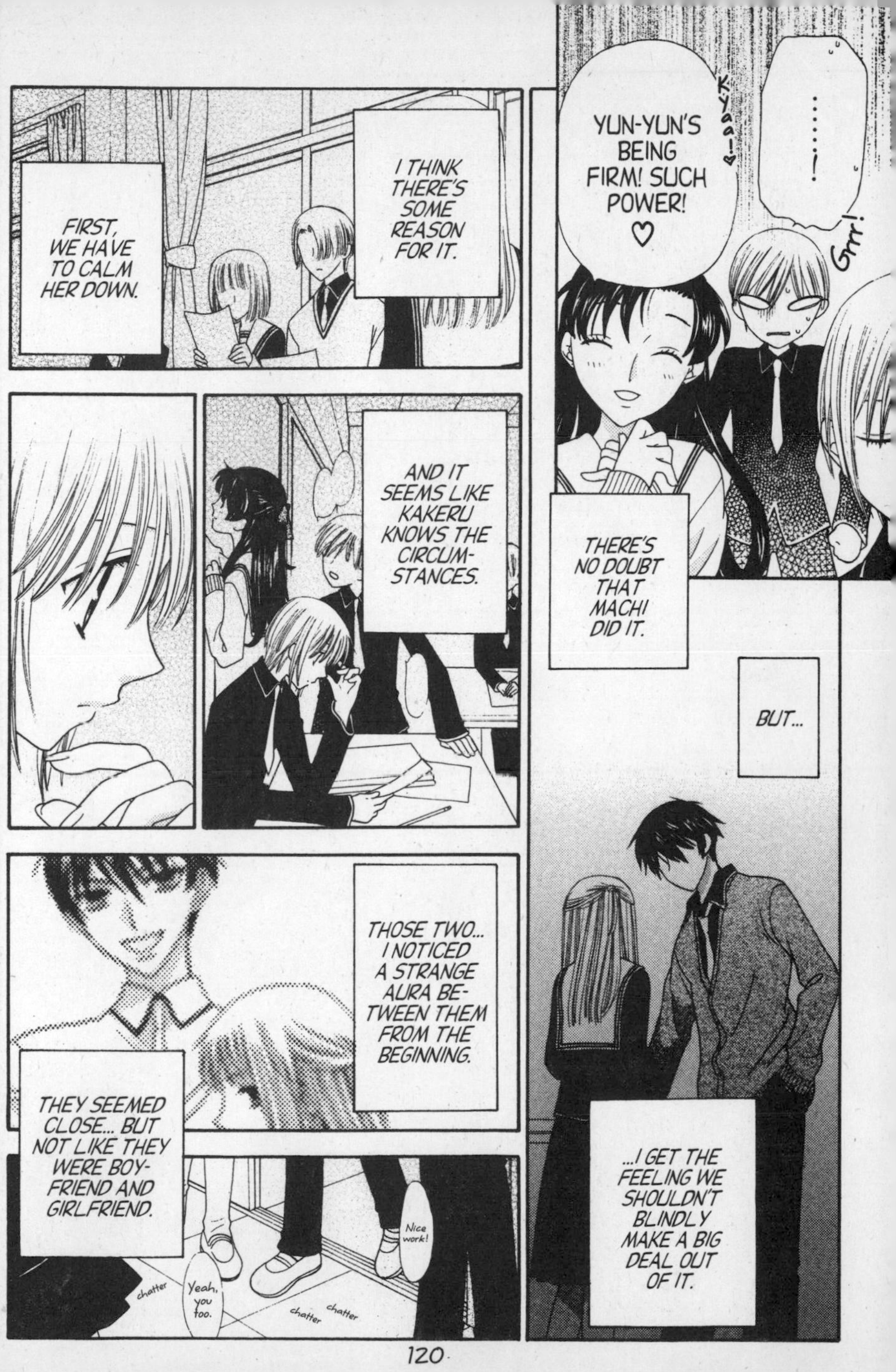

......!
Kyaa!♥
YUN-YUN'S BEING FIRM! SUCH POWER! ♡
Grrr!
THERE'S NO DOUBT THAT MACHI DID IT.
BUT...
...I GET THE FEELING WE SHOULDN'T BLINDLY MAKE A BIG DEAL OUT OF IT.
I THINK THERE'S SOME REASON FOR IT.
FIRST, WE HAVE TO CALM HER DOWN.
AND IT SEEMS LIKE KAKERU KNOWS THE CIRCUM-STANCES.
THOSE TWO... I NOTICED A STRANGE AURA BE-TWEEN THEM FROM THE BEGINNING.
THEY SEEMED CLOSE... BUT NOT LIKE THEY WERE BOY-FRIEND AND GIRLFRIEND.
Nice work!
Yeah, you too.
chatter
chatter
chatter

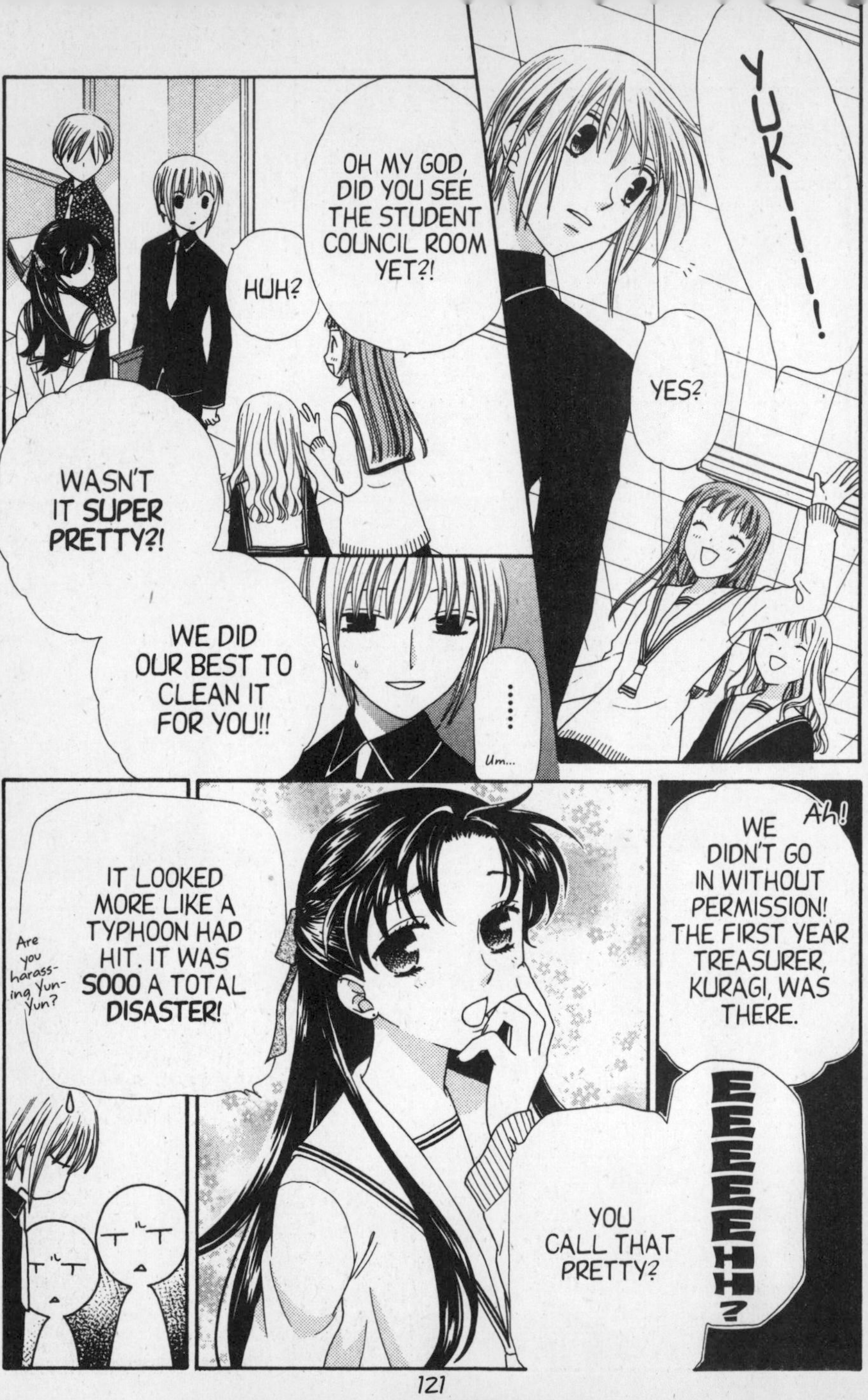
YUKI----!
YES?
OH MY GOD, DID YOU SEE THE STUDENT COUNCIL ROOM YET?!
HUH?
WASN'T IT SUPER PRETTY?!
WE DID OUR BEST TO CLEAN IT FOR YOU!!
......
Um...
Ah!
WE DIDN'T GO IN WITHOUT PERMISSION! THE FIRST YEAR TREASURER, KURAGI, WAS THERE.
EEEEEEHH?
YOU CALL THAT PRETTY?
IT LOOKED MORE LIKE A TYPHOON HAD HIT. IT WAS SOOO A TOTAL DISASTER!
Are you harass-ing Yun-Yun?

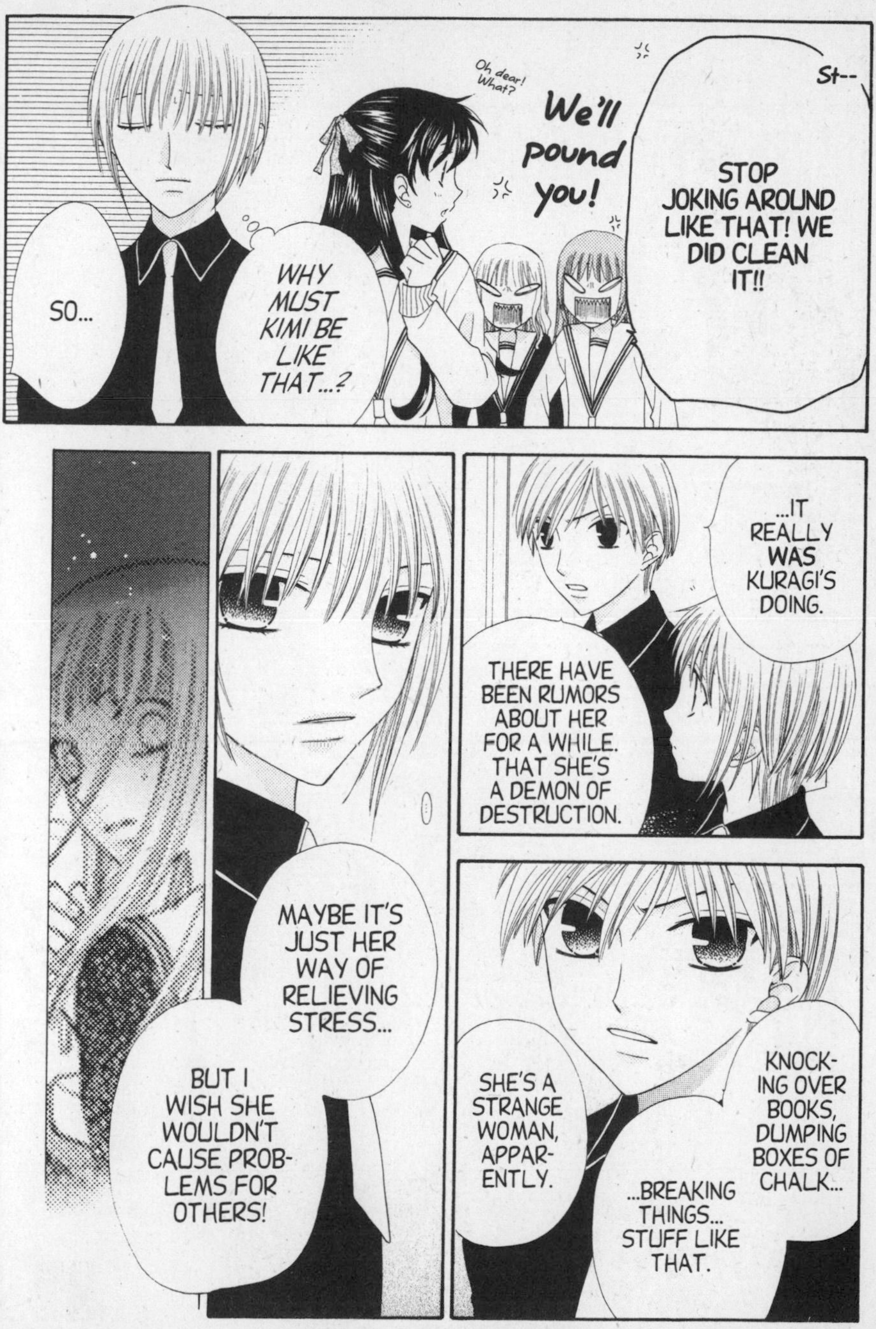
St--
STOP JOKING AROUND LIKE THAT! WE DID CLEAN IT!!
We'll pound you!
Oh dear! What?
WHY MUST KIMI BE LIKE THAT...?
SO...
...IT REALLY WAS KURAGI'S DOING.
THERE HAVE BEEN RUMORS ABOUT HER FOR A WHILE. THAT SHE'S A DEMON OF DESTRUCTION.
KNOCKING OVER BOOKS, DUMPING BOXES OF CHALK...
...BREAKING THINGS... STUFF LIKE THAT.
SHE'S A STRANGE WOMAN, APPARENTLY.
MAYBE IT'S JUST HER WAY OF RELIEVING STRESS...
BUT I WISH SHE WOULDN'T CAUSE PROBLEMS FOR OTHERS!

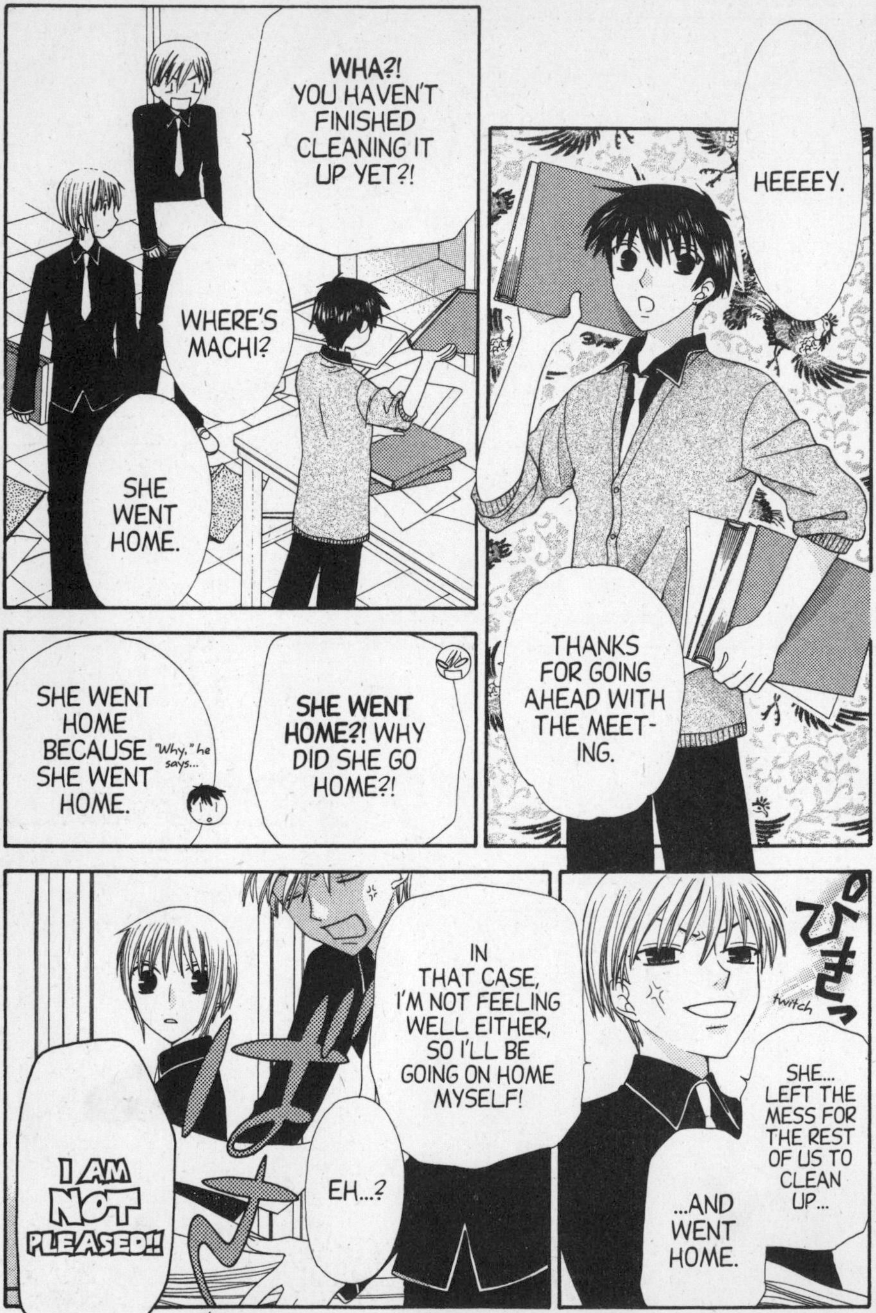
HEEEEY.
THANKS FOR GOING AHEAD WITH THE MEET-ING.
WHA?! YOU HAVEN'T FINISHED CLEANING IT UP YET?!
WHERE'S MACHI?
SHE WENT HOME.
SHE WENT HOME?! WHY DID SHE GO HOME?!
SHE WENT HOME BECAUSE SHE WENT HOME.
"Why," he says...
twitch
SHE... LEFT THE MESS FOR THE REST OF US TO CLEAN UP...
...AND WENT HOME.
IN THAT CASE, I'M NOT FEELING WELL EITHER, SO I'LL BE GOING ON HOME MYSELF!
EH...?
I AM NOT PLEASED!!
slam

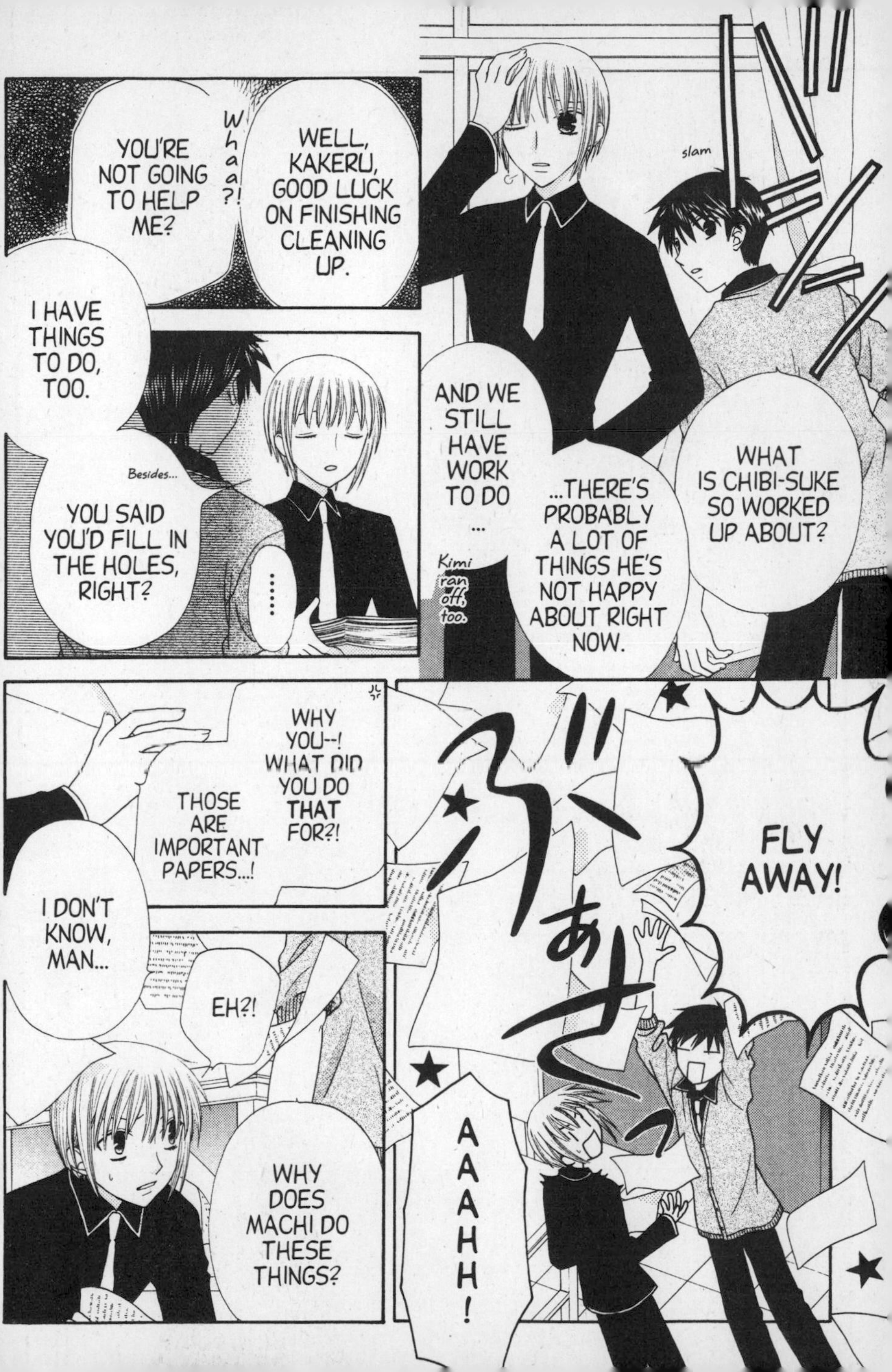
slam
WHAT IS CHIBI-SUKE SO WORKED UP ABOUT?
...THERE'S PROBABLY A LOT OF THINGS HE'S NOT HAPPY ABOUT RIGHT NOW.
AND WE STILL HAVE WORK TO DO ...
Kimi ran off, too.
WELL, KAKERU, GOOD LUCK ON FINISHING CLEANING UP.
Whaa?!
YOU'RE NOT GOING TO HELP ME?
I HAVE THINGS TO DO, TOO.
Besides...
YOU SAID YOU'D FILL IN THE HOLES, RIGHT?
......
FLY AWAY!
ふぁさっ
AAAHH!
WHY YOU--! WHAT DID YOU DO THAT FOR?!
THOSE ARE IMPORTANT PAPERS...!
EH?!
I DON'T KNOW, MAN...
WHY DOES MACHI DO THESE THINGS?

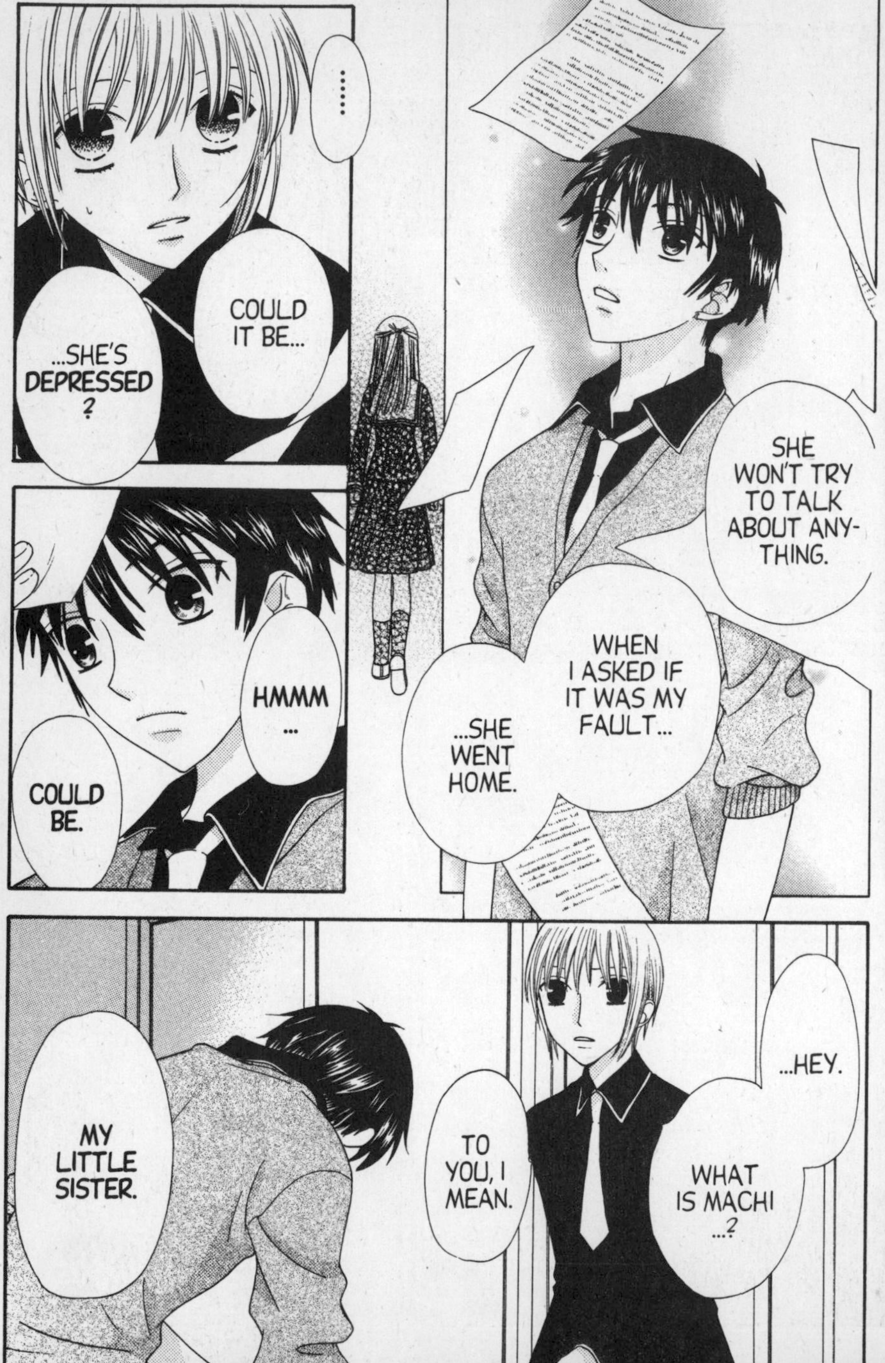

SHE WON'T TRY TO TALK ABOUT ANY-THING.
WHEN I ASKED IF IT WAS MY FAULT...
...SHE WENT HOME.
......
COULD IT BE...
...SHE'S DEPRESSED?
HMMM ...
COULD BE.
...HEY.
WHAT IS MACHI ...?
TO YOU, I MEAN.
MY LITTLE SISTER.

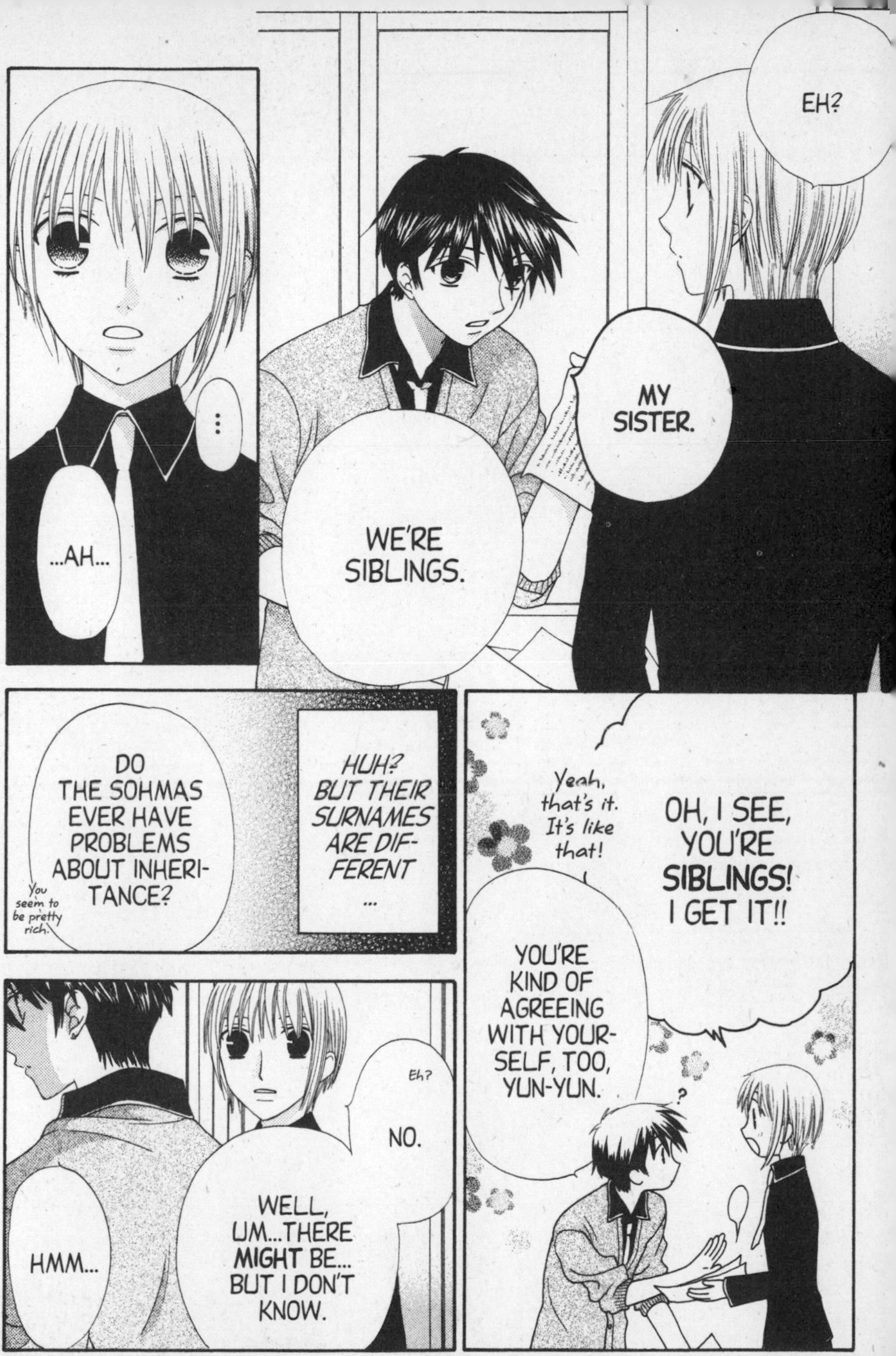
EH?
MY SISTER.
WE'RE SIBLINGS.
...
...AH...
OH, I SEE, YOU'RE SIBLINGS! I GET IT!!
Yeah, that's it. It's like that!
YOU'RE KIND OF AGREEING WITH YOURSELF, TOO, YUN-YUN.
?
HUH? BUT THEIR SURNAMES ARE DIFFERENT ...
DO THE SOHMAS EVER HAVE PROBLEMS ABOUT INHERITANCE?
You seem to be pretty rich.
Eh?
NO.
WELL, UM...THERE MIGHT BE... BUT I DON'T KNOW.
HMM...

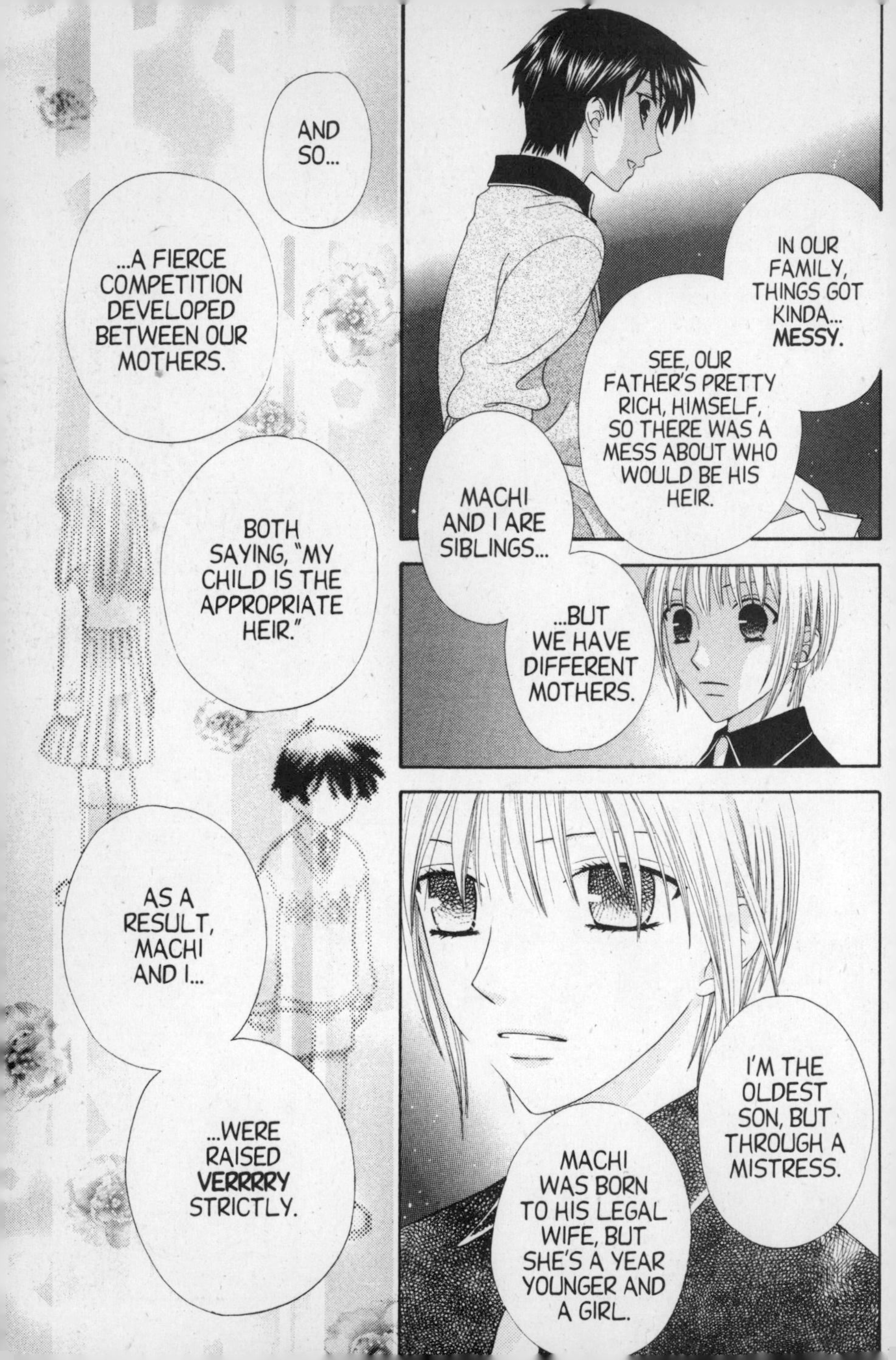
IN OUR FAMILY, THINGS GOT KINDA... **MESSY.**
SEE, OUR FATHER'S PRETTY RICH, HIMSELF, SO THERE WAS A MESS ABOUT WHO WOULD BE HIS HEIR.
MACHI AND I ARE SIBLINGS...
...BUT WE HAVE DIFFERENT MOTHERS.
I'M THE OLDEST SON, BUT THROUGH A MISTRESS.
MACHI WAS BORN TO HIS LEGAL WIFE, BUT SHE'S A YEAR YOUNGER AND A GIRL.
AND SO...
...A FIERCE COMPETITION DEVELOPED BETWEEN OUR MOTHERS.
BOTH SAYING, "MY CHILD IS THE APPROPRIATE HEIR."
AS A RESULT, MACHI AND I...
...WERE RAISED **VERRRRY** STRICTLY.

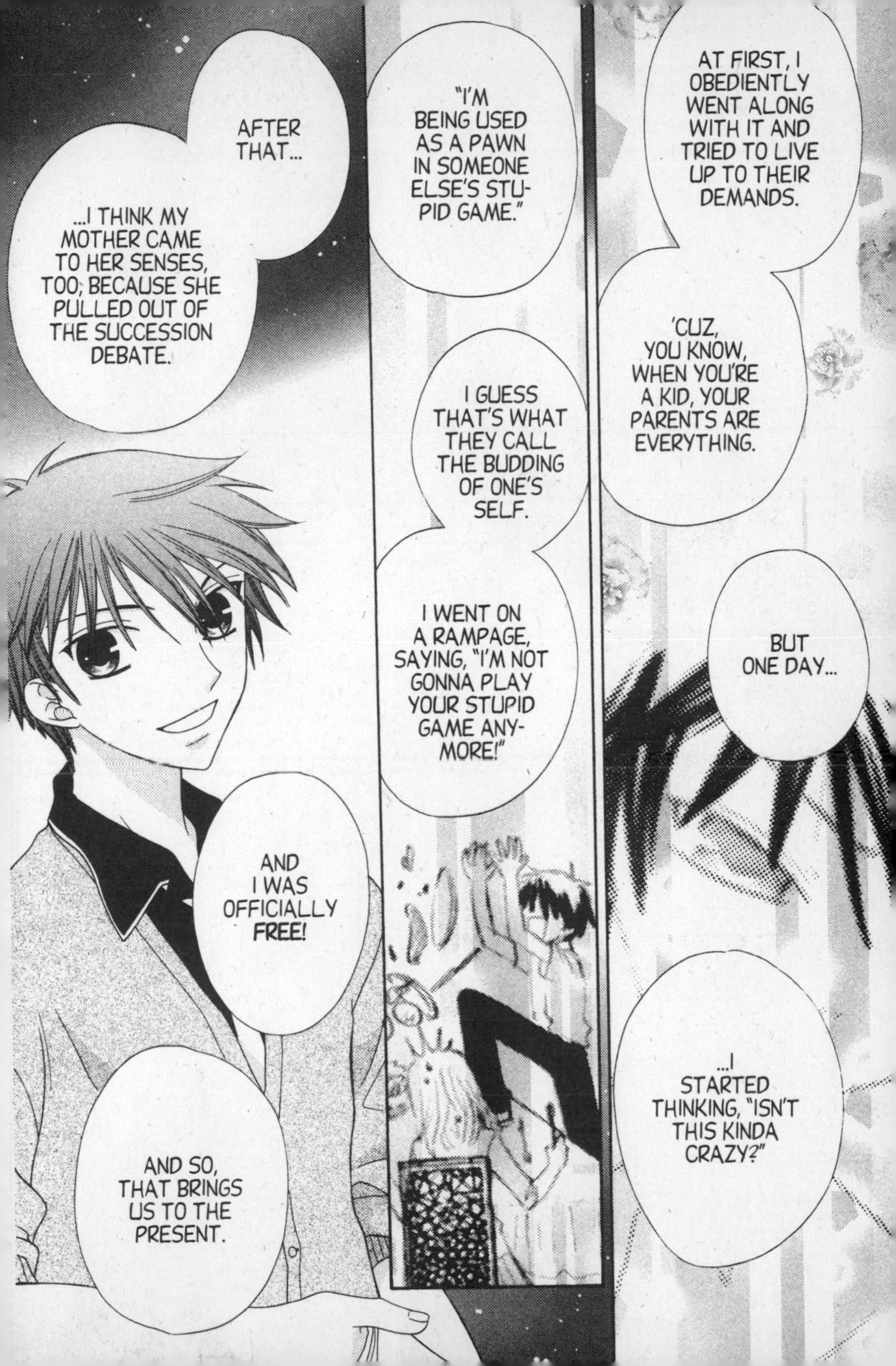
AT FIRST, I OBEDIENTLY WENT ALONG WITH IT AND TRIED TO LIVE UP TO THEIR DEMANDS.
'CUZ, YOU KNOW, WHEN YOU'RE A KID, YOUR PARENTS ARE EVERYTHING.
BUT ONE DAY...
...I STARTED THINKING, "ISN'T THIS KINDA CRAZY?"
"I'M BEING USED AS A PAWN IN SOMEONE ELSE'S STUPID GAME."
I GUESS THAT'S WHAT THEY CALL THE BUDDING OF ONE'S SELF.
I WENT ON A RAMPAGE, SAYING, "I'M NOT GONNA PLAY YOUR STUPID GAME ANYMORE!"
AFTER THAT...
...I THINK MY MOTHER CAME TO HER SENSES, TOO, BECAUSE SHE PULLED OUT OF THE SUCCESSION DEBATE.
AND I WAS OFFICIALLY FREE!
AND SO, THAT BRINGS US TO THE PRESENT.

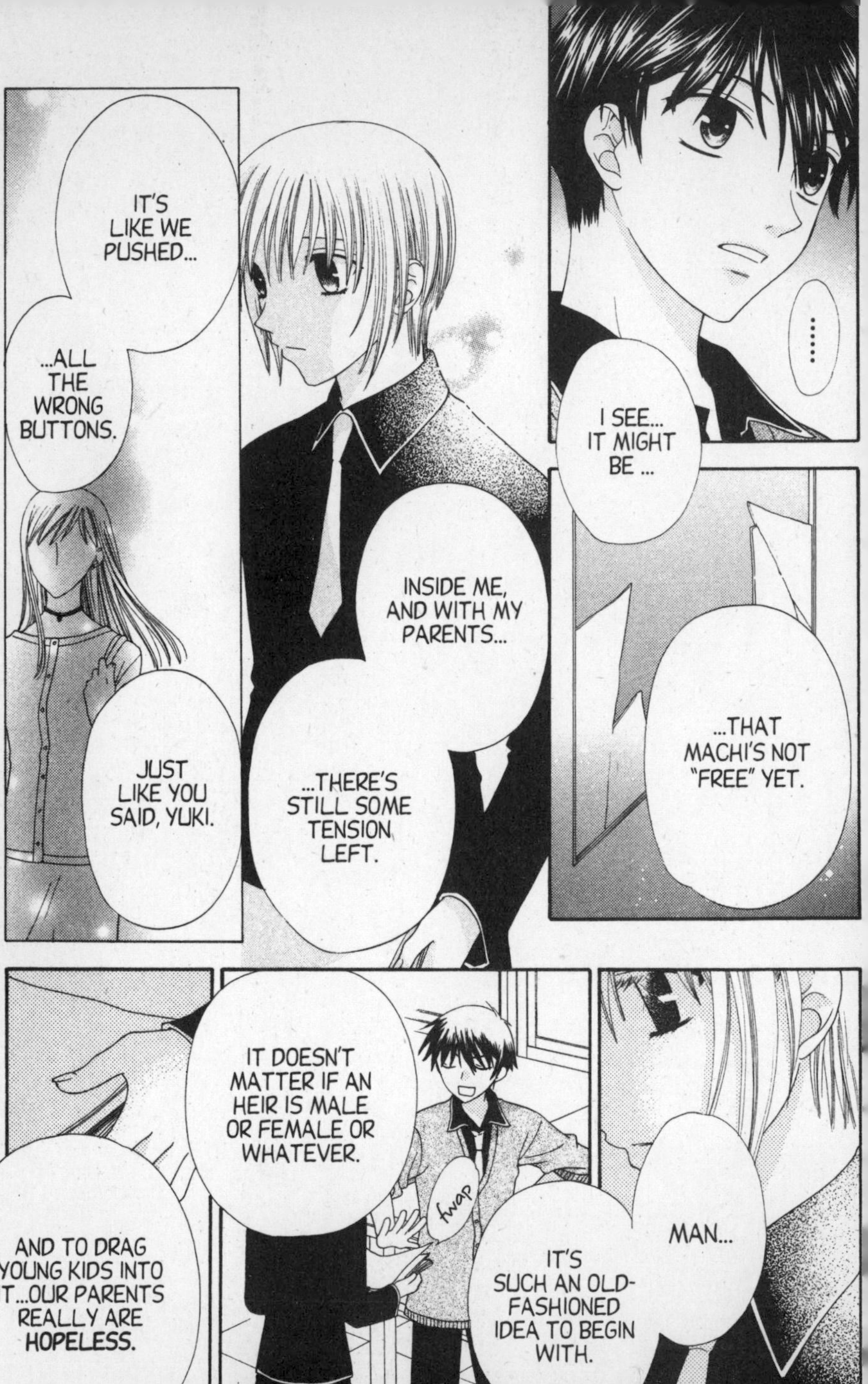
......
I SEE... IT MIGHT BE ...
...THAT MACHI'S NOT "FREE" YET.
INSIDE ME, AND WITH MY PARENTS...
...THERE'S STILL SOME TENSION LEFT.
IT'S LIKE WE PUSHED...
...ALL THE WRONG BUTTONS.
JUST LIKE YOU SAID, YUKI.
MAN...
IT'S SUCH AN OLD-FASHIONED IDEA TO BEGIN WITH.
IT DOESN'T MATTER IF AN HEIR IS MALE OR FEMALE OR WHATEVER.
fwap
AND TO DRAG YOUNG KIDS INTO IT...OUR PARENTS REALLY ARE HOPELESS.

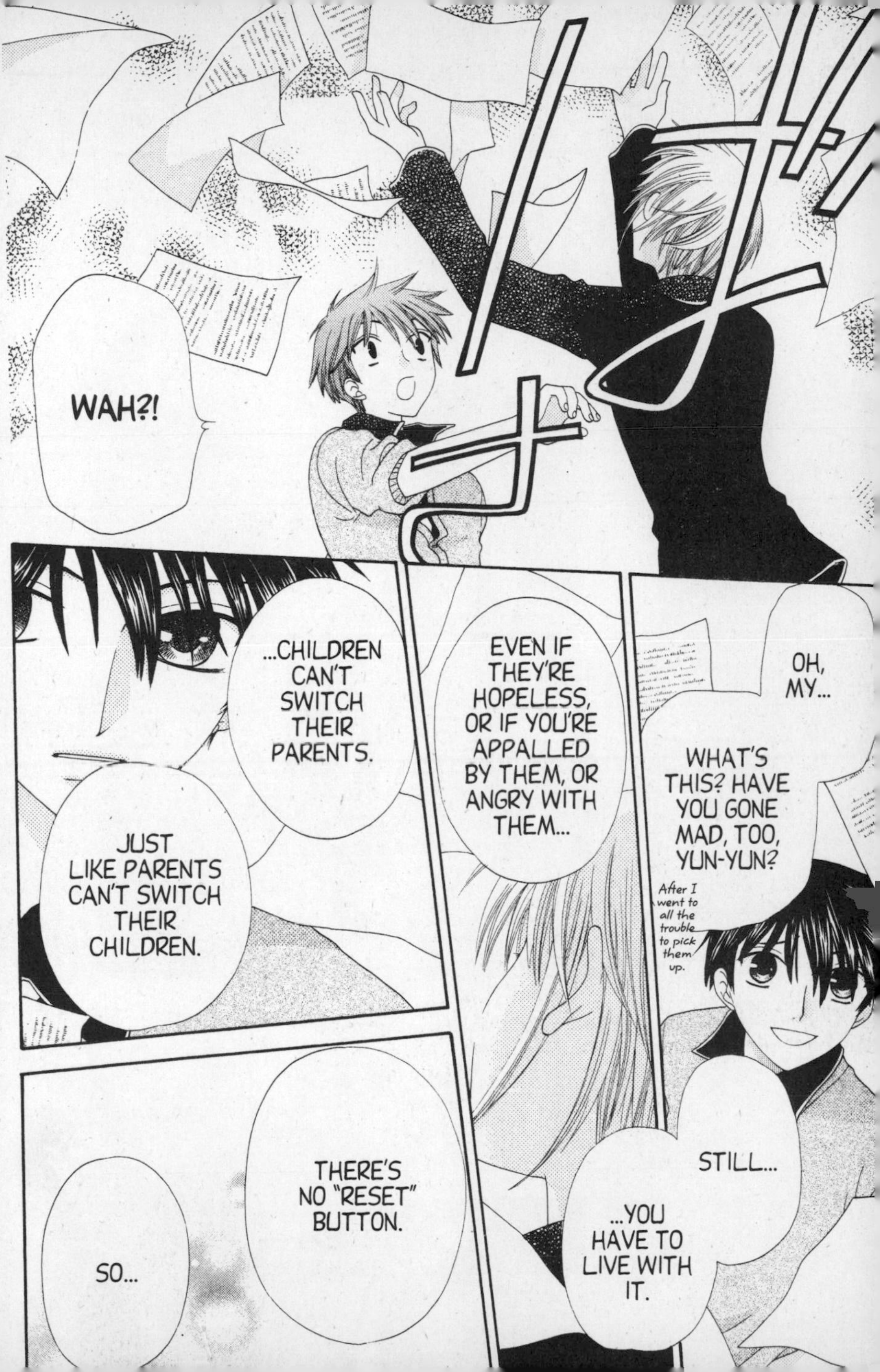
WAH?!
OH, MY...
WHAT'S THIS? HAVE YOU GONE MAD, TOO, YUN-YUN?
After I went to all the trouble to pick them up.
EVEN IF THEY'RE HOPELESS, OR IF YOU'RE APPALLED BY THEM, OR ANGRY WITH THEM...
STILL...
...YOU HAVE TO LIVE WITH IT.
...CHILDREN CAN'T SWITCH THEIR PARENTS.
JUST LIKE PARENTS CAN'T SWITCH THEIR CHILDREN.
THERE'S NO "RESET" BUTTON.
SO...

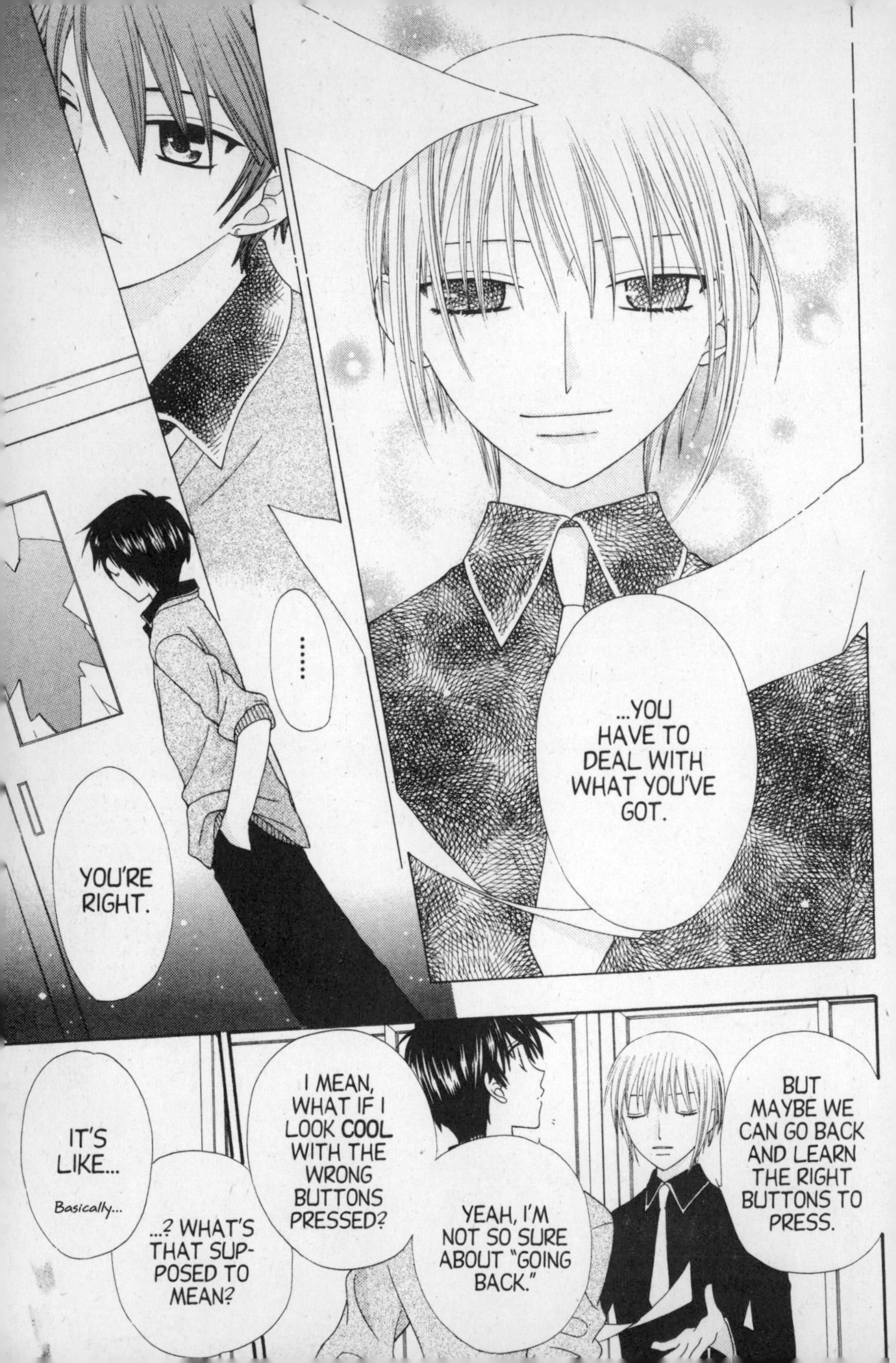
...YOU HAVE TO DEAL WITH WHAT YOU'VE GOT.
......
YOU'RE RIGHT.
BUT MAYBE WE CAN GO BACK AND LEARN THE RIGHT BUTTONS TO PRESS.
YEAH, I'M NOT SO SURE ABOUT "GOING BACK."
I MEAN, WHAT IF I LOOK **COOL** WITH THE WRONG BUTTONS PRESSED?
...? WHAT'S THAT SUP-POSED TO MEAN?
IT'S LIKE...
Basically...

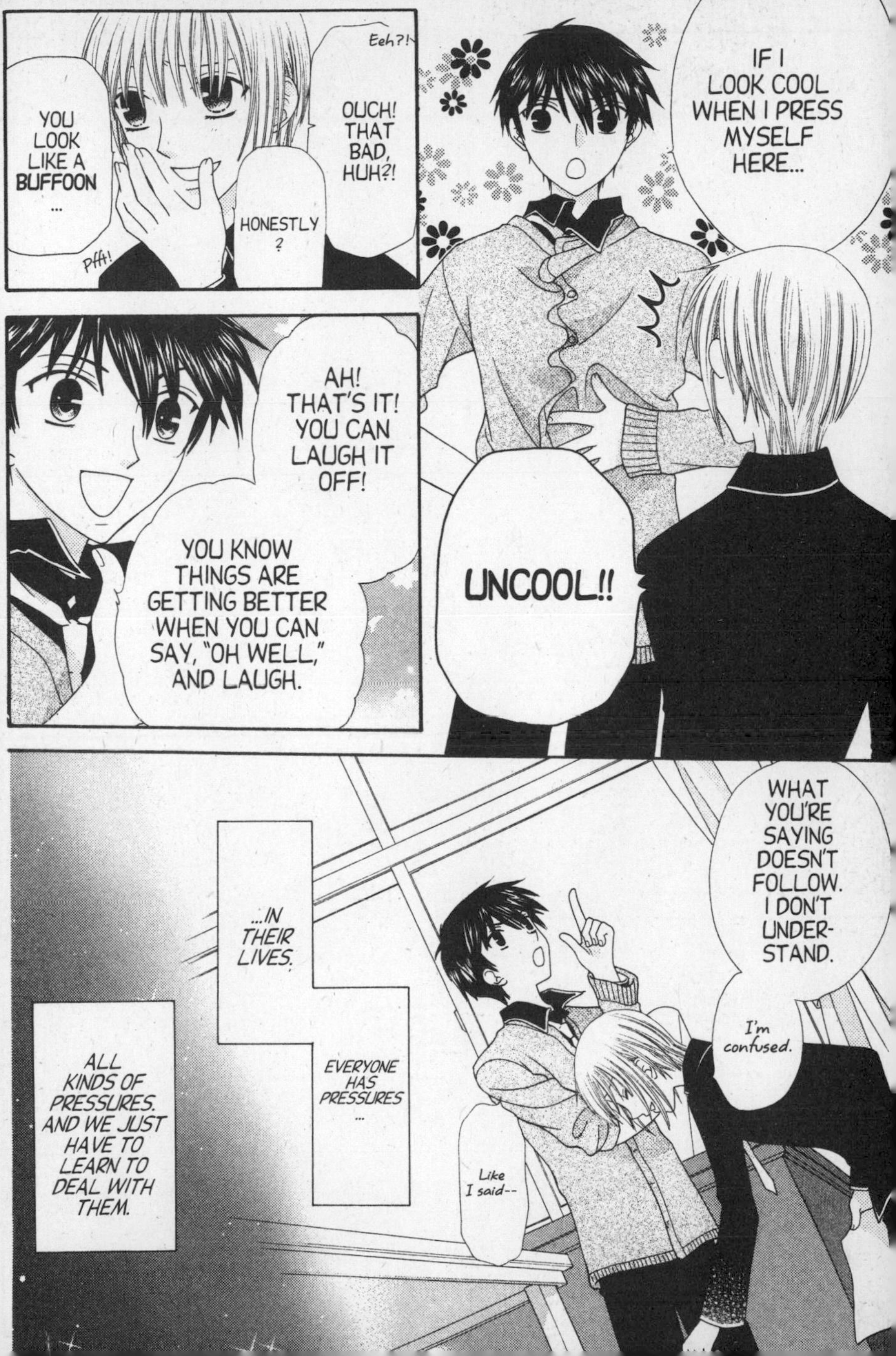
IF I LOOK COOL WHEN I PRESS MYSELF HERE...
UNCOOL!!
Eeh?!
OUCH! THAT BAD, HUH?!
HONESTLY?
YOU LOOK LIKE A BUFFOON...
Pfft!
AH! THAT'S IT! YOU CAN LAUGH IT OFF!
YOU KNOW THINGS ARE GETTING BETTER WHEN YOU CAN SAY, "OH WELL," AND LAUGH.
WHAT YOU'RE SAYING DOESN'T FOLLOW. I DON'T UNDERSTAND.
I'm confused.
Like I said--
EVERYONE HAS PRESSURES...
...IN THEIR LIVES.
ALL KINDS OF PRESSURES. AND WE JUST HAVE TO LEARN TO DEAL WITH THEM.

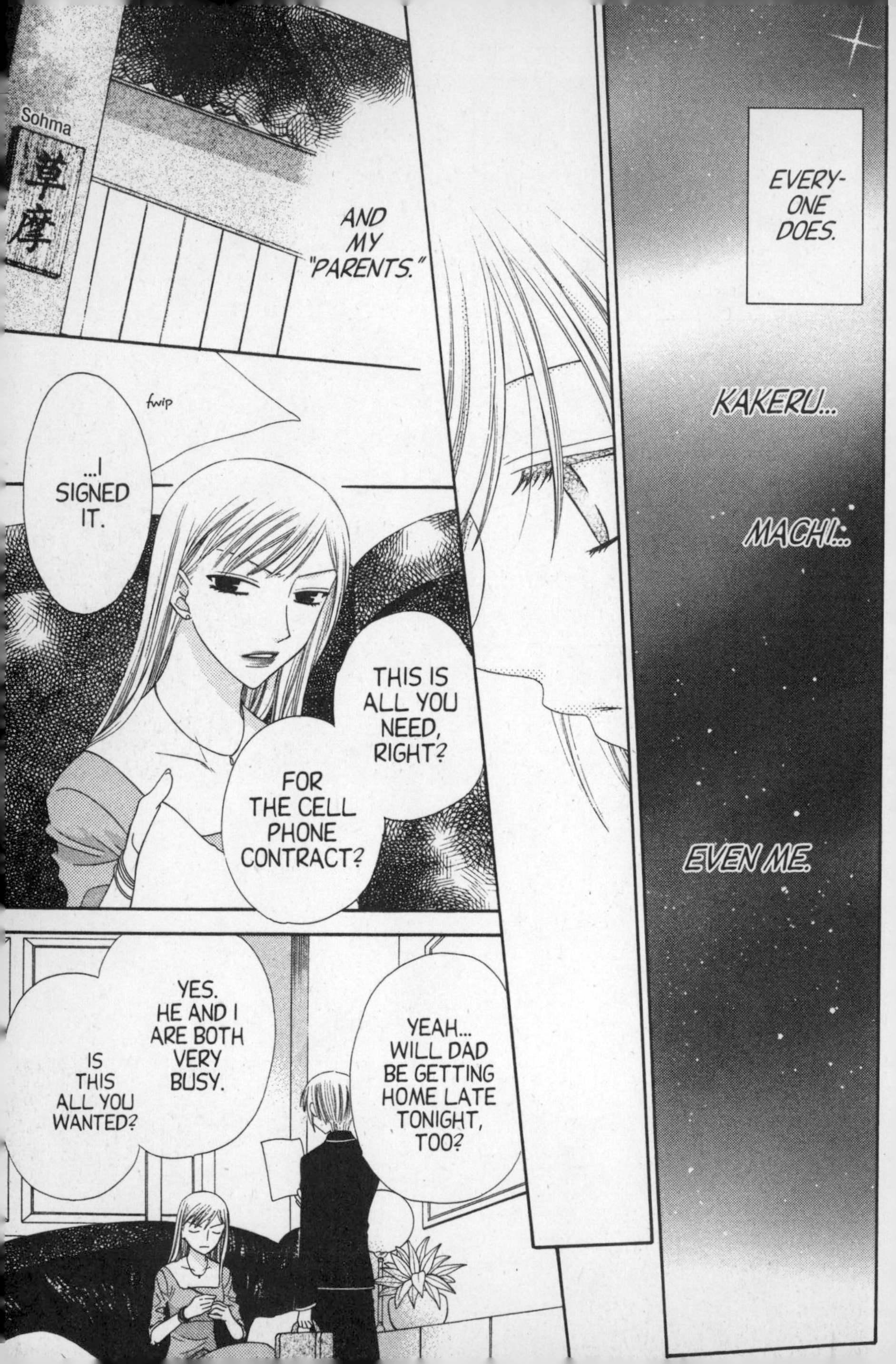
EVERY-ONE DOES.
KAKERU...
MACHI...
EVEN ME.
Sohma
草摩
AND MY "PARENTS."
fwip
...I SIGNED IT.
THIS IS ALL YOU NEED, RIGHT?
FOR THE CELL PHONE CONTRACT?
YEAH... WILL DAD BE GETTING HOME LATE TONIGHT, TOO?
YES. HE AND I ARE BOTH VERY BUSY.
IS THIS ALL YOU WANTED?

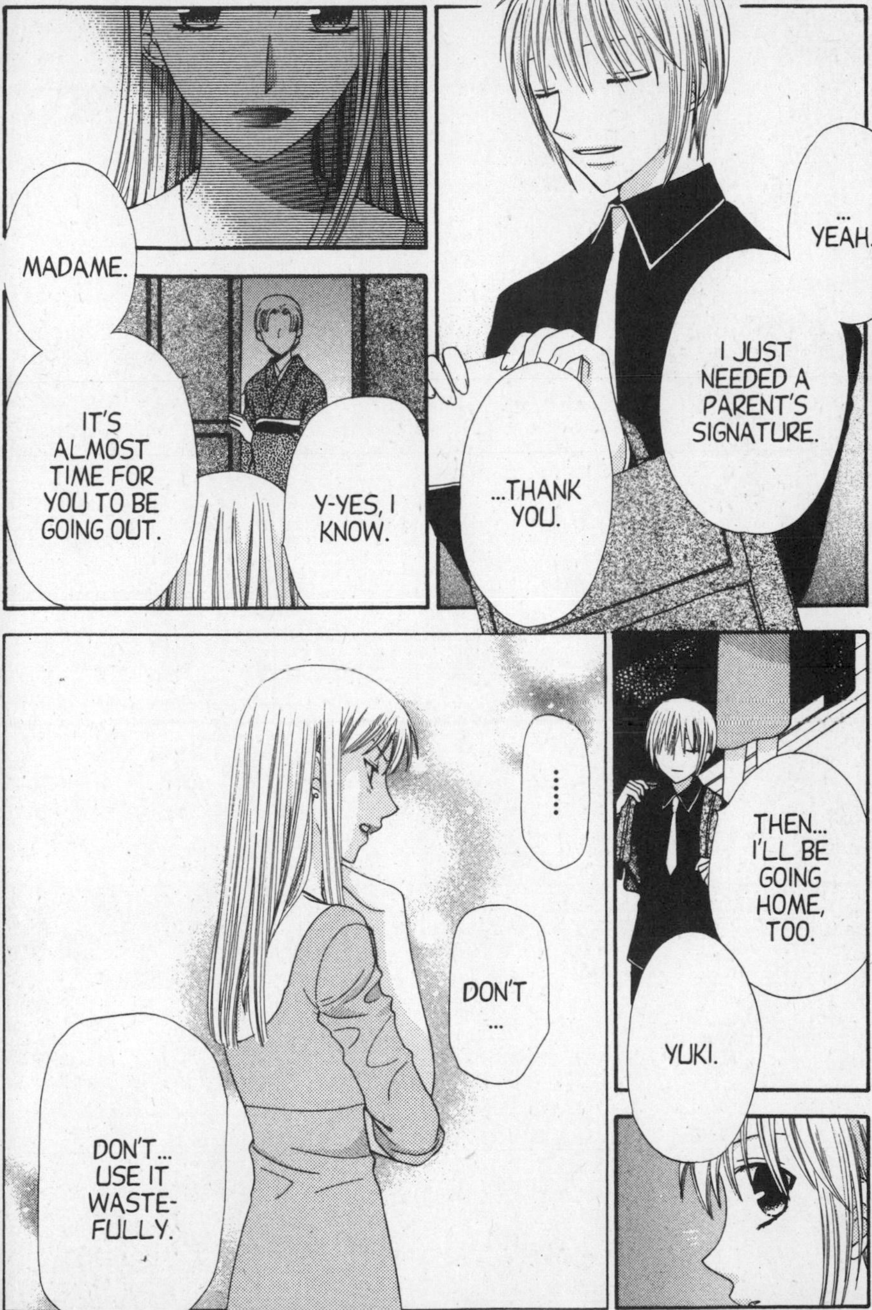
... YEAH.
I JUST NEEDED A PARENT'S SIGNATURE.
...THANK YOU.
MADAME.
IT'S ALMOST TIME FOR YOU TO BE GOING OUT.
Y-YES, I KNOW.
THEN... I'LL BE GOING HOME, TOO.
YUKI.
......
DON'T ...
DON'T... USE IT WASTE-FULLY.

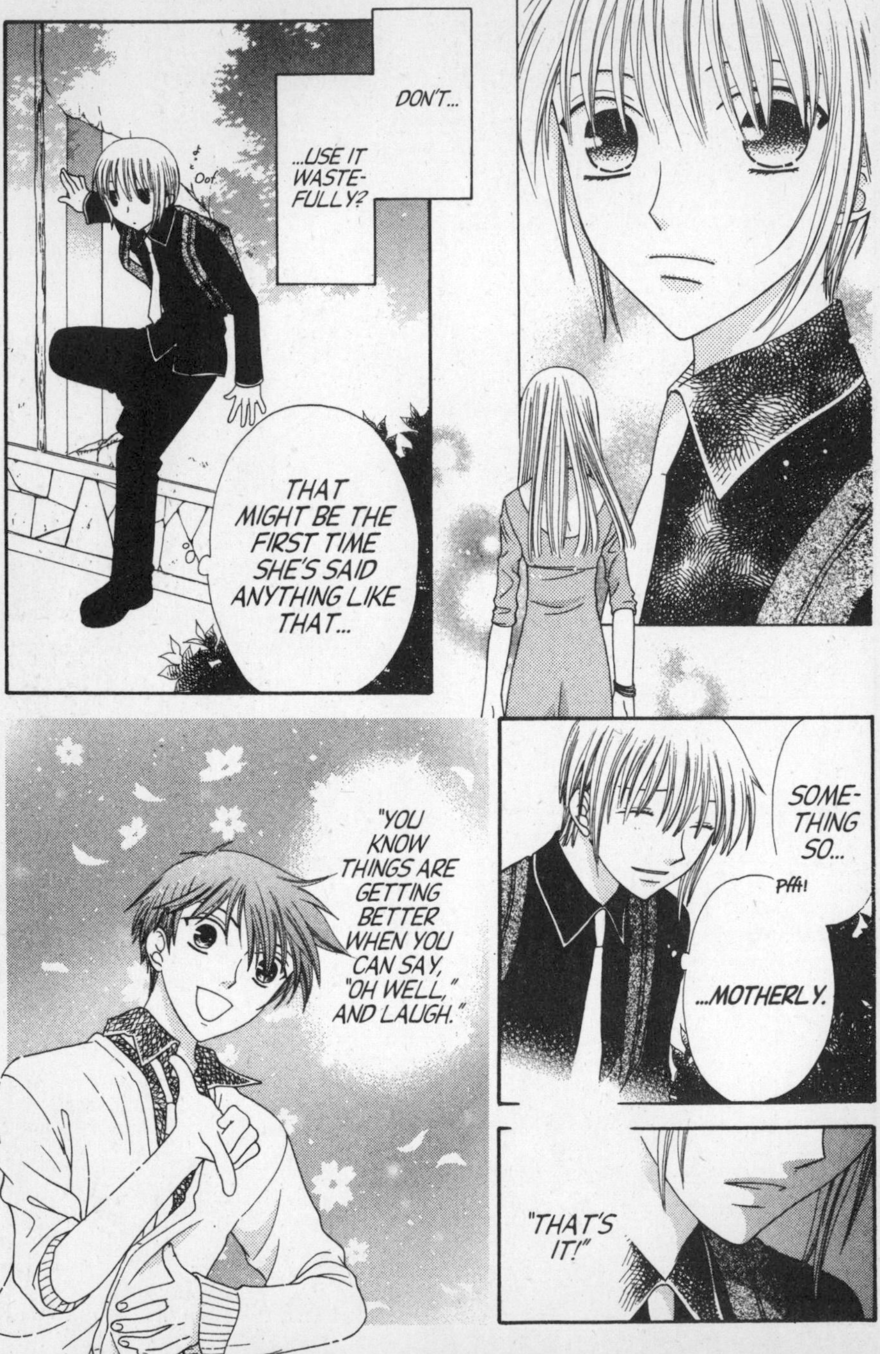
DON'T...
...USE IT WASTEFULLY?
Oof
THAT MIGHT BE THE FIRST TIME SHE'S SAID ANYTHING LIKE THAT...
SOMETHING SO...
Pff!
...MOTHERLY.
"THAT'S IT!"
"YOU KNOW THINGS ARE GETTING BETTER WHEN YOU CAN SAY, "OH WELL," AND LAUGH."

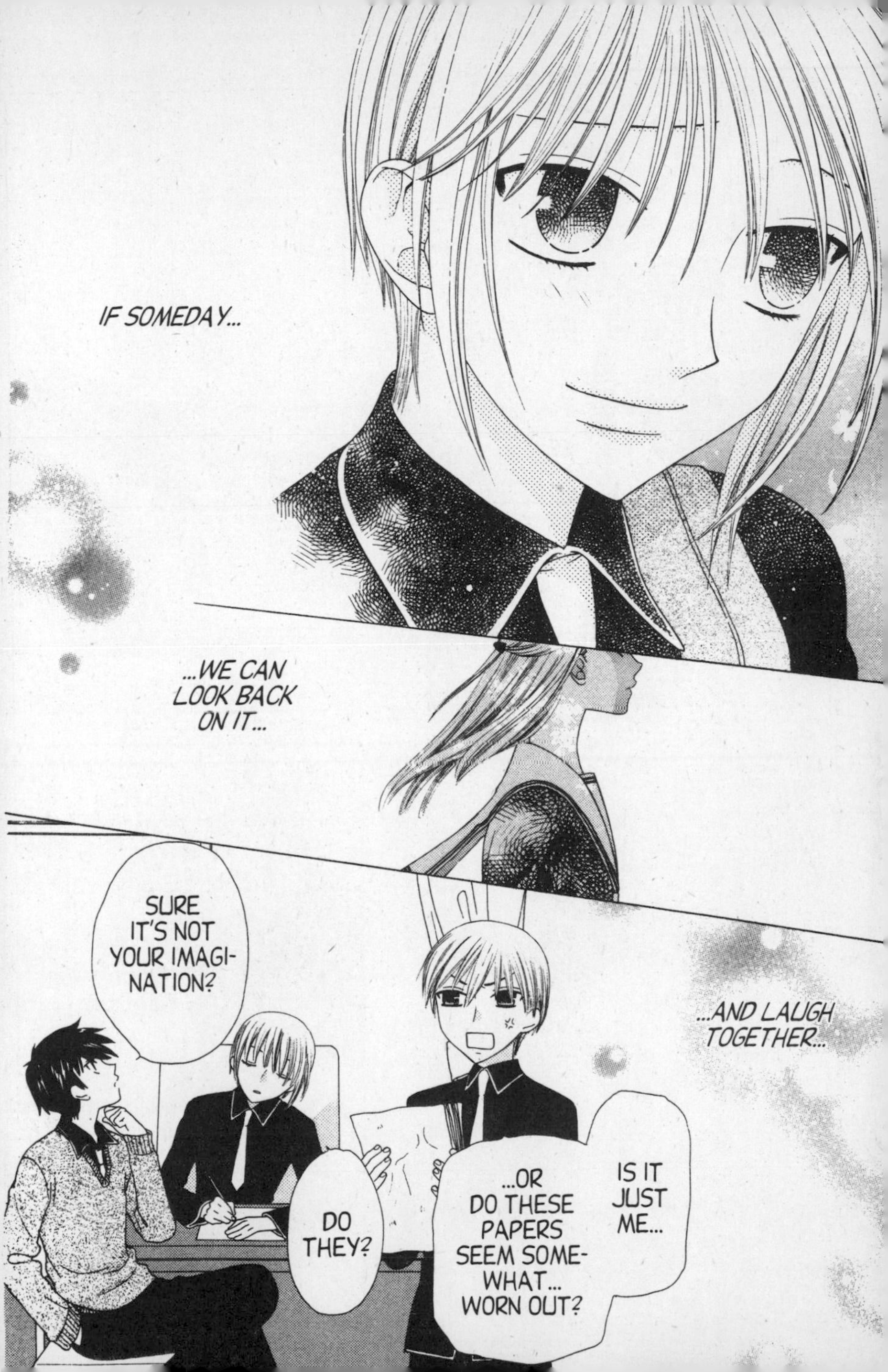
IF SOMEDAY...
...WE CAN LOOK BACK ON IT...
...AND LAUGH TOGETHER...
IS IT JUST ME...
...OR DO THESE PAPERS SEEM SOME-WHAT... WORN OUT?
DO THEY?
SURE IT'S NOT YOUR IMAGI-NATION?

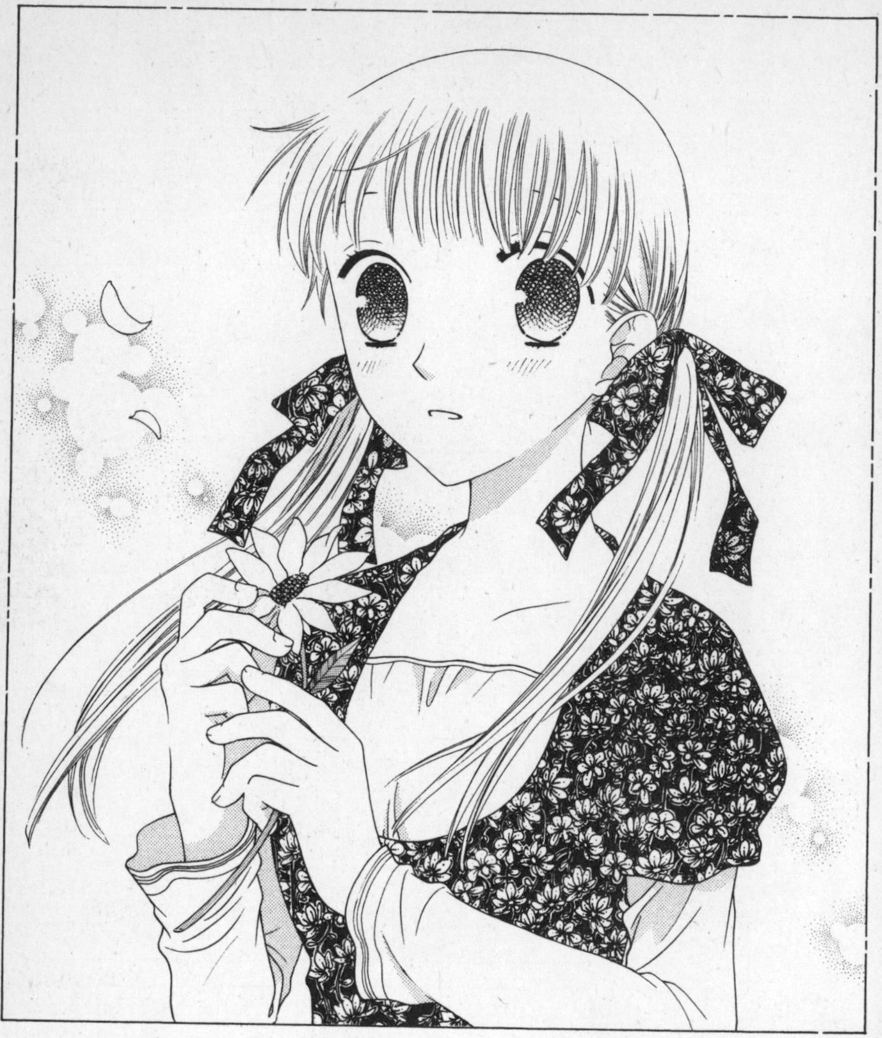

Chapter 82

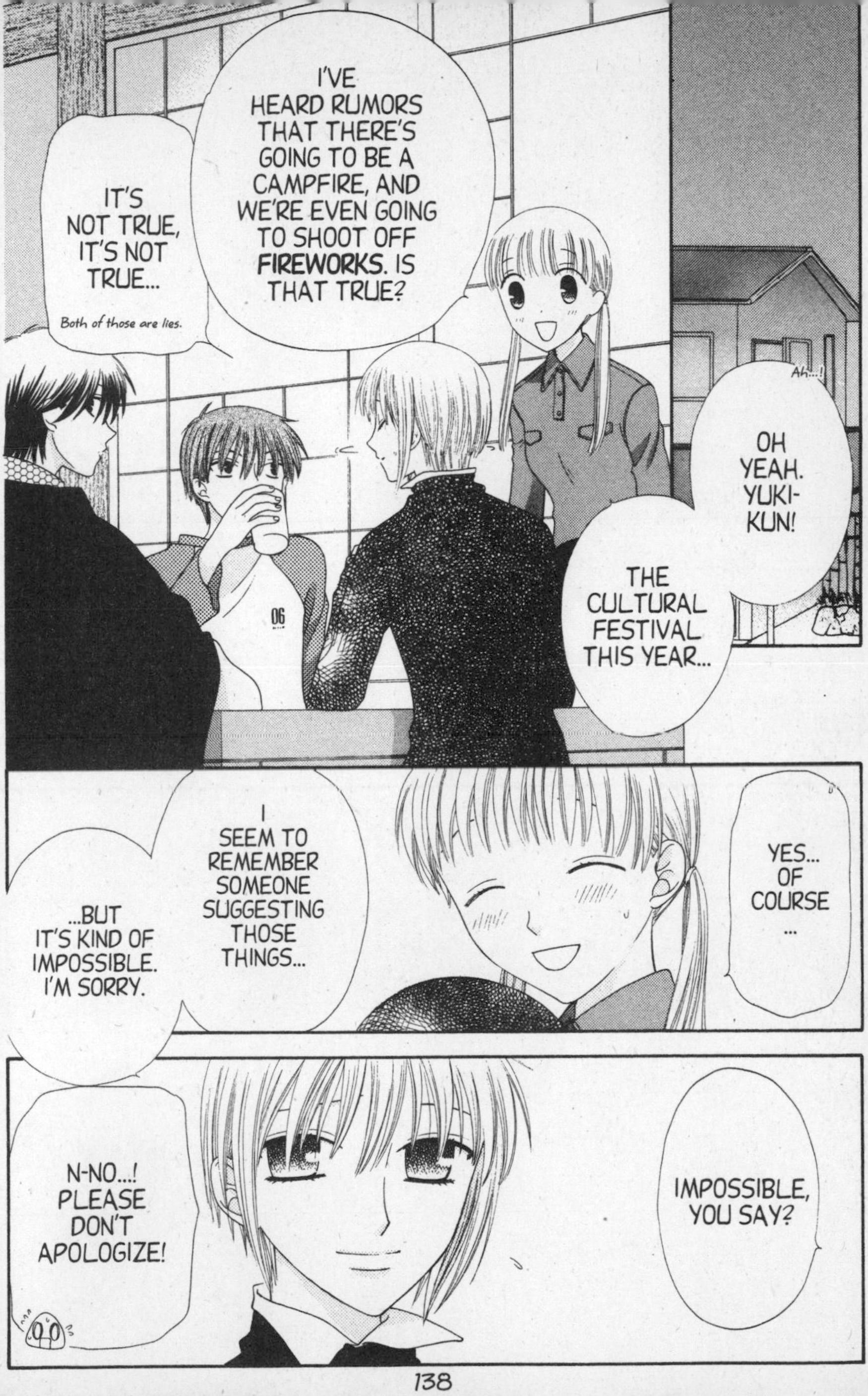
Ah...!
OH YEAH. YUKI-KUN!
THE CULTURAL FESTIVAL THIS YEAR...
I'VE HEARD RUMORS THAT THERE'S GOING TO BE A CAMPFIRE, AND WE'RE EVEN GOING TO SHOOT OFF FIREWORKS. IS THAT TRUE?
IT'S NOT TRUE, IT'S NOT TRUE...
Both of those are lies.
YES... OF COURSE ...
I SEEM TO REMEMBER SOMEONE SUGGESTING THOSE THINGS...
...BUT IT'S KIND OF IMPOSSIBLE. I'M SORRY.
IMPOSSIBLE, YOU SAY?
N-NO...! PLEASE DON'T APOLOGIZE!

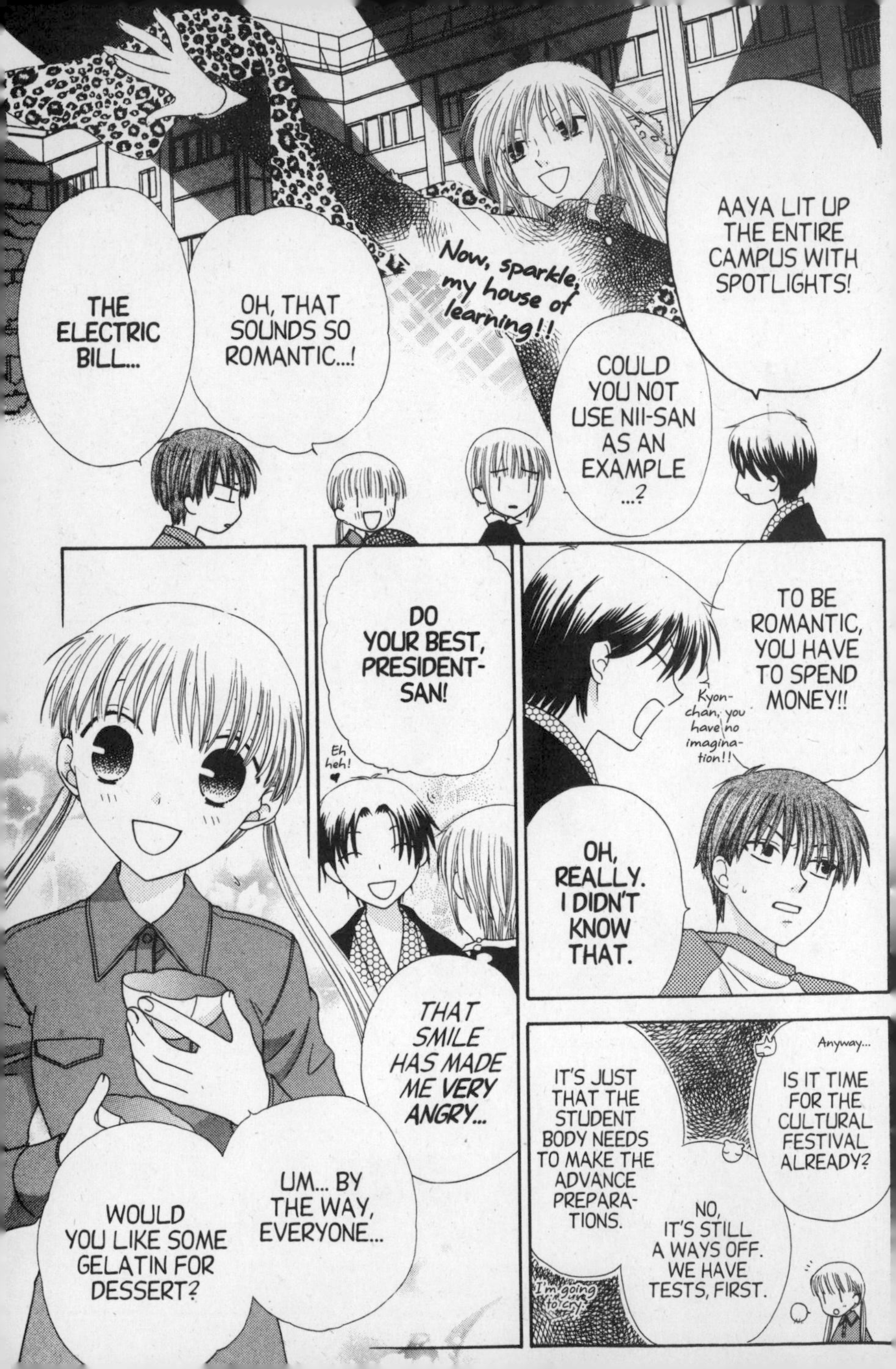
AAYA LIT UP THE ENTIRE CAMPUS WITH SPOTLIGHTS!
Now, sparkle, my house of learning!!
COULD YOU NOT USE NII-SAN AS AN EXAMPLE ...?
OH, THAT SOUNDS SO ROMANTIC...!
THE ELECTRIC BILL...
TO BE ROMANTIC, YOU HAVE TO SPEND MONEY!!
Kyon-chan, you have no imagination!!
OH, REALLY. I DIDN'T KNOW THAT.
DO YOUR BEST, PRESIDENT-SAN!
Eh heh! ♥
THAT SMILE HAS MADE ME VERY ANGRY...
Anyway...
IS IT TIME FOR THE CULTURAL FESTIVAL ALREADY?
NO, IT'S STILL A WAYS OFF. WE HAVE TESTS, FIRST.
IT'S JUST THAT THE STUDENT BODY NEEDS TO MAKE THE ADVANCE PREPARATIONS.
I'm going to cry.
UM... BY THE WAY, EVERYONE...
WOULD YOU LIKE SOME GELATIN FOR DESSERT?

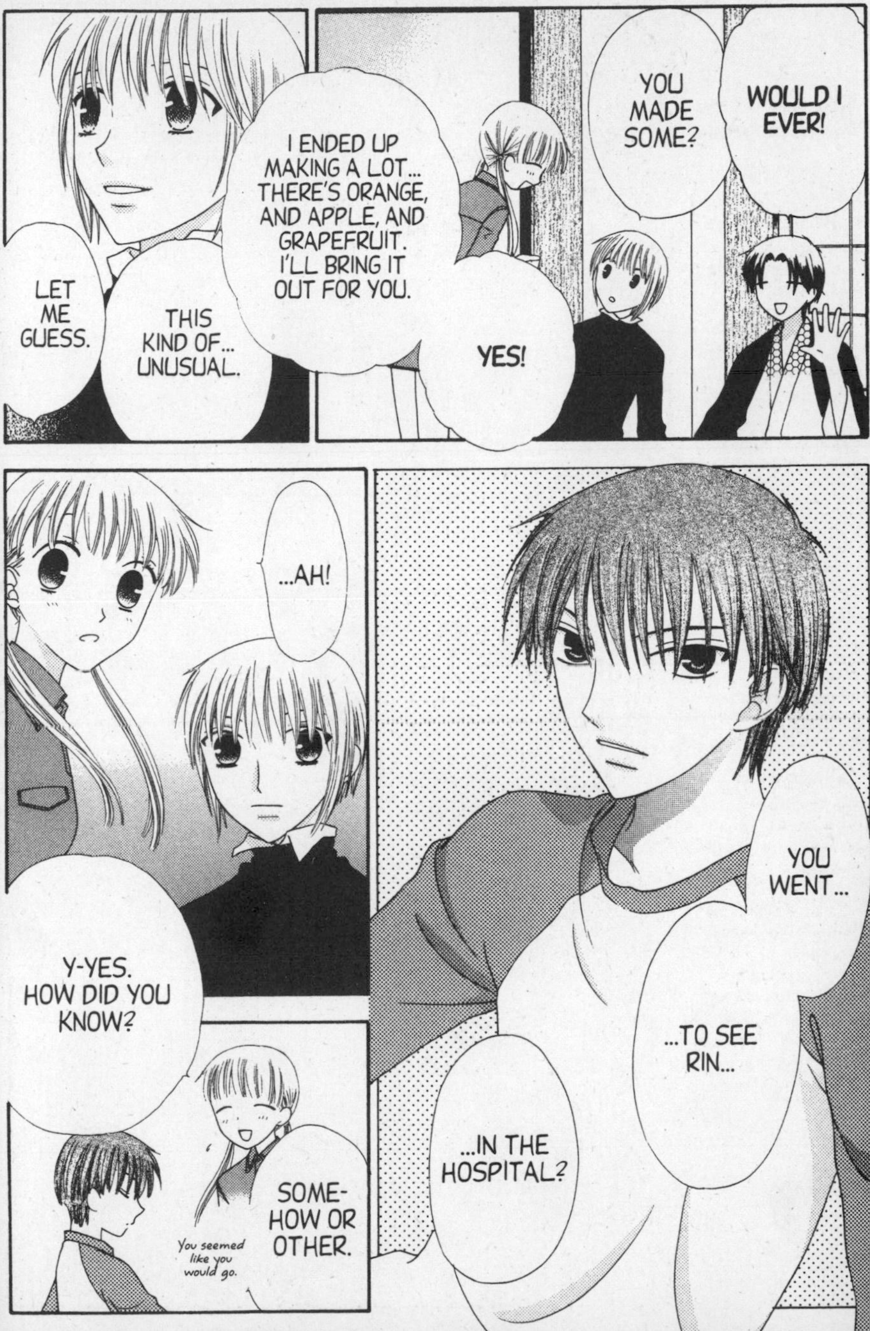

WOULD I EVER!
YOU MADE SOME?
I ENDED UP MAKING A LOT... THERE'S ORANGE, AND APPLE, AND GRAPEFRUIT. I'LL BRING IT OUT FOR YOU.
YES!
THIS KIND OF... UNUSUAL.
LET ME GUESS.
YOU WENT...
...TO SEE RIN...
...IN THE HOSPITAL?
...AH!
Y-YES. HOW DID YOU KNOW?
SOME-HOW OR OTHER.
You seemed like you would go.

Basically, it's like this. Continued...

Sixth month: Isuzu, from Isuzukuretsuki (month of the last cool spring days)

Seventh month: Hiro, from Fumihirogetsuki (month of publication)

Eighth month: Ritsu, from Odakaritsuki (rice harvest month)

Ninth month: Momiji, from Momijitsuki (Autumn leaves month)

Tenth month: Shigure, from Shigurezuki (Autumn showers month)

Eleventh month: Kagura, from Kagurazuki (month of Shinto song and dance)

...like that. T-tired! I really am bad a writing the kanji characters. Especially writing horizontally. I don't know if it's because I'm left-handed or what, though.

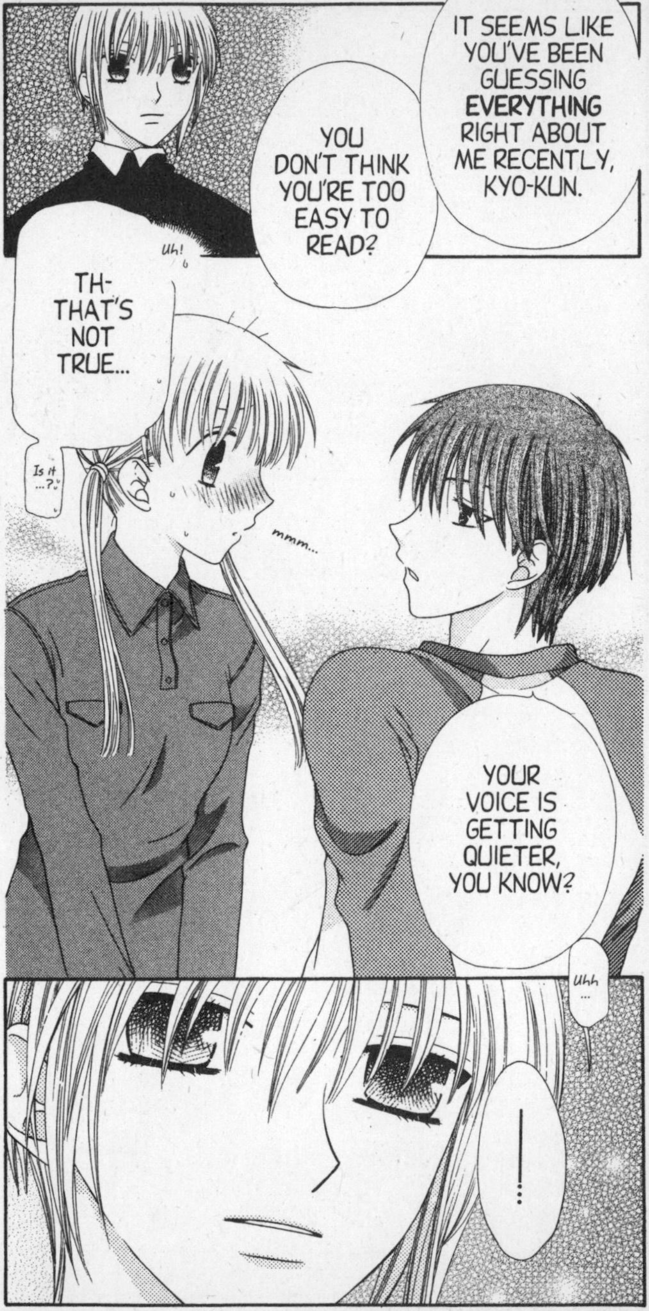
IT SEEMS LIKE YOU'VE BEEN GUESSING **EVERYTHING** RIGHT ABOUT ME RECENTLY, KYO-KUN.
YOU DON'T THINK YOU'RE TOO EASY TO READ?
Uh!
TH-THAT'S NOT TRUE...
Is it ...?
mmm...
YOUR VOICE IS GETTING QUIETER, YOU KNOW?
Uhh ...
......

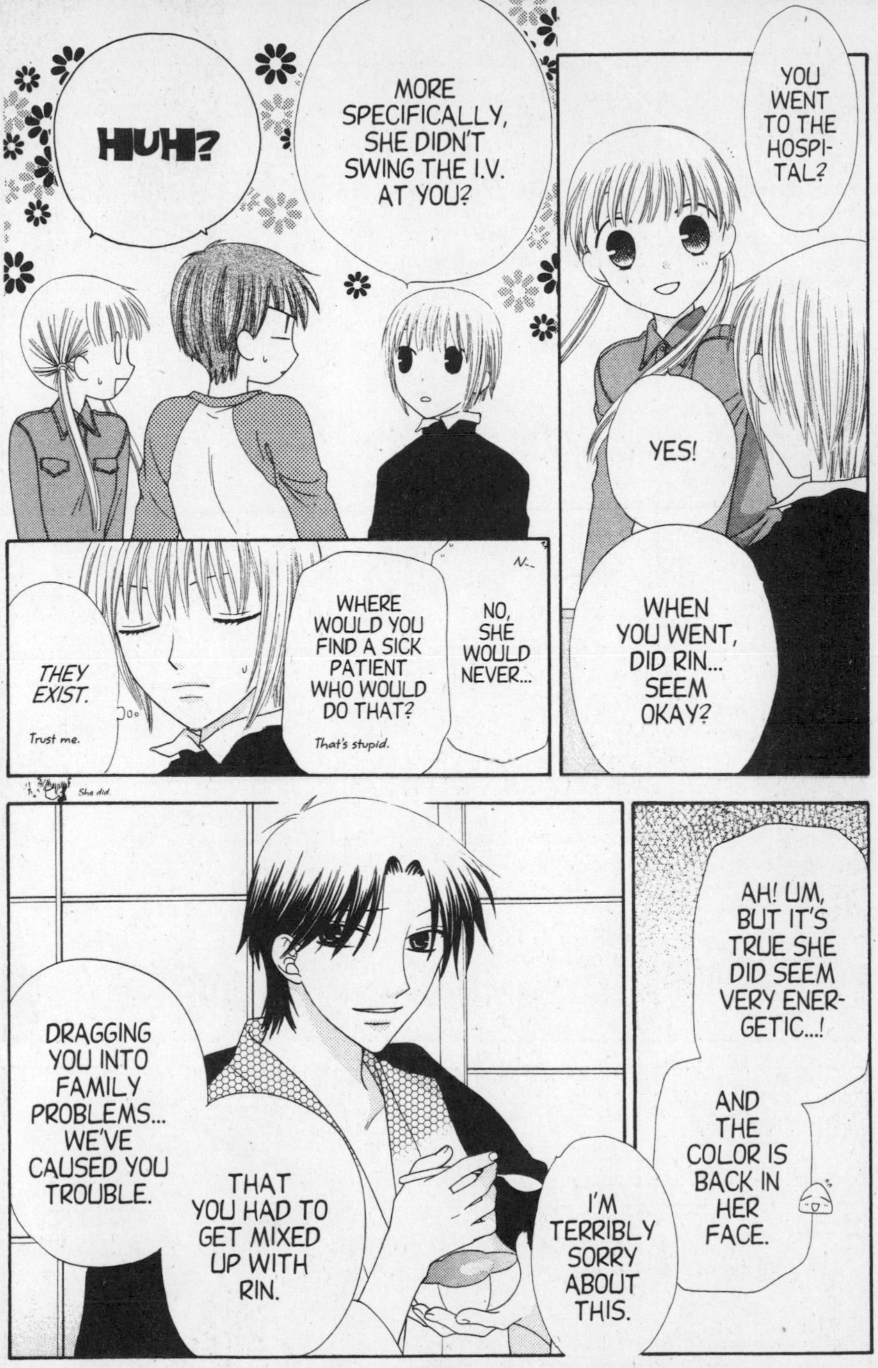
YOU WENT TO THE HOSPI-TAL?
YES!
WHEN YOU WENT, DID RIN... SEEM OKAY?
MORE SPECIFICALLY, SHE DIDN'T SWING THE I.V. AT YOU?
HUH?
N--
NO, SHE WOULD NEVER...
WHERE WOULD YOU FIND A SICK PATIENT WHO WOULD DO THAT?
That's stupid.
THEY EXIST.
Trust me.
She did.
AH! UM, BUT IT'S TRUE SHE DID SEEM VERY ENER-GETIC...!
AND THE COLOR IS BACK IN HER FACE.
I'M TERRIBLY SORRY ABOUT THIS.
THAT YOU HAD TO GET MIXED UP WITH RIN.
DRAGGING YOU INTO FAMILY PROBLEMS... WE'VE CAUSED YOU TROUBLE.

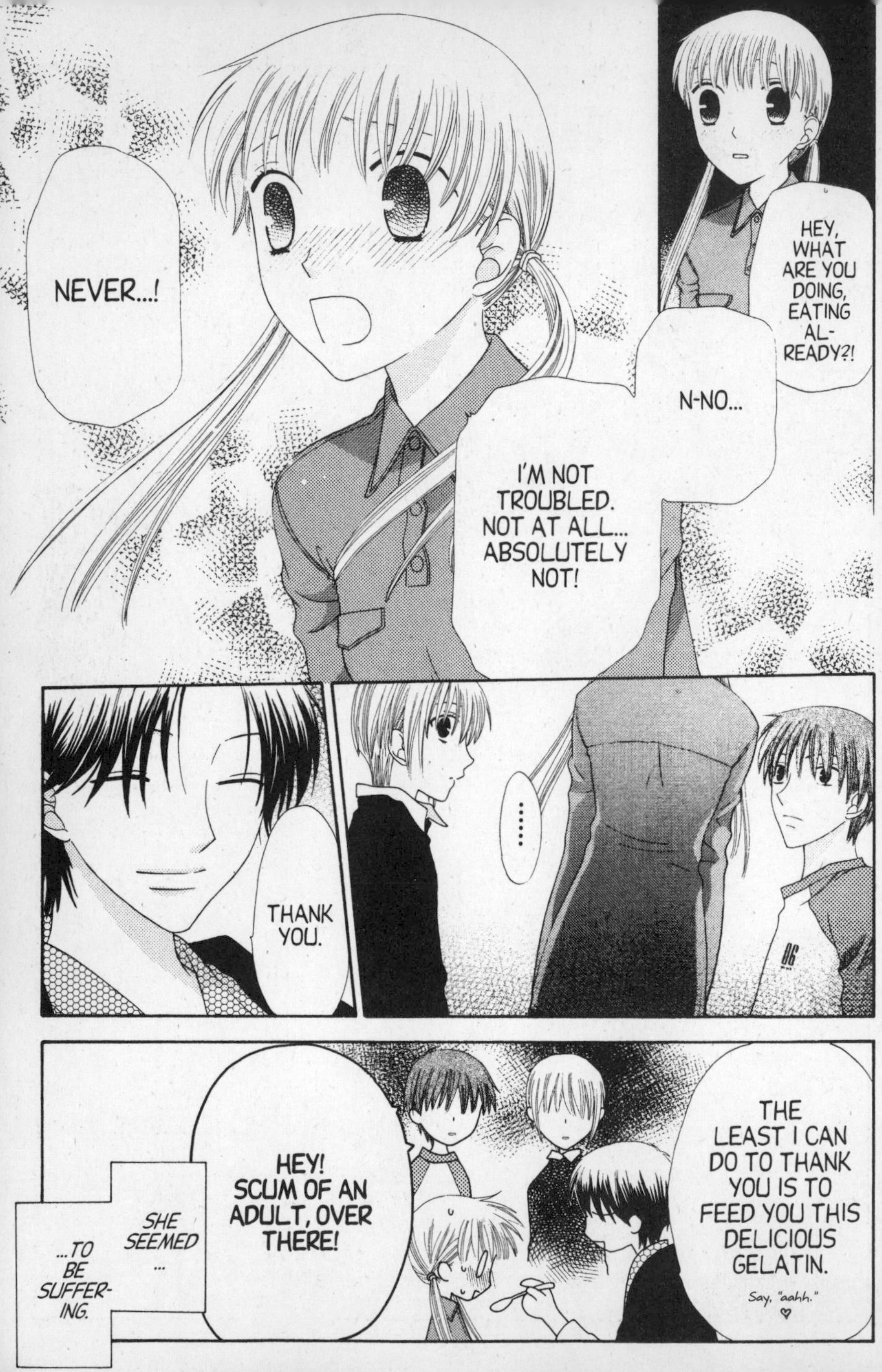
HEY, WHAT ARE YOU DOING, EATING AL-READY?!
N-NO...
I'M NOT TROUBLED. NOT AT ALL... ABSOLUTELY NOT!
NEVER...!
......
THANK YOU.
THE LEAST I CAN DO TO THANK YOU IS TO FEED YOU THIS DELICIOUS GELATIN.
Say, "aahh." ♡
HEY! SCUM OF AN ADULT, OVER THERE!
SHE SEEMED ...
...TO BE SUFFER-ING.

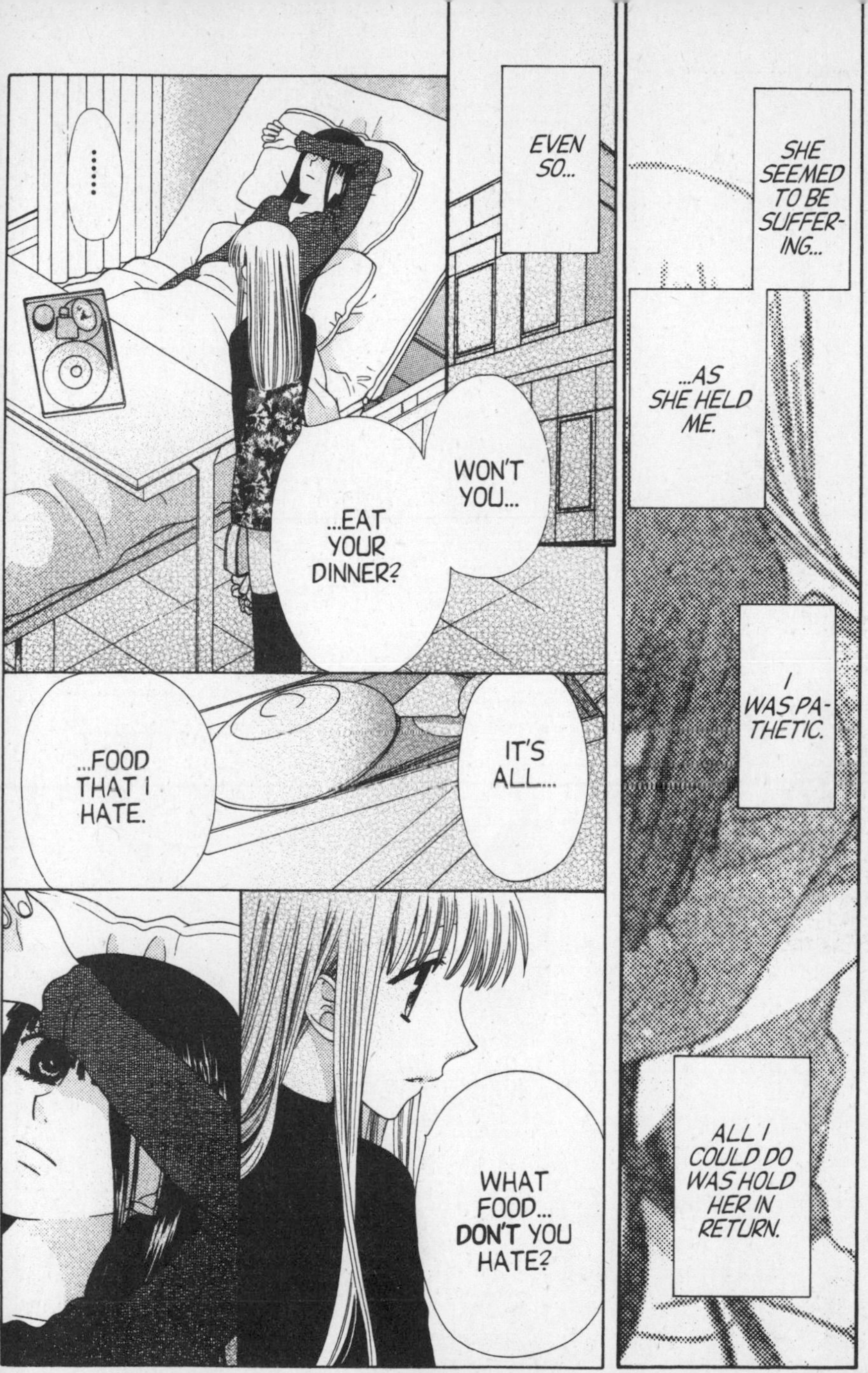

SHE SEEMED TO BE SUFFERING...
...AS SHE HELD ME.
I WAS PATHETIC.
ALL I COULD DO WAS HOLD HER IN RETURN.
EVEN SO...
WON'T YOU...
...EAT YOUR DINNER?
......
IT'S ALL...
...FOOD THAT I HATE.
WHAT FOOD... DON'T YOU HATE?

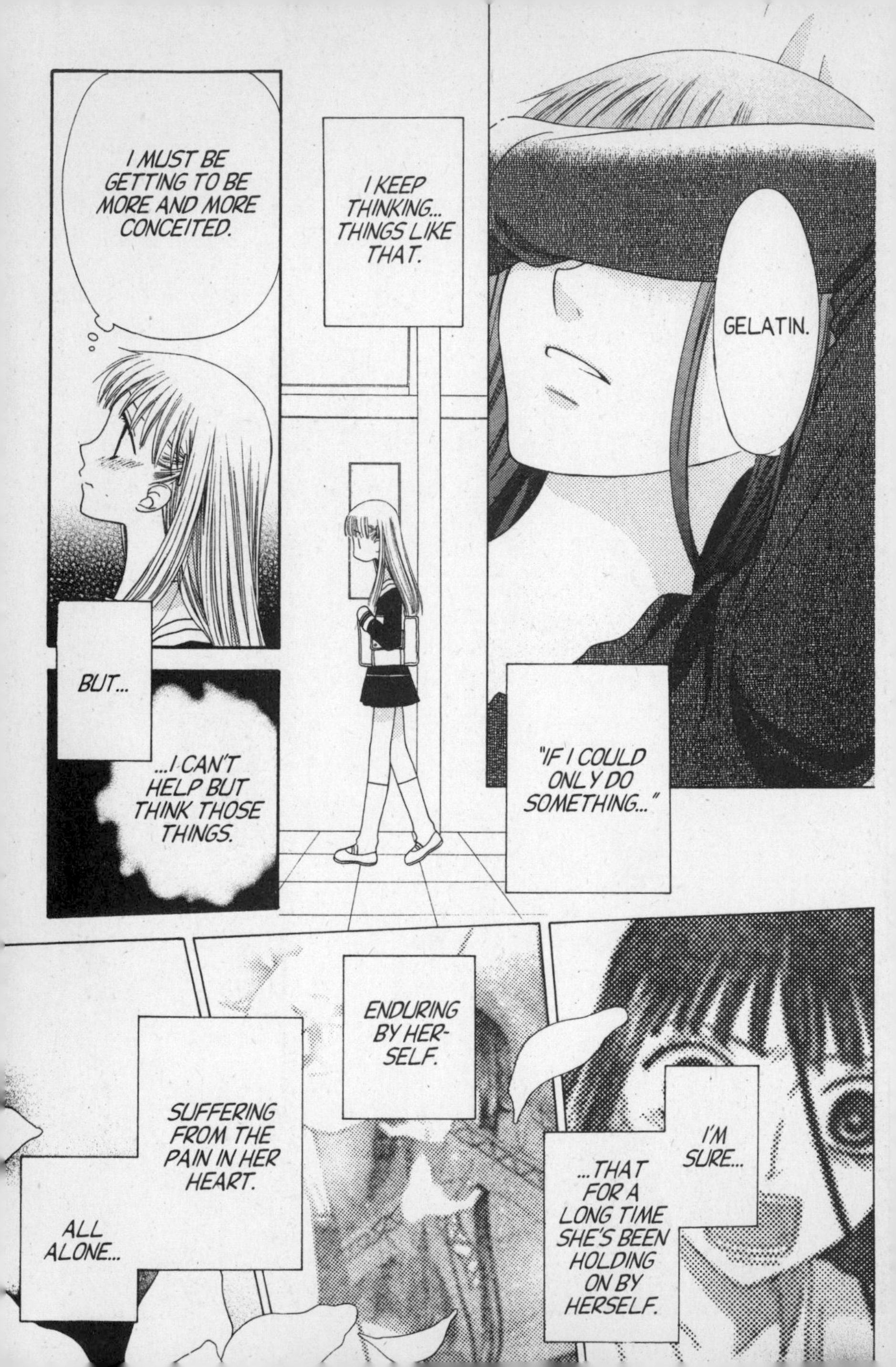
GELATIN.
"IF I COULD ONLY DO SOMETHING..."
I KEEP THINKING... THINGS LIKE THAT.
I MUST BE GETTING TO BE MORE AND MORE CONCEITED.
BUT...
...I CAN'T HELP BUT THINK THOSE THINGS.
I'M SURE...
...THAT FOR A LONG TIME SHE'S BEEN HOLDING ON BY HERSELF.
ENDURING BY HER-SELF.
SUFFERING FROM THE PAIN IN HER HEART.
ALL ALONE...

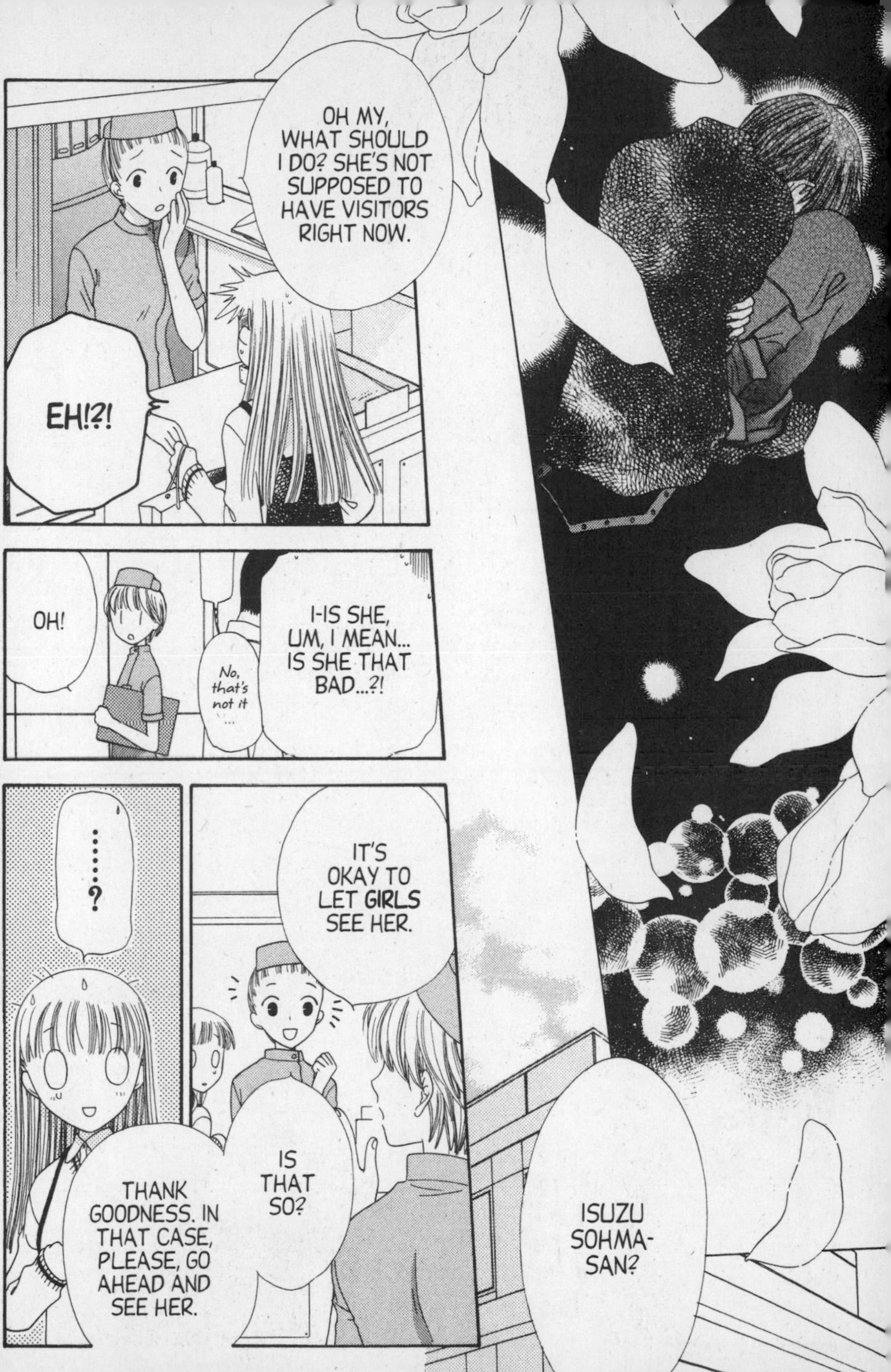
ISUZU SOHMA-SAN?
OH MY, WHAT SHOULD I DO? SHE'S NOT SUPPOSED TO HAVE VISITORS RIGHT NOW.
EH!?!
I-IS SHE, UM, I MEAN... IS SHE THAT BAD...?!
No, that's not it...
OH!
IT'S OKAY TO LET GIRLS SEE HER.
IS THAT SO?
THANK GOODNESS. IN THAT CASE, PLEASE, GO AHEAD AND SEE HER.
......?

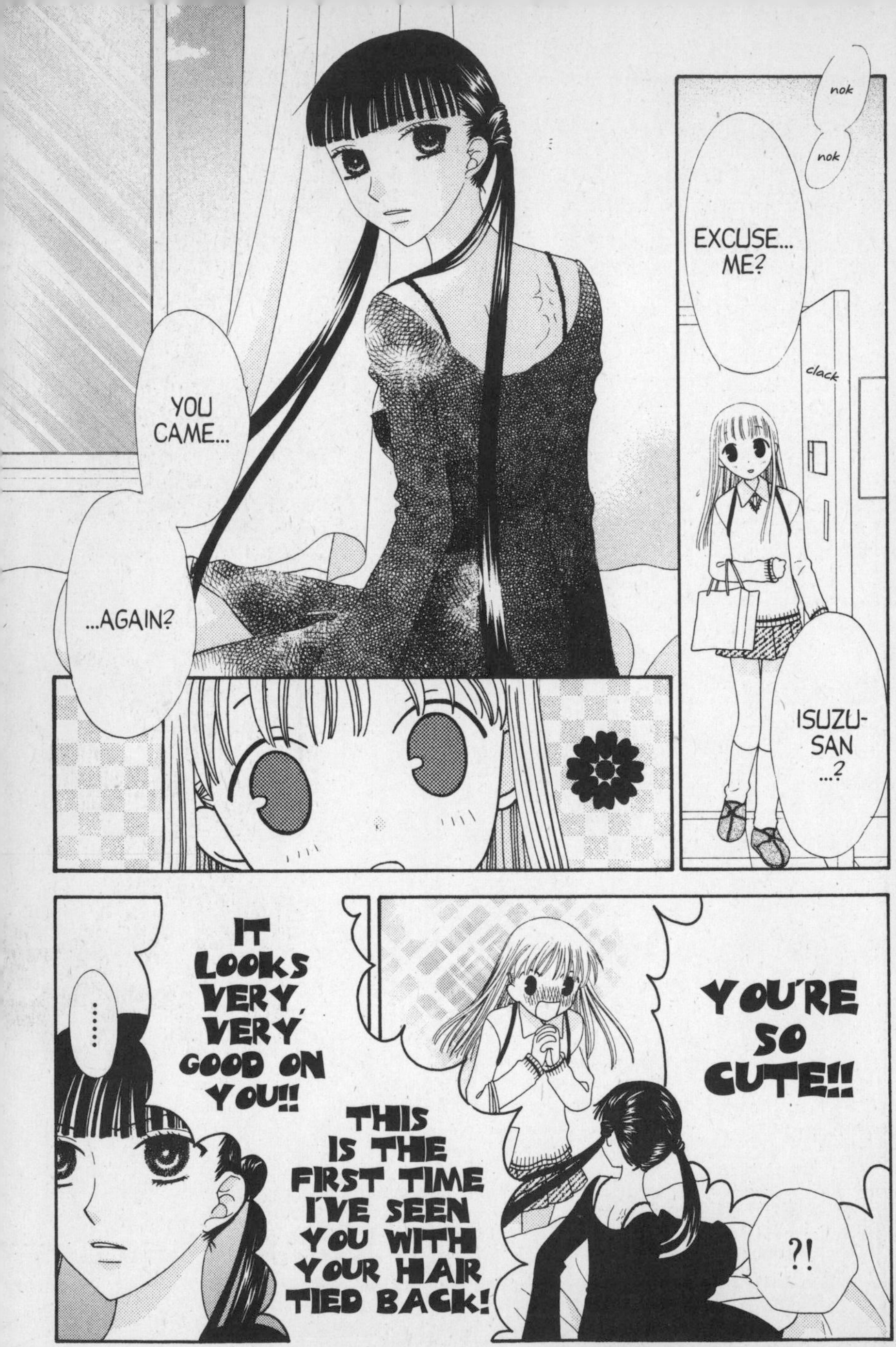
nok
nok
EXCUSE... ME?
clack
ISUZU-SAN ...?
YOU CAME...
...AGAIN?
YOU'RE SO CUTE!!
IT LOOKS VERY, VERY GOOD ON YOU!!
THIS IS THE FIRST TIME I'VE SEEN YOU WITH YOUR HAIR TIED BACK!
?!
......

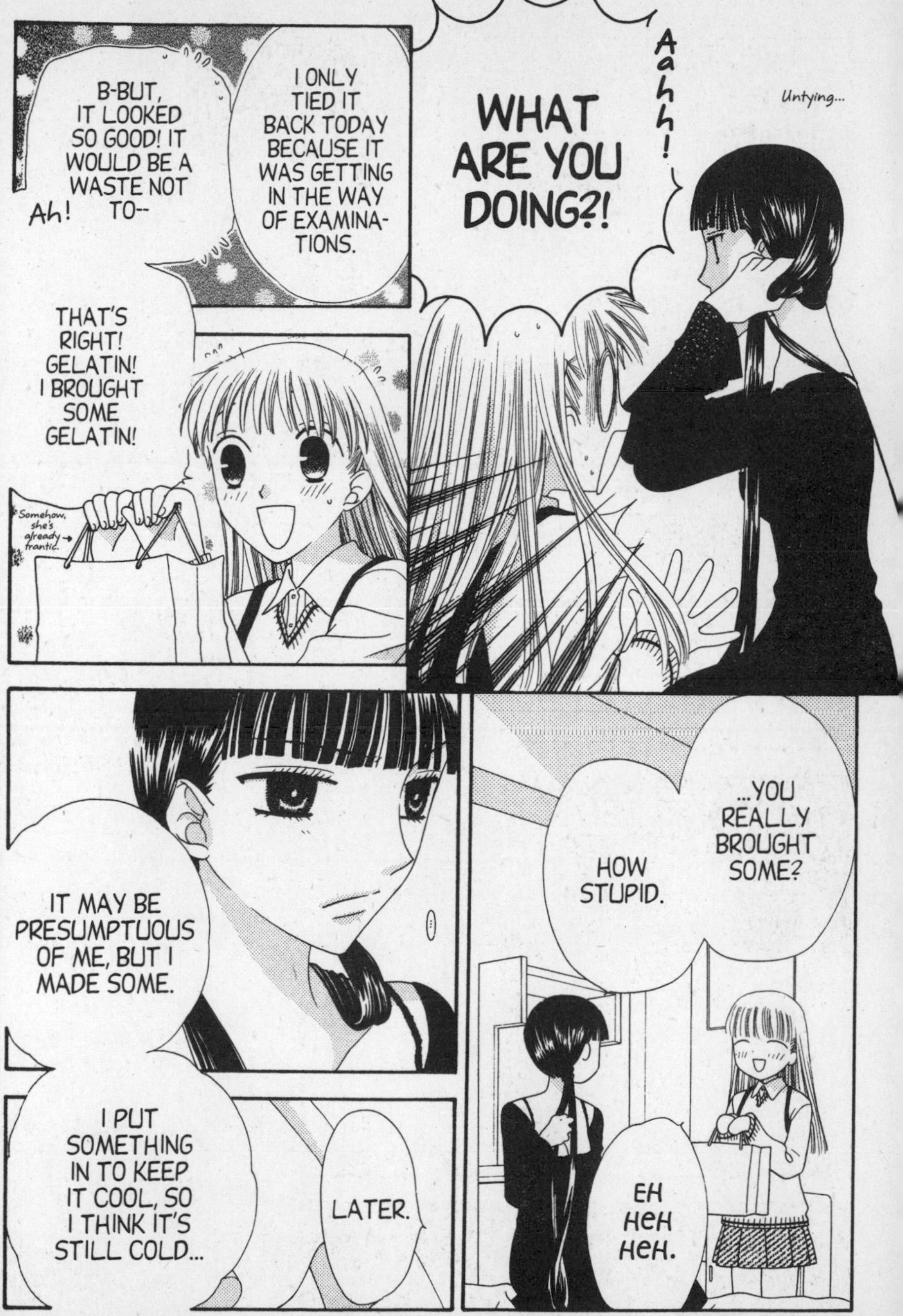
Untying...
Aahh!
WHAT ARE YOU DOING?!
I ONLY TIED IT BACK TODAY BECAUSE IT WAS GETTING IN THE WAY OF EXAMINATIONS.
B-BUT, IT LOOKED SO GOOD! IT WOULD BE A WASTE NOT TO--
Ah!
THAT'S RIGHT! GELATIN! I BROUGHT SOME GELATIN!
Somehow, she's already → frantic.
...YOU REALLY BROUGHT SOME?
HOW STUPID.
EH HEH HEH.
IT MAY BE PRESUMPTUOUS OF ME, BUT I MADE SOME.
LATER.
I PUT SOMETHING IN TO KEEP IT COOL, SO I THINK IT'S STILL COLD...

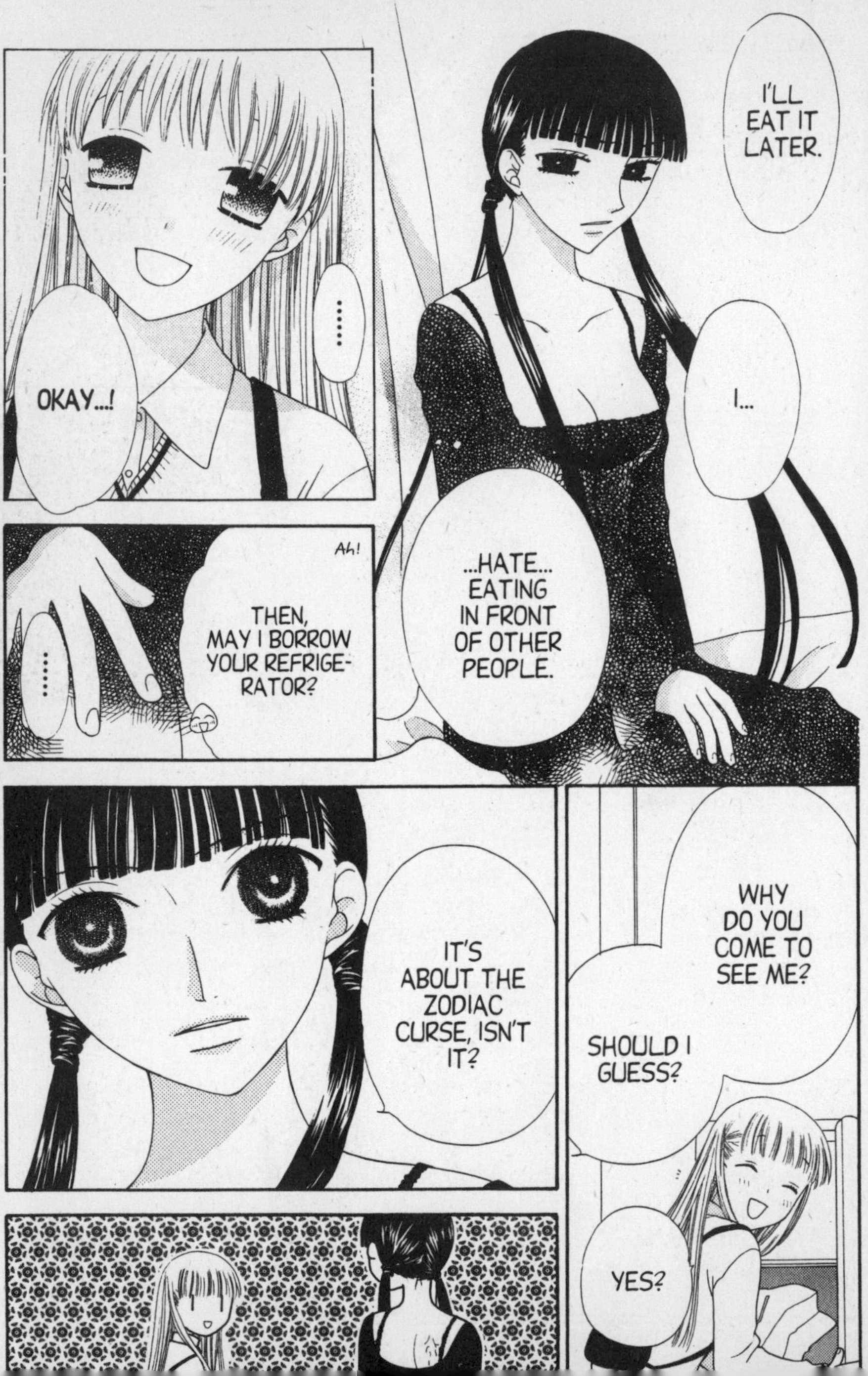
I'LL EAT IT LATER.
I...
...HATE... EATING IN FRONT OF OTHER PEOPLE.
......
OKAY...!
Ah!
THEN, MAY I BORROW YOUR REFRIGE-RATOR?
......
WHY DO YOU COME TO SEE ME?
SHOULD I GUESS?
YES?
IT'S ABOUT THE ZODIAC CURSE, ISN'T IT?

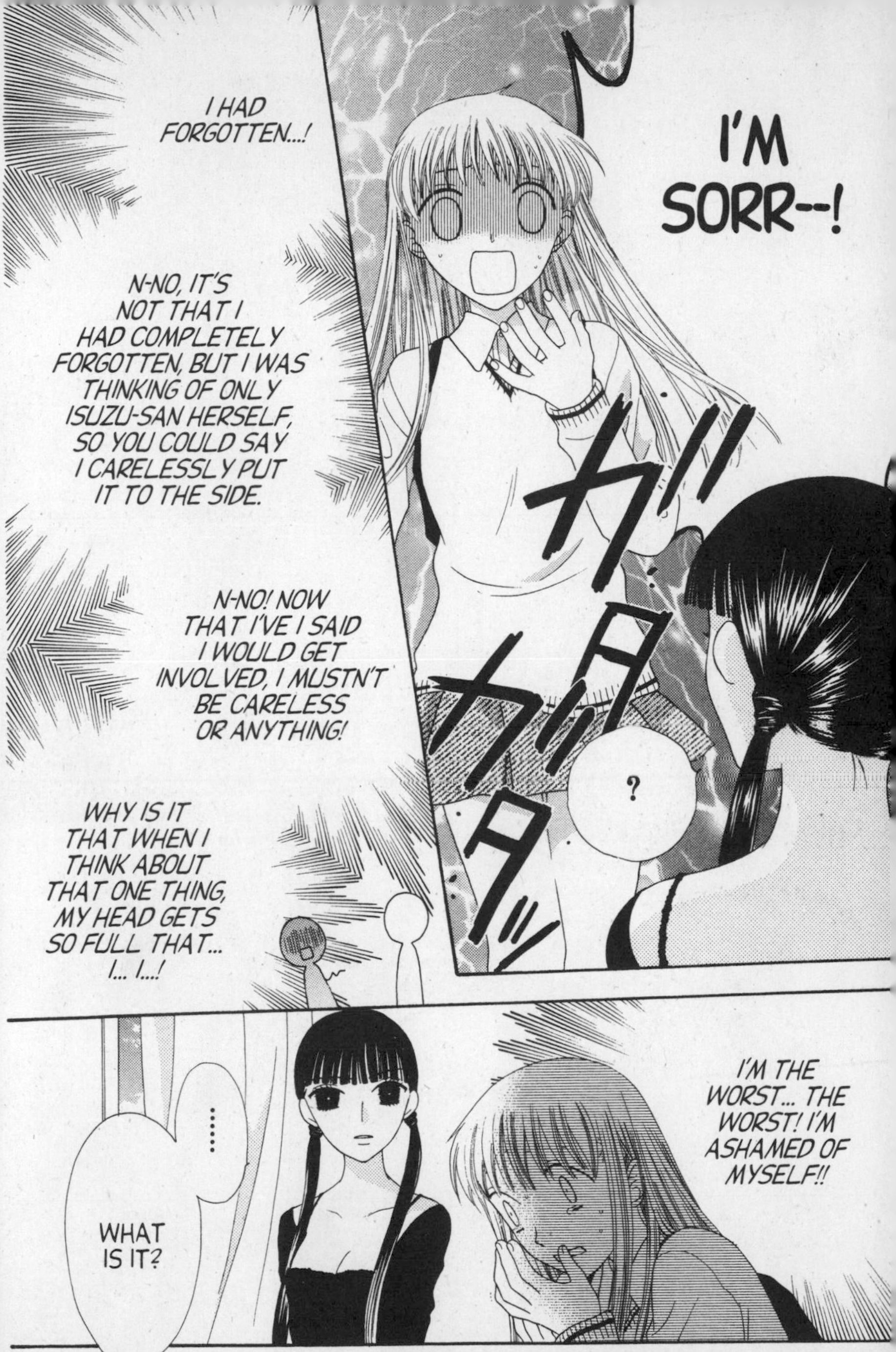
I'M SORR--!
I HAD FORGOTTEN...!
N-NO, IT'S NOT THAT I HAD COMPLETELY FORGOTTEN, BUT I WAS THINKING OF ONLY ISUZU-SAN HERSELF, SO YOU COULD SAY I CARELESSLY PUT IT TO THE SIDE.
N-NO! NOW THAT I'VE I SAID I WOULD GET INVOLVED, I MUSTN'T BE CARELESS OR ANYTHING!
?
WHY IS IT THAT WHEN I THINK ABOUT THAT ONE THING, MY HEAD GETS SO FULL THAT... I... I...!
I'M THE WORST... THE WORST! I'M ASHAMED OF MYSELF!!
......
WHAT IS IT?

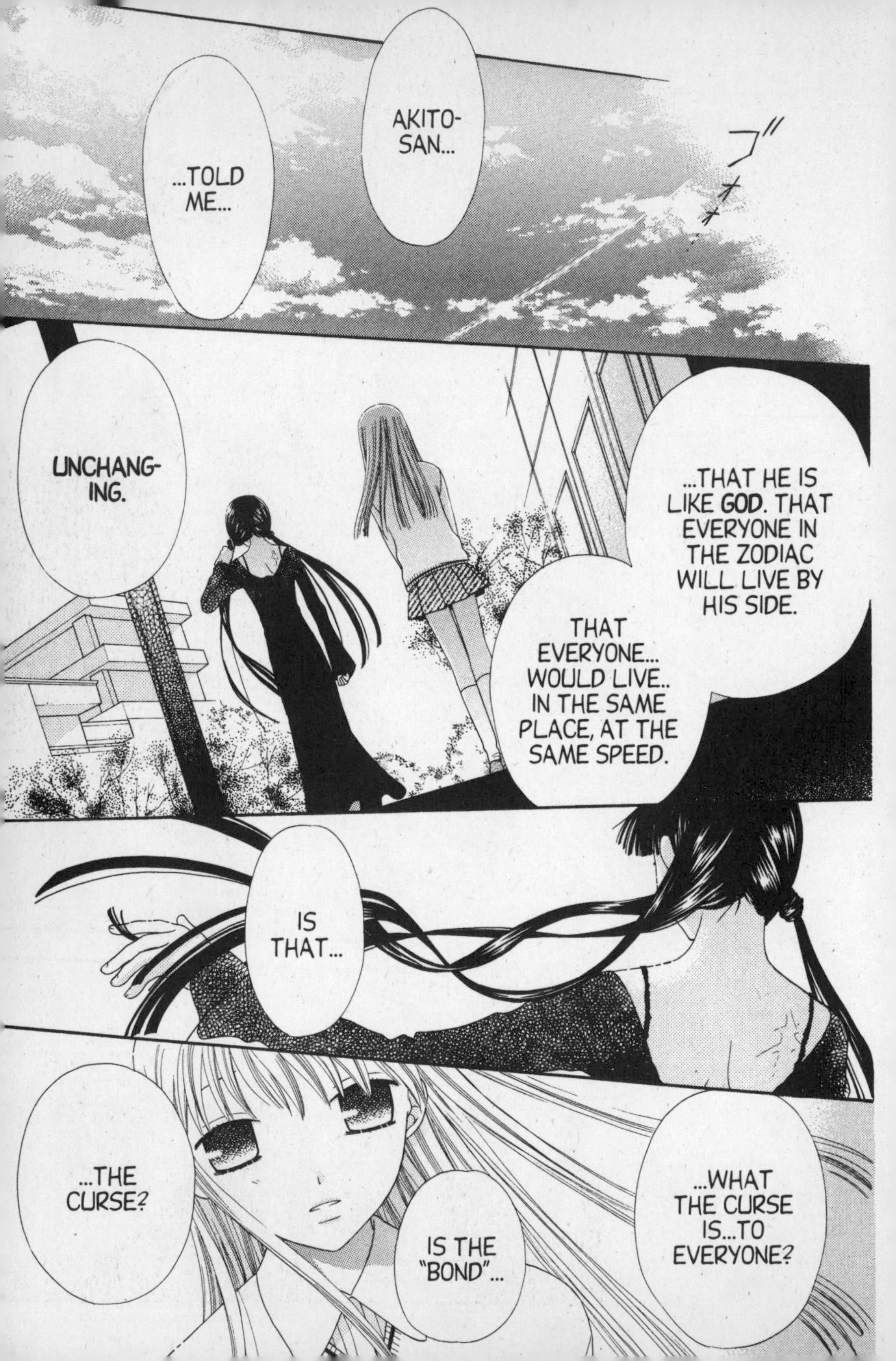

ゴォォ
AKITO-SAN...
...TOLD ME...
...THAT HE IS LIKE **GOD**. THAT EVERYONE IN THE ZODIAC WILL LIVE BY HIS SIDE.
THAT EVERYONE... WOULD LIVE.. IN THE SAME PLACE, AT THE SAME SPEED.
UNCHANGING.
IS THAT...
...WHAT THE CURSE IS...TO EVERYONE?
IS THE "BOND"...
...THE CURSE?

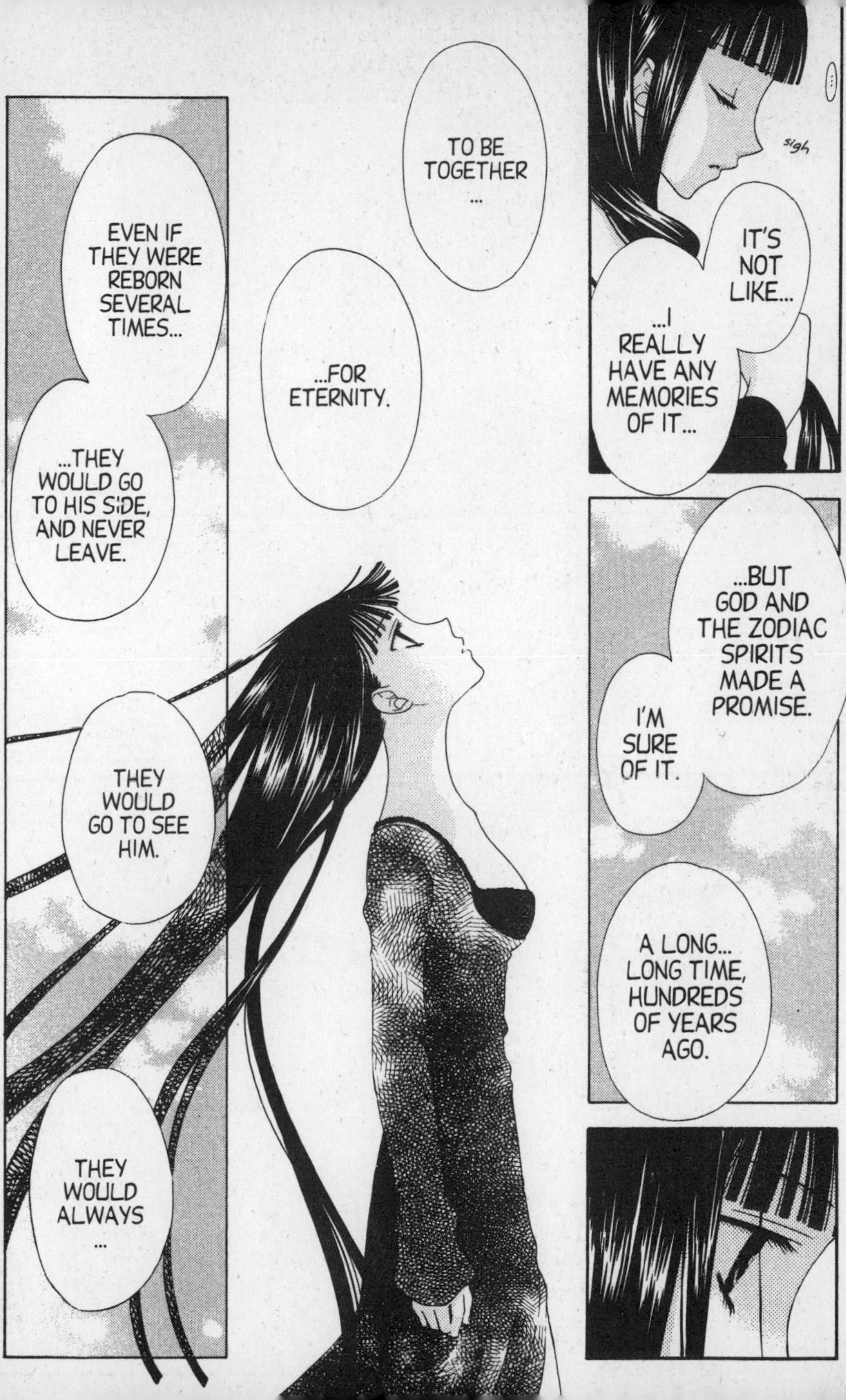
...
sigh
IT'S NOT LIKE...
...I REALLY HAVE ANY MEMORIES OF IT...
...BUT GOD AND THE ZODIAC SPIRITS MADE A PROMISE.
I'M SURE OF IT.
A LONG... LONG TIME, HUNDREDS OF YEARS AGO.
EVEN IF THEY WERE REBORN SEVERAL TIMES...
...THEY WOULD GO TO HIS SIDE, AND NEVER LEAVE.
THEY WOULD GO TO SEE HIM.
THEY WOULD ALWAYS ...
TO BE TOGETHER ...
...FOR ETERNITY.

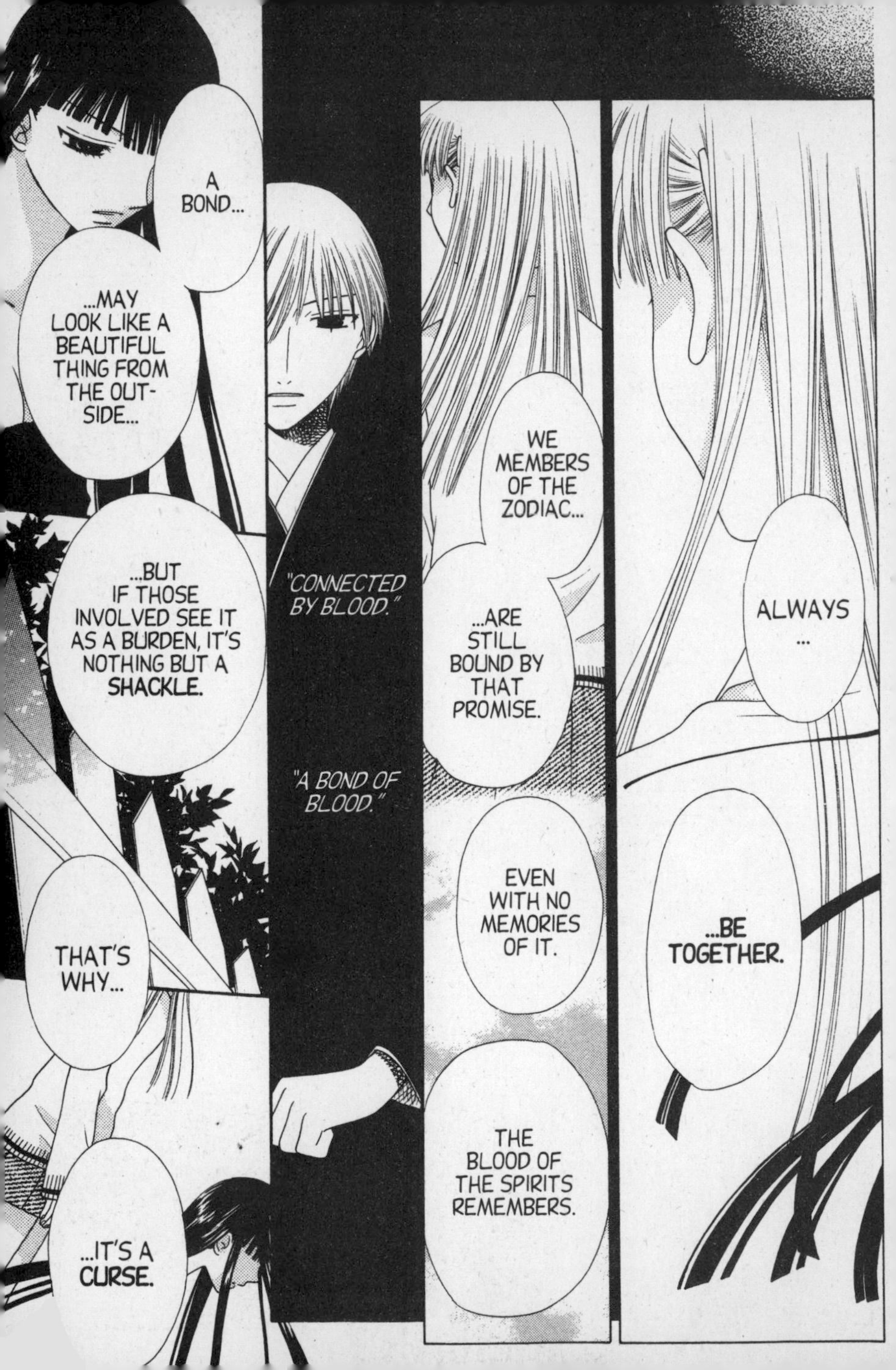
ALWAYS ...
...BE TOGETHER.
WE MEMBERS OF THE ZODIAC...
...ARE STILL BOUND BY THAT PROMISE.
EVEN WITH NO MEMORIES OF IT.
THE BLOOD OF THE SPIRITS REMEMBERS.
"CONNECTED BY BLOOD."
"A BOND OF BLOOD."
A BOND...
...MAY LOOK LIKE A BEAUTIFUL THING FROM THE OUT-SIDE...
...BUT IF THOSE INVOLVED SEE IT AS A BURDEN, IT'S NOTHING BUT A SHACKLE.
THAT'S WHY...
...IT'S A CURSE.

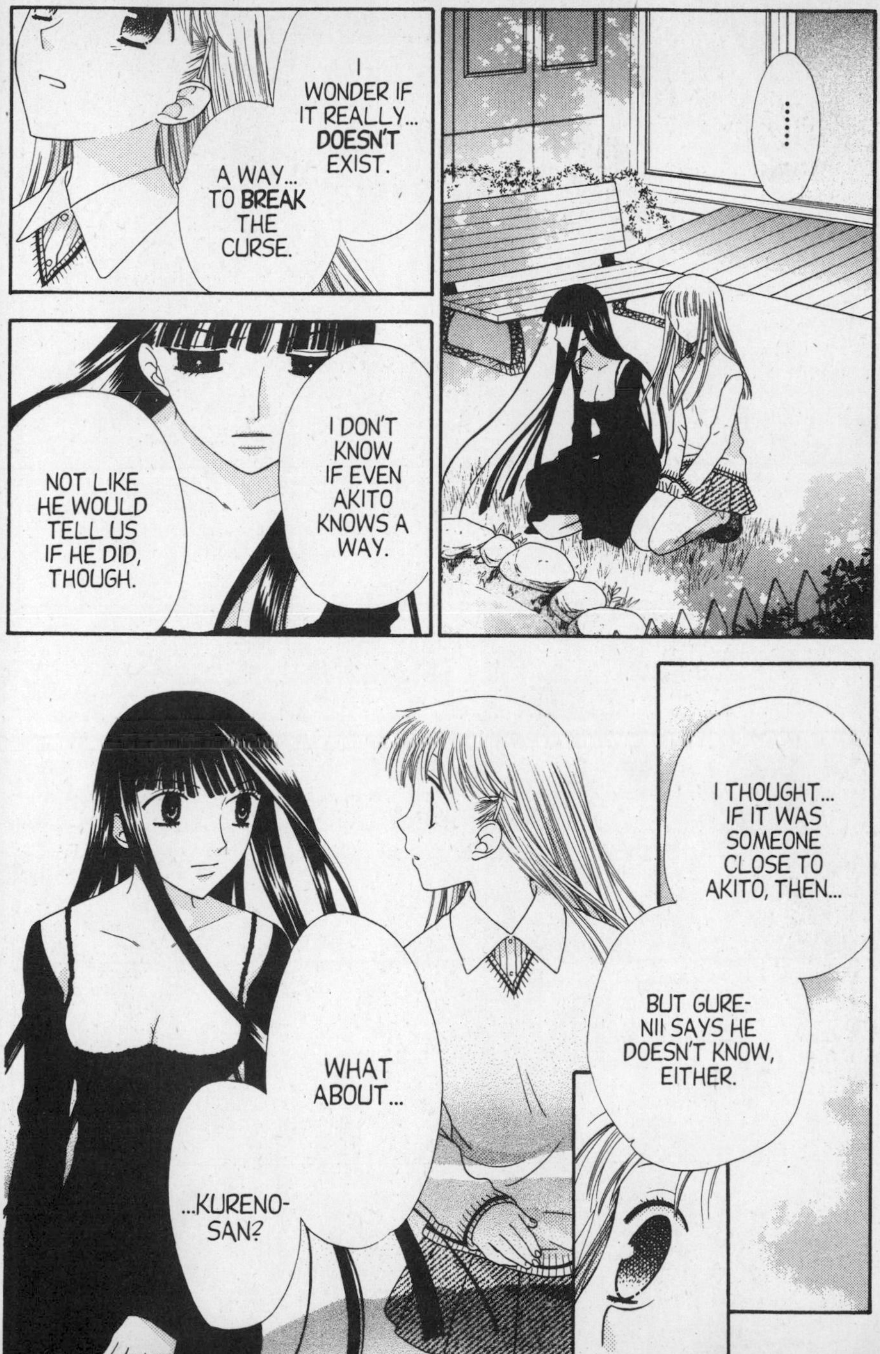
……
I WONDER IF IT REALLY... DOESN'T EXIST.
A WAY... TO BREAK THE CURSE.
I DON'T KNOW IF EVEN AKITO KNOWS A WAY.
NOT LIKE HE WOULD TELL US IF HE DID, THOUGH.
I THOUGHT... IF IT WAS SOMEONE CLOSE TO AKITO, THEN...
BUT GURE-NII SAYS HE DOESN'T KNOW, EITHER.
WHAT ABOUT...
...KURENO-SAN?

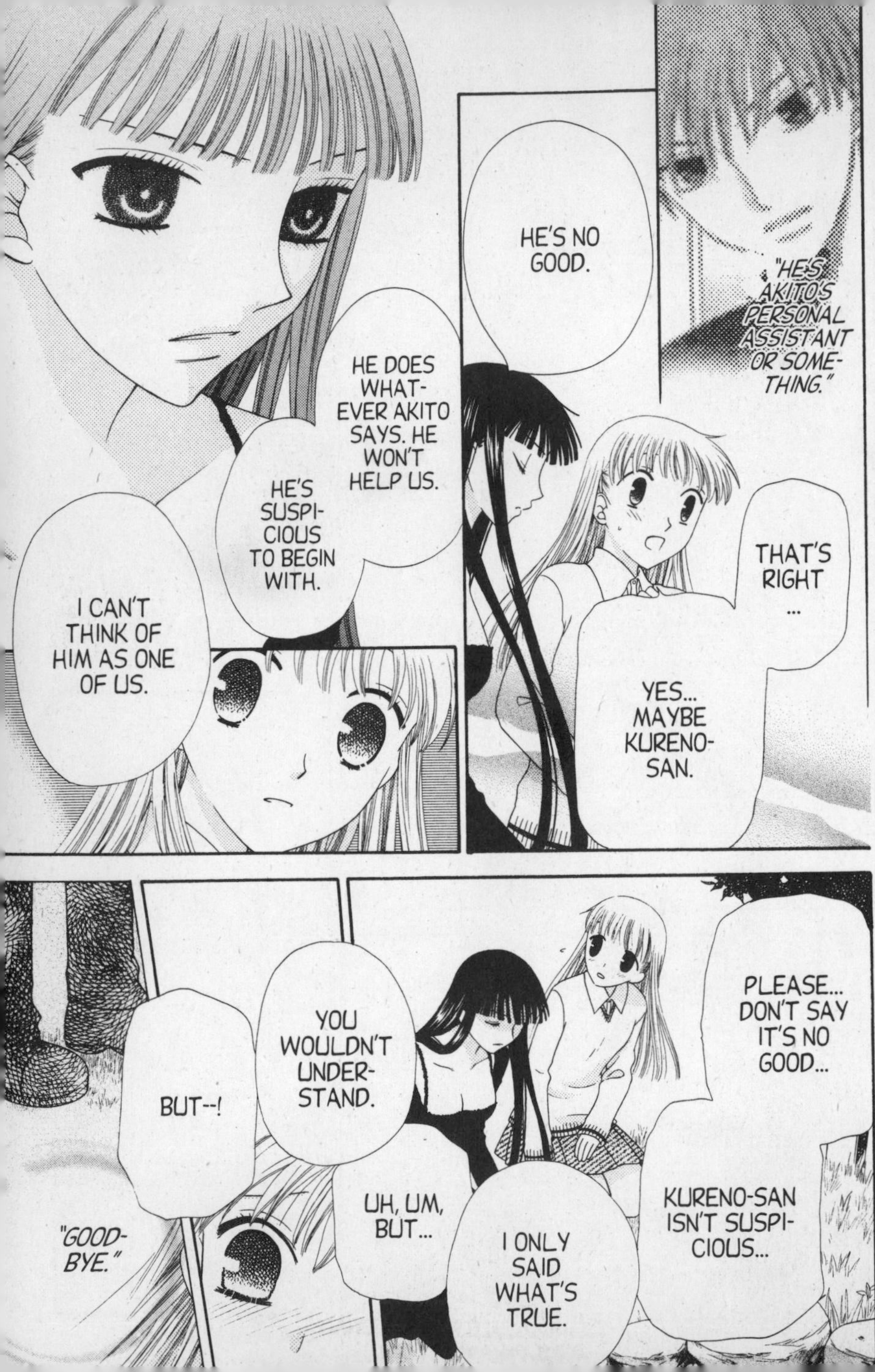
"HE'S AKITO'S PERSONAL ASSISTANT OR SOMETHING."
HE'S NO GOOD.
THAT'S RIGHT ...
YES... MAYBE KURENO-SAN.
HE DOES WHATEVER AKITO SAYS. HE WON'T HELP US.
HE'S SUSPICIOUS TO BEGIN WITH.
I CAN'T THINK OF HIM AS ONE OF US.
PLEASE... DON'T SAY IT'S NO GOOD...
KURENO-SAN ISN'T SUSPICIOUS...
I ONLY SAID WHAT'S TRUE.
UH, UM, BUT...
YOU WOULDN'T UNDERSTAND.
BUT--!
"GOOD-BYE."

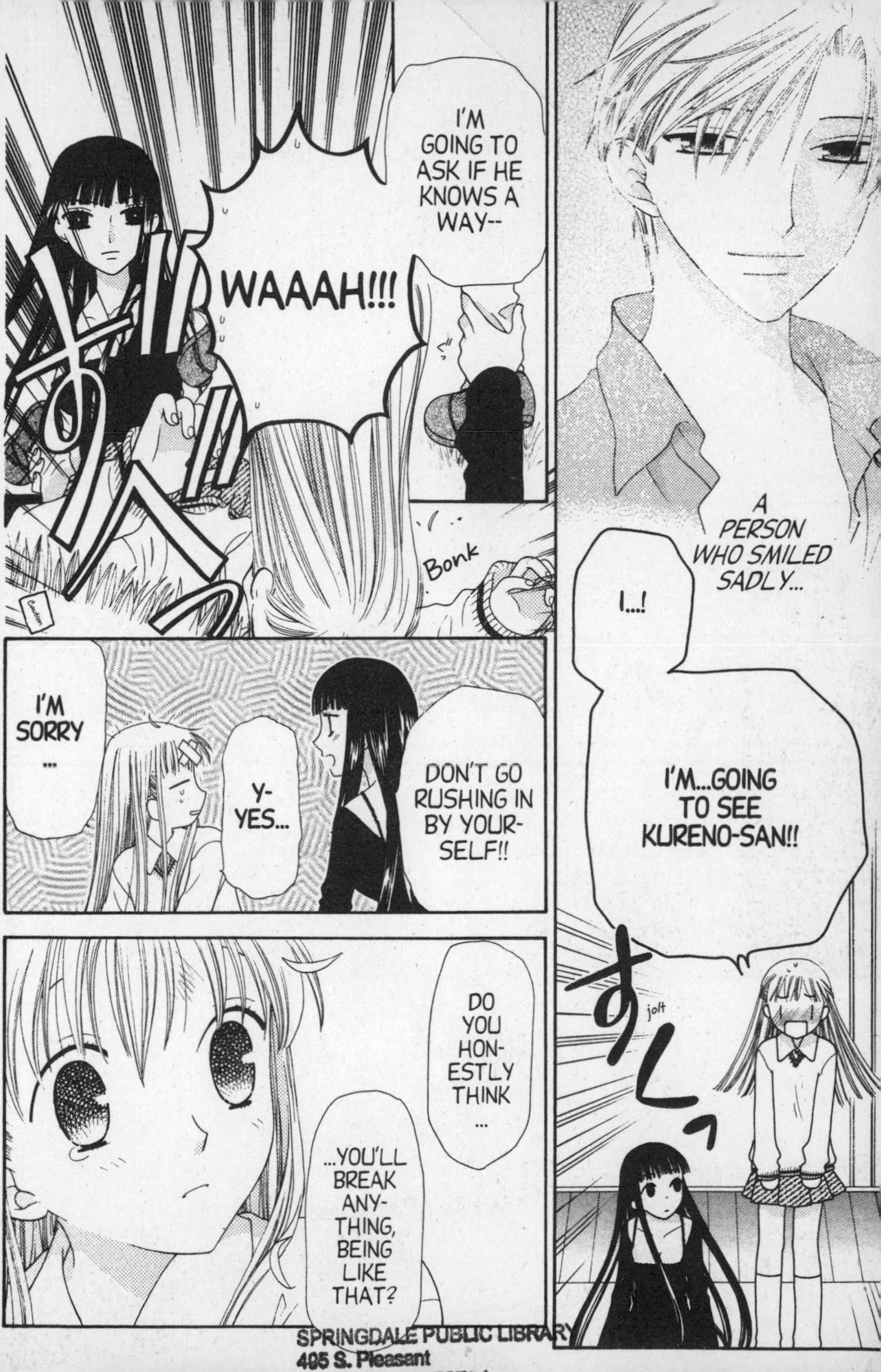
A PERSON WHO SMILED SADLY...
I...!
I'M...GOING TO SEE KURENO-SAN!!
jolt
I'M GOING TO ASK IF HE KNOWS A WAY--
WAAAH!!!
Bonk
DON'T GO RUSHING IN BY YOUR-SELF!!
Y-YES...
I'M SORRY ...
DO YOU HON-ESTLY THINK ...
...YOU'LL BREAK ANY-THING, BEING LIKE THAT?

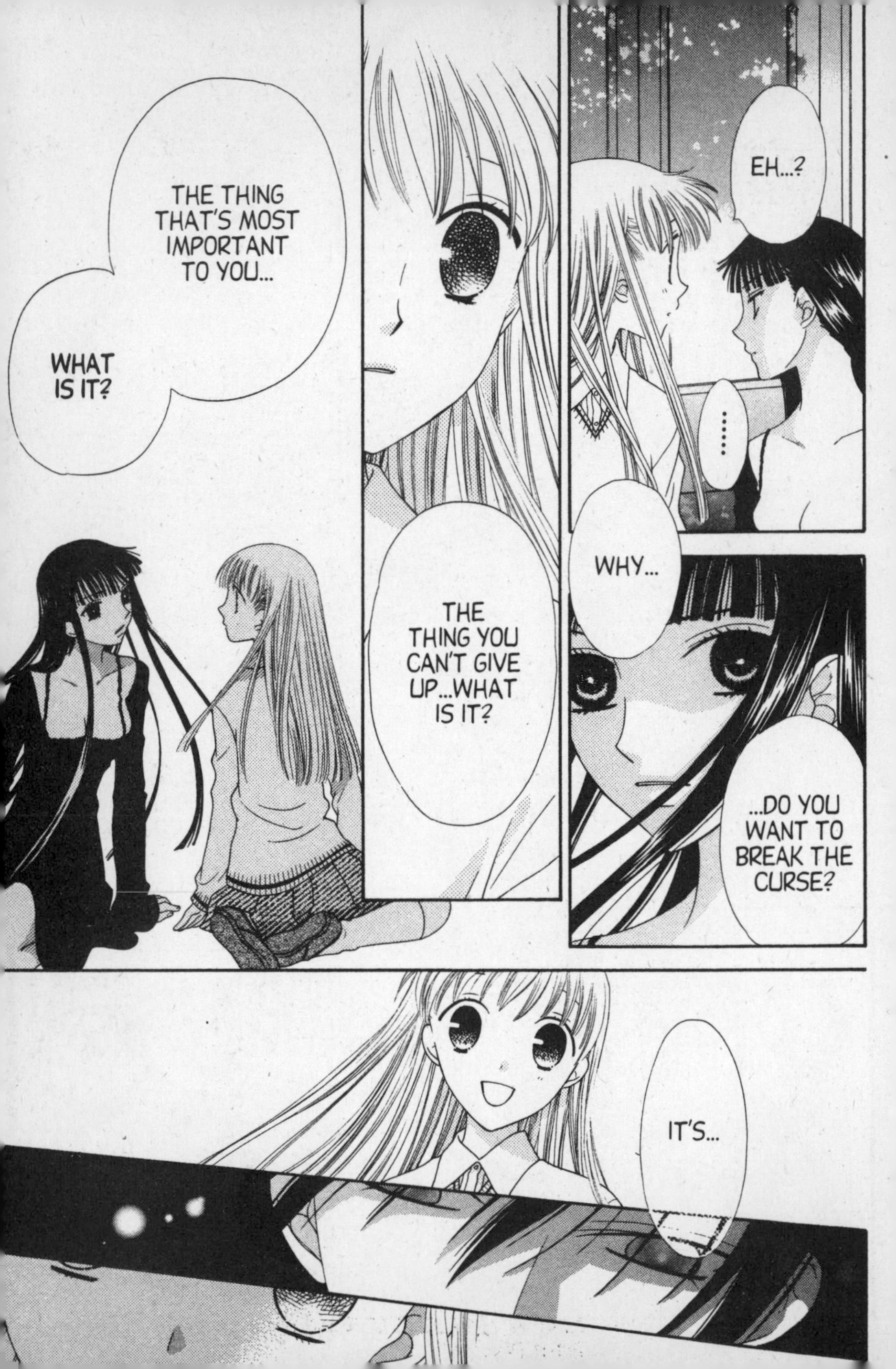
EH...?
......
WHY...
...DO YOU WANT TO BREAK THE CURSE?
THE THING YOU CAN'T GIVE UP...WHAT IS IT?
THE THING THAT'S MOST IMPORTANT TO YOU...
WHAT IS IT?
IT'S...

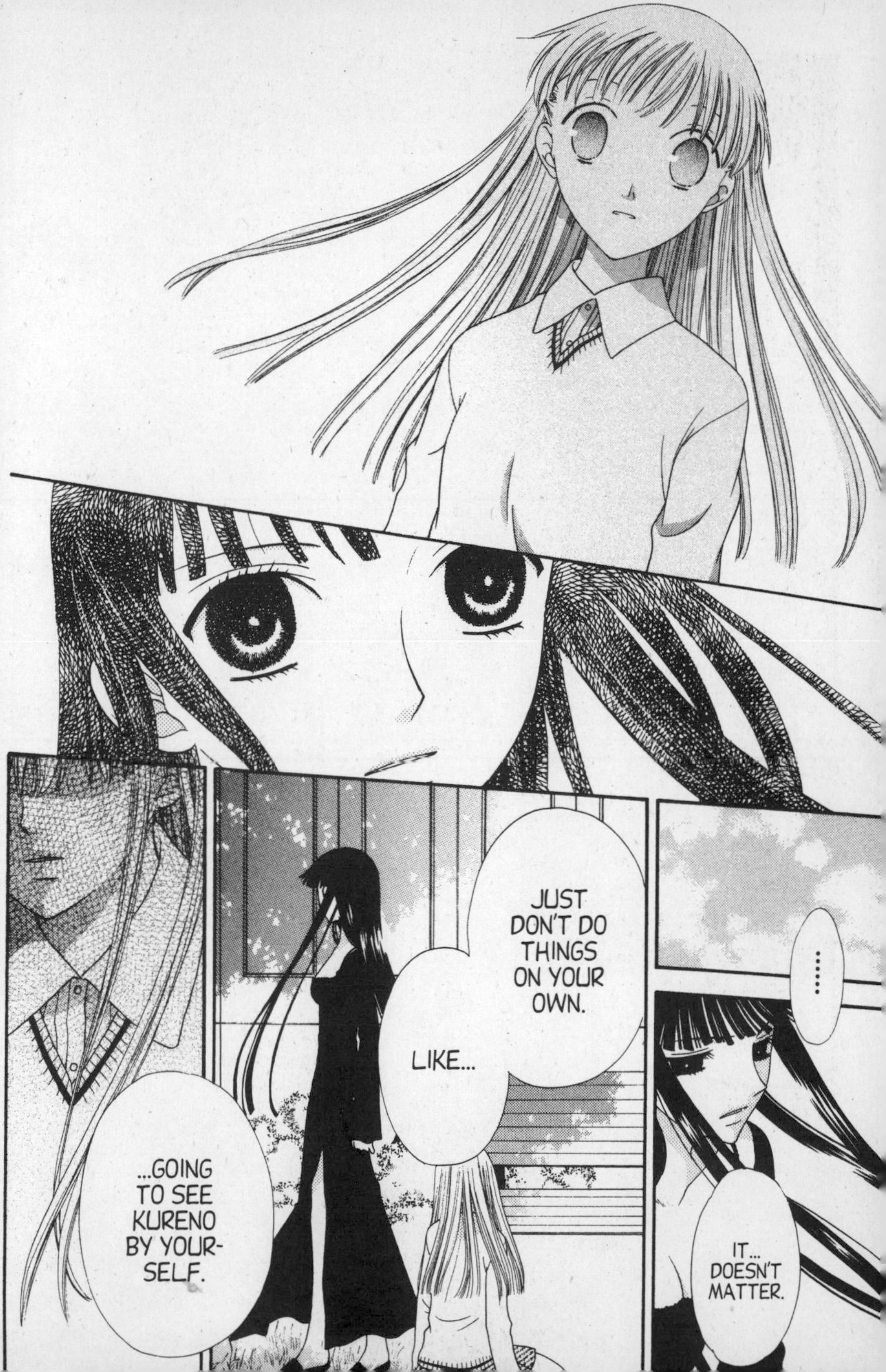
......
IT... DOESN'T MATTER.
JUST DON'T DO THINGS ON YOUR OWN.
LIKE...
...GOING TO SEE KURENO BY YOURSELF.

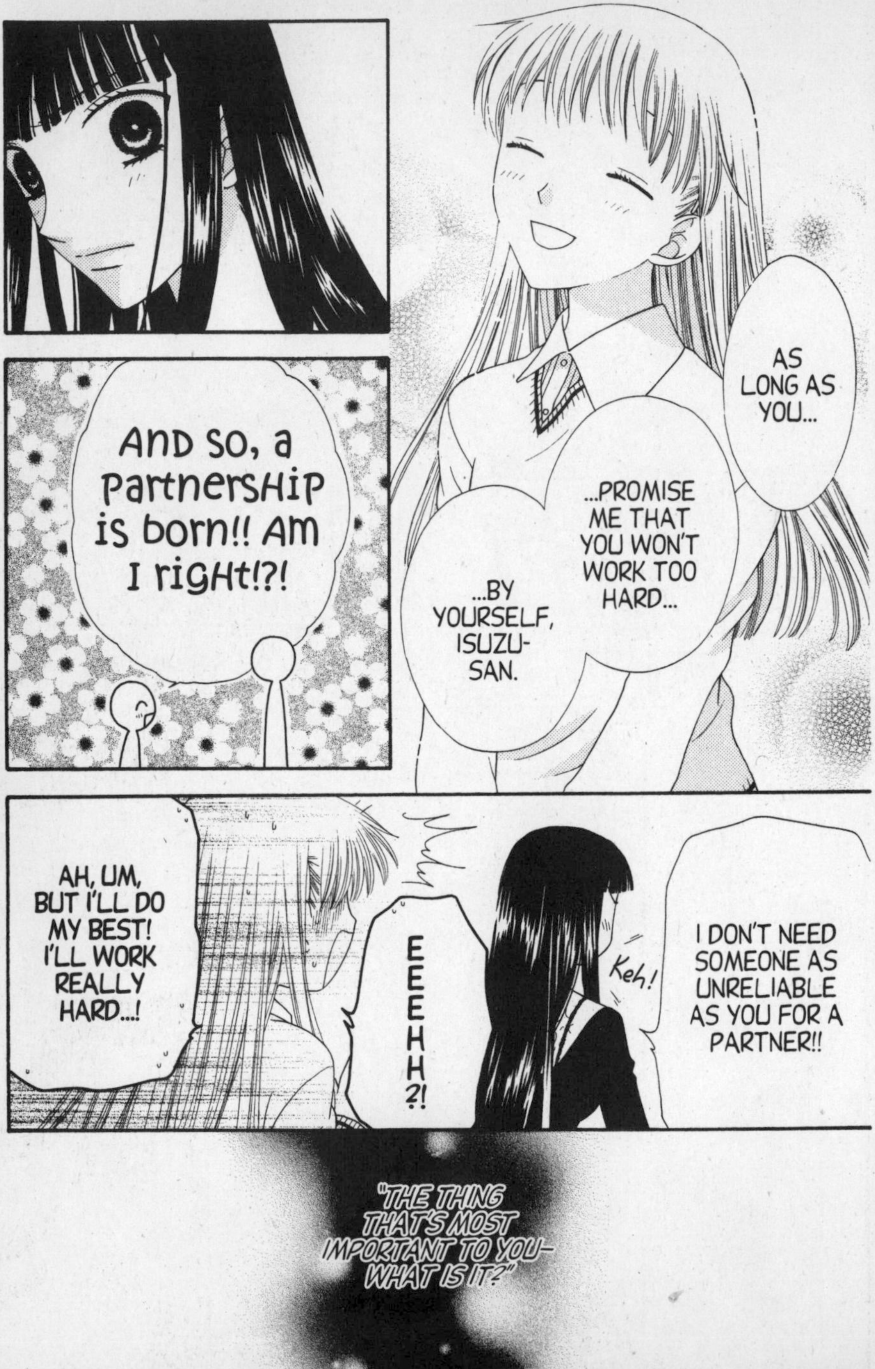
AS LONG AS YOU...
...PROMISE ME THAT YOU WON'T WORK TOO HARD...
...BY YOURSELF, ISUZU-SAN.
And so, a partnership is born!! Am I right!?!
I DON'T NEED SOMEONE AS UNRELIABLE AS YOU FOR A PARTNER!!
Keh!
EEEHH?!
AH, UM, BUT I'LL DO MY BEST! I'LL WORK REALLY HARD...!
"THE THING THAT'S MOST IMPORTANT TO YOU—WHAT IS IT?"

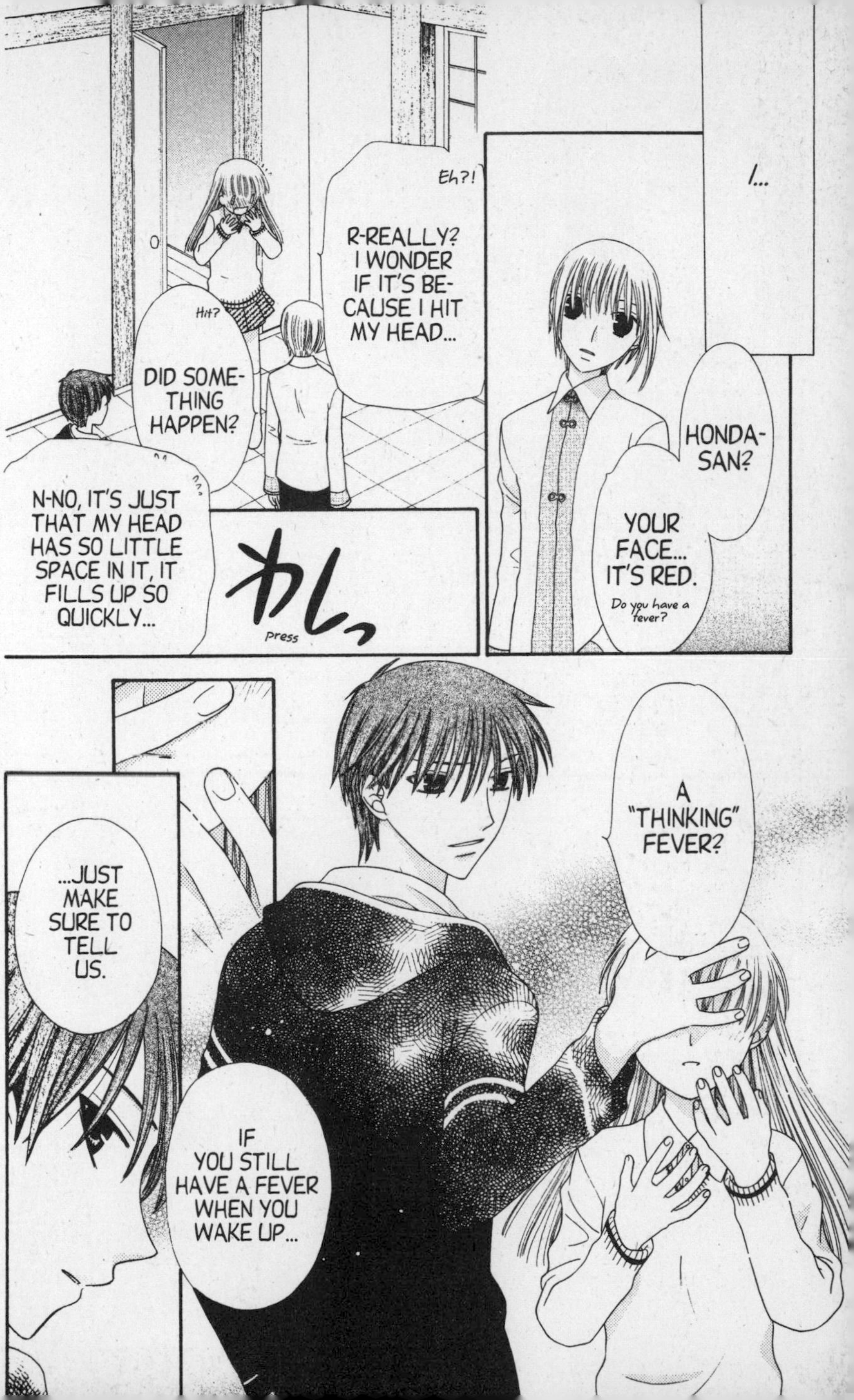
I...
HONDA-SAN?
YOUR FACE... IT'S RED.
Do you have a fever?
Eh?!
R-REALLY? I WONDER IF IT'S BE-CAUSE I HIT MY HEAD...
Hit?
DID SOME-THING HAPPEN?
N-NO, IT'S JUST THAT MY HEAD HAS SO LITTLE SPACE IN IT, IT FILLS UP SO QUICKLY...
press
A "THINKING" FEVER?
IF YOU STILL HAVE A FEVER WHEN YOU WAKE UP...
...JUST MAKE SURE TO TELL US.

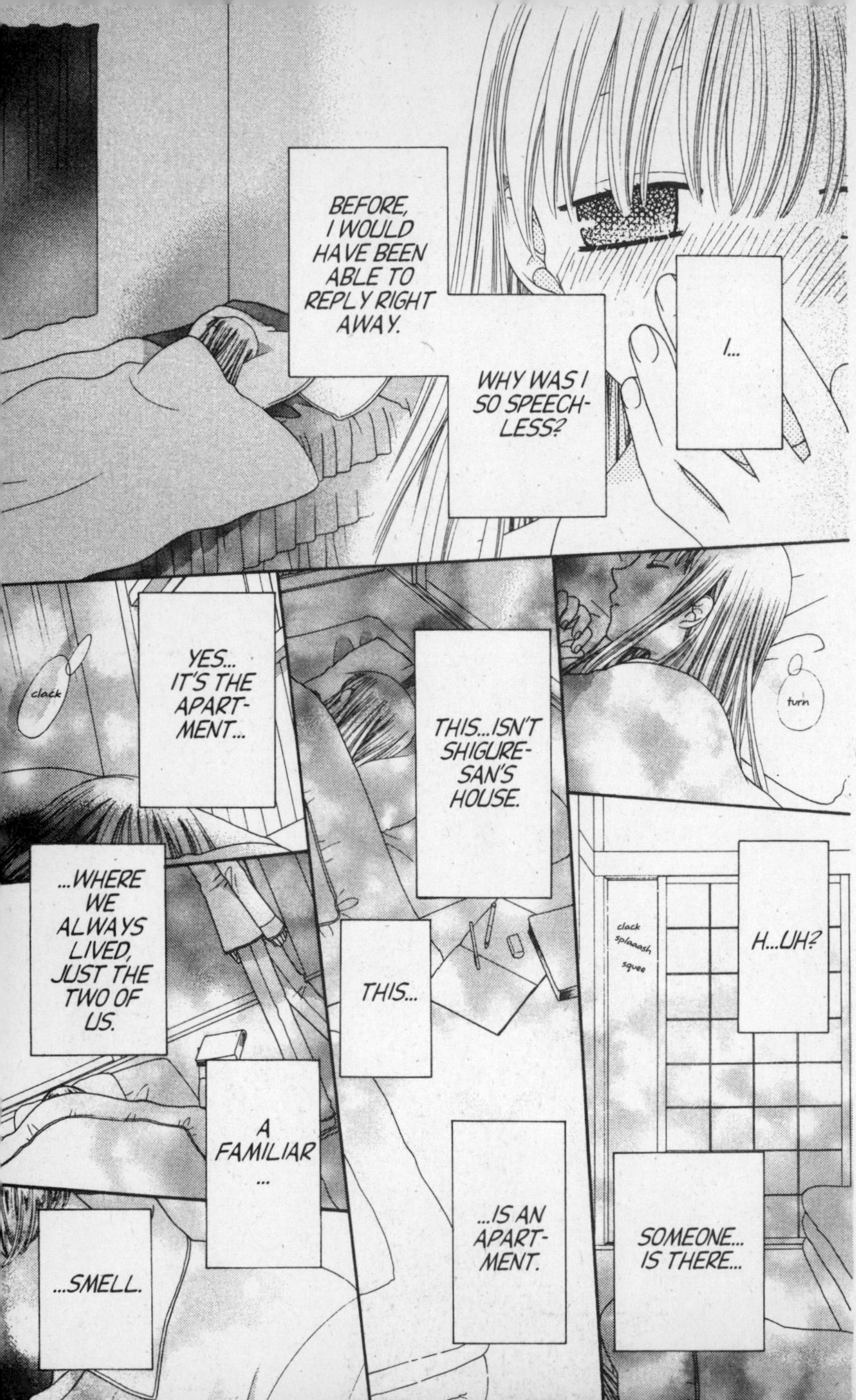
I...
WHY WAS I SO SPEECHLESS?
BEFORE, I WOULD HAVE BEEN ABLE TO REPLY RIGHT AWAY.
turn
H...UH?
clack splaaash squee
SOMEONE... IS THERE...
THIS...ISN'T SHIGURE-SAN'S HOUSE.
THIS...
...IS AN APARTMENT.
clack
YES... IT'S THE APARTMENT...
...WHERE WE ALWAYS LIVED, JUST THE TWO OF US.
A FAMILIAR...
...SMELL.

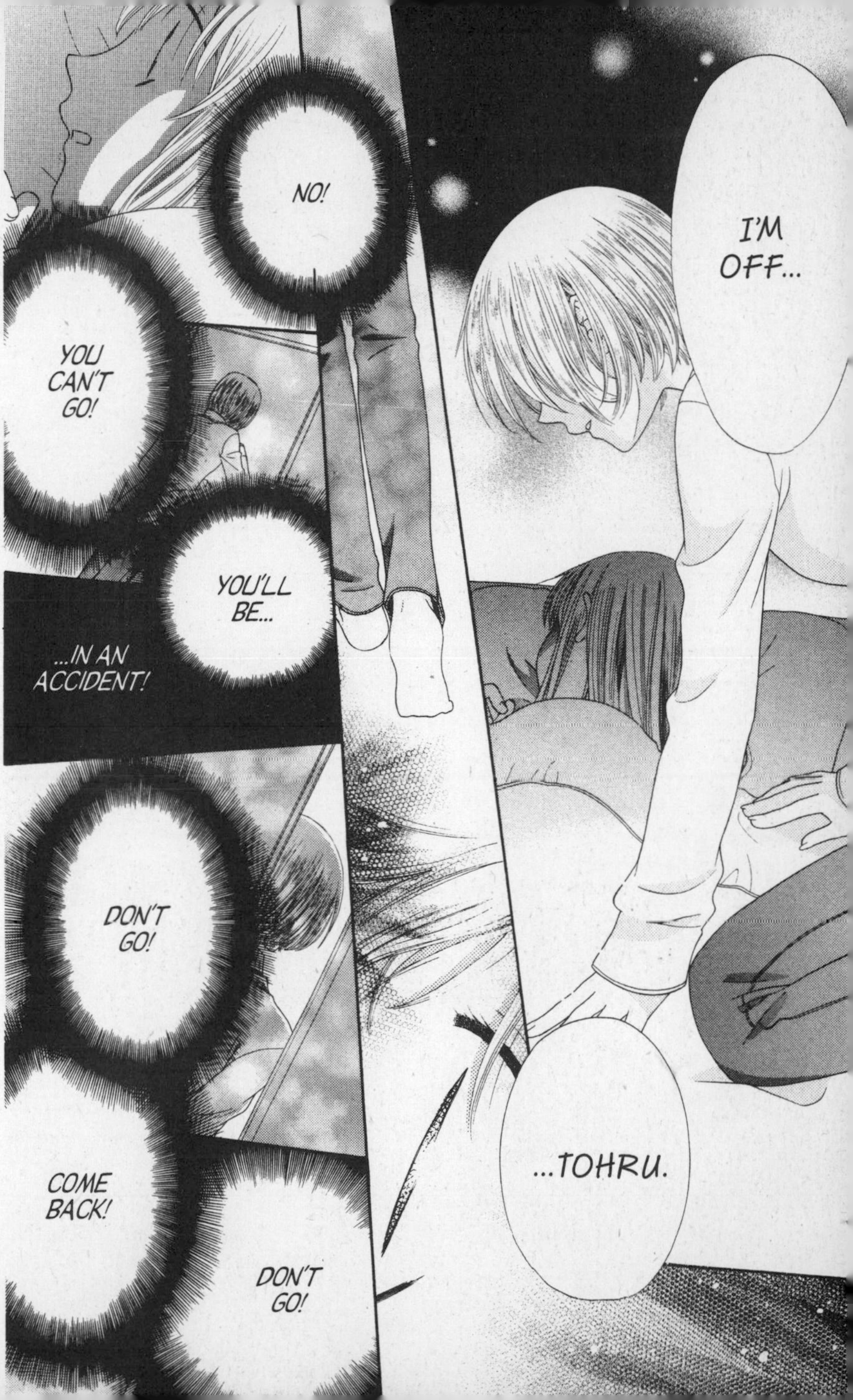
I'M OFF...
...TOHRU.
NO!
YOU CAN'T GO!
YOU'LL BE...
...IN AN ACCIDENT!
DON'T GO!
COME BACK!
DON'T GO!

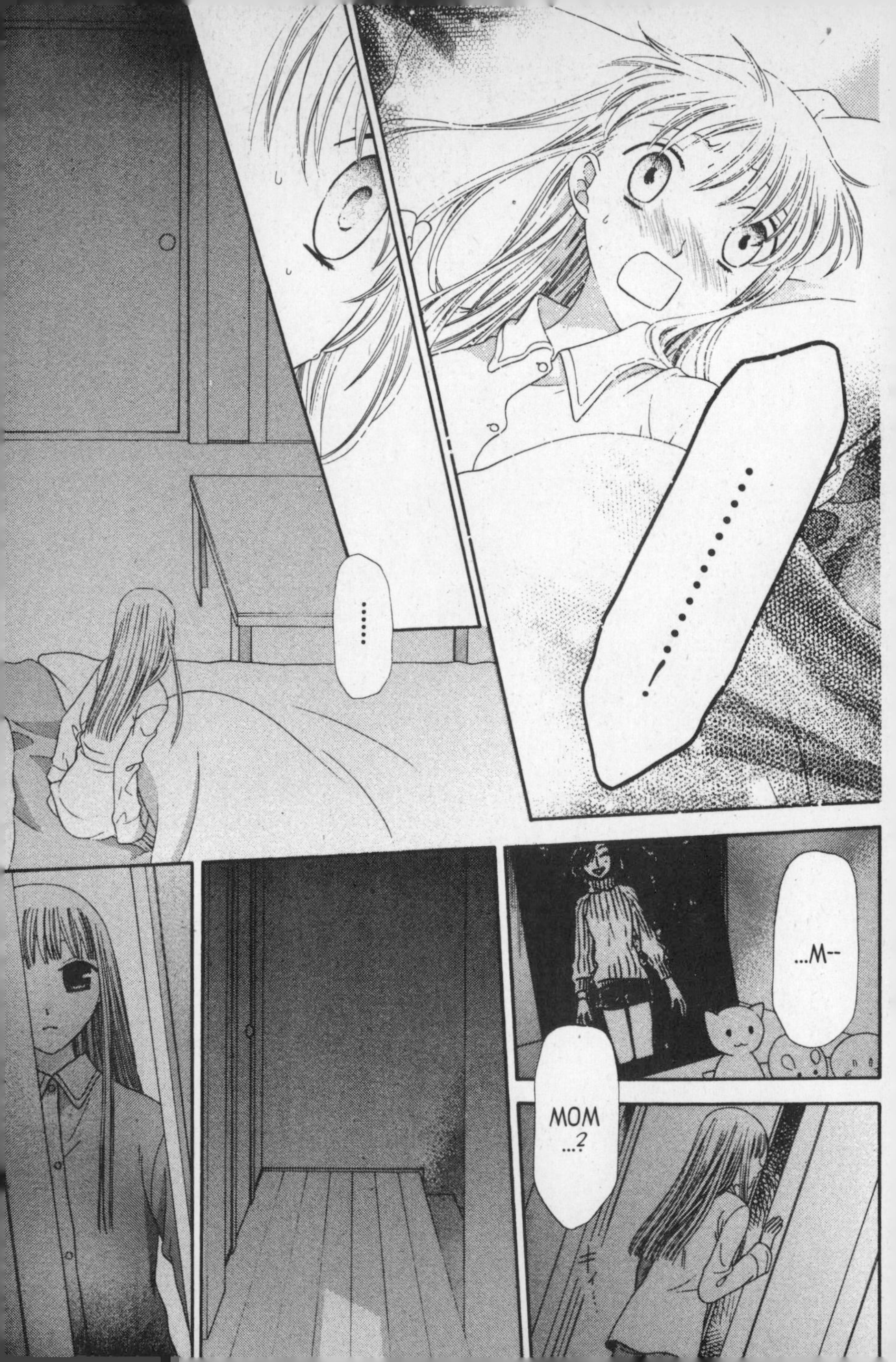
..........!
......
...M--
MOM ...?

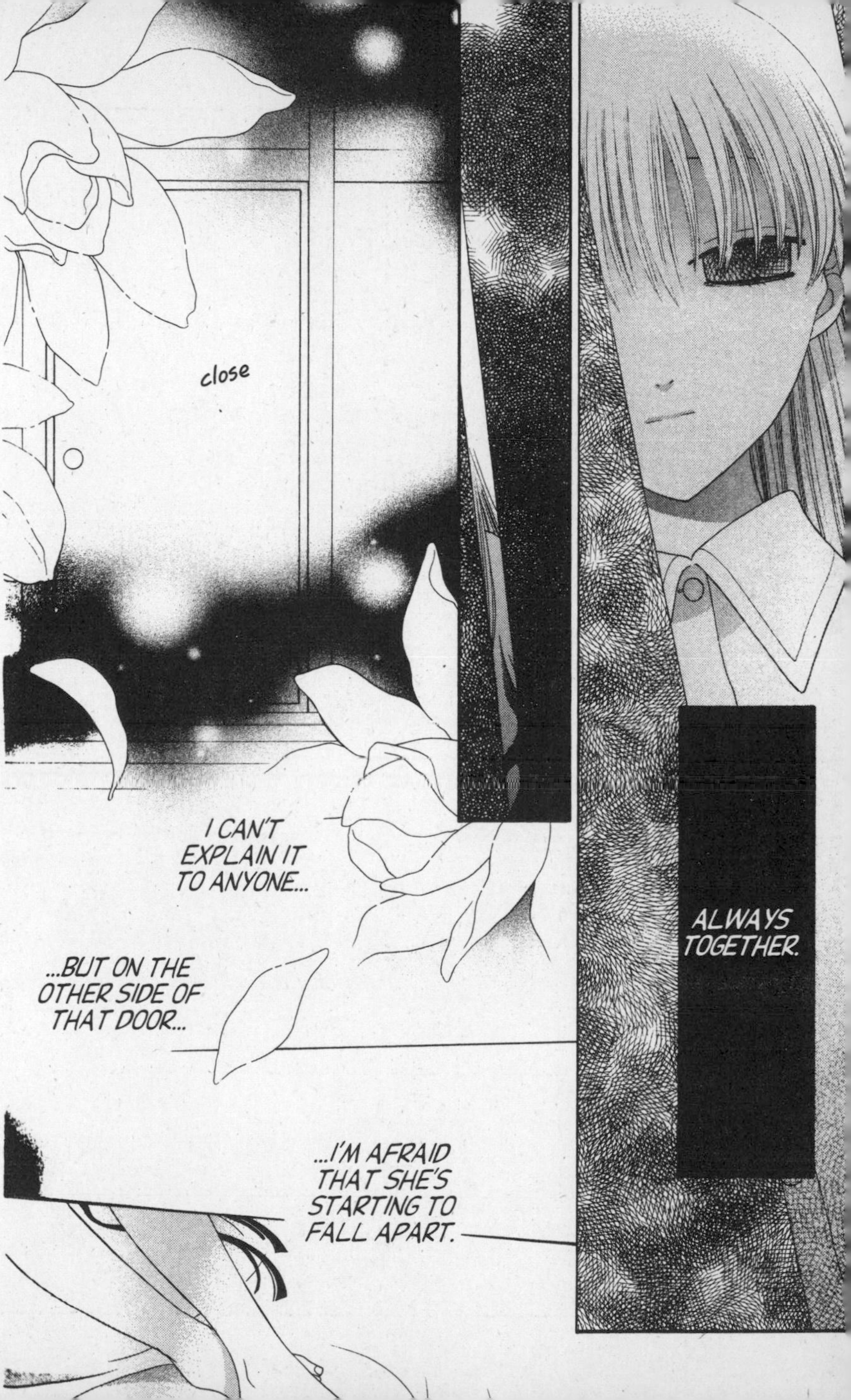
ALWAYS TOGETHER.
close
I CAN'T EXPLAIN IT TO ANYONE...
...BUT ON THE OTHER SIDE OF THAT DOOR...
...I'M AFRAID THAT SHE'S STARTING TO FALL APART.

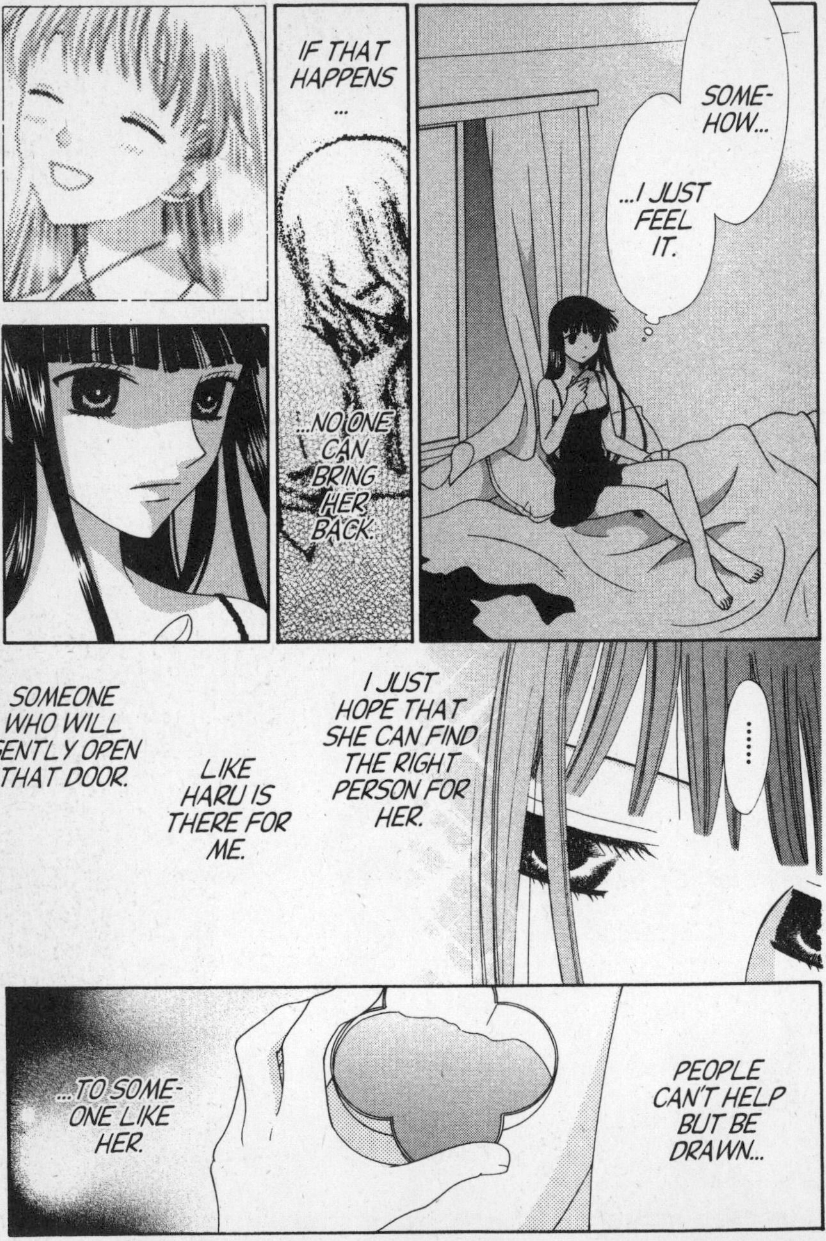
SOME-HOW...
...I JUST FEEL IT.
IF THAT HAPPENS ...
...NO ONE CAN BRING HER BACK.
......
I JUST HOPE THAT SHE CAN FIND THE RIGHT PERSON FOR HER.
LIKE HARU IS THERE FOR ME.
SOMEONE WHO WILL GENTLY OPEN THAT DOOR.
PEOPLE CAN'T HELP BUT BE DRAWN...
...TO SOME-ONE LIKE HER.

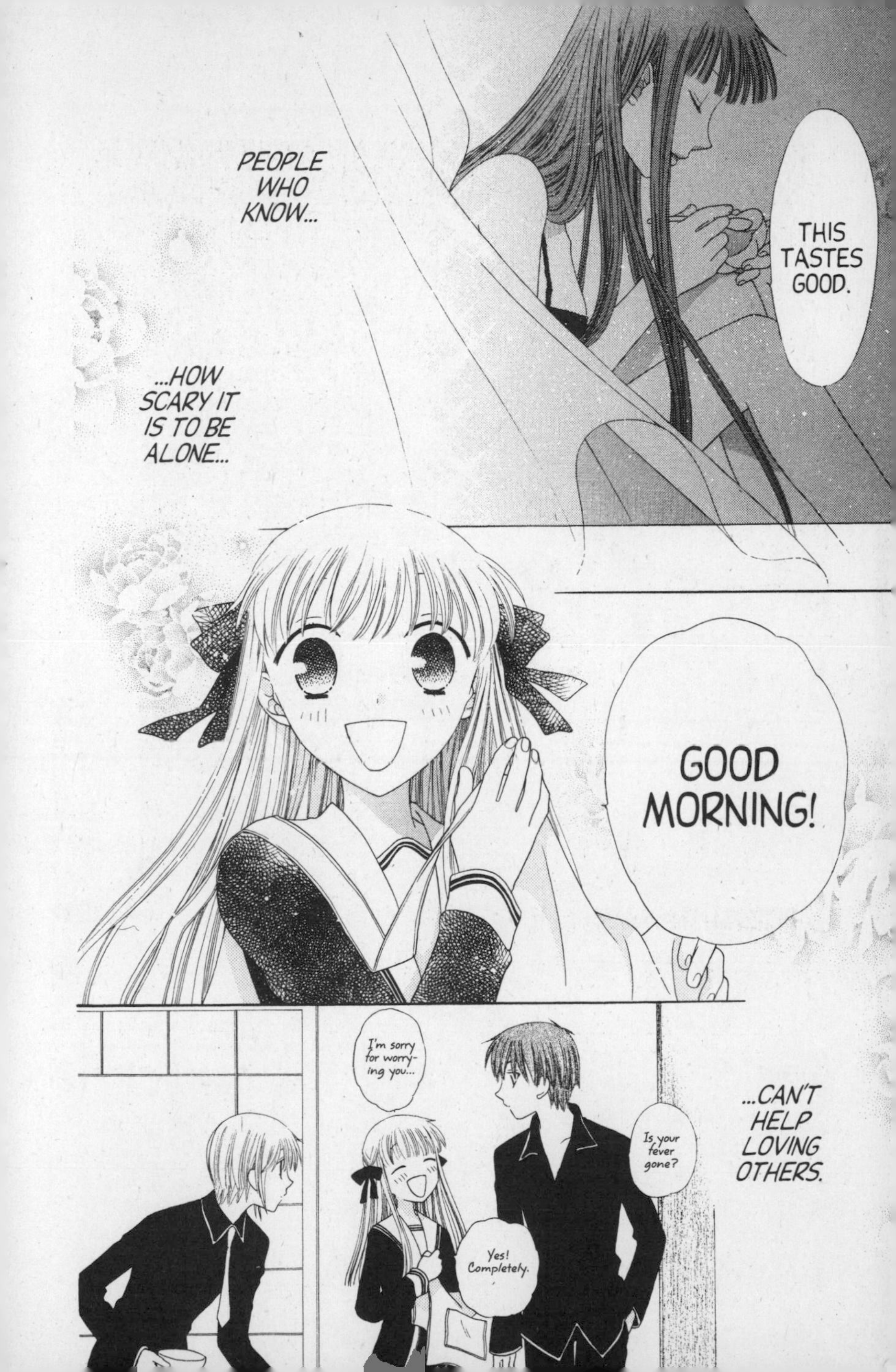
THIS TASTES GOOD.
PEOPLE WHO KNOW...
...HOW SCARY IT IS TO BE ALONE...
GOOD MORNING!
I'm sorry for worrying you...
Is your fever gone?
Yes! Completely.
...CAN'T HELP LOVING OTHERS.

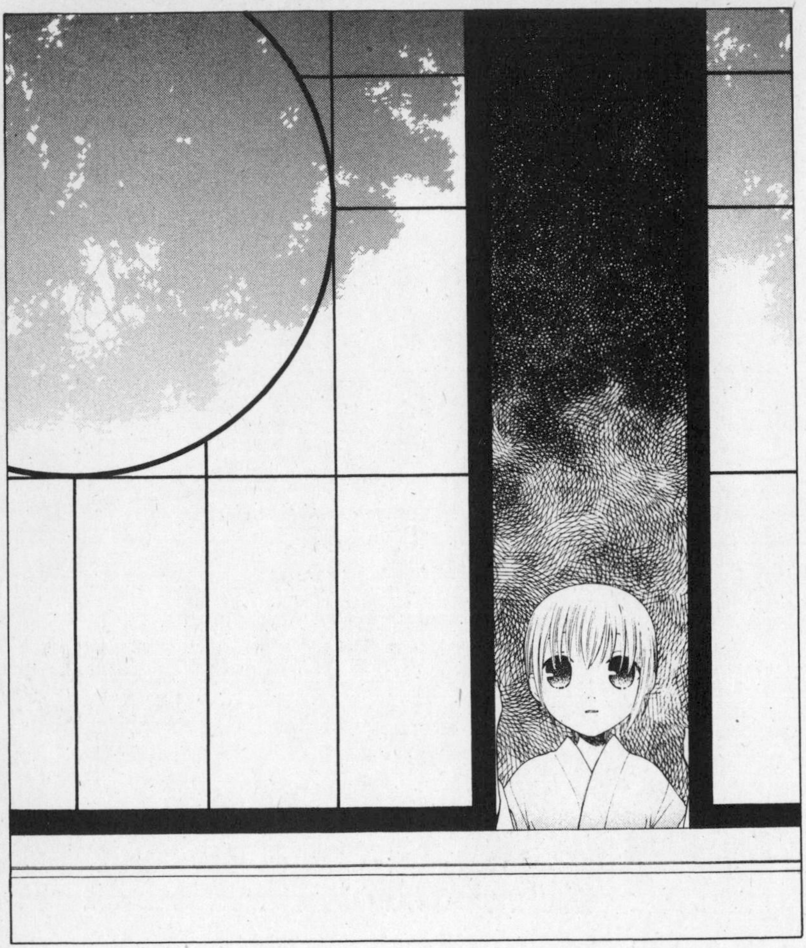

Chapter 83

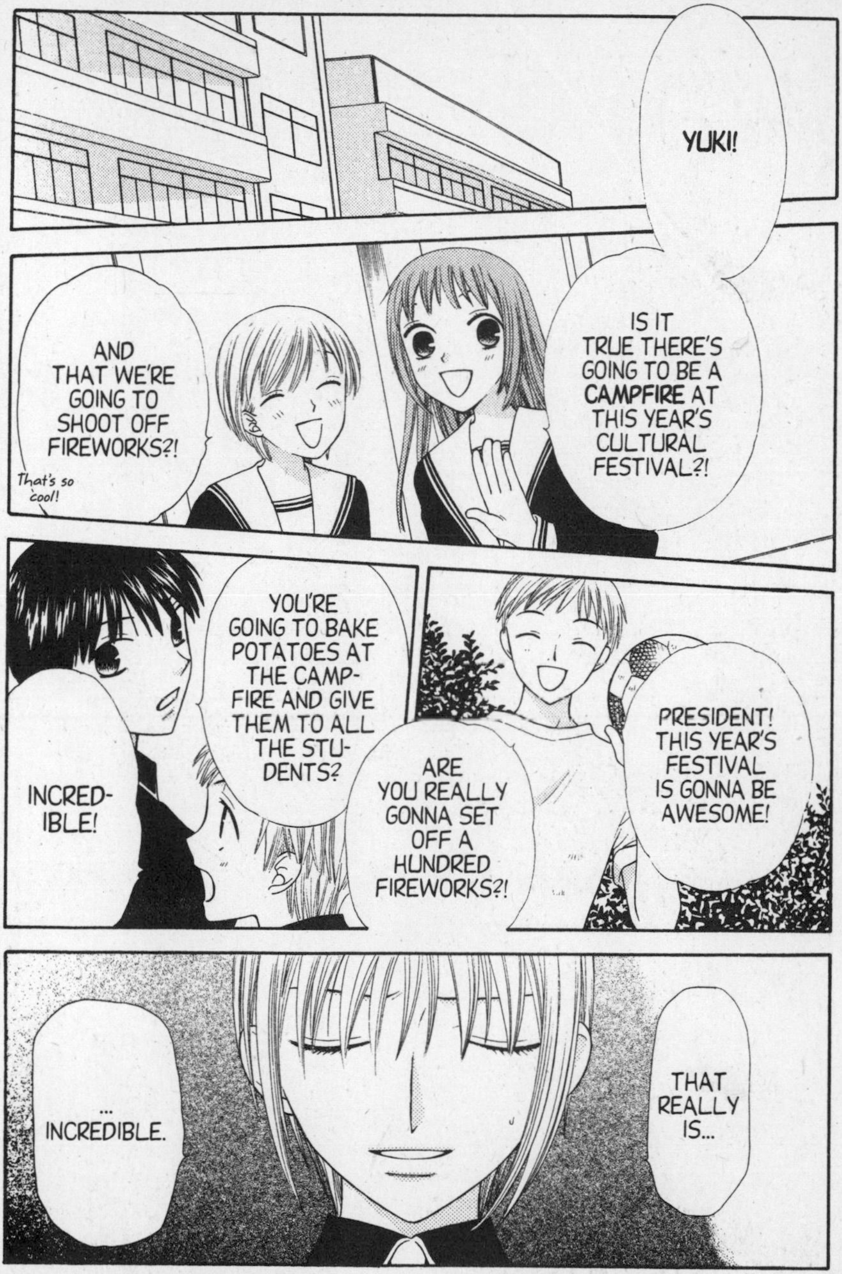
YUKI!
IS IT TRUE THERE'S GOING TO BE A CAMPFIRE AT THIS YEAR'S CULTURAL FESTIVAL?!
AND THAT WE'RE GOING TO SHOOT OFF FIREWORKS?!
That's so cool!
PRESIDENT! THIS YEAR'S FESTIVAL IS GONNA BE AWESOME!
ARE YOU REALLY GONNA SET OFF A HUNDRED FIREWORKS?!
YOU'RE GOING TO BAKE POTATOES AT THE CAMP-FIRE AND GIVE THEM TO ALL THE STU-DENTS?
INCRED-IBLE!
THAT REALLY IS...
... INCREDIBLE.

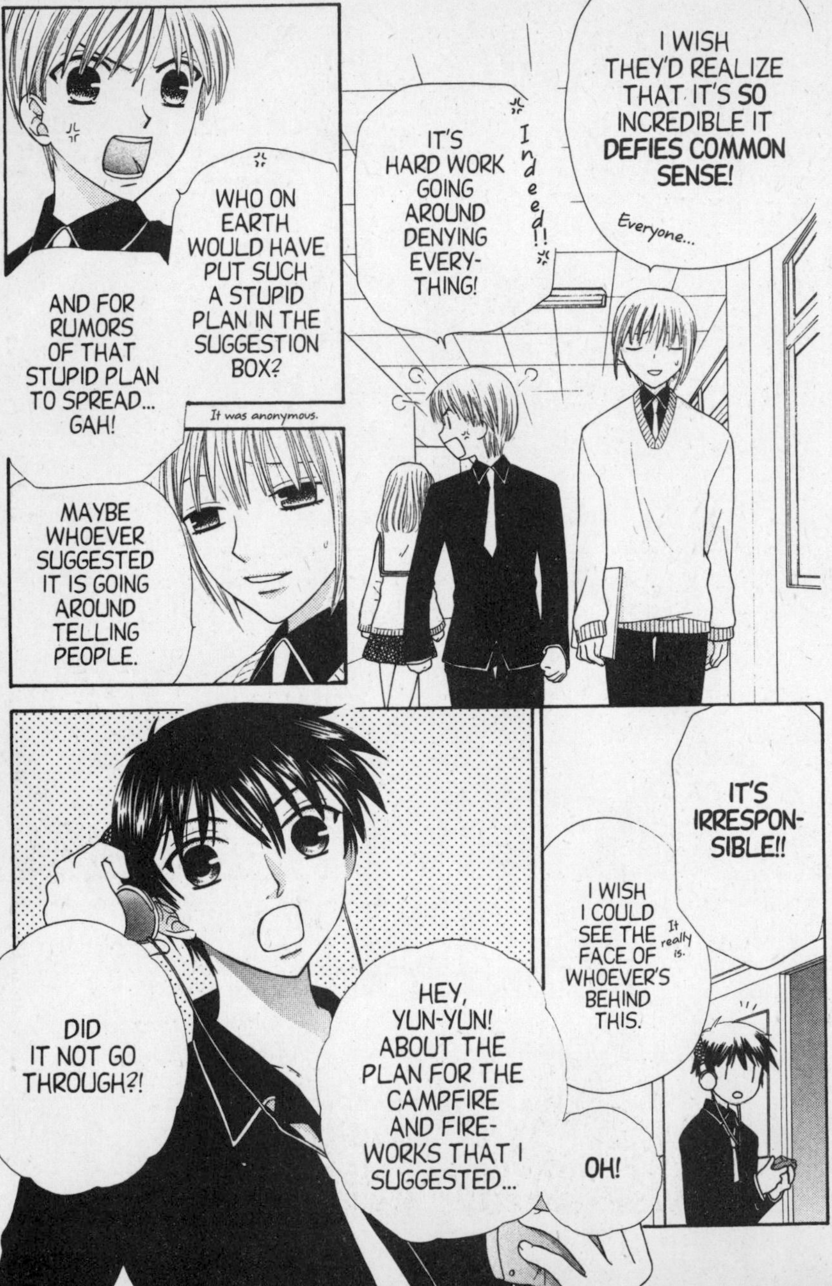

I WISH THEY'D REALIZE THAT IT'S SO INCREDIBLE IT DEFIES COMMON SENSE!
Everyone...
Indeed!!
IT'S HARD WORK GOING AROUND DENYING EVERY-THING!
WHO ON EARTH WOULD HAVE PUT SUCH A STUPID PLAN IN THE SUGGESTION BOX?
AND FOR RUMORS OF THAT STUPID PLAN TO SPREAD... GAH!
It was anonymous.
MAYBE WHOEVER SUGGESTED IT IS GOING AROUND TELLING PEOPLE.
IT'S IRRESPON-SIBLE!!
I WISH I COULD SEE THE FACE OF WHOEVER'S BEHIND THIS.
It really is.
OH!
HEY, YUN-YUN! ABOUT THE PLAN FOR THE CAMPFIRE AND FIRE-WORKS THAT I SUGGESTED...
DID IT NOT GO THROUGH?!

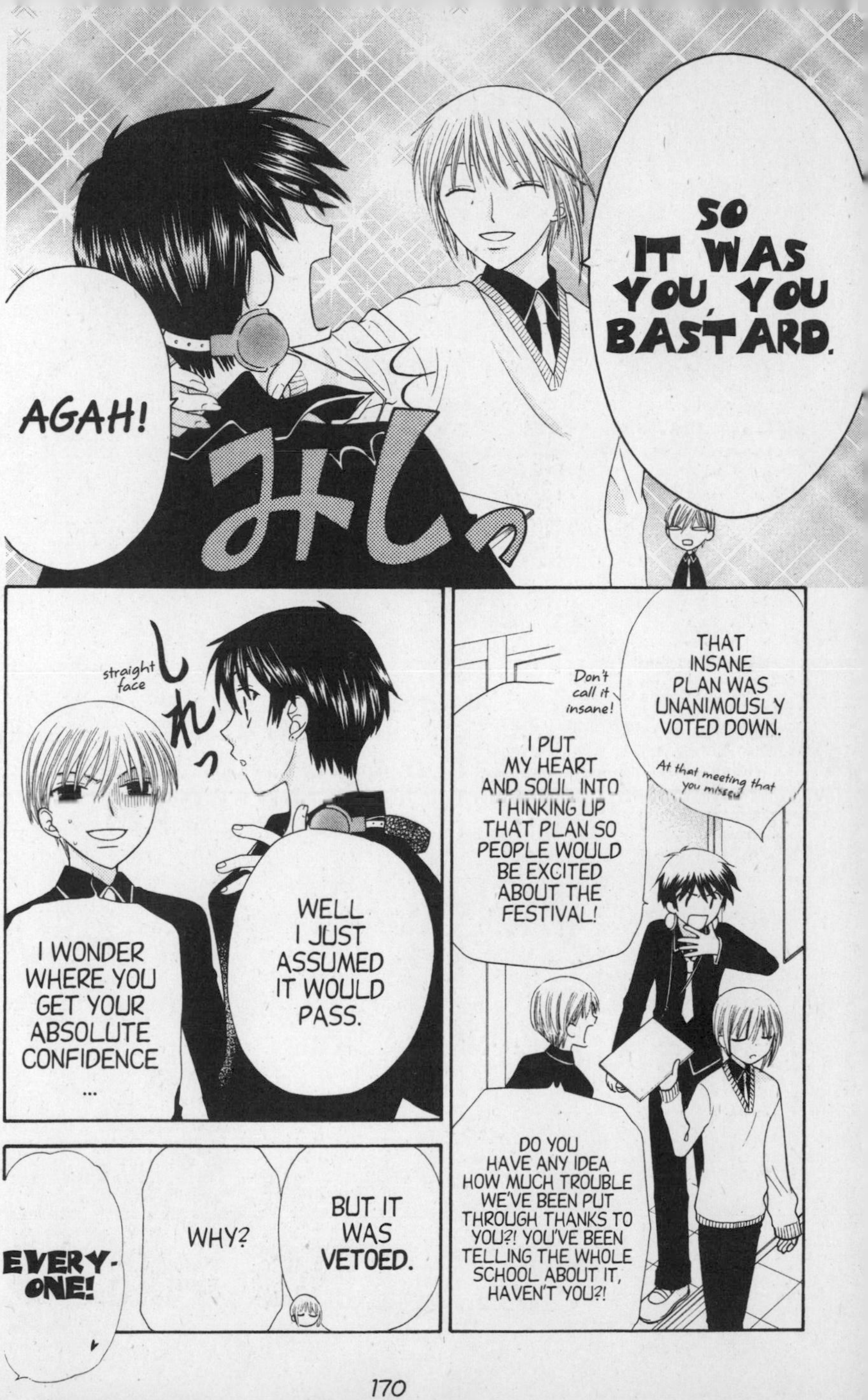
SO IT WAS YOU, YOU BASTARD.
AGAH!
みしっ
THAT INSANE PLAN WAS UNANIMOUSLY VOTED DOWN.
At that meeting that you missed
Don't call it insane!
I PUT MY HEART AND SOUL INTO THINKING UP THAT PLAN SO PEOPLE WOULD BE EXCITED ABOUT THE FESTIVAL!
DO YOU HAVE ANY IDEA HOW MUCH TROUBLE WE'VE BEEN PUT THROUGH THANKS TO YOU?! YOU'VE BEEN TELLING THE WHOLE SCHOOL ABOUT IT, HAVEN'T YOU?!
しれっ
straight face
WELL I JUST ASSUMED IT WOULD PASS.
I WONDER WHERE YOU GET YOUR ABSOLUTE CONFIDENCE ...
BUT IT WAS VETOED.
WHY?
EVERY-ONE!

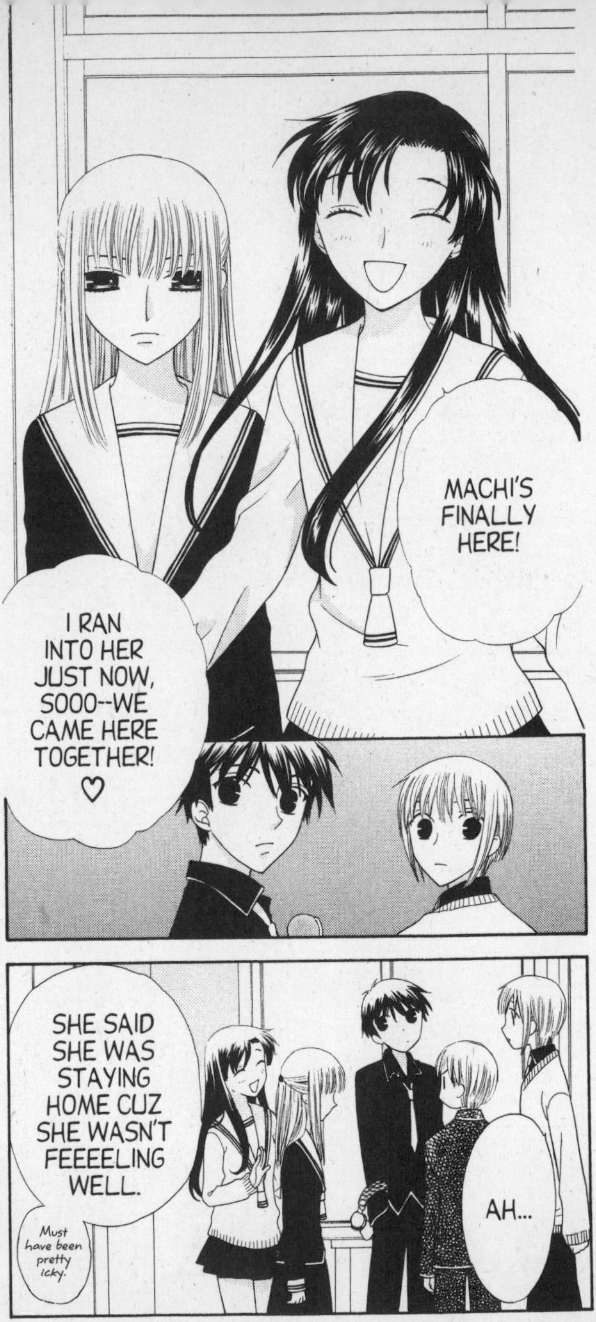
MACHI'S FINALLY HERE!
I RAN INTO HER JUST NOW, SOOO--WE CAME HERE TOGETHER! ♡
AH...
SHE SAID SHE WAS STAYING HOME CUZ SHE WASN'T FEEEELING WELL.
Must have been pretty icky.

...So.

There was one mistake in that Momiji's and Kureno's names are actually reversed. Really... Momitchi is Kureno. Kureno-san is Momiji. That's how it should have been. But what can I say... I'm sorry. When I was coming up with names, by the time I realized I was mistaken, it was too late. The chapter where Momitchi first shows up had already been published in *Hana to Yume Magazine*, and somehow, Momitchi had already become "Momiji!!" (at least from this creator's point of view). So, now, here I am thinking, "Well... c'est la vie." Wow...with flubs like that, you can't tell if I'm the kind of person who thinks things through or not...

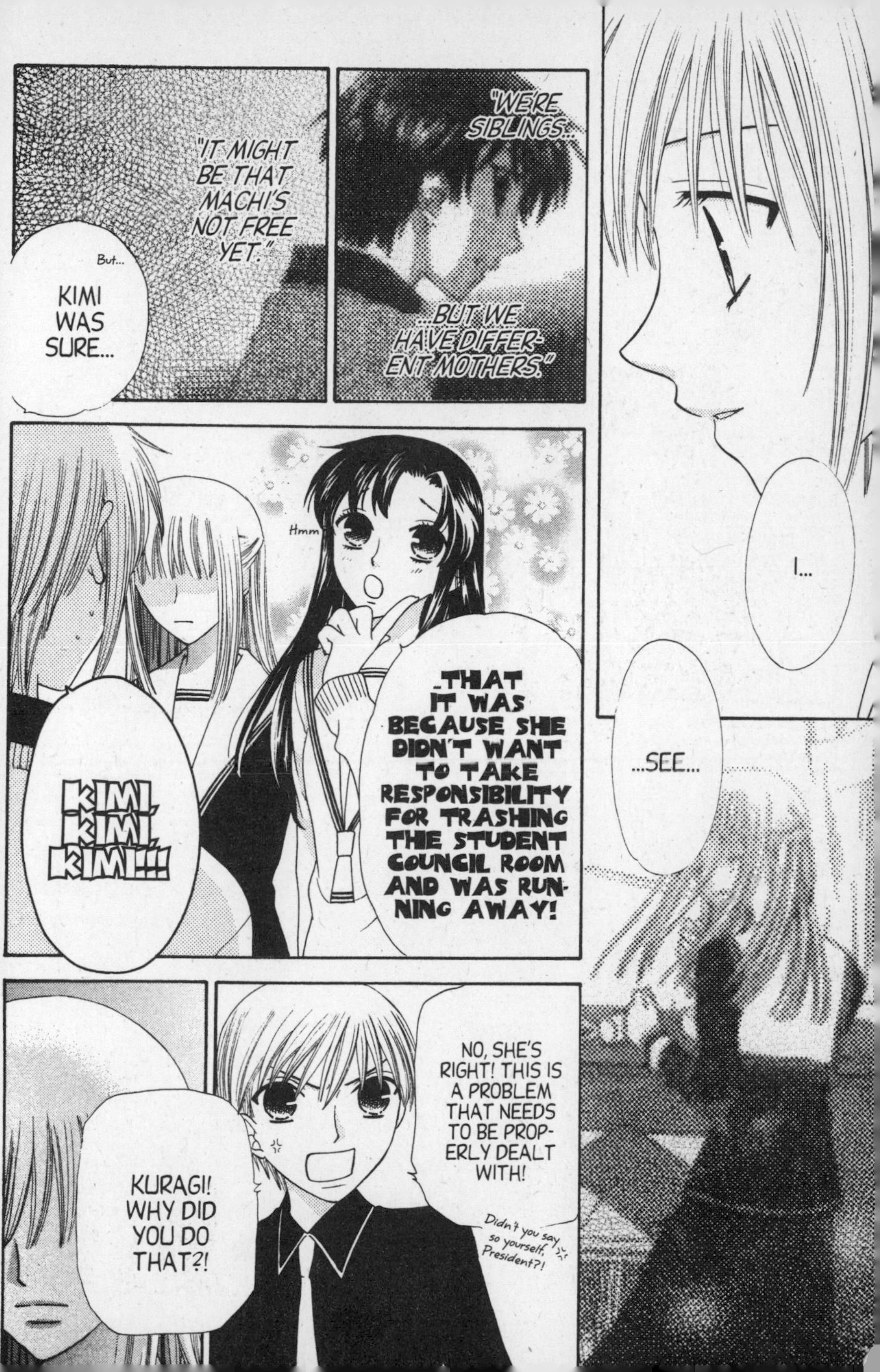
I...
...SEE...
"WE'RE SIBLINGS...
...BUT WE HAVE DIFFERENT MOTHERS."
"IT MIGHT BE THAT MACHI'S NOT FREE YET."
But...
KIMI WAS SURE...
Hmm
...THAT IT WAS BECAUSE SHE DIDN'T WANT TO TAKE RESPONSIBILITY FOR TRASHING THE STUDENT COUNCIL ROOM AND WAS RUNNING AWAY!
KIMI, KIMI, KIMI!!!
NO, SHE'S RIGHT! THIS IS A PROBLEM THAT NEEDS TO BE PROPERLY DEALT WITH!
Didn't you say so yourself, President?!
KURAGI! WHY DID YOU DO THAT?!

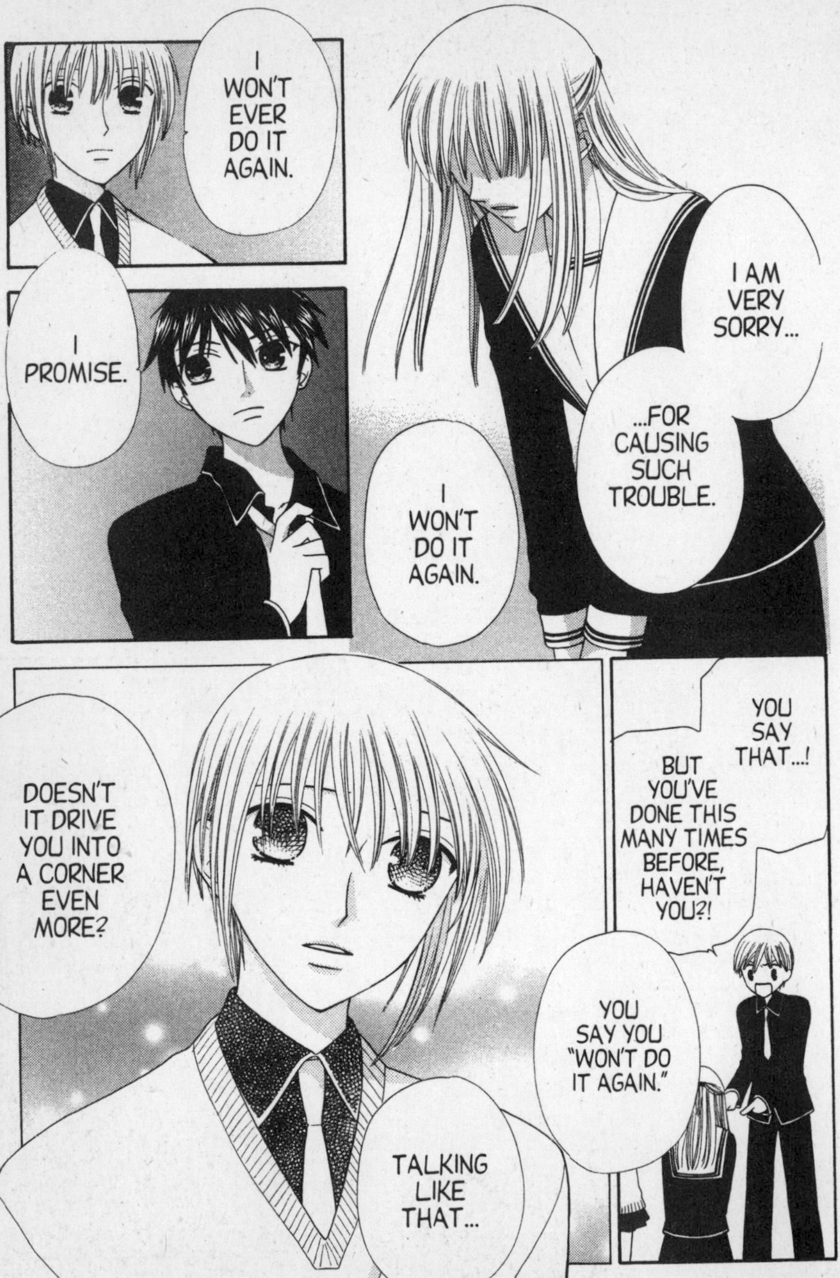
I AM VERY SORRY...
...FOR CAUSING SUCH TROUBLE.
I WON'T DO IT AGAIN.
I WON'T EVER DO IT AGAIN.
I PROMISE.
YOU SAY THAT...!
BUT YOU'VE DONE THIS MANY TIMES BEFORE, HAVEN'T YOU?!
YOU SAY YOU "WON'T DO IT AGAIN."
TALKING LIKE THAT...
DOESN'T IT DRIVE YOU INTO A CORNER EVEN MORE?

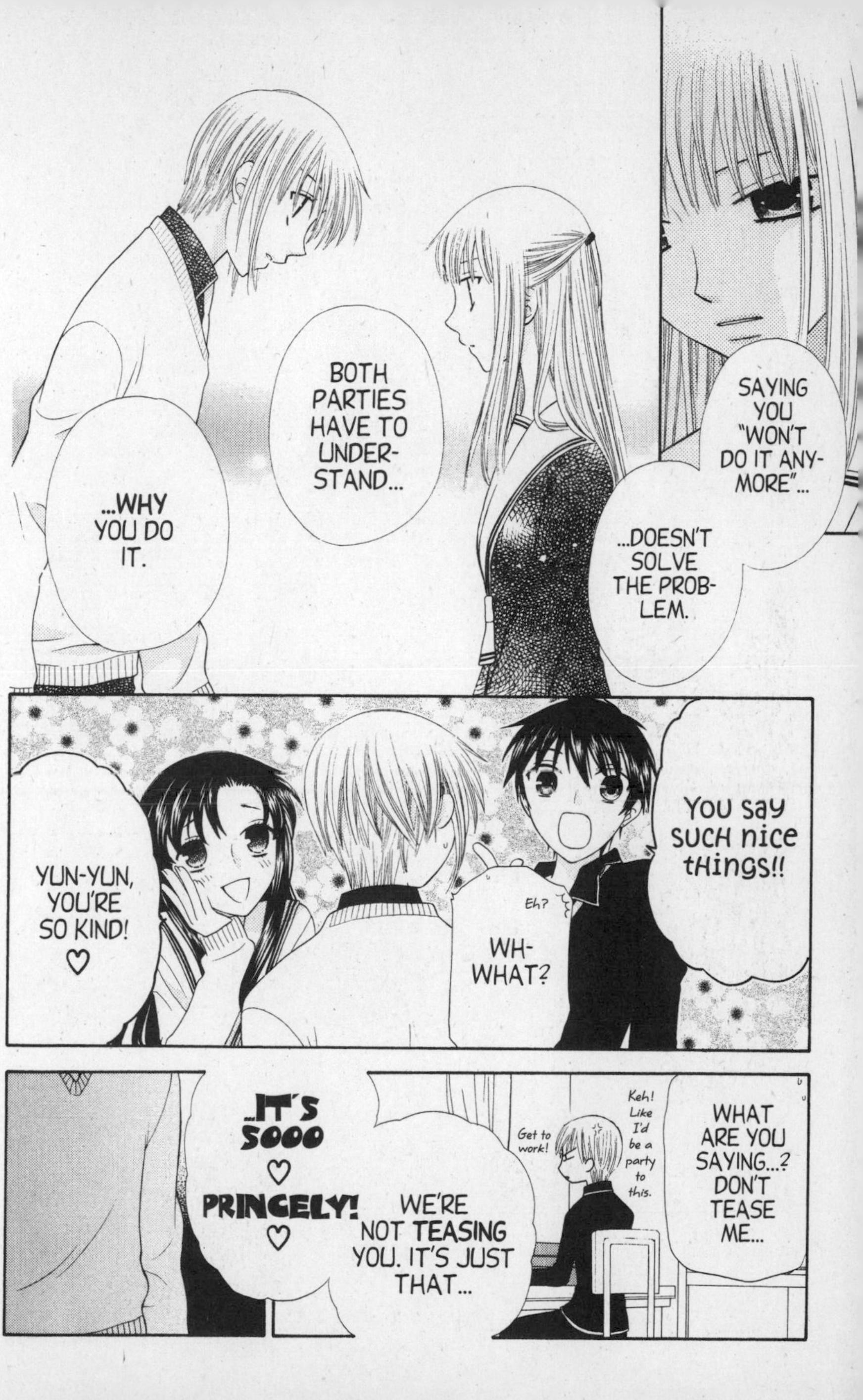
SAYING YOU "WON'T DO IT ANYMORE"...
...DOESN'T SOLVE THE PROBLEM.
BOTH PARTIES HAVE TO UNDERSTAND...
...WHY YOU DO IT.
You say SUCH nice things!!
Eh?
WH-WHAT?
YUN-YUN, YOU'RE SO KIND! ♡
WHAT ARE YOU SAYING...? DON'T TEASE ME...
Keh! Like I'd be a party to this.
Get to work!
WE'RE NOT TEASING YOU. IT'S JUST THAT...
...IT'S SOOO ♡ PRINCELY! ♡

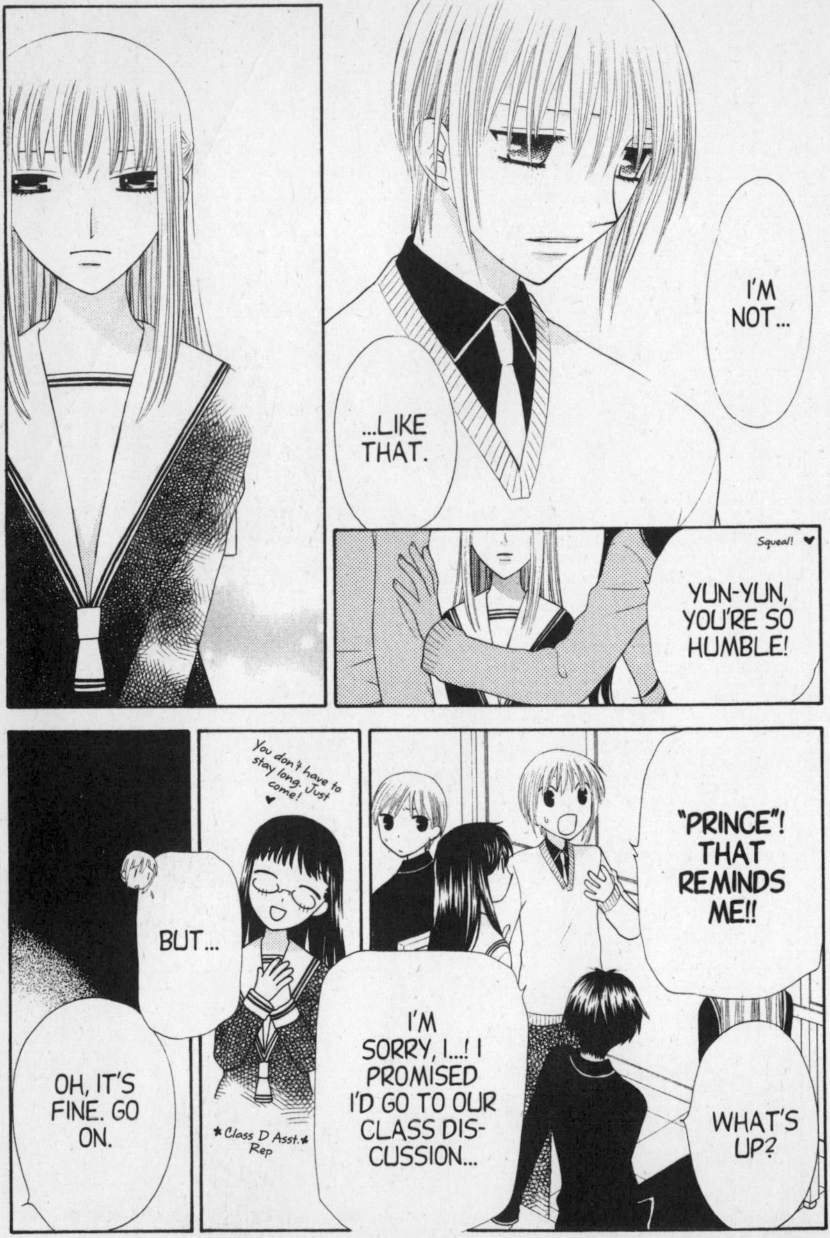
I'M NOT...
...LIKE THAT.
Squeal! ♥
YUN-YUN, YOU'RE SO HUMBLE!
"PRINCE"! THAT REMINDS ME!!
WHAT'S UP?
I'M SORRY, I...! I PROMISED I'D GO TO OUR CLASS DIS-CUSSION...
You don't have to stay long. Just come! ♥
Class D Asst. Rep
BUT...
OH, IT'S FINE. GO ON.

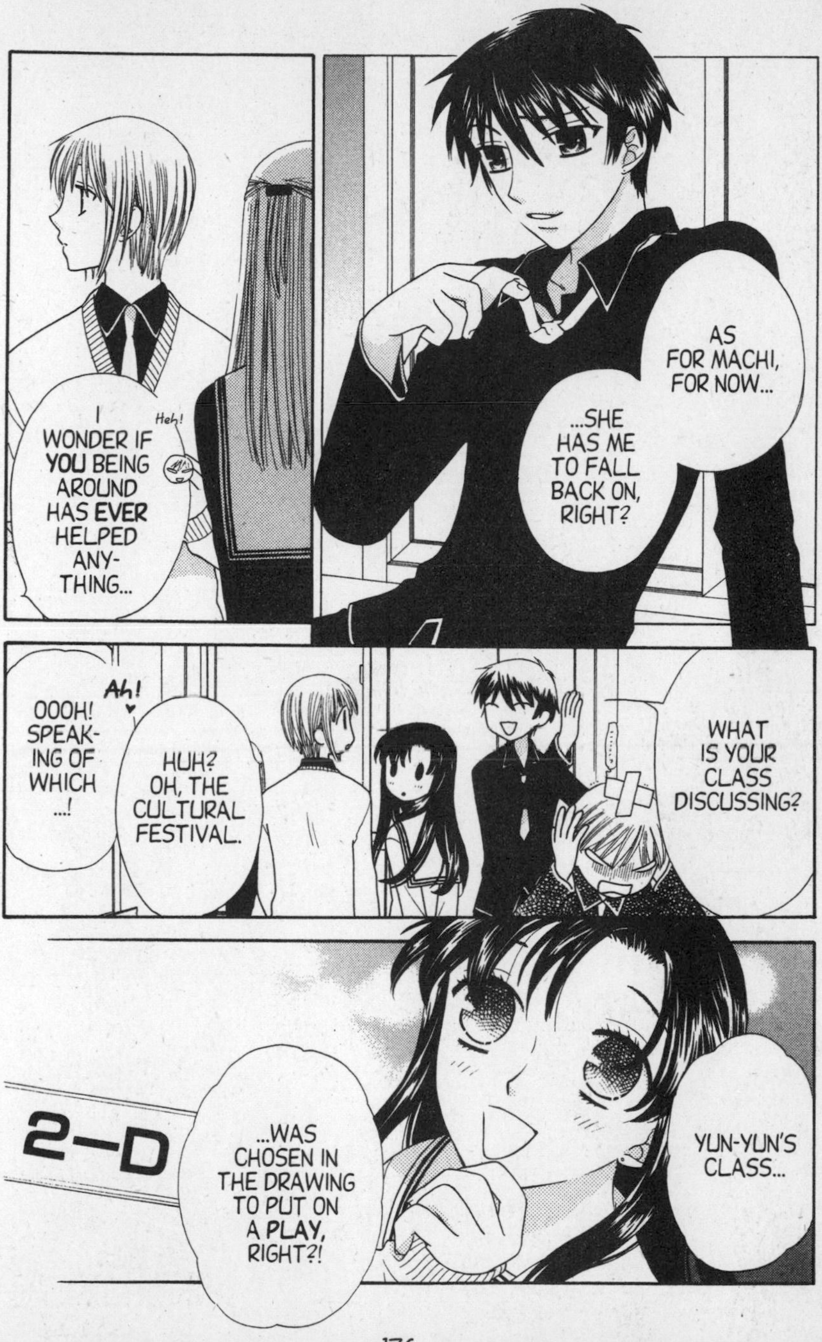
AS FOR MACHI, FOR NOW...
...SHE HAS ME TO FALL BACK ON, RIGHT?
Heh!
I WONDER IF YOU BEING AROUND HAS EVER HELPED ANYTHING...
WHAT IS YOUR CLASS DISCUSSING?
HUH? OH, THE CULTURAL FESTIVAL.
Ah!
OOOH! SPEAKING OF WHICH ...!
YUN-YUN'S CLASS...
2-D
...WAS CHOSEN IN THE DRAWING TO PUT ON A PLAY, RIGHT?!

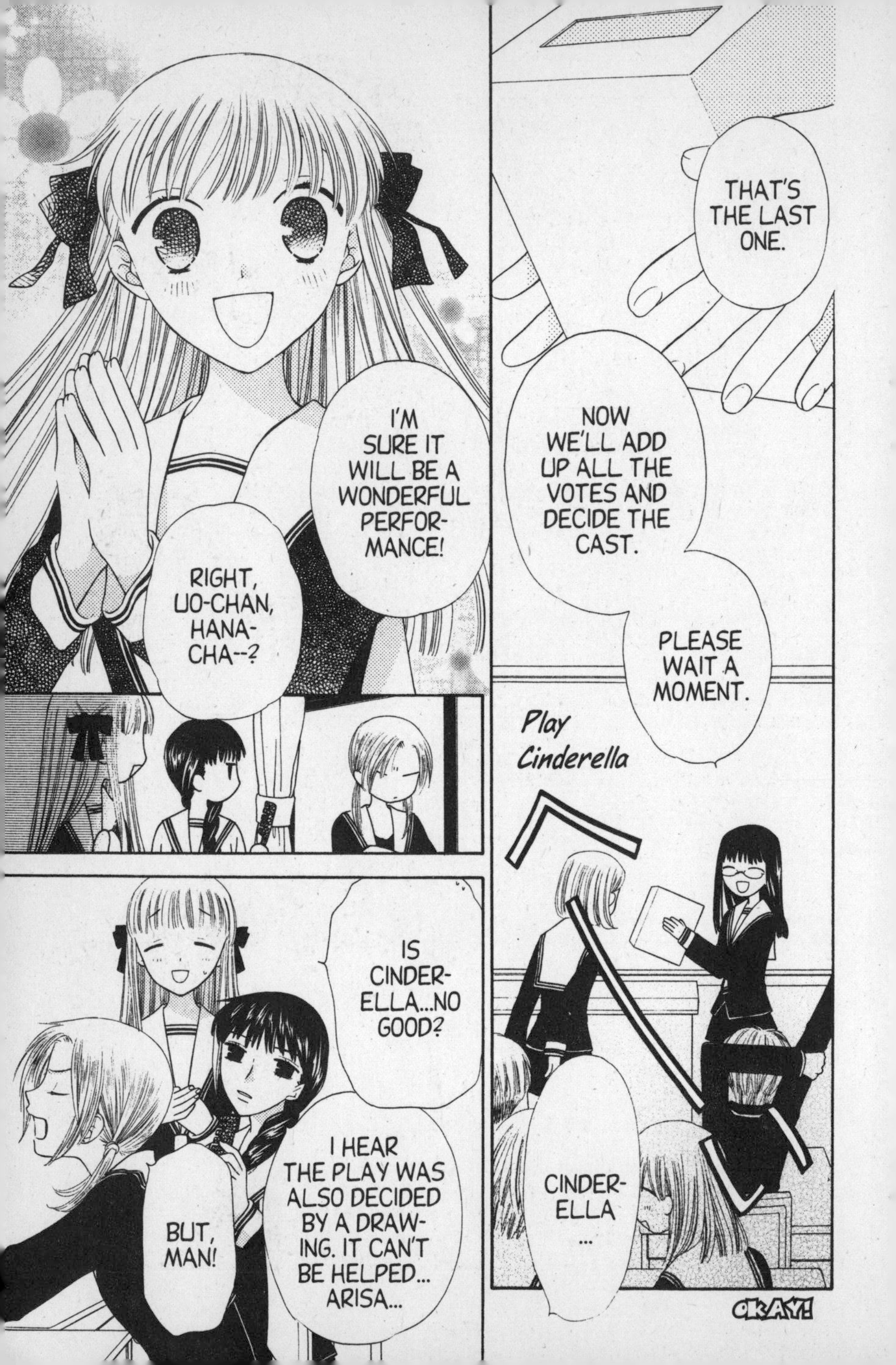

THAT'S THE LAST ONE.
NOW WE'LL ADD UP ALL THE VOTES AND DECIDE THE CAST.
PLEASE WAIT A MOMENT.
Play Cinderella
CINDER-ELLA ...
OKAY!
I'M SURE IT WILL BE A WONDERFUL PERFOR-MANCE!
RIGHT, UO-CHAN, HANA-CHA--?
IS CINDER-ELLA...NO GOOD?
I HEAR THE PLAY WAS ALSO DECIDED BY A DRAW-ING. IT CAN'T BE HELPED... ARISA...
BUT, MAN!

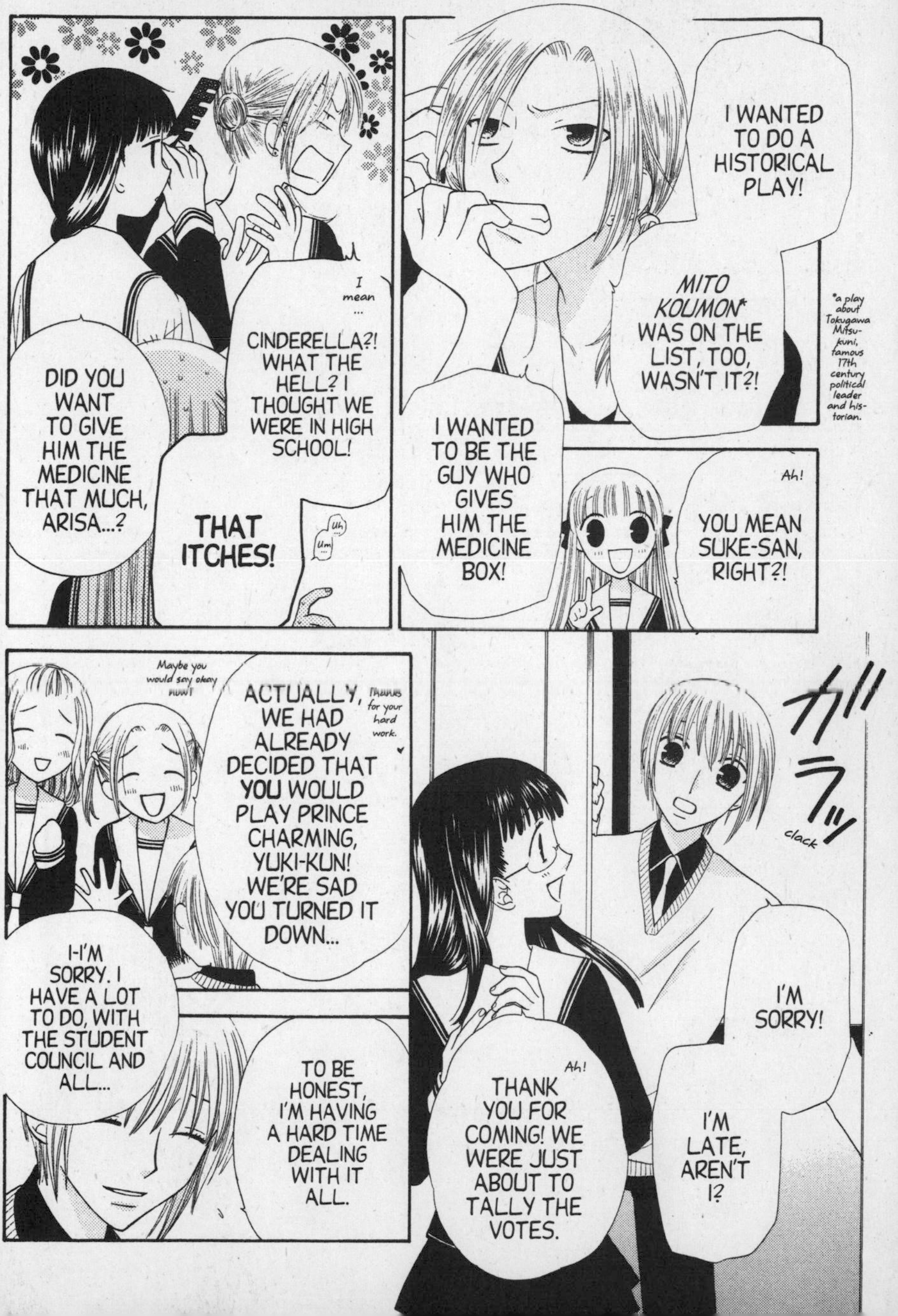
I WANTED TO DO A HISTORICAL PLAY!
MITO KOUMON* WAS ON THE LIST, TOO, WASN'T IT?!
*a play about Tokugawa Mitsu-kuni, famous 17th century political leader and his-torian.
Ah!
YOU MEAN SUKE-SAN, RIGHT?!
I WANTED TO BE THE GUY WHO GIVES HIM THE MEDICINE BOX!
I mean ...
CINDERELLA?! WHAT THE HELL? I THOUGHT WE WERE IN HIGH SCHOOL!
THAT ITCHES!
Uh ...
Um ...
DID YOU WANT TO GIVE HIM THE MEDICINE THAT MUCH, ARISA...?
ガラッ
clack
I'M SORRY!
I'M LATE, AREN'T I?
Ah!
THANK YOU FOR COMING! WE WERE JUST ABOUT TO TALLY THE VOTES.
Thanks for your hard work.
ACTUALLY, WE HAD ALREADY DECIDED THAT YOU WOULD PLAY PRINCE CHARMING, YUKI-KUN! WE'RE SAD YOU TURNED IT DOWN...
Maybe you would say okay
TO BE HONEST, I'M HAVING A HARD TIME DEALING WITH IT ALL.
I-I'M SORRY. I HAVE A LOT TO DO, WITH THE STUDENT COUNCIL AND ALL...

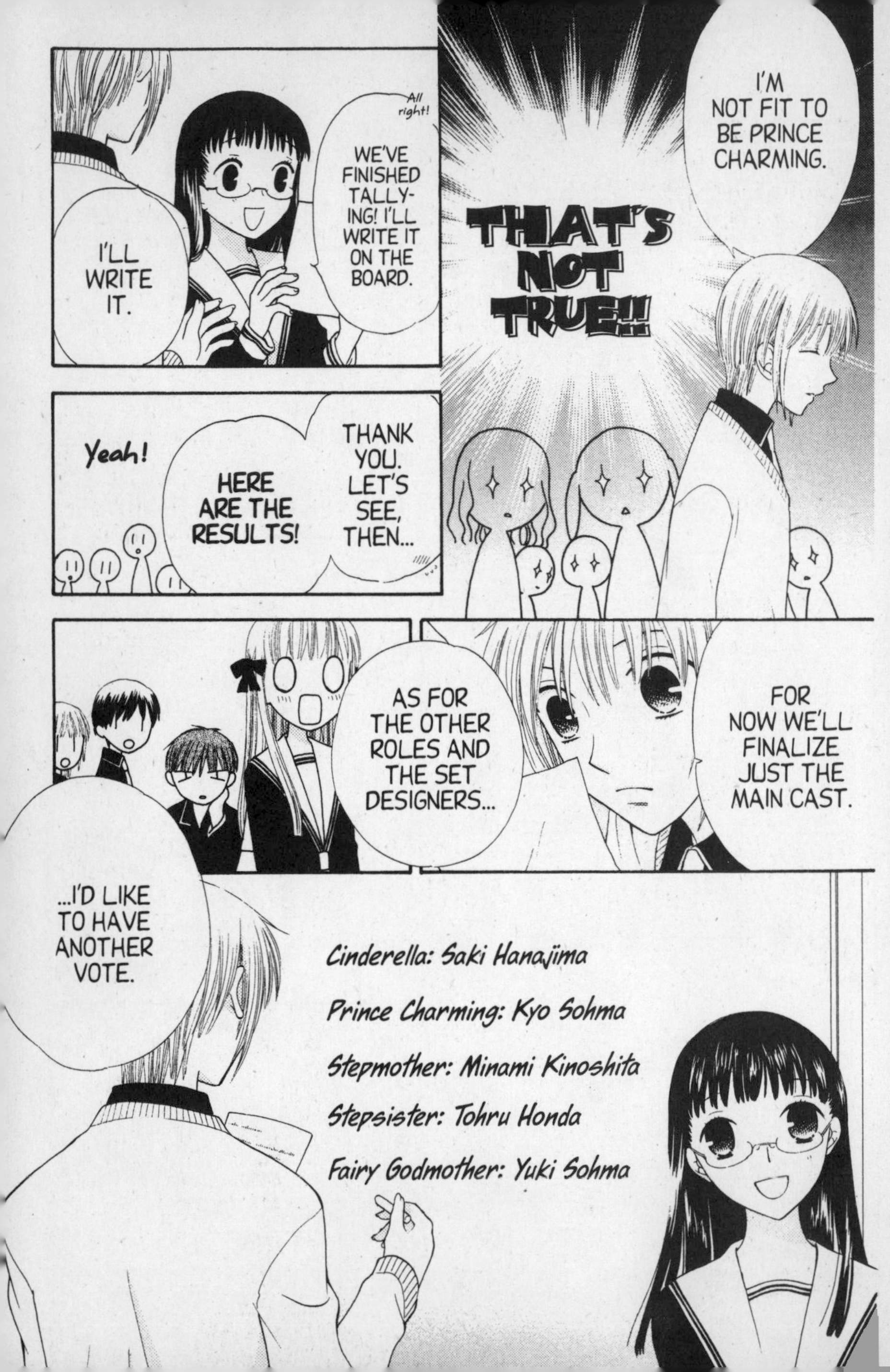
I'M NOT FIT TO BE PRINCE CHARMING.
THAT'S NOT TRUE!!
All right!
WE'VE FINISHED TALLY-ING! I'LL WRITE IT ON THE BOARD.
I'LL WRITE IT.
THANK YOU. LET'S SEE, THEN...
HERE ARE THE RESULTS!
Yeah!
FOR NOW WE'LL FINALIZE JUST THE MAIN CAST.
AS FOR THE OTHER ROLES AND THE SET DESIGNERS...
Cinderella: Saki Hanajima
Prince Charming: Kyo Sohma
Stepmother: Minami Kinoshita
Stepsister: Tohru Honda
Fairy Godmother: Yuki Sohma
...I'D LIKE TO HAVE ANOTHER VOTE.

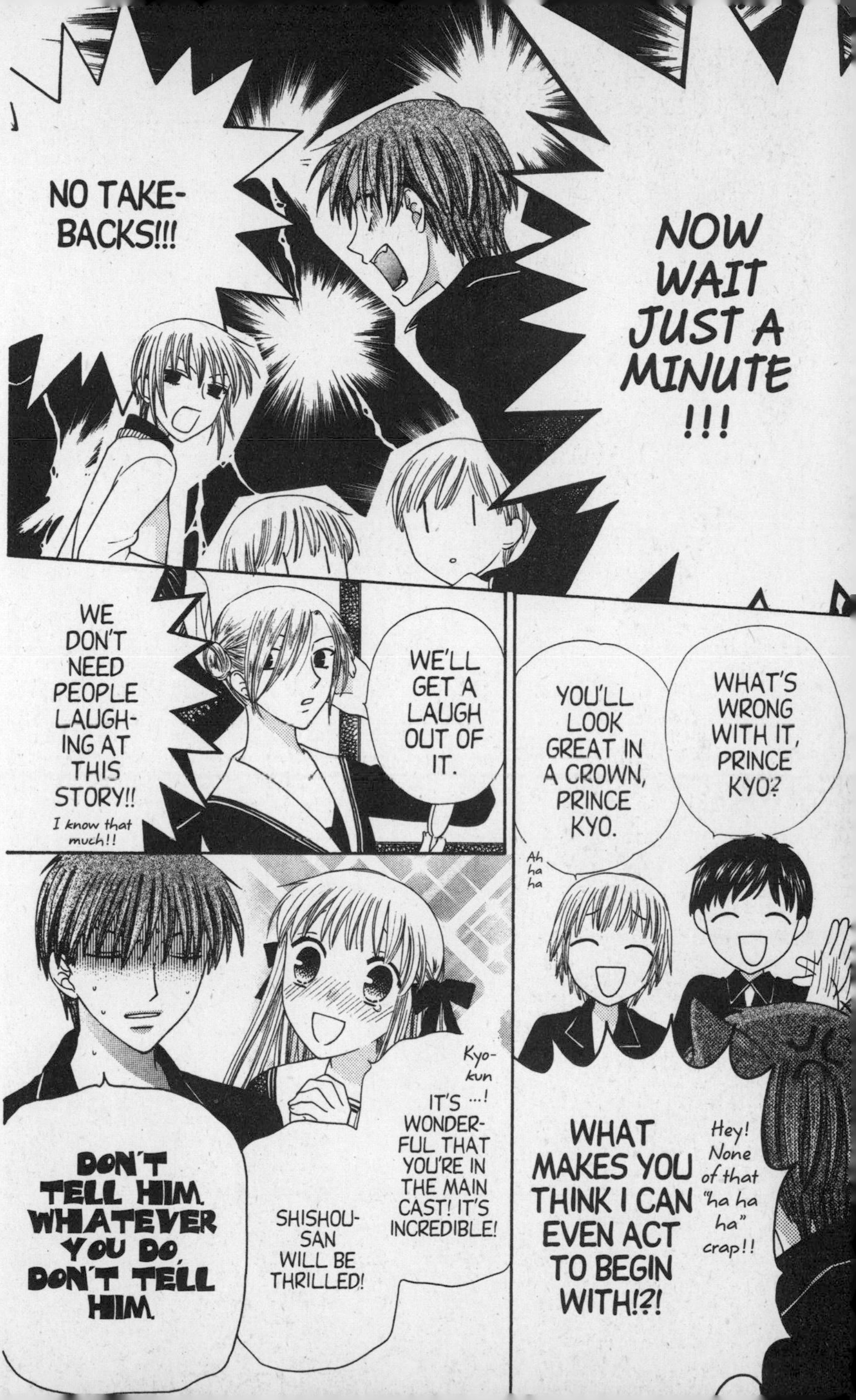
NOW WAIT JUST A MINUTE!!!
NO TAKE-BACKS!!!
WHAT'S WRONG WITH IT, PRINCE KYO?
YOU'LL LOOK GREAT IN A CROWN, PRINCE KYO.
Ah ha ha
Hey! None of that "ha ha ha" crap!!
WHAT MAKES YOU THINK I CAN EVEN ACT TO BEGIN WITH!?!
WE'LL GET A LAUGH OUT OF IT.
WE DON'T NEED PEOPLE LAUGHING AT THIS STORY!!
I know that much!!
Kyo-kun ...!
IT'S WONDERFUL THAT YOU'RE IN THE MAIN CAST! IT'S INCREDIBLE!
SHISHOU-SAN WILL BE THRILLED!
DON'T TELL HIM. WHATEVER YOU DO, DON'T TELL HIM.

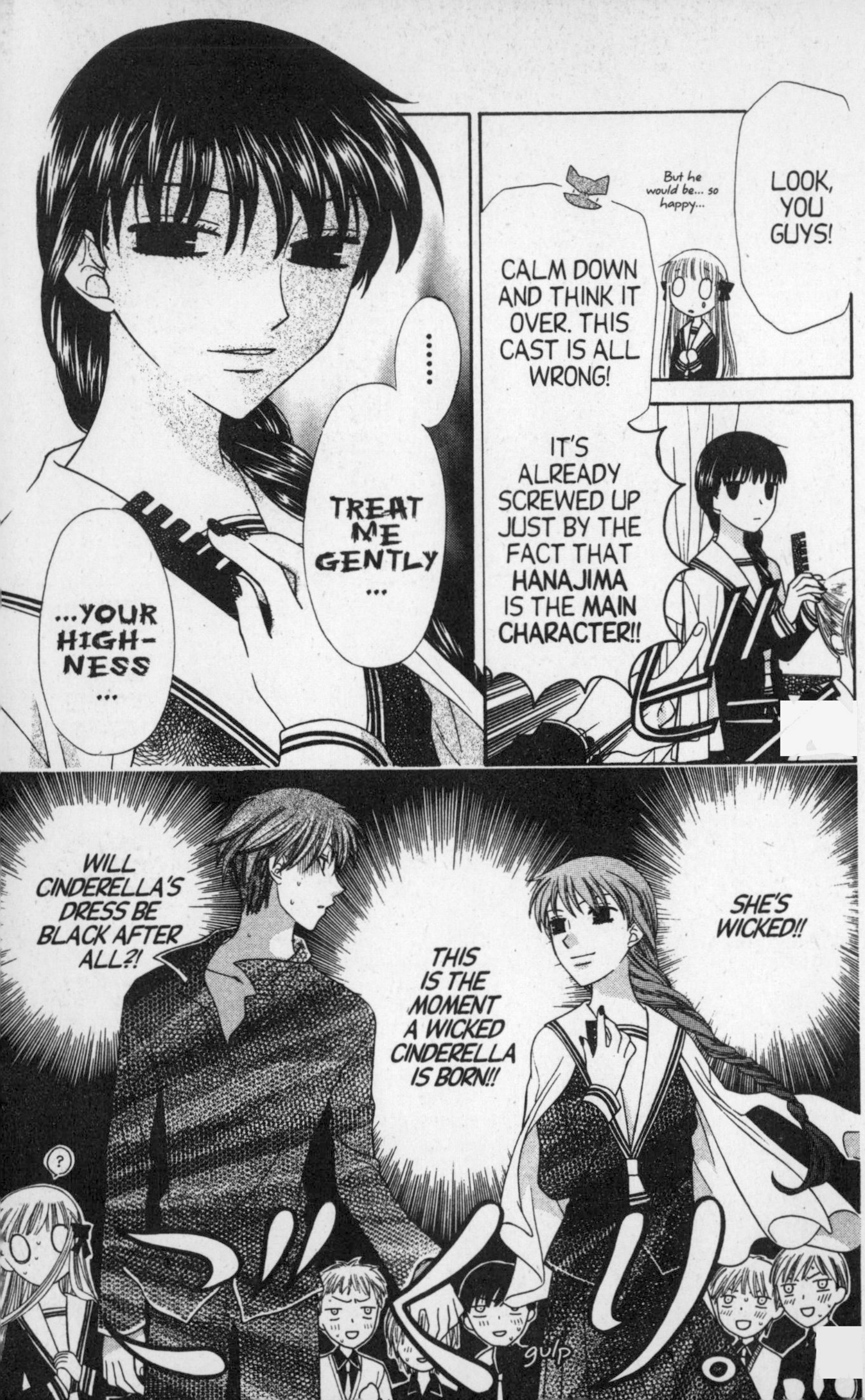
LOOK, YOU GUYS!
But he would be... so happy...
CALM DOWN AND THINK IT OVER. THIS CAST IS ALL WRONG!
IT'S ALREADY SCREWED UP JUST BY THE FACT THAT HANAJIMA IS THE MAIN CHARACTER!!
......
TREAT ME GENTLY...
...YOUR HIGHNESS...
SHE'S WICKED!!
THIS IS THE MOMENT A WICKED CINDERELLA IS BORN!!
WILL CINDERELLA'S DRESS BE BLACK AFTER ALL?!
?
gulp

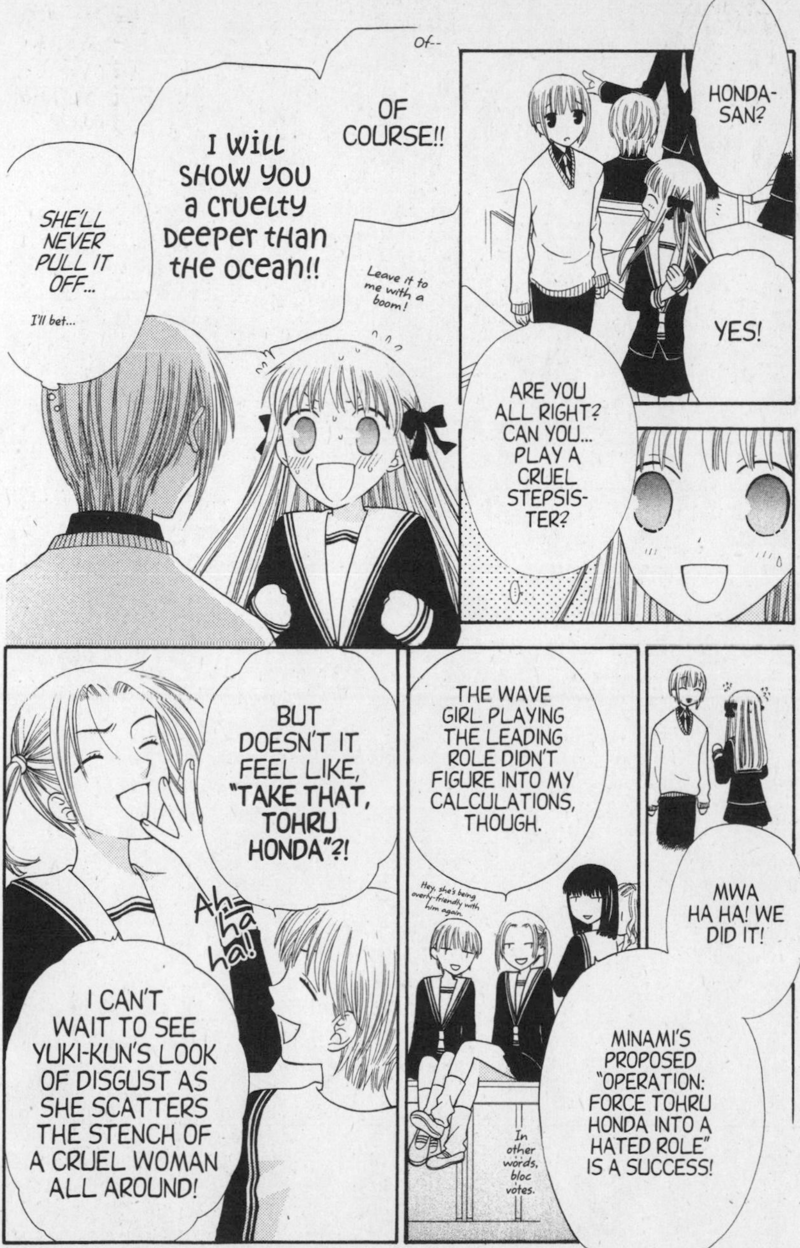
HONDA-SAN?
YES!
ARE YOU ALL RIGHT? CAN YOU... PLAY A CRUEL STEPSISTER?
Of--
OF COURSE!!
I WILL SHOW YOU A CRUELTY DEEPER THAN THE OCEAN!!
Leave it to me with a boom!
SHE'LL NEVER PULL IT OFF...
I'll bet...
MWA HA HA! WE DID IT!
MINAMI'S PROPOSED "OPERATION: FORCE TOHRU HONDA INTO A HATED ROLE" IS A SUCCESS!
In other words, bloc votes.
THE WAVE GIRL PLAYING THE LEADING ROLE DIDN'T FIGURE INTO MY CALCULATIONS, THOUGH.
Hey, she's being overly-friendly with him again.
BUT DOESN'T IT FEEL LIKE, "TAKE THAT, TOHRU HONDA"?!
Ah-ha ha ha!
I CAN'T WAIT TO SEE YUKI-KUN'S LOOK OF DISGUST AS SHE SCATTERS THE STENCH OF A CRUEL WOMAN ALL AROUND!

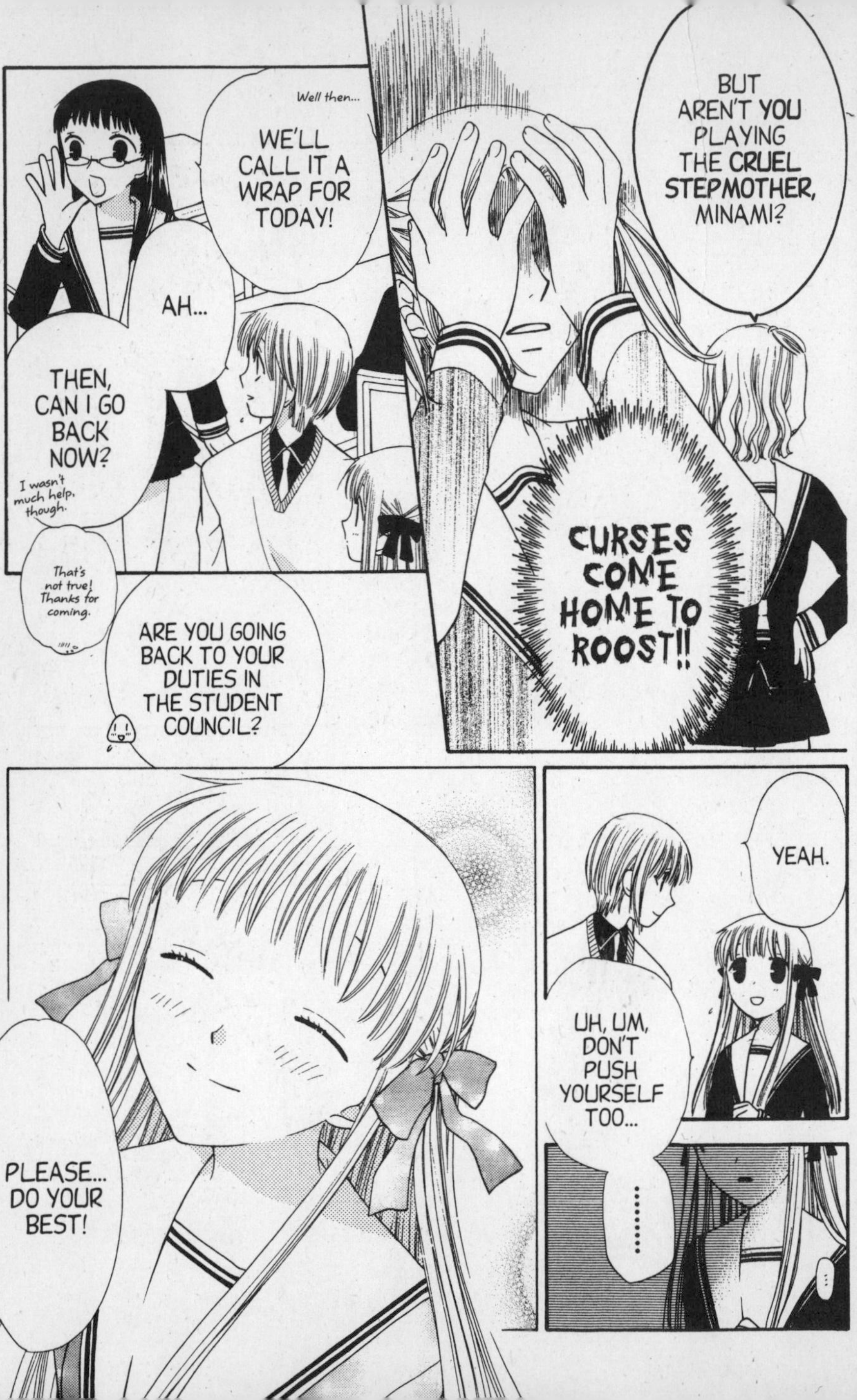
BUT AREN'T YOU PLAYING THE CRUEL STEPMOTHER, MINAMI?
CURSES COME HOME TO ROOST!!
Well then...
WE'LL CALL IT A WRAP FOR TODAY!
AH...
THEN, CAN I GO BACK NOW?
I wasn't much help, though.
That's not true! Thanks for coming.
ARE YOU GOING BACK TO YOUR DUTIES IN THE STUDENT COUNCIL?
YEAH.
UH, UM, DON'T PUSH YOURSELF TOO...
......
...
PLEASE... DO YOUR BEST!

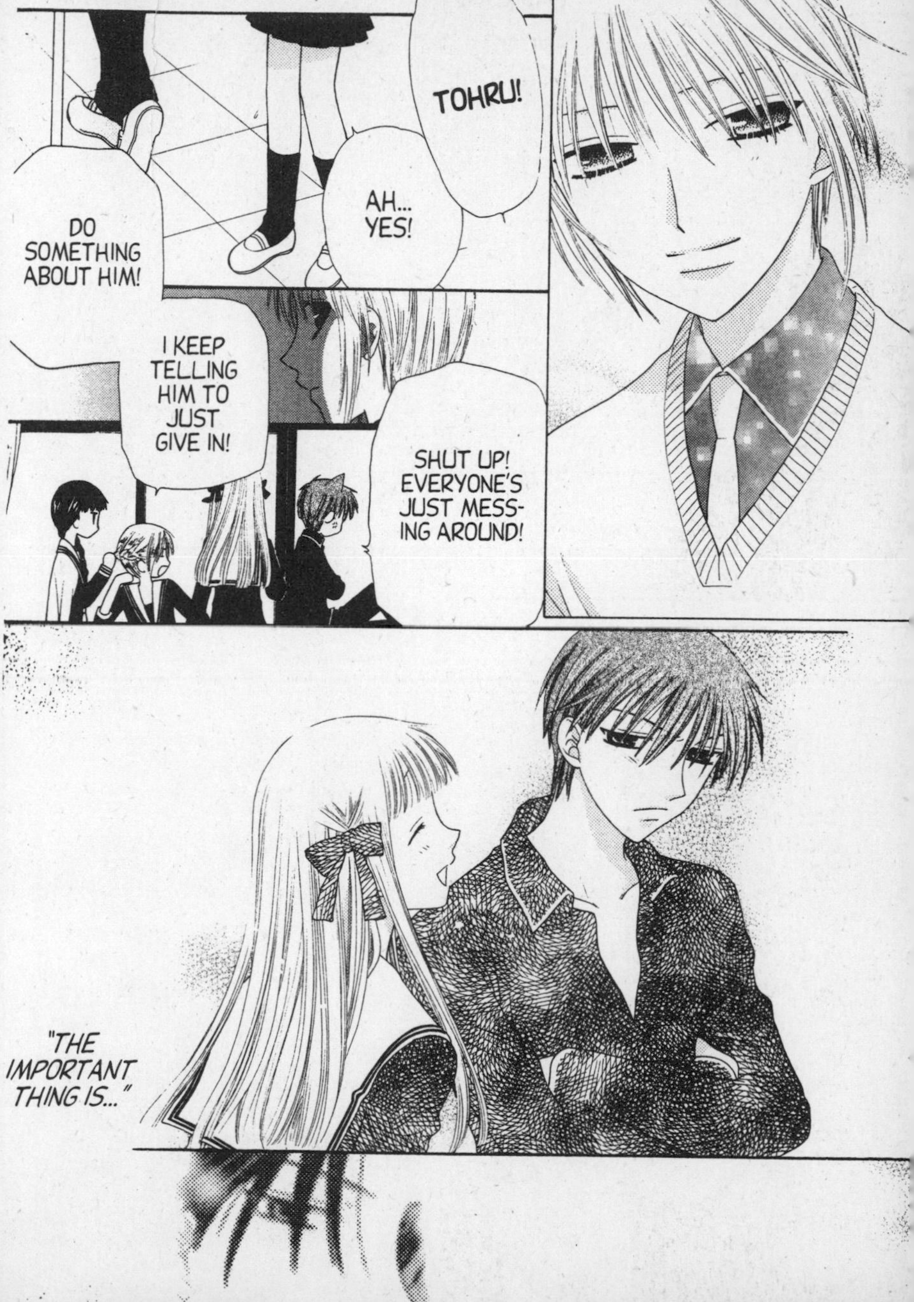

TOHRU!
AH... YES!
DO SOMETHING ABOUT HIM!
I KEEP TELLING HIM TO JUST GIVE IN!
SHUT UP! EVERYONE'S JUST MESS-ING AROUND!
"THE IMPORTANT THING IS..."

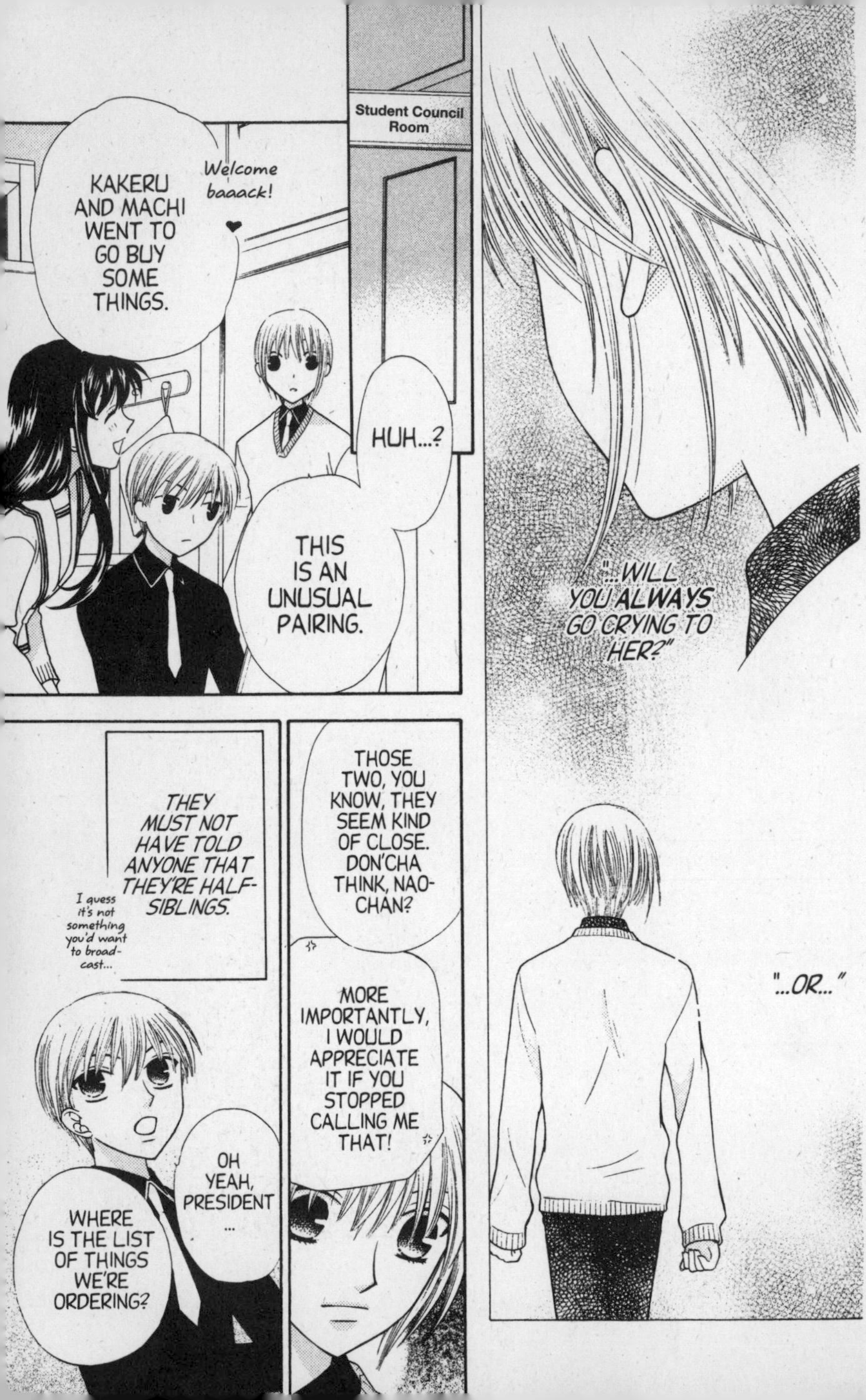
"...WILL YOU ALWAYS GO CRYING TO HER?"
"...OR..."
Student Council Room
Welcome baaack!
KAKERU AND MACHI WENT TO GO BUY SOME THINGS.
HUH...?
THIS IS AN UNUSUAL PAIRING.
THOSE TWO, YOU KNOW, THEY SEEM KIND OF CLOSE. DON'CHA THINK, NAO-CHAN?
MORE IMPORTANTLY, I WOULD APPRECIATE IT IF YOU STOPPED CALLING ME THAT!
THEY MUST NOT HAVE TOLD ANYONE THAT THEY'RE HALF-SIBLINGS.
I guess it's not something you'd want to broad-cast...
OH YEAH, PRESIDENT...
WHERE IS THE LIST OF THINGS WE'RE ORDERING?

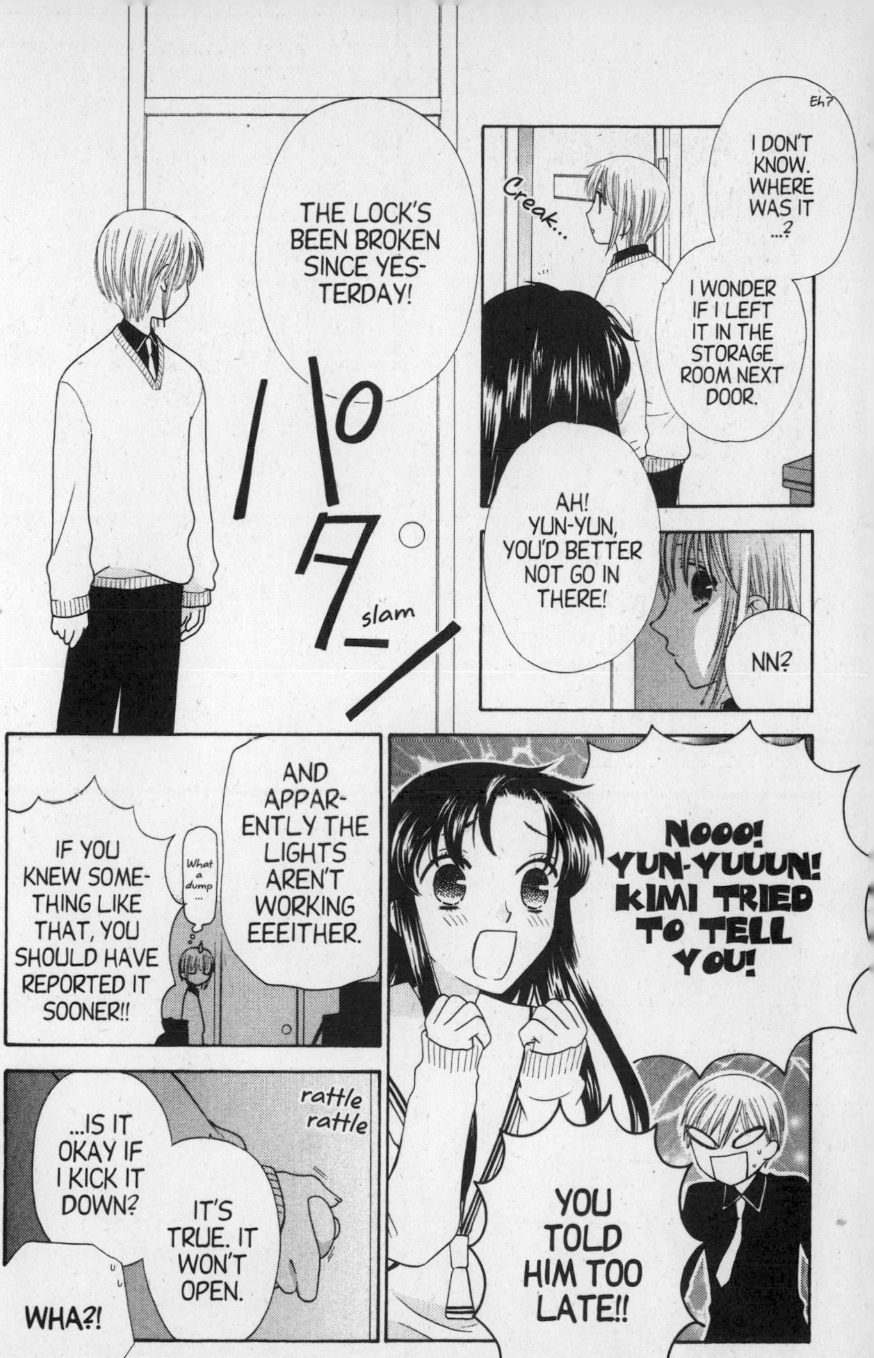
Eh?
I DON'T KNOW. WHERE WAS IT ...?
Creak...
I WONDER IF I LEFT IT IN THE STORAGE ROOM NEXT DOOR.
AH! YUN-YUN, YOU'D BETTER NOT GO IN THERE!
NN?
THE LOCK'S BEEN BROKEN SINCE YESTERDAY!
slam
NOOO! YUN-YUUUN! KIMI TRIED TO TELL YOU!
YOU TOLD HIM TOO LATE!!
AND APPARENTLY THE LIGHTS AREN'T WORKING EEEITHER.
IF YOU KNEW SOMETHING LIKE THAT, YOU SHOULD HAVE REPORTED IT SOONER!!
What a dump...
rattle rattle
IT'S TRUE. IT WON'T OPEN.
...IS IT OKAY IF I KICK IT DOWN?
WHA?!

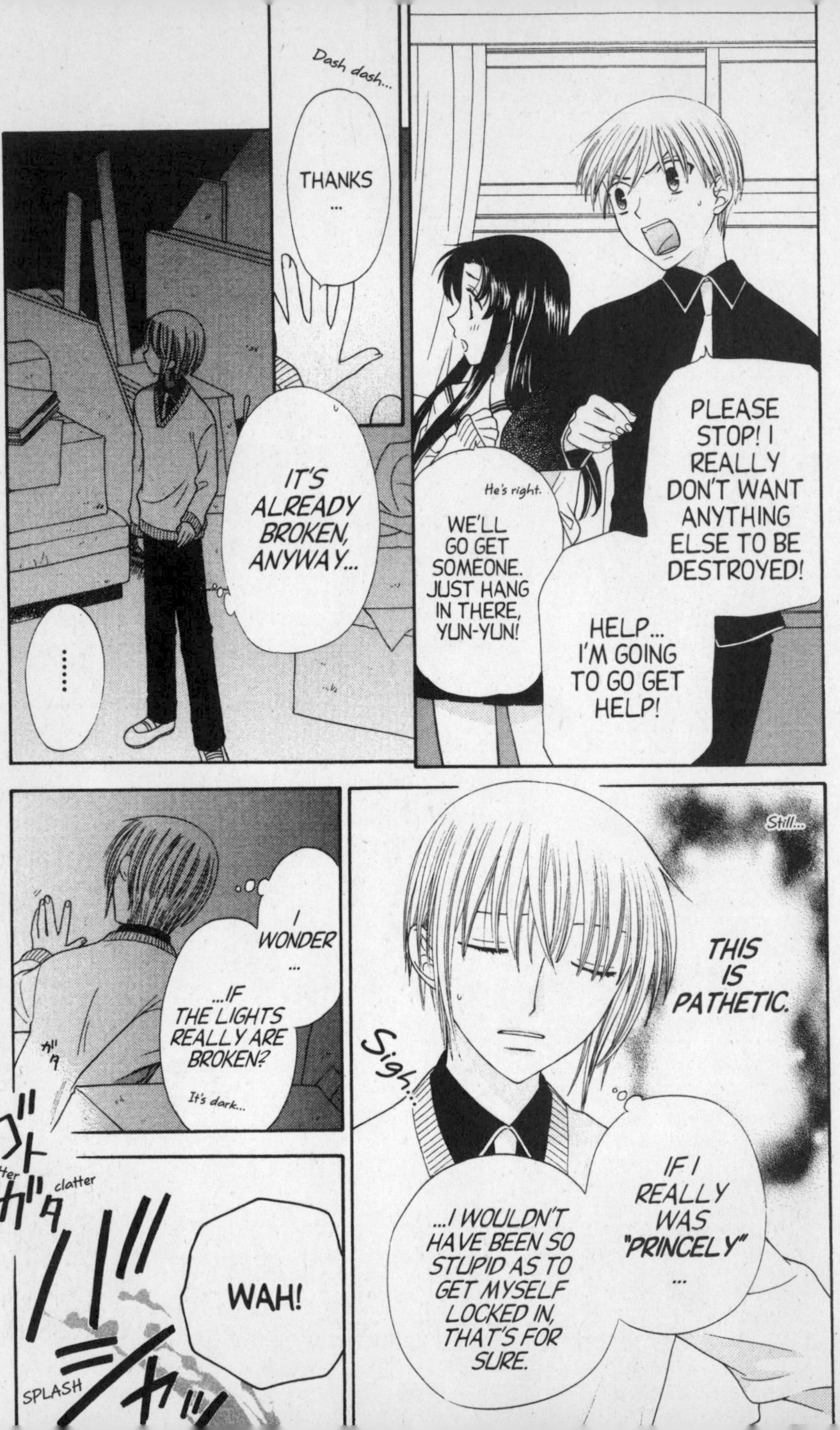
PLEASE STOP! I REALLY DON'T WANT ANYTHING ELSE TO BE DESTROYED!
HELP... I'M GOING TO GO GET HELP!
He's right.
WE'LL GO GET SOMEONE. JUST HANG IN THERE, YUN-YUN!
Dash dash...
THANKS ...
IT'S ALREADY BROKEN, ANYWAY...
......
Still...
THIS IS PATHETIC.
Sigh...
IF I REALLY WAS "PRINCELY" ...
...I WOULDN'T HAVE BEEN SO STUPID AS TO GET MYSELF LOCKED IN, THAT'S FOR SURE.
I WONDER ...
...IF THE LIGHTS REALLY ARE BROKEN?
It's dark...
ガタ
ゴト
clatter
ガタ
clatter
WAH!
バシャッ
SPLASH

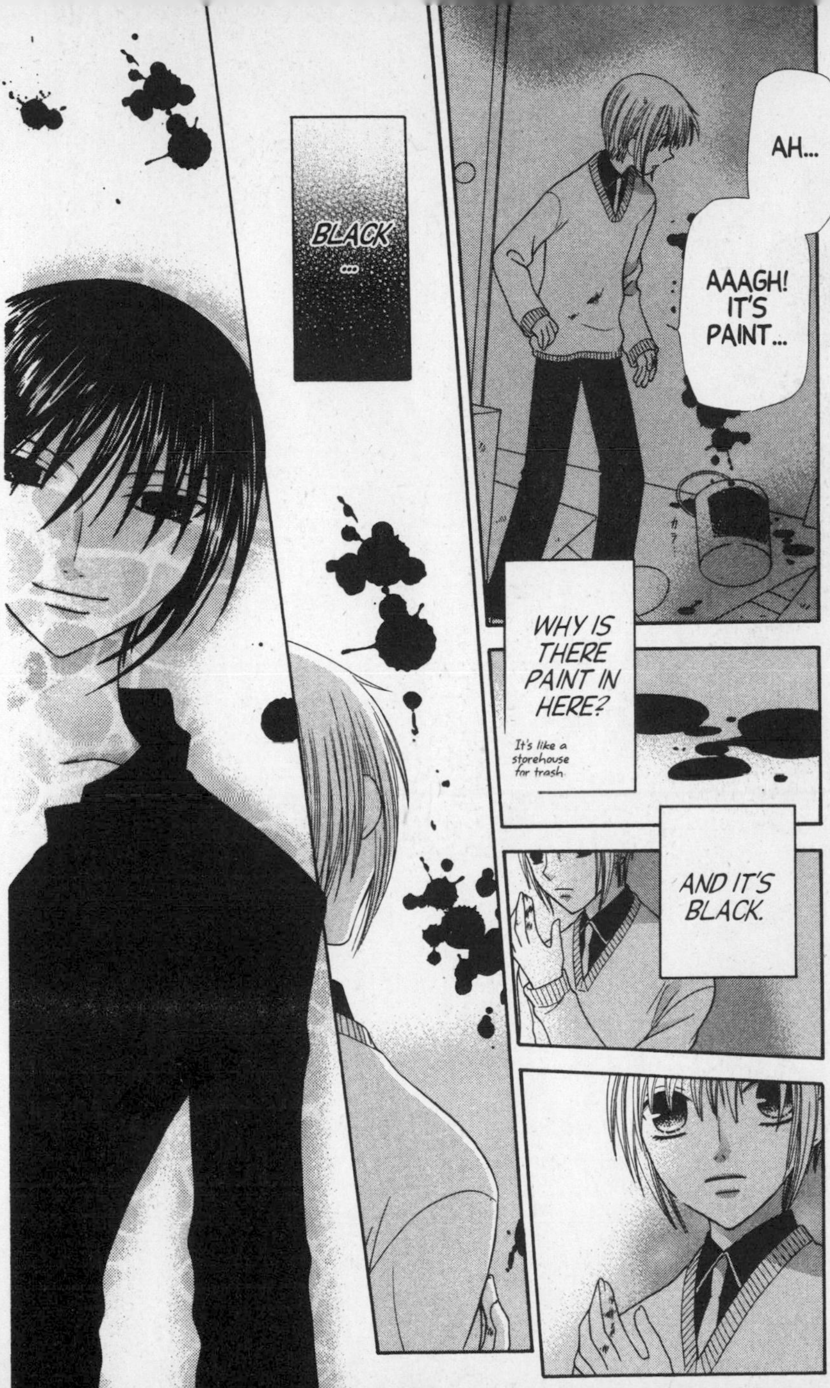
AH...
AAAGH! IT'S PAINT...
WHY IS THERE PAINT IN HERE?
It's like a storehouse for trash.
AND IT'S BLACK.
BLACK...

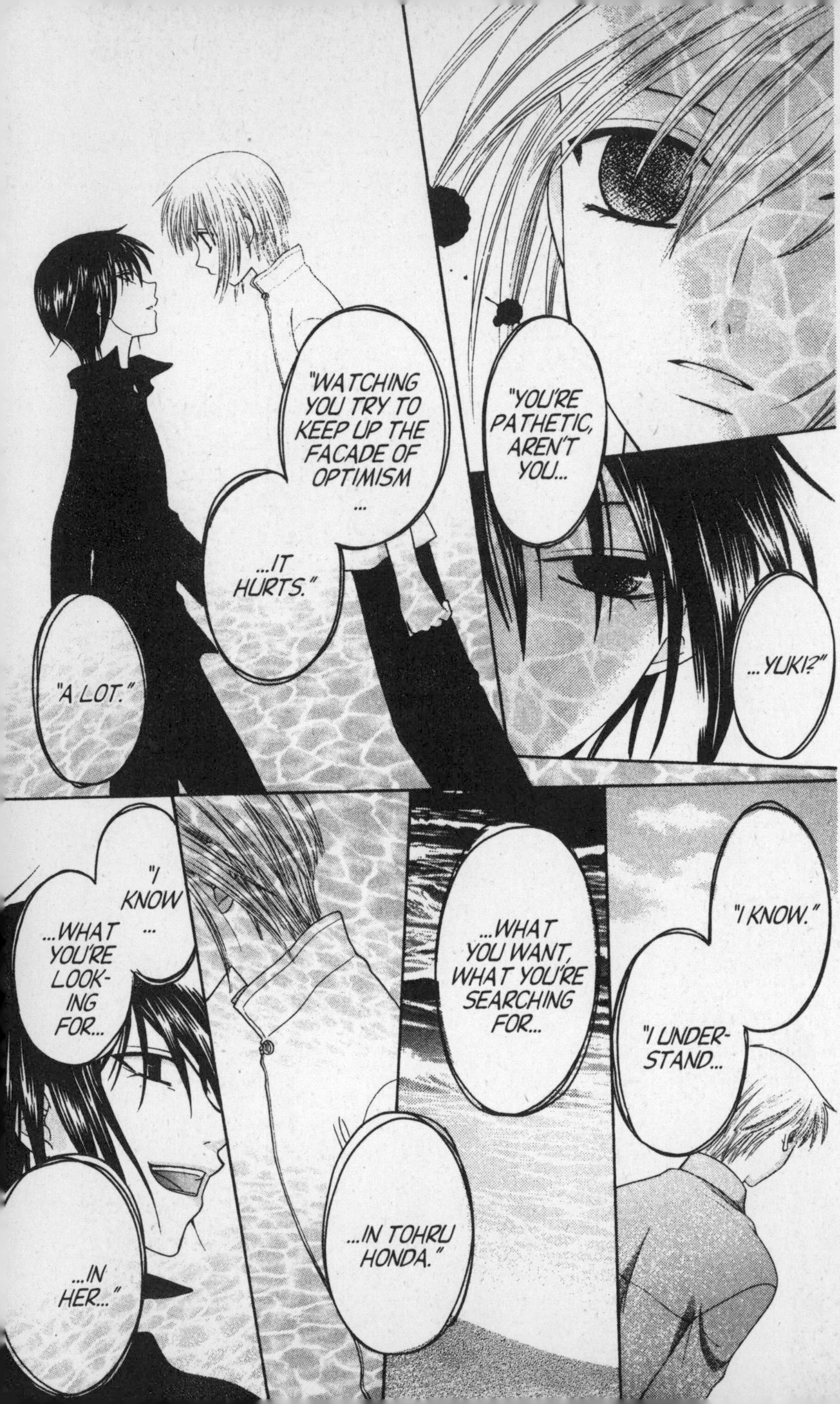
"YOU'RE PATHETIC, AREN'T YOU...
...YUKI?"
"WATCHING YOU TRY TO KEEP UP THE FACADE OF OPTIMISM ...
...IT HURTS."
"A LOT."
"I KNOW."
"I UNDER-STAND...
...WHAT YOU WANT, WHAT YOU'RE SEARCHING FOR...
...IN TOHRU HONDA."
"I KNOW ...
...WHAT YOU'RE LOOK-ING FOR...
...IN HER..."

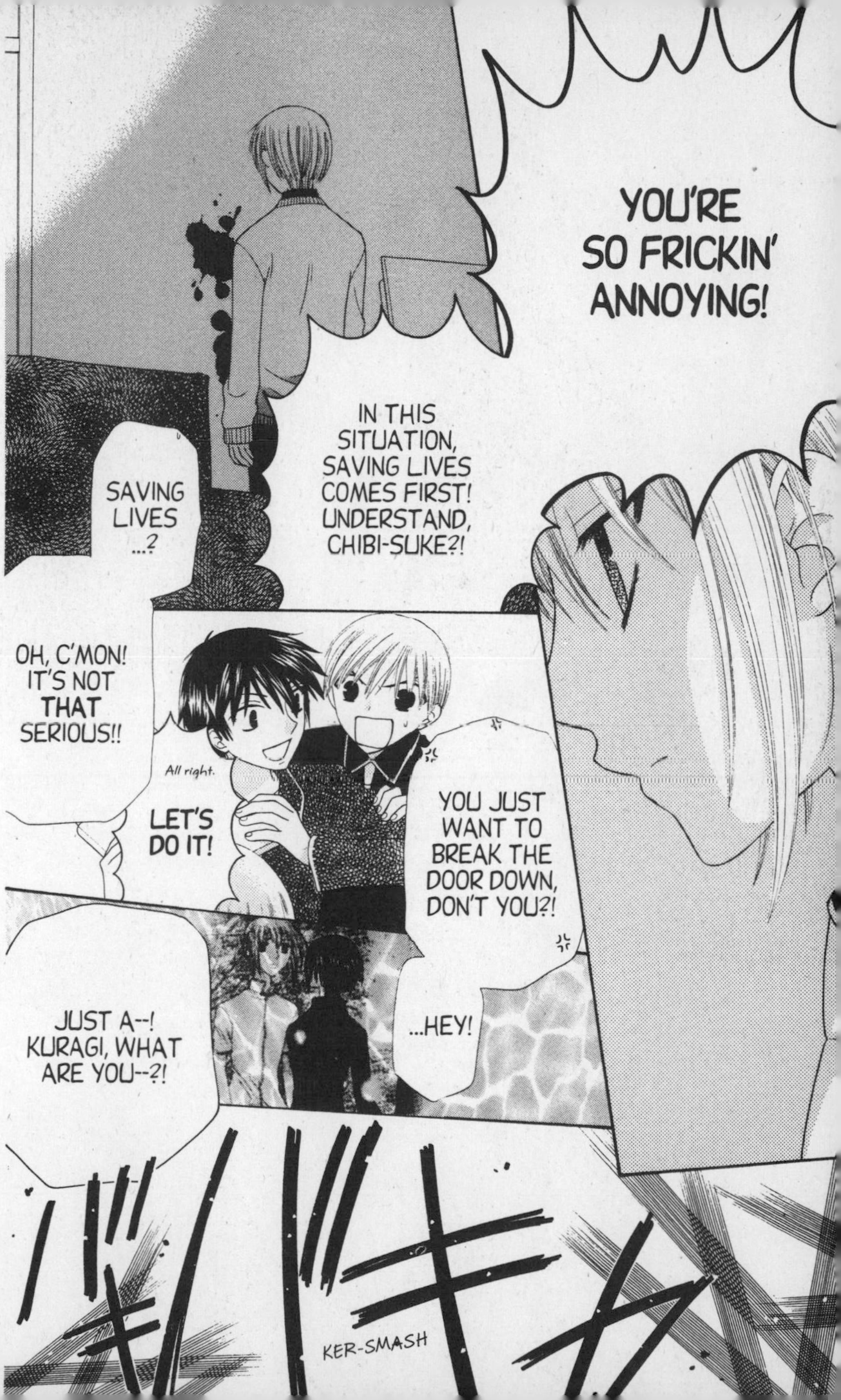
YOU'RE SO FRICKIN' ANNOYING!
IN THIS SITUATION, SAVING LIVES COMES FIRST! UNDERSTAND, CHIBI-SUKE?!
SAVING LIVES ...?
YOU JUST WANT TO BREAK THE DOOR DOWN, DON'T YOU?!
OH, C'MON! IT'S NOT THAT SERIOUS!!
All right.
LET'S DO IT!
...HEY!
JUST A--! KURAGI, WHAT ARE YOU--?!
KER-SMASH

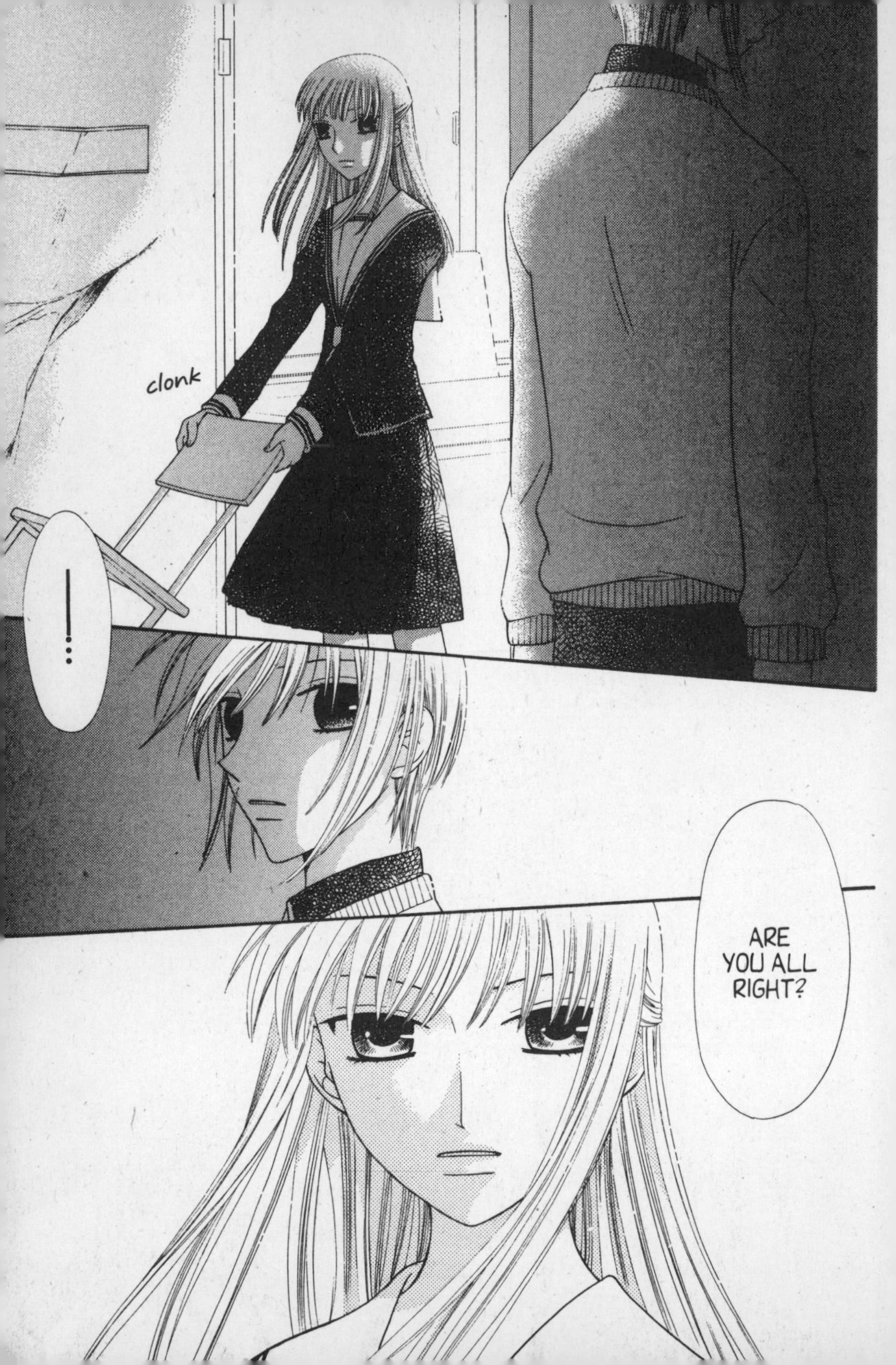
clonk
ARE YOU ALL RIGHT?

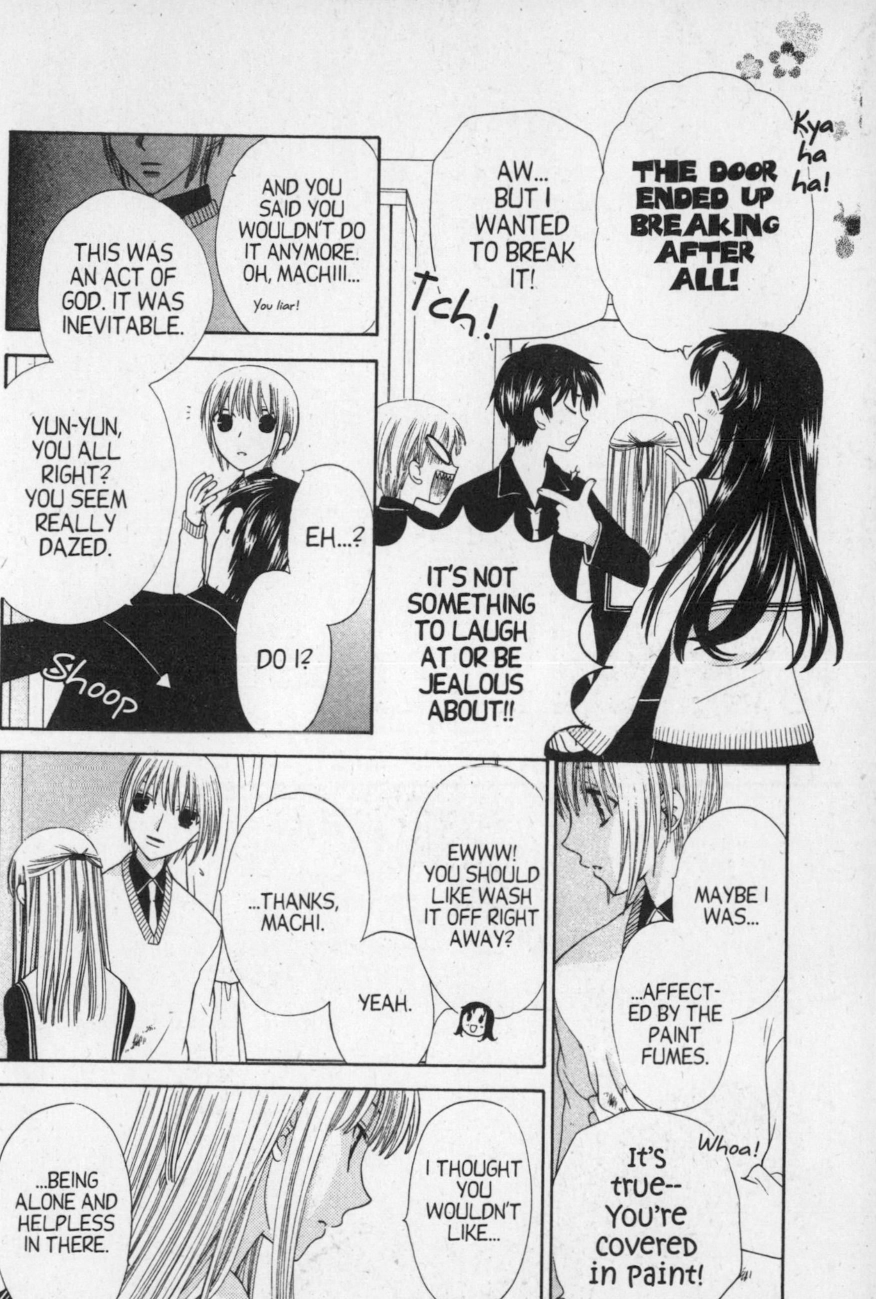
Kya ha ha!
THE DOOR ENDED UP BREAKING AFTER ALL!
AW... BUT I WANTED TO BREAK IT!
Tch!
IT'S NOT SOMETHING TO LAUGH AT OR BE JEALOUS ABOUT!!
AND YOU SAID YOU WOULDN'T DO IT ANYMORE. OH, MACHIII...
You liar!
THIS WAS AN ACT OF GOD. IT WAS INEVITABLE.
YUN-YUN, YOU ALL RIGHT? YOU SEEM REALLY DAZED.
EH...?
DO I?
Shoop
MAYBE I WAS...
...AFFECTED BY THE PAINT FUMES.
Whoa!
It's true-- You're covered in paint!
EWWW! YOU SHOULD LIKE WASH IT OFF RIGHT AWAY?
...THANKS, MACHI.
YEAH.
I THOUGHT YOU WOULDN'T LIKE...
...BEING ALONE AND HELPLESS IN THERE.

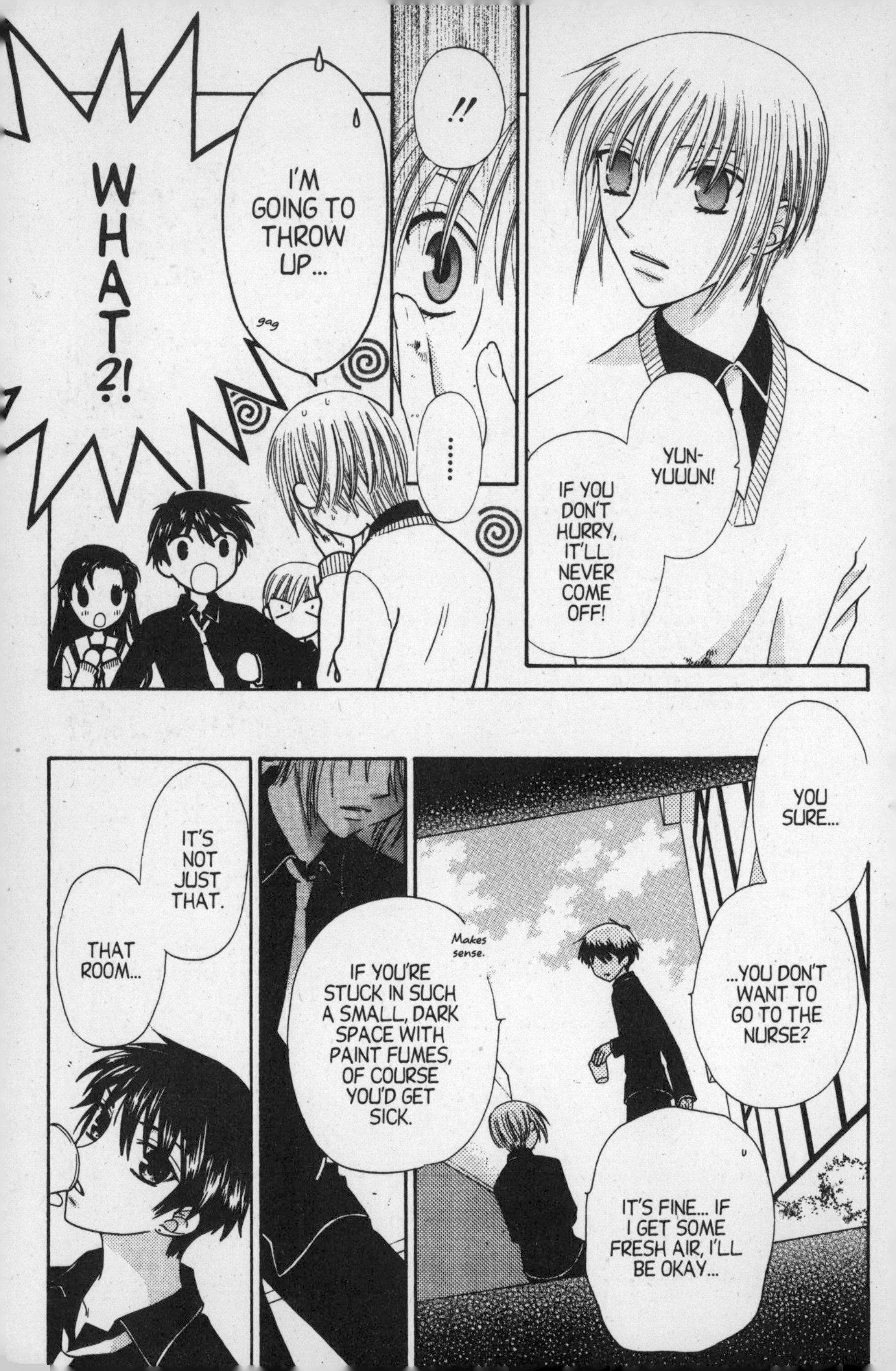
YUN-YUUUN!
IF YOU DON'T HURRY, IT'LL NEVER COME OFF!
!!
......
I'M GOING TO THROW UP...
gag
WHAT?!
YOU SURE...
...YOU DON'T WANT TO GO TO THE NURSE?
IT'S FINE... IF I GET SOME FRESH AIR, I'LL BE OKAY...
Makes sense.
IF YOU'RE STUCK IN SUCH A SMALL, DARK SPACE WITH PAINT FUMES, OF COURSE YOU'D GET SICK.
IT'S NOT JUST THAT.
THAT ROOM...

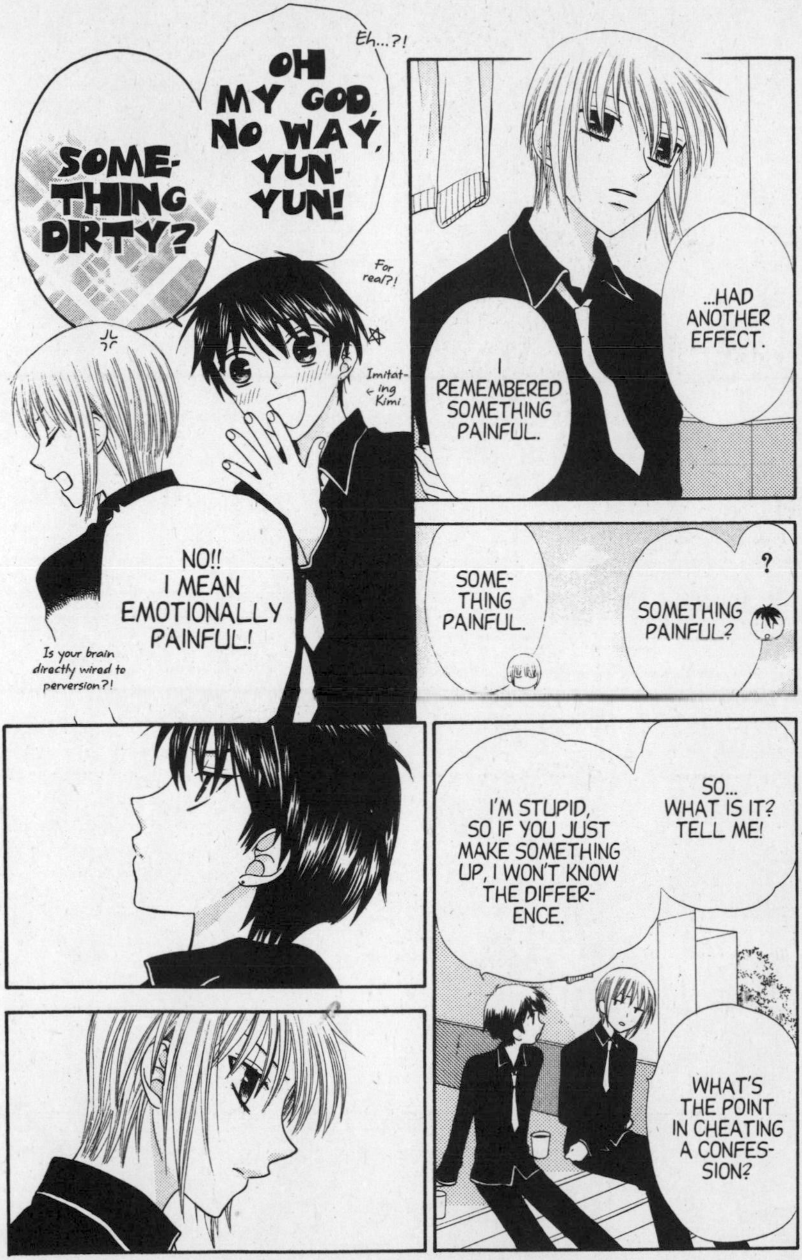
...HAD ANOTHER EFFECT.
I REMEMBERED SOMETHING PAINFUL.
SOMETHING PAINFUL?
SOME-THING PAINFUL.
Eh...?!
OH MY GOD, NO WAY, YUN-YUN!
For real?!
Imitat-ing Kimi
SOME-THING DIRTY?
NO!! I MEAN EMOTIONALLY PAINFUL!
Is your brain directly wired to perversion?!
SO... WHAT IS IT? TELL ME!
I'M STUPID, SO IF YOU JUST MAKE SOMETHING UP, I WON'T KNOW THE DIFFER-ENCE.
WHAT'S THE POINT IN CHEATING A CONFES-SION?

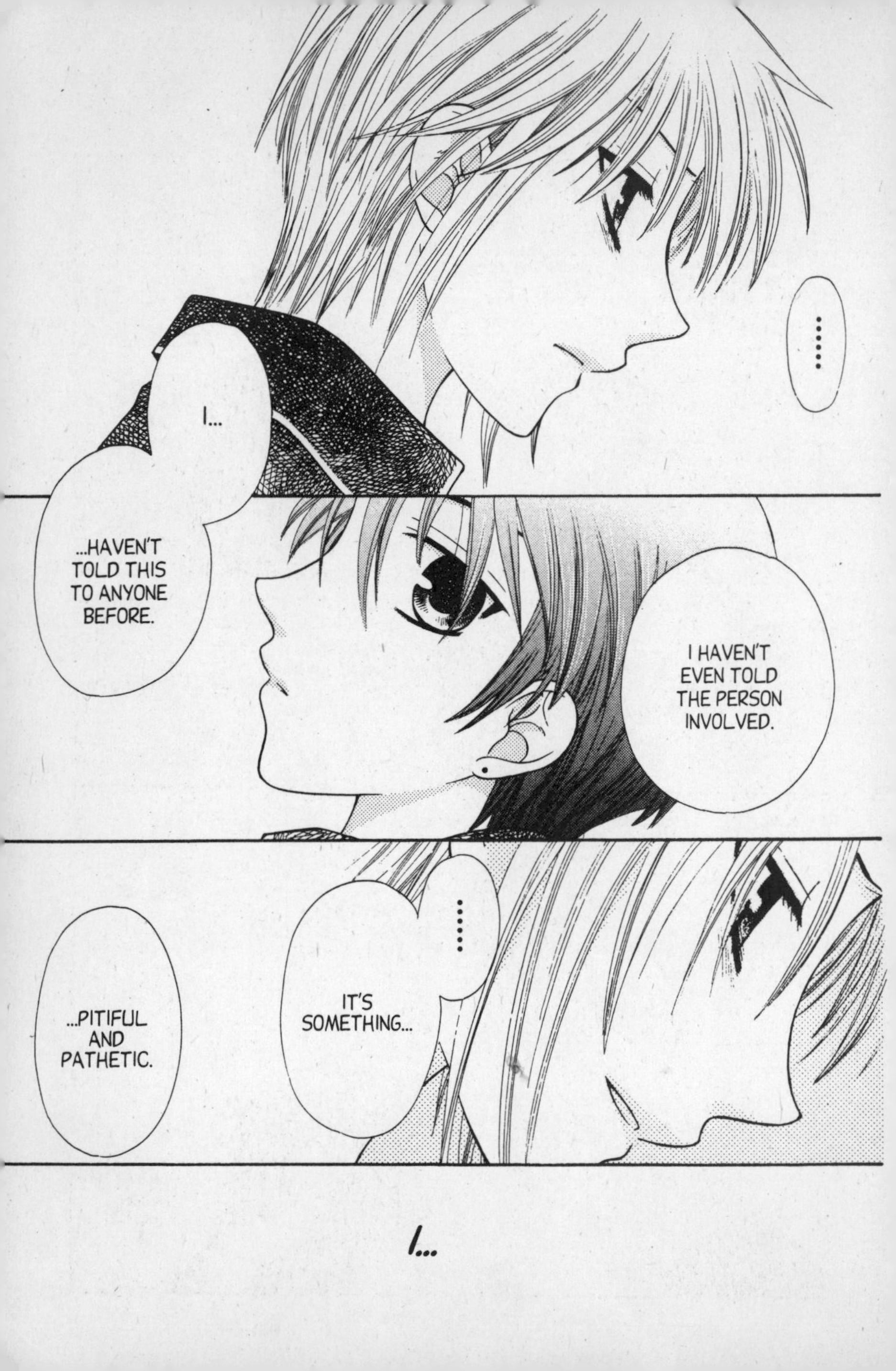
......
I...
...HAVEN'T TOLD THIS TO ANYONE BEFORE.
I HAVEN'T EVEN TOLD THE PERSON INVOLVED.
......
IT'S SOMETHING...
...PITIFUL AND PATHETIC.
I...

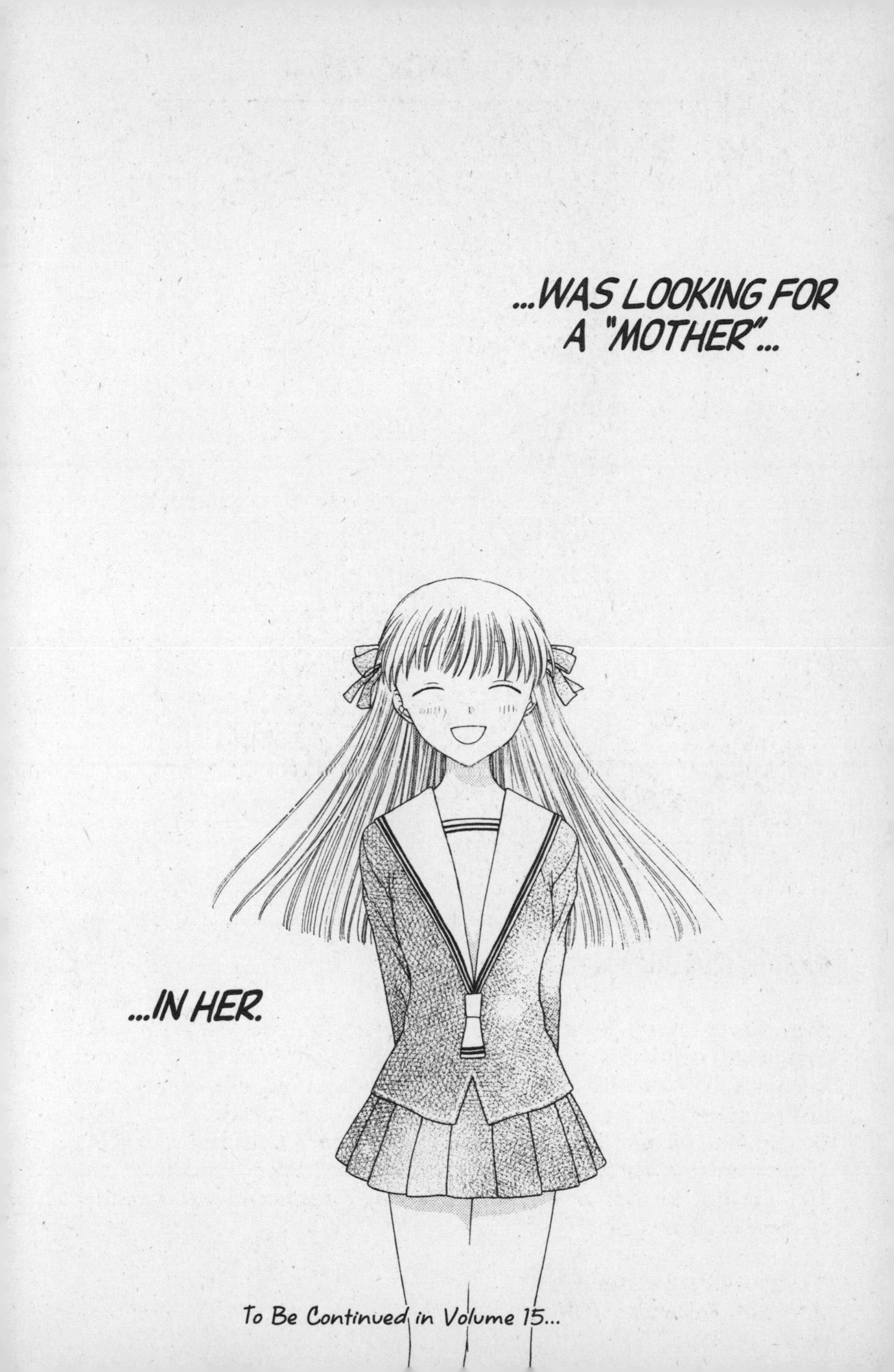
...WAS LOOKING FOR A "MOTHER"...
...IN HER.
To Be Continued in Volume 15...

Next time in...

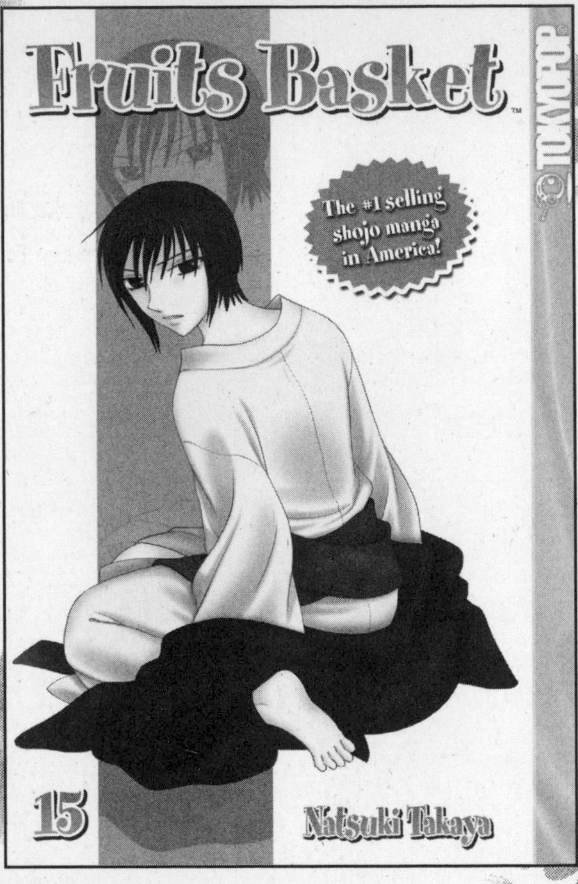
Fruits Basket™
TOKYOPOP
The #1 selling shojo manga in America!
15
Natsuki Takaya

Yuki's Painful Past...

Yuki finally comes to grips with his troubled past, recalling the events that culminated in his mother selling him to Akito. Yuki also remembers being told by Akito that he was worthless and deserving of everyone's hate and scorn. When Yuki is snapped out of his rueful reverie, he confesses that he sees Tohru as a mother figure. But before Tohru can give Yuki the gentle nurturing that he craves, she must prepare for the "Cinderella" play. Will the show be a hit, or will Arisa's feelings for Kureno cause the curtain to come crashing down?

Fruits Basket Volume 15
Available December 2006

Year of the Rooster: A Wake-Up Call

By nature, Roosters are highly organized individuals that tend to overwork themselves and get very depressed if they should fail in even the smallest of areas. It is their constant thirst for knowledge and their lone devotion to their work that keeps them going. Nonetheless, Roosters are always interesting and extremely adventurous in everything that they do and fame tends to follow their every move.

While men born in this year are quite boastful, women tend to focus more on the job at hand and let their influence be its own reward. Women are also very forgiving and let previous ills be forgotten instead of holding a grudge. When it comes to their appearance, Roosters are perfectionists, and these birds love nothing more than going out on the town and dancing until dawn with friends and lovers.

Celebrity Roosters:
Hayden Christensen
Craig David
Bryce Dallas Howard
Christina Milian
Britney Spears
Kelly Rowland
Foghorn Leghorn
Cornelius Rooster (Corn Flakes)
Rooster Cogburn

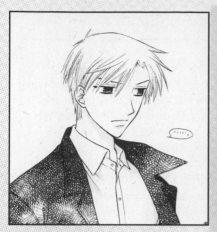

Rooster

Years*: 1945, 1957, 1969, 1981, 1993, 2005, 2017, 2029, 2041
Positive Qualities: Courageous, Hard-working, Alert, Perfectionist, Aggressive
Grievances: Arrogant, Selfish, Timid
Suitable Jobs: Business Owner, Publicist, Journalist, Soldier, Teacher
Compatible With: Snake, Ox, Dragon
Must Avoid: Rabbits
Ruling Hours: 5 PM to 7 PM
Season: Fall
Ruling Month: September
Sign Direction: West
Fixed Element: Fire
Corresponding Western Sign: Virgo

Considered a favorable sign, the Rooster is the only creature among the twelve animals of the Chinese Zodiac to bear wings, making it the perfect messenger to bridge the gap between Heaven and Earth. Its morning crow also serves to wake the farmer from his slumber and drive away any evil spirits that might be lingering in the fields.

For anyone fortunate enough to be born in the Year of the Rooster, they are endowed with its same virtues: knowledge, credibility, courage, military expertise and benevolence. Roosters are deep thinkers and highly talented, but very prideful by nature and quite arrogant. They always think they are right and even if proven wrong, they will persist in disputing any facts thrown at them. They are often seen as being selfish or even eccentric by others, but they tend to spend what they earn quite fast knowing that what is here today may be gone tomorrow.

*Note: It is important to know what day Chinese New Year's was held on as that changes what Zodiac animal you are. Example: 1981 actually began on February 5 and anyone born before that date is actually a Monkey.

Fans Basket

For Volume 14 of *Fruits Basket*, I need to give a very special shout-out to Stephanie Duchin. As a recent TOKYOPOP intern, Stephanie had the enviable task of opening piles and piles of Fans Basket letters and sketches. She'd run excitedly over to my desk and show me her favorite drawings from all of you die-hard readers. And just so you know, Stephanie happens to be a huge *Furuba* freak in her own right! In any case, she and I really bonded over all the wonderful things you all keep sending to me. Many thanks, Stephanie! I wish you were still here, because the fan mail is piling up again!

- Paul Morrissey, Editor

Kamryn G.
Age 13
Boerne, TX

Seriously, how adorable is Kisa in this sketch?! I guess I haven't exactly made it a secret that she's one of my favorite characters, since I keep getting drawings of her! I also love how Momiji's shirt is way too big for him.

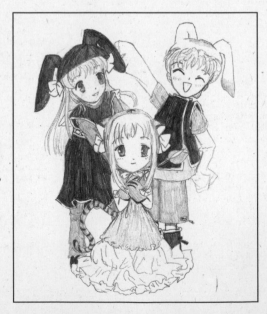

Kathy Phan
Age 12
Oakland, CA

This sketch is so utterly precious! Tohru looks soooooo sweet and vulnerable. Thanks for sending this in, Kathy. It made me say, "Awwwwwwww!"

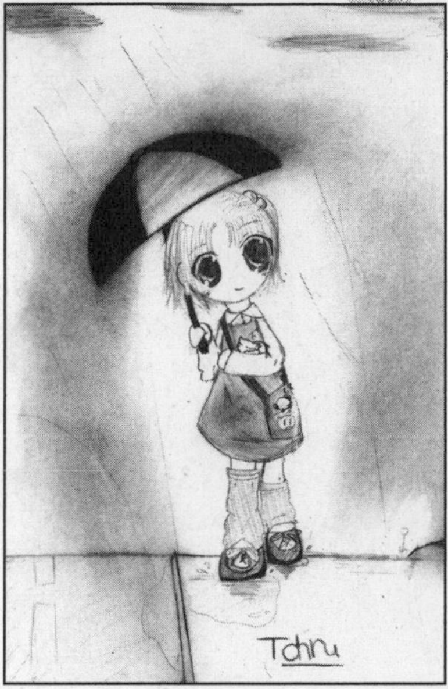
Tohru

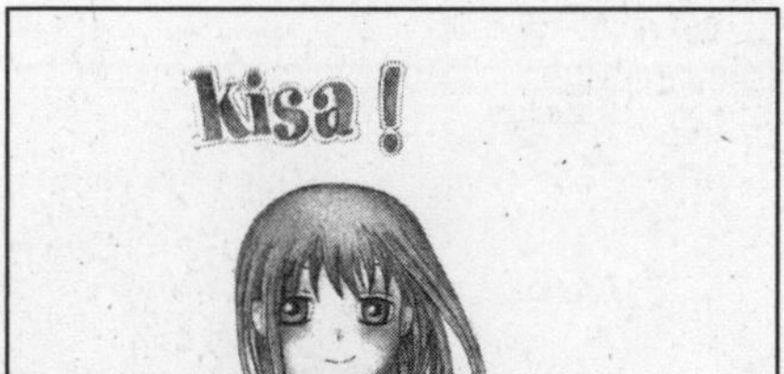
Kisa !

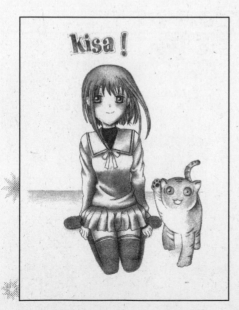

Michelle Pimentel
Age 14
El Cajon, CA

Here's another Kisa drawing. I am really impressed by Michelle's shading, especially with Kisa's clothes. However, the playful little tiger is what totally sold me!

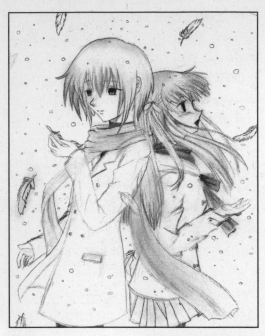

Samantha Johnson
Age 18
South Charleston, OH

You have a great, unique style, Samantha. Your sketch really makes me yearn for Autumn.

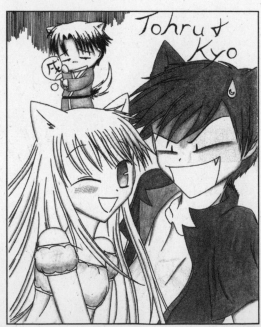

Tohru ♥ Kyo

Austa Joye
Age 17
Columbia, SC

This is so awesome, Austa! I *love* Kyo's attitude, and giving Tohru cat ears was a nice touch!

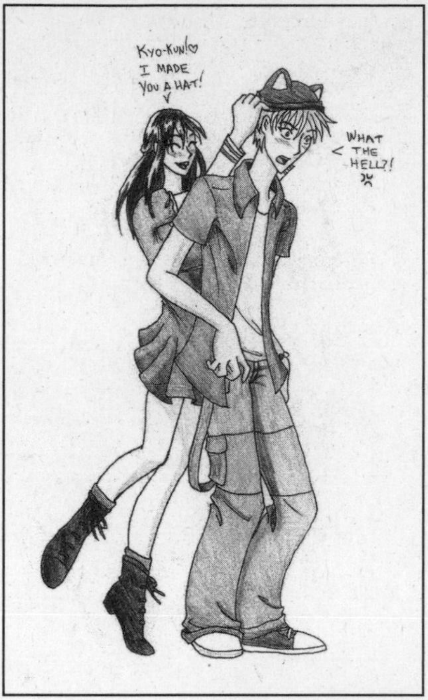
KYO-KUN!♡ I MADE YOU A HAT!
WHAT THE HELL?!

Amy Tanguay
Age 19
Sugar Land, TX

Like Samantha Johnson, Amy has her own style. I love the fun, playful body language in this drawing.

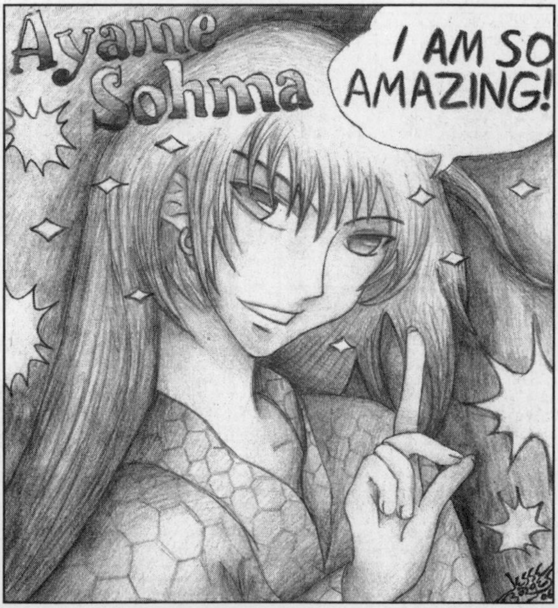
Ayame Sohma
I AM SO AMAZING!

Jesse Borges
Age 21
San Francisco, CA

Whoa! Jesse, you *totally* captured the essence of Ayame!

Do you want to share your love for *Fruits Basket* with fans around the world? "Fans Basket" is taking submissions of fan art, poetry, cosplay photos, or any other Furuba fun you'd like to share!

How to submit:

1) Send your work via regular mail (NOT e-mail) to:

"Fans Basket"
c/o TOKYOPOP
5900 Wilshire Blvd.
Suite 2000
Los Angeles, CA 90036

2) All work should be in black-and-white and no larger than 8.5" x 11". (And try not to fold it too many times!)

3) Anything you send will not be returned. If you want to keep your original, it's fine to send us a copy.

4) Please include your full name, age, city and state for us to print with your work. If you'd rather us use a pen name, please include that, too.

5) IMPORTANT: If you're under the age of 18, you must have your parent's permission in order for us to print your work. Any submissions without a signed note of parental consent cannot be used.

6) For full details, please check out our website: http://www.tokyopop.com/aboutus/fanart.php

Disclaimer: Anything you send to us becomes the exclusive property of TOKYOPOP Inc. and, as we said before, will not be returned to you. We will have the right to print, reproduce, distribute, or modify the artwork for use in future volumes of *Fruits Basket* or on the web royalty-free.

Mary Le
Age 14
Modesto, CA

Yes, Mary, *Furuba* does indeed rock! There are so many fun details in this sketch! I especially like Tohru's skirt.

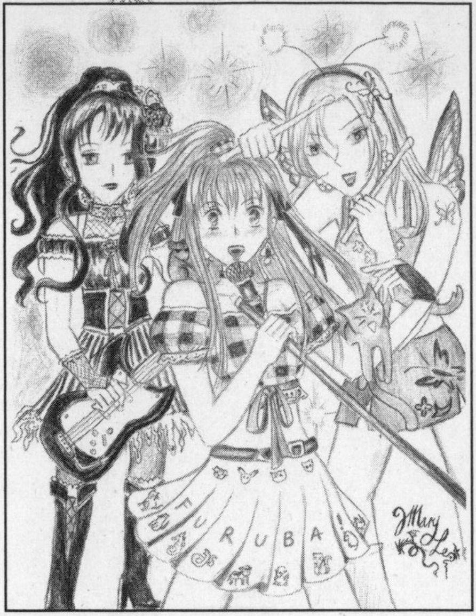
F U R U B A !
Mary Le

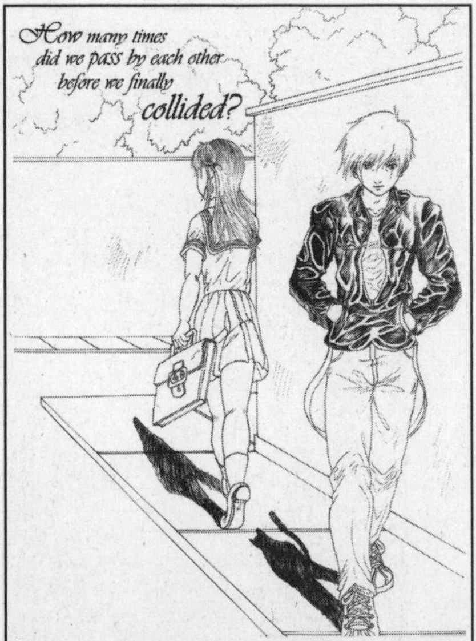
How many times did we pass by each other before we finally collided?

Kimberly Chadwick
Age 18
Hattiesburg, MS

Oooh! Great piece, Kimberly. I really like your pen work--especially with Kyo's jacket. And his shadow is a clever touch.

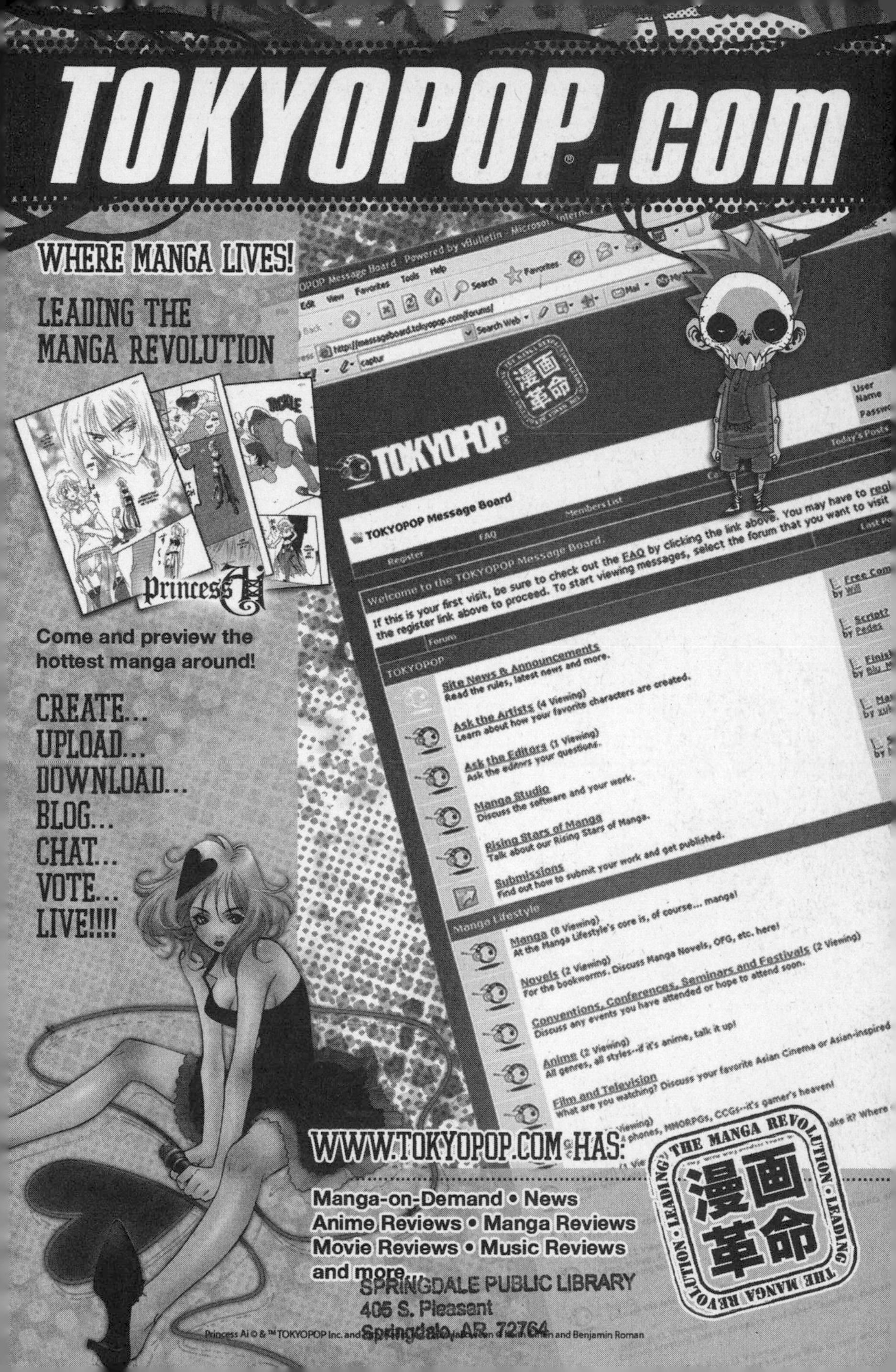
TOKYOPOP.com
WHERE MANGA LIVES!
LEADING THE MANGA REVOLUTION
Princess Ai
Come and preview the hottest manga around!
CREATE...
UPLOAD...
DOWNLOAD...
BLOG...
CHAT...
VOTE...
LIVE!!!!
TOKYOPOP Message Board
Welcome to the TOKYOPOP Message Board.
If this is your first visit, be sure to check out the FAQ by clicking the link above. You may have to register before you can post: click the register link above to proceed. To start viewing messages, select the forum that you want to visit
Site News & Announcements
Read the rules, latest news and more.
Ask the Artists (4 Viewing)
Learn about how your favorite characters are created.
Ask the Editors (1 Viewing)
Ask the editors your questions.
Manga Studio
Discuss the software and your work.
Rising Stars of Manga
Talk about our Rising Stars of Manga.
Submissions
Find out how to submit your work and get published.
Manga Lifestyle
Manga (8 Viewing)
At the Manga Lifestyle's core is, of course... manga!
Novels (2 Viewing)
For the bookworms. Discuss Manga Novels, OFG, etc. here!
Conventions, Conferences, Seminars and Festivals (2 Viewing)
Discuss any events you have attended or hope to attend soon.
Anime (2 Viewing)
All genres, all styles--if it's anime, talk it up!
Film and Television
What are you watching? Discuss your favorite Asian Cinema or Asian-inspired
WWW.TOKYOPOP.COM HAS:
Manga-on-Demand • News
Anime Reviews • Manga Reviews
Movie Reviews • Music Reviews
and more...
THE MANGA REVOLUTION • LEADING • THE MANGA REVOLUTION • LEADING
漫画革命
Princess Ai © & ™ TOKYOPOP Inc. and ... Keith Giffen and Benjamin Roman

TOKYOPOP MANGA SUPPLEMENT

Every life has a story...
Every story has a life of its own.

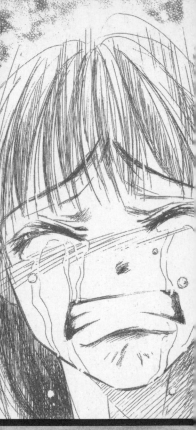

LIFE™

When Ayumu gets in the school
of her choice but her best
bud does not, the pain of being
separated from her friend is
too much to handle...But a new
school year begins and a fresh
start is presented to her,
until she takes solace in her
new friend Manami...

OT
OLDER TEEN
AGE 16+

DRAMA

© Keiko Suenobu

Volumes 1 and 2 Available Now!

FOR MORE INFORMATION VISIT: WWW.TOKYOPOP.COM

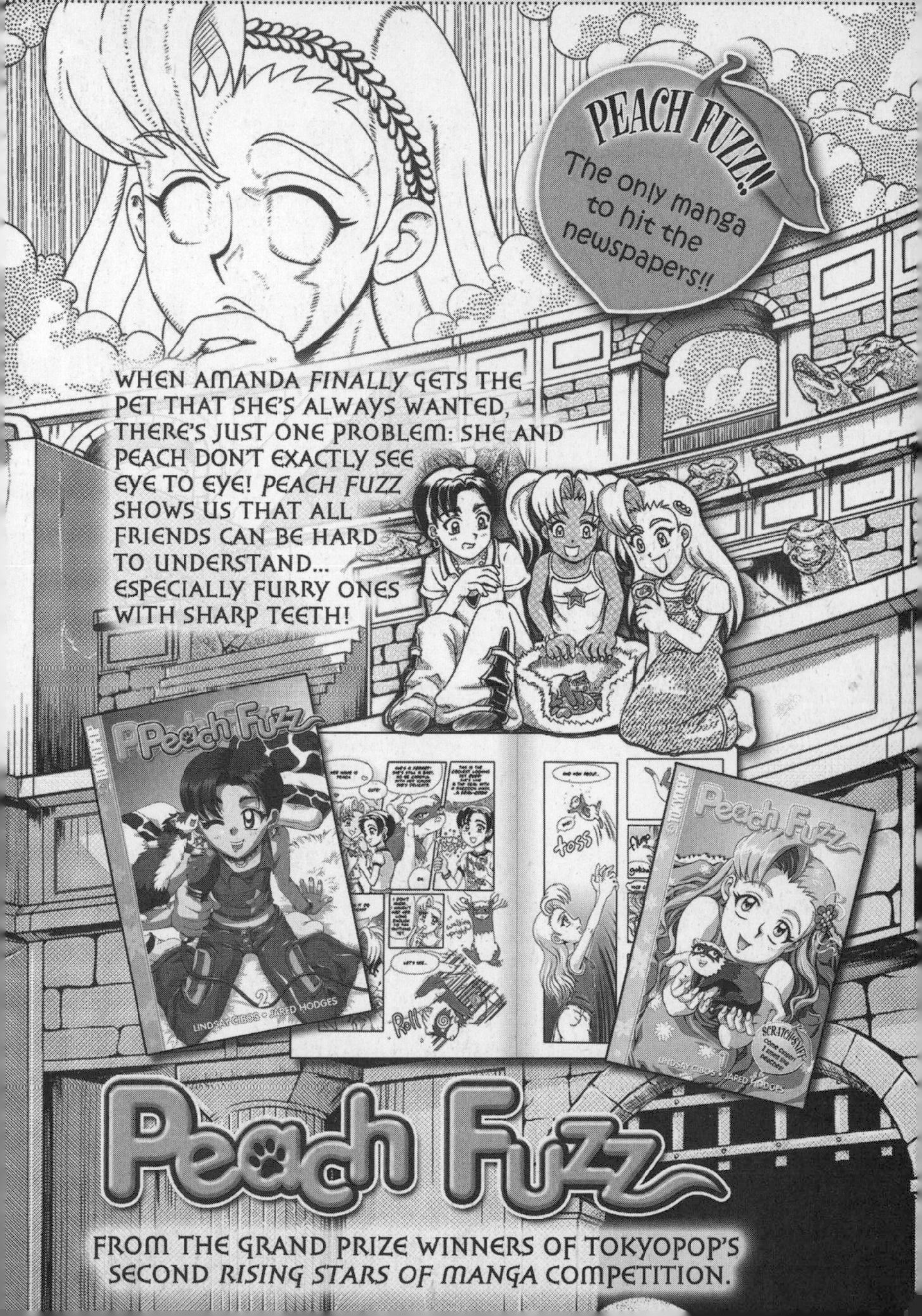
PEACH FUZZ!!
The only manga to hit the newspapers!!
WHEN AMANDA *FINALLY* GETS THE PET THAT SHE'S ALWAYS WANTED, THERE'S JUST ONE PROBLEM: SHE AND PEACH DON'T EXACTLY SEE EYE TO EYE! *PEACH FUZZ* SHOWS US THAT ALL FRIENDS CAN BE HARD TO UNDERSTAND... ESPECIALLY FURRY ONES WITH SHARP TEETH!
Peach Fuzz
LINDSAY CIBOS • JARED HODGES
toss
Roll
Peach Fuzz
LINDSAY CIBOS • JARED HODGES
Peach Fuzz
FROM THE GRAND PRIZE WINNERS OF TOKYOPOP'S SECOND *RISING STARS OF MANGA* COMPETITION.

PEACHFUZZ

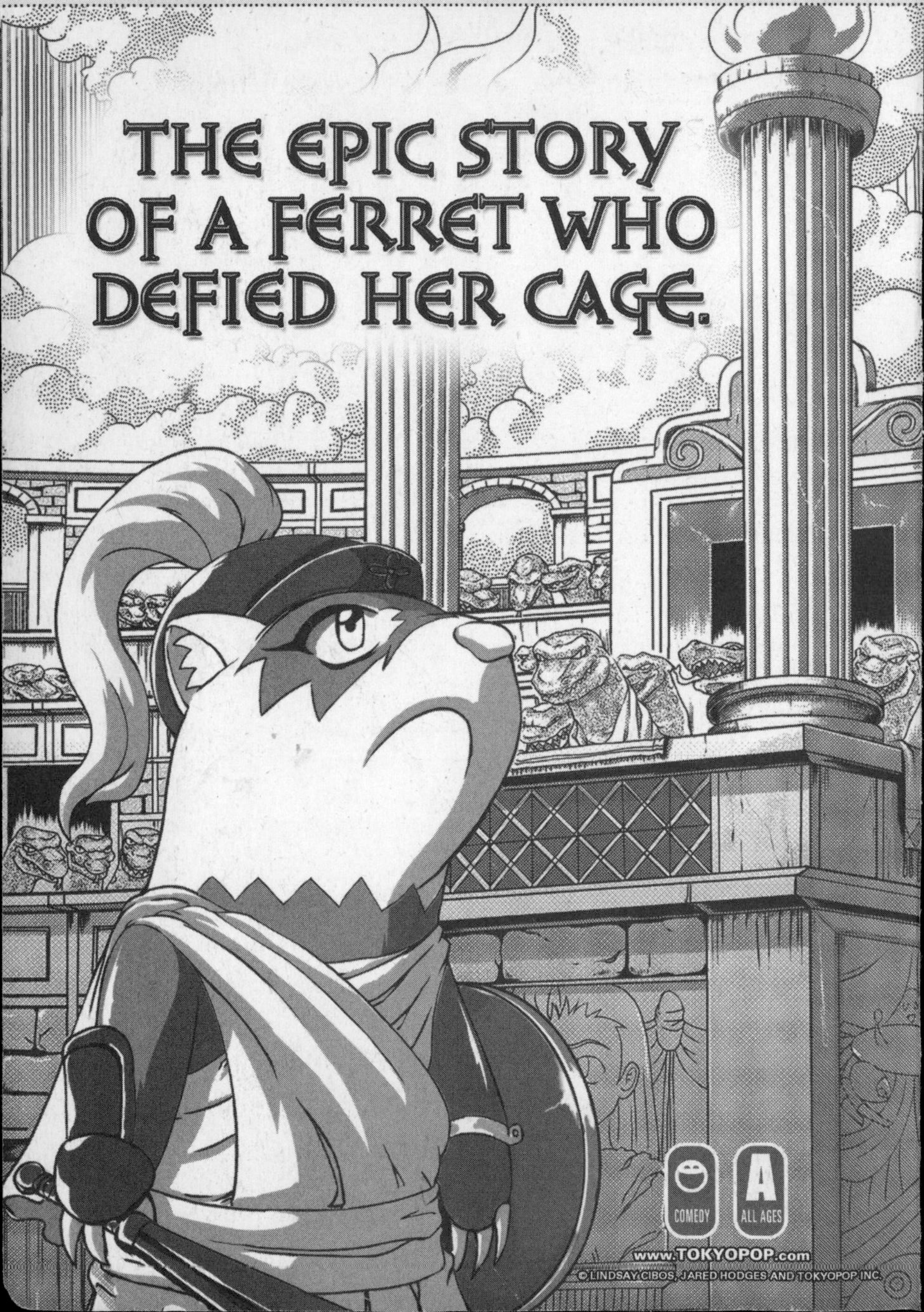
THE EPIC STORY
OF A FERRET WHO
DEFIED HER CAGE.
COMEDY
A
ALL AGES
www.TOKYOPOP.com
© LINDSAY CIBOS, JARED HODGES AND TOKYOPOP INC.

P9-CNC-806

STOP!

This is the back of the book.
You wouldn't want to spoil a great ending!

This book is printed "manga-style," in the authentic Japanese right-to-left format. Since none of the artwork has been flipped or altered, readers get to experience the story just as the creator intended. You've been asking for it, so TOKYOPOP® delivered: authentic, hot-off-the-press, and far more fun!

DIRECTIONS

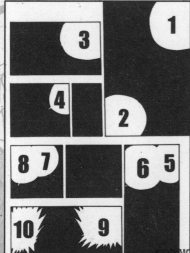

If this is your first time reading manga-style, here's a quick guide to help you understand how it works.

It's easy... just start in the top right panel and follow the numbers. Have fun, and look for more 100% authentic manga from TOKYOPOP®!

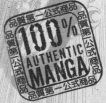

SPRINGDALE PUBLIC LIBRARY
405 S. Pleasant
Springdale, AR 72764